THE
ETIQUETTE
ADVANTAGE IN
BUSINESS

THIRD EDITION

THE
ETIQUETTE
ADVANTAGE IN
BUSINESS

THIRD EDITION

PERSONAL SKILLS FOR
PROFESSIONAL SUCCESS

PETER POST

with Anna Post, Lizzie Post, and Daniel Post Senning

WILLIAM MORROW
An Imprint of HarperCollinsPublishers

EMILY POST'S THE ETIQUETTE ADVANTAGE IN BUSINESS, THIRD EDITION. Copyright © 2014 by The Emily Post Institute, Inc. All rights reserved. Printed in the United States of America. No part of this book may be used or reproduced in any manner whatsoever without written permission except in the case of brief quotations embodied in critical articles and reviews. For information address HarperCollins Publishers, 195 Broadway, New York, NY 10007.

HarperCollins books may be purchased for educational, business, or sales promotional use. For information please e-mail the Special Markets Department at SPsales@harpercollins.com.

FIRST EDITION

Designed by Kris Tobiassen / Matchbook Digital

Library of Congress Cataloging-in-Publication Data has been applied for.

ISBN 978-0-06-227046-7

18 19 20   OV/LSC   10 9 8 7 6 5 4 3

WE DEDICATE THIS BOOK TO PEGGY POST

who has in turn dedicated more than twenty years as an author, spokesperson, seminar presenter, columnist, and director of The Emily Post Institute. During this time she has carried on the tradition of bringing etiquette to America that began with Emily Post in 1922.

Peggy's dedication to the Institute and to making people's lives more pleasant has been instrumental in raising people's awareness of and interest in etiquette. Peggy has been a wonderful mentor to the next generation as they prepare to take up the mantle of Emily Post.

CONTENTS

PART 4: RISING TO THE OCCASION

PART 5: COMMUNICATION

PART 6: ON THE ROAD

ACKNOWLEDGMENTS

While this is the third edition of *The Etiquette Advantage in Business*, we could not have gotten here without the help and support of people who contributed to the first and second editions. Fred DuBose and Royce Flippin were instrumental in helping make those two editions successful with both their writing and editing skills.

Thanks to all who helped with research and great ideas for the first and second editions: Courtney Denby, Inge Dobelis, Martha Leslie Hailey, Tad Harvey, Beth Landis, Alexis Lipsitz, Dierdre Van Dyk, Bryce Walker, Regis Canning, Lois Ebin, John Fowler, Greg Gregory, Dr. Judy Harkins, Mimi Irwin, Nancy Maniscalco, Knox Massey, James B. Miller Jr., Bob Moore, Susan Onaitis, Morgan Rich, and Evan P. Spingarn.

For their critical eye editing the first and second editions, thanks go to: Linda Ambrose, Keith Anderson, Kate DuBose, Stacy Kravetz, Kenneth Santor, and Burke Stinson.

Our warmest appreciation to Tricia Post for overseeing the rewrite process for the third edition. Tricia is the behind-the-scenes writer and editor at The Emily Post Institute.

We also want to extend a special thank you to Emily Krump, our editor at HarperCollins, who has worked doggedly to keep us on track and to make this, the third edition, the best edition yet.

INTRODUCTION
PERSONAL SKILLS FOR PROFESSIONAL SUCCESS

At The Emily Post Institute we've often discussed if we got the title of this book wrong. Perhaps the subtitle, *Personal Skills for Professional Success*, is a better, more descriptive one. That, after all, is what the book is really about—how you can achieve success in your business life.

Our own experience teaching business etiquette over the years has given us a deep appreciation of Emily Post's belief that everyday manners and workplace manners are inseparable. Just as people everywhere strive for pleasant personal encounters, people in business want and need standards of behavior that make their professional relationships smooth, enjoyable, and productive. Knowing the best way to behave can make all the difference between getting ahead . . . and getting left behind.

Your personal skills are what help you forge good business relationships, and relationships are at the heart of business etiquette. Not rules; not which fork you use, or if you called someone by their first name instead of their title and last name, or put paper in the photo copier when it ran out, or cleaned your dishes and wiped the table after finishing your lunch in the office cafeteria.

Knowing how to behave in a wide variety of professional settings not only makes you a more pleasant, confident, and enjoyable person to work with, but it also provides you with the all-important tools for building solid, productive relationships with your business associates—relationships that will help propel you and your company toward your mutual goals. Given today's greater job mobility, the growing popularity of the team concept in business, and the increased need to take different cultural and generational sensitivities into account in a global marketplace, your personal skills are now, more than ever, the key to your professional success, and it is etiquette that helps you build relationships.

The goal of *The Etiquette Advantage in Business* is to help you develop the self-assurance that comes with knowing not just *what* to do but also *why* that behavior is appropriate. Throughout this book, our advice is grounded in etiquette's bedrock principles of consideration, respect, and honesty and how these inform and guide what others consider good manners. With this knowledge, you will be able to judge for yourself what constitutes "correct behavior" in any given situation.

WHAT YOU'LL FIND

Reflecting the ever-accelerating pace of business, this revised edition of *The Etiquette Advantage in Business* has been extensively reviewed and updated to reflect the realities of today's business world, particularly as it strives to integrate digital life into the workplace.

In 1999, *The Etiquette Advantage in Business* was written to address a major issue in the workplace: incivility. Incivility alone wouldn't have warranted the book, but the growing frustration of workers about incivility did. Employees were no longer willing to be silent about being treated rudely. A survey in 2000 revealed how serious the issue had become: more than 50 percent of workers had been treated rudely. As a result, 22 percent of them were decreasing their work effort and 12 percent were leaving their jobs because of it. Profits and productivity were directly being affected by incivility on the workplace.

At the same time technology was having a major impact on how people communicated. With the advent of the desktop computer, executives no longer had assistants typing memos, letters, and reports from dictation. They were crafting emails and using word processors to create their own documents, and in doing so they were making mistakes in tone, grammar, and proofing that directly affected business in a negative way. Likewise cell phones began to impact relationships as businesspeople used them in ways that was perceived by others as rude.

Six years later, the second edition of *The Etiquette Advantage in Business* focused on the changing attitudes toward a more informal workplace. Casual dress, teams, home offices, cubicle areas, and open office relationships between managers and employees all fostered this more informal workplace. A new generation—millennials—was about to make its presence felt on the scene just as the workplace was coming to grips with the different ideas and attitudes that Gen Xers brought with them into the business world. Technology continued to be a boon to the workplace. However, as more work could be done by fewer people, technology made it possible for businesspeople to be available 24/7, rather than merely from nine to five. Email communication and inappropriate use of cell phones continued to demand special attention.

While all three editions are written for businesspeople of all types, levels, and backgrounds—including office workers, those who work at home, and executives who regularly do business overseas—the third edition pays special attention to the fact that for the first time in history four generations are actively working side by side in the workplace. Learning how to interact with people from generations other than your own is key to being successful in business today. For instance, a fifty-something baby boomer may find himself working for a twenty-four-year-old millennial dot-com start-up owner. They both need to consider carefully their respective attitudes toward the work environment, means of communicating, comfort with technology, and even the importance of work compared to personal time.

The third edition also brings added emphasis to the growth of digital communication and social networking. Texting, tweeting, blogging, LinkedIn, Facebook, and even Pinterest now can be used to build relationships or be abused and hurt relationships and even cost people their jobs. Smartphones have supplanted cell phones with their added capabilities to surf the Internet and communicate by email and text, bringing another level of distraction and interruption to face-to-face interactions.

The third edition devotes considerable space to the needs of employees in the junior to midlevel range. It also offers counsel to top management on matters such as how to maintain good relations with employees and how to deal with knotty ethical problems. Much of the book's advice is universal: Whether you're a pin-striped corporate executive or a sneaker-wearing dot-commer, knowing the ins and outs of cell phone etiquette, picking an appropriate business gift, or hosting a business dinner will always be valuable.

Part by part, here's what you'll encounter:

THE KEYS TO SUCCESS. Part 1 concentrates on the most important part of the etiquette equation: you. It addresses the basic principles of etiquette, including why and how it enhances your interactions with others; explains the importance of behaving ethically at all times, including guidelines for setting and maintaining high ethical standards; and finally, gives soup-to-nuts advice on all aspects of business attire and grooming for men and women.

THE JOB APPLICANT. Part 2 explores how to use etiquette to your advantage when conducting a job search, applying for a job, updating your résumé and cover letter, using online resources, and going through the job-interview process.

AT THE WORKPLACE. Nowhere is etiquette more important than in your work environment, where harmonious relationships are essential for business success. Part 3 covers every aspect of office life, including how to get along with your coworkers and supervisors; your attitude toward your work space (be it cubicle or corner office); relations between the sexes and generations; how to be a considerate and effective manager; the art of running a productive, on-time meeting; and the issues that can arise when you're telecommuting or working out of a home office.

RISING TO THE OCCASION. The practical advice offered in Part 4 will help you feel confident and at ease when dealing with business associates both inside and outside your workplace. These chapters include tips on fostering customer satisfaction, choosing an appropriate business gift, and decoding even the most formal table setting at a business dinner or lunch. You'll also find comprehensive etiquette advice for when you are entertaining or being entertained.

COMMUNICATION. Part 5 is devoted to the etiquette of self-expression. Its six chapters cover the importance of introductions; the art of speaking clearly; considerate phone and digital phone behavior; and how to express yourself skillfully in writing, both in the traditional way (on paper) and in electronic form. A new chapter on the ins and outs of social networking in the workplace rounds out this section.

ON THE ROAD—HERE AND ABROAD. Part 6 focuses on the etiquette of business travel, including advice on domestic travel; conventions and trade shows; and the special challenges of international travel, where understanding and respecting your hosts' culture is the very first step in any successful business negotiation.

The Etiquette Advantage in Business brings a level of comfort to the businessperson who never had the chance to learn the basics of etiquette, provides a refresher course for those who did, equates good manners with good business sense, and instills the self-confidence that sets every businessperson on the road to success. We hope our book will make a difference for employees and executives everywhere and serve as a helpmate that grounds people in the timeless fundamentals as they work their way through a fast-changing world.

PETER POST, ANNA POST, LIZZIE POST, AND DANIEL POST SENNING
April 30, 2014

PART ONE

THE KEYS TO SUCCESS

CHAPTER 1
ETIQUETTE AND ETHICS

Emily Post once said, "Etiquette is a house built on ethics." In the first edition of *Etiquette* published in July 1922, she described the relationship she saw between etiquette and ethics this way: "Etiquette must, if it is to be of more than trifling use, include ethics as well as manners."

Interestingly, she saw ethics as a subset of etiquette rather than the other way around. To understand that relationship is to have an understanding and appreciation of what etiquette really is, because it is not simply some rigid code of manners. Even Emily said so.

Emily was an inveterate scrapbook keeper, and newspaper and magazine articles written about her are all preserved. In one of the articles in one of those scrapbooks, a reporter must have pressed her on the issue of etiquette being just a bunch of rules, because her answer got right to the heart of the matter: "Whenever two people come together and their behavior affects one another, you have etiquette. Etiquette is not some rigid code of manners; it's simply how persons' lives touch one another."

When two people come together and their behavior affects each other, what you also have is a society. Each and every one of us is a social animal. We don't simply live alone, independent of the people around us. We can't live without regard for the people around us. If we did, humanity would have been doomed long ago.

One of the hallmarks of good etiquette is that it never calls attention to itself. When everything is going well as far as your actions, appearance, and words are concerned, your focus—and the focus of the people you are with—will be on the content of your discussion. Slip up with any one of these factors, however, and the focus instantly shifts to the error ("I can't believe he just did that"). By being aware of your actions, appearance, and words, and working to improve your performance in all three areas, you can directly enhance the quality of your relationships.

We live together. As a group—a society—we identify and then codify behaviors that are acceptable and behaviors that are unacceptable and then we expect people to abide by those expectations, which become laws and manners. Laws are rules for which the society defines specific penalties and imposes those penalties. Manners are those behaviors society has identified as ways we will interact with each other so we are comfortable in the presence of one another. In essence, manners tell us what to do, whereas laws tell us what not to do.

That's what your boss could tell you in a performance review. If she did, how would you go about fulfilling such a request? Chances are you wouldn't have a clue where to begin. If, however, you shift your focus from improving your "relationships" in general to evaluating how well you handle the specific factors that influence all relationships, this goal will start to look much more attainable. This is easier than you might think, because there are three fundamental things that can affect a relationship: your actions, your appearance, and your words.

1. ACTIONS. Our actions impact the image others have of us. Imagine: You sit down at a restaurant table with a client. After a few minutes, your cell phone starts ringing. You answer it and start talking. This action, without some sort of regard for the people you are with, would create a negative atmosphere at your business lunch. What is a better action, one that will improve your relationship with your client? Simple: Either turn off your phone before meeting your client or let your client know that you're expecting a call and then excuse yourself to the lobby or a private area when your phone vibrates.

2. APPEARANCE. The importance of clothes and grooming is obvious. Dress like a slob, and the people you are with will think of you as a slob. Body odor and bad breath—those are no-brainers. But what about body language? That falls under appearance as well: Twitching your foot during a meeting says you are either nervous or apprehensive, or worse, you can't wait for the meeting to end. Improve your appearance by keeping your foot still—and staying calm, alert, and twitch-free in general—and you will build better relationships with the people you do business with.

3. WORDS. Coarse language is out of bounds. But say you're in a meeting and you blurt out, "Oh my god, Sally, what a great idea!" Later, you discover that some of the people present were offended that you took the Lord's name in vain. Instead of thinking about Sally's great idea, those participants were focused on you and their negative perception of you.

While it may seem that we unconsciously observe hundreds of manners each day, there are situations that cause us to pause because there seems to be no particular manner to apply. How, then, do we know what to do? Fortunately, etiquette is more than just manners. It also embodies the principles on which all manners are built, principles that can help a person identify the best course of action when there is no particular manner to guide her.

When Emily wrote, "Etiquette must, if it is to be of more than trifling use, include ethics as well as manners," in the very next sentence she expounded on what etiquette meant to her:

> "Certainly what one is, is of far greater importance than what one appears to be. A knowledge of etiquette is of course essential to one's decent behavior, just as clothing is essential to one's decent appearance."

You can cloak yourself to appear to be anything, but Emily understood that doing so creates just a hollow shell for yourself, and eventually, that shell will disintegrate. The real you is what really matters in your interactions with everyone you come into contact.

WHO IS THE REAL YOU?

You get dressed in the morning, and as you look in the mirror, you think to yourself, "I look great today!"

The problem? When you walk into the meeting room that day, the other people there, including your boss, wonder, "What on earth is he wearing *that* for?"

Mistake.

Why? Because you forgot a cardinal rule of business etiquette: The perspective of the other person matters. Every day at work you interact with people and those actions leave impressions on them about you. You may think it doesn't matter because they are a colleague or they work for you. But it does matter because one day they may be your boss or a client who decides if you are someone she wants to work with, or a prospect who is deciding who gets a new contract, or a future boss who decides if you get a job or get promoted.

Perspective in business matters. And that fact leads directly to three goals that can help you build better, stronger relationships.

THE THREE GOALS

Throughout the day, you are faced with choices as you interact with people. Which choice you act on will determine not only if you resolve whatever the

---

MANNERS

Manners are guidelines, not rules. In many situations, manners can help us determine the right thing to do, but there are always exceptions, and so we use our judgment and common sense to decide when a manner applies and when we should do something differently.

Manners tell us two types of things:

What to do in all kinds of situations

- What fork to use
- When to hold a door for someone
- How to introduce yourself to another person

What we can expect other people to do

- When you extend your hand to shake hands, you fully expect the other person to reciprocate.
- When you hold a door for someone, you expect him to say "Thank you."
- When you are in line, you expect those in the line to wait their turn also.

In essence, manners are guidelines to help us as we interact with the people around us, by sketching out the appropriate actions, appearance, and words that will help us build successful relationships.

---

situation is but also if your relationship is enhanced or hurt by it. In essence: *How* you do things matters.

Recognizing that the *how* matters in business leads directly to the first goal: Think before you act. Too often people act impulsively without thinking, and sometimes, as a result, they end up having to apologize. That apology often takes the form of "I'm sorry. I can't believe I did that. I don't know what I was thinking." Thinking before you act will reduce the number of times you have to apologize for your actions because instead of making impulsive decisions you will make considered decisions. And usually, when we consider (i.e., think), we make better choices. And that leads directly to the second goal.

Make choices that build relationships. Once you've done the thinking, you will inevitably consider options. Some of those options will be nonstarters, some will be good for you, and some will be harder on or less advantageous to you. In examining your choices, the key is to identify the option that not only resolves the situation but also builds the relationship. Sometimes the best option is *not* the easiest choice for you, but if it is best for everyone else involved, then it is the best solution for you, too.

Answering a phone call while having a conversation with another person is a perfect example. Instead of reflexively answering the phone, you hesitate and quickly realize you have another option: You can send the call to voice mail. If you answer it, you know that the person you are with may feel annoyed at being put "on hold" while you deal with your call. If you don't answer it, you'll miss the call but will improve your image in the other person's eyes because you have tacitly said, "You're more important to me than my phone." Realizing that the perspective of the person you are with matters to your image today and in the future, you push the button sending the call to voice mail. Good choice.

Now, those two goals don't work to build your image without a third: sincerity. Your actions need to be grounded in sincerity because when they are, people develop confidence in you, and confidence begets trust, and relationships are built on trust. Try to fool someone, be someone who you are not, use flattery to get what you want, and that person will soon see through you and consequently have little if any trust in your motives—at which point regaining that person's trust will be very difficult.

That's it. Three goals to help you be more successful in business:

1. Think before you act.

2. Make choices that build relationships.

3. Do it sincerely.

THE THREE PRINCIPLES THAT GOVERN ALL ETIQUETTE

Interestingly, those three goals go hand in hand with the three principles that govern all etiquette. The principles are the guiding concepts on which all manners are based. Among other things, they tell us

- What to do when there is no prescribed manner or a particular manner doesn't work

- How to resolve relationship situations

For example, while attending a business dinner, an elderly client begins to excuse herself from the table. Because business etiquette is meant to be non–gender specific, the appropriate "manner" states that you, as a male, shouldn't stand as she gets ready to leave the table. But you also know the client is old school—and so you decide that, despite the latest guideline or "rule," you will stand. As you do, she smiles and says, "Thank you." By understanding the unique circumstances of the situation and showing respect for your dinner companion by standing in spite of what the current rule says, you have made her appreciate you just that much more. In turn, you've helped yourself and your company build a better relationship with her.

Virtually all the manners that you'll find in etiquette books—and, indeed, all the choices that you'll ever make about your actions, appearance, and words—are governed by three principles: *consideration*, *respect*, and *honesty*.

- Consideration means looking at the current situation and assessing how it affects everyone who is involved.

- Respect means identifying how a possible action will affect others.

- Honesty means acting sincerely and being truthful, not deceitful.

Having a command of good etiquette really means knowing how to use your own common sense in applying one or more of the above principles to determine the best course of action in any situation.

The man standing up at the dinner table knows that in this case being respectful of his companion was more important than following the rule—so he rose. He put the principles into action by applying the three goals. He was considerate in taking just a moment to think before he simply acted. He applied the principle of respect by examining each possible action to identify not only if it resolved the situation but also if it built the relationship. Finally, he was honest and sincere with himself in his choice to rise

---

THE IMPORTANCE OF SINCERITY

Contrary to what some people may think, a concerted effort to make a good impression through the use of etiquette doesn't mean putting on airs, playing games, betraying yourself, or compromising your integrity. Phoniness and pretentiousness are one thing; observing guidelines of behavior that have evolved over time to serve the common good is quite another. Therefore, it's not enough to be considerate, respectful, and honest; you must also be sincere in the use of these principles. If you aren't, people will see through your veneer. "Jim seems like a nice guy, but there's something about him that strikes me as phony"—that's not the impression you want to make.

---

because it would honor the woman who would be pleased by his action.

Consideration	Thinking before you act
Respect	Making choices that build relationships
Honesty	Doing it sincerely

WHERE DO ETHICS FIT IN?

So why is ethics a subset of etiquette? Whereas every ethical situation is governed by the three principles, not every manner addresses an ethical situation.

For instance, knowing which fork to use at a dinner party is not an ethical issue but it is an etiquette rule. Other examples of etiquette rules that aren't ethical issues include: not picking your nose, standing when greeting a person, and responding to an invitation.

When you face a decision that involves a moral right and wrong and isn't just a matter of how to resolve a situation like how to hold a fork, that's when the issue becomes an ethical issue. Its resolution is governed by those same principles—consideration, respect, and honesty. For instance, taking credit for work that's not yours is certainly an ethical issue, but it is also an etiquette issue as its resolution is governed by etiquette's three principles.

The Ethics Resource Center[*] identified a number of different types of unethical behavior that were reported by employees as behaviors they had witnessed:

- Abusive or intimidating behavior toward other employees (18 percent)
- Lying to other employees (17 percent)
- Discriminating on the basis of race, color, gender, age, or similar categories (12 percent)
- Conflicts of interest (15 percent)
- Violating company policies related to Internet use (12 percent)
- Misreporting of hours worked (10 percent)
- Violations of health or safety regulations (10 percent)
- Stealing, theft, or related fraud (9 percent)
- Employee benefits violations (9 percent)

[*] Ethics Resource Center National Business Ethics Survey 2013

HIDING AN OFFICE ROMANCE—AN ETHICAL ISSUE

Q. The junior staffer whom I directly supervise told me she is dating another coworker. She told me this in confidence on a Friday evening when we went out for a few drinks. The coworker she is dating is a midlevel manager like me. I consider them both my friends as well. She told me not to tell our department head and not to tell the coworker she is dating that I know. The coworker and I work together on many projects. In hindsight, I can see where their romance has impacted a few tasks in the past months. I am concerned our team performance will be negatively impacted. I do not want my job or title or reputation to be on the line because I knew about their relationship.

I am not sure if I should confide in my manager, confront the junior staffer saying to keep her relationship outside of work, or not say anything at all. Any advice would be helpful.

A. By confiding in you, the junior staffer has put you in a position where your silence has the potential to boomerang on you. You need to act. First step, talk to the junior staffer and explain that her revelation has put you in an ethical bind and that she and your coworker need to own up to the relationship. Let her know that you are concerned both because teamwork may be negatively impacted and because if (or more likely "when") the cat is out of the bag, you may be implicated in hiding the information.

While it's expected that the couple maintain a strictly professional demeanor at work, it's only fair that coworkers and managers be aware that there might be a relationship factor in play. If the company has a policy regarding office romances, the couple will need to be prepared to abide by it.

- Falsifying time reports or hours worked (12 percent)
- Sexual harassment (11 percent)
- Giving or accepting bribes, kickbacks, or inappropriate gifts (5 percent)

All of these unethical behaviors can be defined as inconsiderate, disrespectful, and dishonest—just the opposite of the principles of etiquette. So ethical behavior is behavior grounded in consideration, respect, and honesty, and that's why, as Emily said, "Etiquette must, if it is to be of more than trifling use, include ethics as well as manners."

Ethics Is Grounded in Intent

We can all agree that lying about time worked is an ethical issue. When does an ethical issue no longer qualify as an ethical issue? Are the following ethical dilemmas?

- Taking $100 from petty cash
- Taking a quarter from petty cash for the parking meter
- Falsifying financial records
- Copying your résumé on the office copier
- Lying about hours worked
- Taking a pen from the office home with you

Some of these examples are serious breaches and come with consequences when discovered. There's no wiggle room to put a spin on the action that excuses it.

Other actions seem petty. Really, who is going to worry about a quarter from petty cash or two pieces of paper in the copier or a pen? Probably no one.

Still, they are ethical issues because of the intent behind them. "I'll just take a quarter from petty cash" has a very different intent from "I'll borrow a quarter now and return it after lunch." In both cases, only the perpetrator knows what has happened, but the intent changes the action from an excusable one, an action in which others would continue to have trust in a person, to an inexcusable one, an action that engenders mistrust if the person is caught.

And unfortunately, when ethical situations like this arise, that's when Murphy raises his ugly head and you get caught. And once caught, dealing with the larger, more serious issue of an ethical violation is much worse than handling the situation ethically to begin with.

REPORTING ETHICAL MISBEHAVIOR

The fellow in the next cubicle has been gone all afternoon—for the third day in a row. What do you do? While you may feel a tug of loyalty toward the guy (he's really not such a bad egg), your duty is clear. Besides behaving ethically yourself, it is also your responsibility to report unethical behavior on the part of your coworkers.

In practice, how you actually respond to such behavior will vary depending on the severity and nature of the transgression. If it's a matter of a few ballpoint pens slipped into a briefcase or someone ducking out of the office an hour early now and then, you may weigh the pros and cons of saying something and then decide to remain silent for the time being. If the transgression is more serious—such as repeatedly going missing from the office for hours at a time, acting abusively toward a fellow employee, or lying about a work-related issue—you should approach your colleague and give him the opportunity to redress the situation before you do: "Jack, lying about that sales call reflects badly on the company and the rest of us. You need to approach [the manager] and explain what really happened—and if you don't, I will."

If the other person ignores you and continues the unethical behavior or tells you to take a hike—or if the transgression violates the law or is so serious that you don't feel you should approach your colleague about it—then your next step is to talk to someone in your firm's management. Your choices could include your immediate supervisor, your company's human resources department, or your firm's ethics officer.

One thing to bear in mind is that supervisors and human resources staff are obligated to investigate any complaints brought to them. The advantage of going to your firm's ethics officer first—especially if you are uncertain about whether the behavior is ethical or not or want to learn more about your company's guidelines before acting—is that the ethics officer is not required to take any action and doesn't have to divulge your name to management, the courts, or any regulatory agency.

If you are worried about repercussions, or simply want to keep your name out of the affair, many companies—including all publicly held corporations—now offer a simpler option: The Sarbanes-Oxley Act of 2002 requires public companies to have anonymous "hotlines" or similar whistleblower systems so that employees can report ethical violations without revealing their identities.

ETHICS ISSUES IN THE WORKPLACE

Behaving ethically toward your coworkers involves more than simply being honest with them. Good ethics also means treating your colleagues fairly and without discrimination and giving them whatever support and information they need to do their jobs effectively.

The following are key areas to be aware of.

Engaging in Abusive Behavior

You may disagree with the way a colleague is doing her job, or even dislike her for some reason, but that is *never* an excuse to berate or intimidate a coworker. If you're so upset that you can't conduct a job-related discussion calmly and professionally, put off the discussion for another day or sit down with the other person and your manager to hash out a constructive solution.

When Someone Is Abusive Toward You

While remaining calm yourself, respond immediately by telling the abusive colleague that his behavior is not only inappropriate but also unethical. Then offer to continue the discussion at another time when emotions have cooled. If the other person's abusive behavior continues, bring it to your immediate supervisor's attention.

Discrimination

Just like abusive behavior, treating a coworker differently because of his race, color, religion, national origins, marital status, parental or family status, gender, sexuality, disability, or age is an affront to workplace ethics as well as being illegal.

Sexual Harassment

Any sexually oriented talk or behavior in the workplace that makes a fellow employee uncomfortable is unethical and illegal and should not be tolerated. If you believe you are the victim of sexual harassment or have witnessed it, see "What Is Sexual Harassment?" (see page 123).

Keeping Confidences

If a coworker tells you something in confidence, whether it's work-related or personal, you are ethically obligated to keep the conversation private—*unless* that information involves something clearly harmful to your company, a fellow employee, or the public. At that point, it becomes incumbent on you to tell the person that this cannot remain confidential—and that if he doesn't take the issue to the appropriate person, you will have to do so.

Taking Credit

Taking credit for someone else's ideas—either passively or actively—is a form of stealing. One way to prevent this sort of thing from happening to you is to write up your idea in memo form at its very inception and email it or circulate a hard copy prior to any meetings or discussions.

Accepting Blame

When you cause a problem at work, it's incumbent on you to stand up at once and openly accept responsibility. If someone blames you unfairly, you have every right to demand that your colleague set the record straight—and to do it yourself if he refuses.

Backstabbing and Undermining

The ethical employee does not backstab or undermine his or her colleagues. On the other hand, when asked to discuss a colleague with management, it is his responsibility to objectively outline the positive and negative aspects of his colleague's performance, focusing only on work-related matters, while avoiding any overtly personal criticism. As for bull sessions among your peers about a colleague's work performance, the ethical thing is to demur politely—explaining simply, "I don't care to get into that sort of thing."

YOU AND YOUR COMPANY

When you joined your firm, you entered into an agreement to abide by all company policies and to fulfill the contractual obligations of your job. In return, your company took on the obligations of living up to its financial agreement with you and treating you fairly. There are several key ethical issues that commonly arise on both sides of this arrangement.

Your Things or Theirs?

Even the smallest pilfering could easily be the first step down a slippery slope. The best ethical approach is simply to avoid taking any office supplies out of the workplace. The only exception would be if you are explicitly working on work-related projects at home and you have your company's permission to bring home any needed supplies.

An Honest Day's Work

Avoid padding even a few minutes to the hours you're contracted to work or to what you report on your time sheet. If you are forced to miss work time—to keep a doctor's or dentist's appointment, for example—schedule the appointment for the beginning or end of the day to minimize the impact on your work schedule, and offer to work late or through lunch to make up for the lost time. Minimize the time spent on personal phone calls and emails, or in nonwork-related conversation with colleagues.

TELECOMMUTING

Taking a strong ethical position on your work hours is even more important when you're telecommuting. Since no one is watching to see if you're actually at your desk, it's up to you—and your inner ethical compass—to make sure that you're providing your employer with and reporting on an honest day's effort.

Sick Days

Sick days are strictly for illnesses that are debilitating or contagious enough to require you to stay out of the office. Using a sick day to catch up on your shopping or go to the ball game is unethical—and could also put your job in jeopardy if someone spots you in the act.

Respecting Proprietary Information

If you stumble across data that are not meant for your eyes, it is your ethical obligation not only to avoid scrutinizing this information but also to call attention to the lapse in confidentiality.

Expense Reports

Asking your firm to reimburse you for expenses that aren't actually business-related is a form of stealing. Make sure you know exactly what your company's expense reimbursement policy is and follow it.

Company Perks

Unless your company's policy explicitly says otherwise, you must assume that company perks are intended strictly for you and your coworkers and are to be used only for business-related purposes. If there is any uncertainty, offer to pay the full value of any perks in question.

Conflict of Interest

Most companies have strict conflict-of-interest rules, and it is your responsibility to know the details of your firm's policy. Beyond this, the ethical business-person is careful to avoid even the *appearance* of a conflict. For example, if you have a particularly close personal relationship with someone who is a potential vendor and it could possibly leave you open to a charge of favoritism, you should pass this information on to your company's management, along with a request that you not be involved in any procurement decisions involving that firm.

WHEN THE CULPRIT IS YOU

What if—through ignorance, carelessness, or a lapse in judgment—you do something yourself that is clearly unethical?

There will always be a strong temptation in such cases to keep quiet about your misstep and hope that no one notices, but ethics experts agree that the best move is to admit what you've done and offer to make restitution as appropriate. Tell your supervisor that you're sorry for your actions and that you'd like to start over with a clean slate. While you may still lose your job, this is better than living with the knowledge of what you've done and the anxiety that your actions may eventually be uncovered.

IT'S A LEGAL MATTER

From the ban on insider trading by investment bankers to the Hippocratic oath taken by doctors, every profession has its own unique set of legal and ethical requirements. It's your responsibility to keep abreast of all the legalities regarding your particular trade. Review these rules carefully when you first join a firm, and periodically update your knowledge. One of the best ways to do this is to confer regularly with someone from your company's legal department. Insist, too, that your company have a policy of quickly disseminating any changes or modifications in your field's legal requirements. In a courtroom, ignorance of the law is no excuse—which means that if you're not up to speed, it's your head that could be on the chopping block.

LYING FOR YOUR BOSS—AND OTHER ETHICAL DILEMMAS

You should *never* lie for your boss or be put in a situation where you're forced even to consider it. If your boss doesn't want to deal with a visitor or a telephone call, it's better to say your boss is "unavailable" rather than telling a fib like "He's in a meeting" or "She's out of the office." The same holds true, by the way, when it comes to keeping confidences your boss has shared with you.

In a more troubling situation—if, for example, your boss asks you to alter the minutes of a meeting—your best response is to say, "I'm sorry, but I'm uncomfortable with that." Most managers will respect your ethical stance and back down.

Perhaps the toughest of all dilemmas is when a manager or colleague asks you to do something that you feel is unethical "for the good of the company." If you're feeling pressure to do something questionable—or observe someone else being so pressured—your first step should be to discuss the pros and cons of the situation with a supervisor who isn't directly involved in the assignment. If that doesn't clear up the matter, contact your firm's human resources department or ethics officer (if you have one). As a last resort, you can go to your company's legal counsel or compliance officer.

If you attempt to turn down the questionable assignment but the pressure to act unethically continues, you'll need to consider resigning. At the very least, you'll want to take an unflinching look at your entire company. Is the pressure you're feeling an aberration, or is it reflective of the general corporate culture?

The final step, in cases in which you believe your firm's activities are dangerous or illegal, is to become a whistle-blower and report the company's ethics lapses to the appropriate oversight agency.

THE ETHICAL MANAGER

As a company manager, you have three additional sets of ethical responsibilities beyond your obligations as an employee:

- You have a responsibility not to abuse your position when interacting with your subordinates.
- You have a responsibility to serve as an ethical role model for others in the company.
- You have a responsibility to actively promote an ethical environment within your firm, including putting systems into place to help accomplish this goal and encouraging employees to come to you with their concerns.

Let's consider these points one at a time.

Not Abusing Your Position

The ethical manager will never ask an employee to lie or misrepresent the facts or to perform an action that is ethically dubious. The ethical manager is also scrupulously fair in her treatment of all subordinates, including hiring and promoting employees. Finally, the ethical manager never exploits her position to demand a favor or other consideration from an employee; to harass or vent displeasure toward an employee in an abusive, belittling, or intimidating way; or to ask an employee to put in more work than he is being paid for.

Conversely, the ethical manager makes every effort to support her staff members within the company and also in regard to their long-term career paths. She works with each employee in good faith to resolve any problems or difficulties that might arise. The ethical manager is also careful to be clear and accurate in all interoffice communications and to pass along important information about the company in an appropriate and timely fashion.

Serving as an Ethical Role Model

Experts agree that corporate ethics are defined from the top down. When a company's leaders are perceived as having high personal ethics, that company's employees are more likely to have high ethical standards as well. The higher your leadership position, the more effect your words and actions will have.

Promoting an Ethical Workplace

The ethical leader insists that his firm adopt ethical goals and means and encourages an open decision-making process that includes a full discussion of the ethical implications of various business opportunities.

The role of an ethical leader also involves making sure the company has systems in place that support ethical behavior. These include a corporate code of ethics that applies to all employees at all times; in-house communication strategies that emphasize the importance of ethical behavior and encourage the discussion of ethical issues within the company; training programs to help educate employees on how to make good ethical decisions; resources for employees who wish to seek guidance on ethical issues; a mechanism for reporting unethical behavior; and an established process for dealing with ethics lapses if and when they occur, including an ethics officer who reports directly to the CEO.

THE ETHICAL VENDOR

Clients and customers are the lifeblood of any business. Treating your customers ethically is not just the right thing to do, it will also help ensure that they remain your customers over the long haul. The ethical vendor

- Works diligently to finish every assignment professionally within the agreed-upon time frame, while charging a fair price for it

- Gives honest reasons for any problems and/or delays and offers legitimate, honorable solutions

- Provides an accurate estimate of the costs for any services or goods ahead of time, when appropriate, and makes good on that estimate

- Never promises anything that can't be delivered

- Never offers cash or other unethical inducements in an attempt to secure business

- Never colludes with a customer to get around regulations, manipulate fees or prices, or secure business in an unethical fashion

- Avoids even the appearance of any unethical behavior in its business relationships

An ethical company will typically have a policy against working for two clients who are competitors, for example, and will place a limit on the value of gifts that be given to or received from clients. What should you do if you do get a present that's too expensive? Simply return the item in question with a note saying, "I appreciate your gift, but I'm afraid the rules here won't allow me to keep it." (See also "Accepting and Declining Gifts," page 173.)

THE ETHICAL CUSTOMER

Being an ethical customer or client doesn't mean you can't push hard for the best possible service or product at the best possible price. It does mean, however, that you always conduct your negotiations in an open, honest fashion and are careful not to use your position to exploit or manipulate the vendor—for instance, by asking a firm to spend time preparing a proposal "on spec" when you know that you have no intention of hiring that company. In addition, the ethical customer

- Pays vendors within the agreed-upon time period

- Lives up to all contractual obligations

- Doesn't pressure the vendor to provide goods or services beyond the scope of their agreement

- Never allows a choice of vendor to be influenced by favors, gifts, or kickbacks

- Avoids even the appearance of any conflict of interest or discrimination when selecting vendors

- Works in good faith with creditors to resolve outstanding debts if financial difficulties make it impossible to meet contractual obligations

THE ETHICAL JOB SEEKER

Whether you're between jobs, looking to change positions, or just starting out on your career path, searching for new employment has its own set of ethical hurdles. It's always a good idea to head off disruptive speculation by being as discreet as possible when looking for a new job—for example, by conducting all interviews and job-related phone calls at a safe distance from your office. These activities should be done only on your own time, either outside normal work hours or in the context of a personal or vacation day. You also owe it to your employer to give at least two weeks' notice before leaving your current job.

In addition, the ethical job-seeker

- Never lies or exaggerates in a résumé or cover letter

- Focuses only on legitimate accomplishments during interviews

- Avoids bad-mouthing his or her former employer when leaving a job

Ethics experts also suggest taking advantage of the job-interview process to inquire about your prospective employer's ethical policies and enforcement systems. If a firm has shaky or nonexistent ethical standards and practices, the time to learn this is *before* you jump on board—not after.

CHAPTER 2
DRESS AND GROOMING

Business dress has undergone such radical shifts in the past ten years that people simply no longer know what is appropriate anymore. Standards that used to speak for the entire work world now barely suffice for an individual profession. For instance, some law offices still require men to wear suits, whereas others opt for a jacket-and-tie look and some go so far as to permit full-blown business casual anytime. A few firms still subscribe to a casual Friday mode, although that particular trend is fast dying out. We've even heard of casual firms going to a formal Friday routine.

Does all this change mean that anything goes? Of course not. Figuring out which clothes are appropriate for your business simply means assessing the par-ticulars. It boils down to (1) dressing to fit in at your company and (2) dressing to meet the expectations of those with whom you do business. In a word, it's situational. But that doesn't mean you should get complacent. Some things about clothing never change: People judge you by your clothes; dressing appropriately at your company is a vital ingredient in making a good first impression as well as in maintaining a good image at work. Knowing how to dress yourself well will give you an advantage over your peers.

ATTITUDE AND ADAPTATION

Today's work environment emphasizes situational dress, with an employee's choice of what to wear to work determined by his or her profession and the attitudes of the company. Fields such as finance, law, banking, and insurance typically call for traditional business clothing in almost every case, whereas industries that provide design or content—advertising, publishing, entertainment, fashion, and information technology—tend to allow for more personal expression.

The modern business worker is chameleon-like. What to wear to work depends on what he plans for

> **TIP:** Dressing for "what I'm doing today" can be risky. You never know when an invitation to see a valued customer, client, or contractor may come out of the blue. Avoid getting caught by either (1) keeping a change of dress clothes in your office or (2) dressing daily in a way that's appropriate regardless of the situation—the wiser of the two choices.

that day. If he's doing nothing special, a man might wear his usual open-collar shirt; if meeting with clients who are sure to be wearing ties, he will wear one, too. Or, if he's going to be meeting with clients who wear nothing but jeans and T-shirts, he knows that wearing a suit could build a wall between him and his clients, so he'll opt for jeans and an open-collar dress shirt.

SEVEN KEY POINTS

Whether your workplace is stodgily conservative or more casual, here are seven pointers that always apply to business dress:

1. **Keep it understated.** Understatement—allowing your clothes to speak without shouting—has always been the hallmark of the well dressed. Coco Chanel famously said that you should always remove one accessory before stepping out, a way of putting "less is more" into practice. Yet this,

too, is relative. What is considered too flashy by a conservative law firm is a far cry from what's too "out there" at a recording studio.

2. **Dress for the job you want, not the job you have.** Take a look at how your manager dresses, or the people in the sales division where you really want to work. Use your own style, but match your dress style to their level of formality, at least occasionally, to show your employers that you're focused on growing with the company, rather than pushing the envelope on corporate dress policy.

3. **Represent your company.** Whenever you deal with people from outside, your clothes reflect on your company. No matter what the dress code is at the office, be prepared to look your best.

4. **Keep it neat and clean.** The blouse with the ripped seam and the unpressed trousers should stay in the closet until they can be mended and

---

OWN YOUR LOOK

Q. I have heard the phrase "You should dress for the job you want, not the job you have." I work at a large software company where most people wear business attire. I'm one of the youngest people. I'm concerned that if I wear business attire, I'll be seen as the kid playing dress up.

A. A professional appearance goes a long way to enhancing your image at work. You will be judged by your appearance and dressing down can make you seem younger and less qualified than

you are. If most people at your firm wear business attire, then you certainly can as well. By wearing appropriate business attire, you show respect for your coworkers and the culture, as well as making it clear that you belong. When you demonstrate respect, you have a much better chance of having respect shown to you in return. Be sure to have your clothes properly fitted to you; this will go a long way to ensuring that you look professional, as well as making you feel comfortable in your new look and not just "playing dress up."

ironed. The same goes for footwear, even on casual days: Dirty canvas shoes, beat up flip-flops, or well-worn heels should be saved for home and not worn to work. Soiled jeans and a T-shirt speak more of slovenliness and poor personal habits than of rebellion and cool.

5. **Don't reveal too much.** Clothes that are too revealing are unsuitable in any workplace. Whether intentional or not, low-cut blouses, tight pants, short skirts, and see-through fabrics send a sexual message. The smart business dresser knows that the key is to have your colleagues, bosses, and clients focus on your work, not your body.

6. **Dress for the time of day.** Arriving at work in clothes more suitable for evening is also a bad idea. Bring in your after-work attire and change your outfit after the official workday is done.

7. **Don't be a fashion victim.** Because your work clothes are the kind of investment that should last for several years, don't let "what's in" or "what's cheap" be your guide. Following a trend can be a giant mistake if it doesn't fit who you are and an even bigger mistake if it doesn't fit your company's culture.

BUSINESS CLOTHES FOR MEN

The following notes on clothes and accessories are to help men make choices when they shop and dress, no matter what field they are in. Choosing suitable fabrics has to do with seasonality and practicality. Personal style will always play a part, but erring on the side of subtlety is generally the best course.

> **TIP:** Not only will wool wrinkle less, but also a lightweight variety is actually cooler than linen and some cottons for summer.

The Suit

Your business suit may spend more time hanging in the closet than it used to, but it remains an essential in every man's wardrobe. While you want to select a suit with care, think less of making a fashion statement than of finding something that fits well and feels comfortable and that will stand the test of time.

There's only one ironclad rule in choosing a fabric for a suit: No matter what the color, the surface should be matte—not shiny, iridescent, or fuzzy. The choice in fabrics boils down to wool, cotton, or microfiber.

- **Wool.** With its many textures, wool is the suit fabric of choice because of its ability to stretch yet still keep its shape, its matte finish, its ability to breathe (keeping you warmer in winter and cooler in summer), and its long shelf life.

- **Cotton.** In summer, cotton and linen are popular suit fabrics because they're so comfortable and lightweight. But be careful, especially with linen. Unless you aspire to the fashionable nonchalance associated with wrinkles, remember that linen will look as if you slept in it after only a few hours.

- **Microfibers.** Microfiber suits are a great alternative. They come in as many colors and patterns as wool and cotton options but have the added bonus of being wrinkle resistant, which make them fantastic for travel and frequent wear.

Dark colors have always been associated with authority, but tradition has also embraced suits in lighter shades of brown (tan and beige) and gray. Solids are always a safe choice, but pinstripes are a handsome alternative, with a very thin, light gray stripe being the most common choice.

Sport Jackets and Blazers

The most versatile style is the single-breasted jacket in a classic shape. Small checks, muted patterns, and tweeds are the usual designs, while solids come in almost every color imaginable. If the sport coat is the most casual item of business wear and the three-piece suit the dressiest, the navy blue blazer occupies the middle ground. A blazer paired with gray flannel pants creates a classic look that's unsurpassed.

Slacks

Slacks should be worn with the waist high enough to rest the waistband over your hipbones. Nonpleated pants tend to make you look slimmer. Cuffs are classic, whereas no cuffs present a more modern look.

Dress Shirts

At work, more muted colors work better than loud ones. The only qualification is to make sure the jacket, shirt, and tie complement one another. White remains the dressiest choice. A collar with stays instead of buttons is more formal. The button-down collar offers a wide range of formality as it can be worn with a suit or with jeans and no tie.

Overcoats and Raincoats

The traditional and most versatile length for an overcoat is just below the knee. Shorter coats such as pea coats, parkas, and duffle coats are also perfectly fine to wear with casual clothes or even a suit, especially in colder climates where practicality has to prevail over style. The trench coat is one of the more popular coat styles, and this raincoat can double as a dress coat.

Shoes

From the dressiest on down, the traditional business shoes are the oxford (plain toe or cap toe), the wing tip, and the plain or tasseled loafer. Your shoes should harmonize with your outfit: black with gray, brown with tan, either with navy.

Socks

Beyond these three basics, few rules apply to socks: (1) Use dark socks for business wear, (2) match them to your pants, and (3) make sure they're high enough not to show your bare shins when you sit down. Natural fibers such as cotton and wool are preferable to synthetics because they are better insulators and are more breathable, keeping feet warmer and deterring foot odor.

Accessories

As basic as a tie, as small as a pen, as infrequently used as an umbrella—the smaller items of the businessman's wardrobe can dress up your look, giving it an expensive sheen, or dress it down. And, like clothing, these accessories should change character according to the situation.

THE TIE

For the great majority of men who dress for business, the tie remains the most important of all accessories. Wide, skinny, striped, solid—even ties are subject to fashion whims. There are two schools of thought about ties: The first says that your tie is a way for you to express your individuality. The second says that defining your personality with your tie may make you feel good, but nobody else really cares. Some people find idiosyncratic ties unprofessional—your coworkers might get a kick out of your tie with the mermaid motif, but some of your customers may not be amused. One solution to this problem is to keep a "safe" tie in your office. Regardless of the design, make sure your tie color coordinates with your shirt and jacket.

HATS

Crowned hats for men fell out of fashion in the 1960s and '70s but have been making a comeback in the last decade or so. The most popular hat for business attire is the fedora, followed by the homburg and the porkpie. In the western and southwestern United States, the Stetson is often worn with business attire. Definitely wear your suit when shopping for a hat. You'll want to be sure the hat complements your suit. Keep your hat clean, brushed (if needed), and blocked to retain its shape.

BELTS AND SUSPENDERS

Belts should be coordinated with your shoe color, and that means you need at least two—a black one and a brown one. The standard belt width is one or one and a quarter inches, which fits the belt loops on suit pants, flannels, and khakis. Materials of choice are fine-grade leather and for casual wear, braided leather, suede, or canvas. Avoid showy buckles, obvious stitching, and other trimmings for your business belts.

THE UBIQUITOUS BASEBALL CAP

The most important consideration for the cap-wearing businessperson is to know when to take it off. Wearing a baseball cap to work is perfectly fine, but keeping it on once you've stepped through the door is not. The cap is so much a part of some men that they forget they have it on, and more than one worker has come to an early-morning meeting and had to be reminded to remove it. Never wear a hat, including the baseball hat, in a restaurant or any time you are at a table for a meal. Be aware, too, that those of an older generation do not consider a baseball cap appropriate for business attire.

Suspenders are coordinated to the tie, with the quietness or wildness of the pattern determined by the company culture in which the wearer works.

JEWELRY

Two words sum up the well-dressed businessman's use of jewelry: minimalist and subtle. A wedding band, a class ring, and a good watch aren't quite the limit, but they're close. Anything else on the hands or wrists should be limited to a very simple ring, cuff links, or a simple bracelet. Tie tacks, pins, and bars are all appropriate. Chains around the neck are never suitable in a conventional work environment and are often out of place even in casual settings.

WATCHES

Think simple. The classic analog watch has always been a traditional businessman's accessory and is popular

PROFESSIONAL AND CASUAL BUSINESS CLOTHES FOR MEN

Men—Professional / Formal

ACCEPTABLE

Suits—three piece, two piece, two button or three button, wool or cotton

Vests

Blazers or sport jackets

Slacks

Dress shirts or oxford shirts, button-down or with collar stays

Ties

Overcoats or raincoats

Oxfords, wing tips, or loafers, tasseled or plain

Dark socks

NOT ACCEPTABLE

Loud colors or bold patterns

Spread collars without ties

Athletic shoes

White socks

Fur coats

Showy belt buckles

Men—Casual

ACCEPTABLE

Blazers or sport jackets

Oxford shirts, button down or with collar stays

Turtlenecks

Short-sleeved knit polo shirts

Khaki or flannel slacks

Dress jeans (dark, pressed)

V-neck or crewneck sweaters

Informal ties, optional

NOT ACCEPTABLE

T-shirts with slogans, sayings, or cartoon characters

Torn or worn-out jeans

Anything shiny or too tight

Sandals

Tank tops

Shorts, unless specifically approved at your workplace

---

even in the age of digital timepieces. Keep that dive watch with several timers and multiple buttons for non-business situations. Even more important than the style you choose is making sure you turn off any electronic sounds your watch makes. A sudden beep announcing the hour can interrupt a meeting or presentation.

SUNGLASSES

Don't wear sunglasses when you're meeting with people for business unless you're walking outside in bright sun. Obviously, you should make eye contact, and sunglasses render that impossible while at the same time making you look inscrutable (or worse, suspicious). Wearing sunglasses indoors is an affectation that's going to make most people think you're trying to shout "Hollywood!"

BRIEFCASES

Laptop computer cases are now challenging the traditional briefcase in popularity, especially since many now build in additional room for documents and other materials. Whichever you use, it should be in excellent condition. For a simple sheaf of papers, another option is a leather envelope carried under the arm.

STAYING WELL GROOMED

Staying well groomed means staying clean, odor-free, and untousled. It's a practical thing: A man with greasy hair and dandruff is going to be less appealing to be around, his sloppy personal habits creating a wall between him and his coworkers and—perhaps even more important—his clients. The idea is to attract, not repel. Here's an everyday grooming checklist, including some items to keep on hand:

HAIR. Wash your hair often enough to keep it from looking greasy. Avoid both the super-blow-dried look and the gelled-to-the-skull look. If you tend to have dandruff, use a dandruff shampoo and keep a small clothes brush in the office for whisking flakes off your shoulders. When it comes to style, for most business fields, you'll want to go with something low key and simple. Anything that makes someone focus on your hair rather than your work is probably not the style you should choose.

FINGERNAILS. Dirt can mysteriously appear under your fingernails when you least expect it. Keep a nail clipper with a cleaning tool in your desk drawer, but be sure to use it in the restroom, not at your desk.

FIVE O'CLOCK SHADOW. This can be a problem if you have very dark hair. An electric shaver will smarten you up if you have a late-afternoon meeting, so keep one in your desk drawer if necessary, and remember to take it to the restroom if you need to use it.

NECK, NOSE, AND EAR HAIR. One morning a week, check to see if your nose hairs need to be clipped (special blunt-end scissors and clippers are made for the purpose) or your ears tweezed. Your barber or

TATTOOS AND PIERCINGS

A tattoo on a part of your body that no one will see is not an issue, but one on a hand, forearm, neck, or any other potentially visible place is different. Will the exotic tiger tattooed on your arm or upper neck affect your chances of getting a job or being promoted? No one knows for sure—but as soon as the tattoo becomes part of the image you project, it may affect what people think of you.

By comparison, most body piercings are benign. Unlike tattoos, most piercing ornaments can be removed at will, which means that people who like them can have their cake and eat it, too. Most American businesses, however, still think piercings are strictly for earlobes. The smart man or woman in business takes cues from his or her peers and bosses before wearing any piercings to work.

stylist can take care of the neck and ear hair and eyebrows, too.

BODY ODOR. A daily shower is the best defense against body odor, and a deodorant or antiperspirant is the second best, but avoid those with a heavy scent. This is another good item to stash at your desk and use in the restroom if you need to later in the day.

BREATH. To keep your breath fresh, keep a toothbrush at work and brush after lunch. Brushing the back of the tongue helps control odor, and a breath mint or two during the day should keep you from offending. Flossing is also a huge contributor to keeping your breath fresh. Think about it: Rotting old food stuck between your teeth collecting bacteria? That can't be good. Just be sure to brush and floss in the restroom.

WELL-HEELED, SHINED SHOES. Shoes with the heels worn down should be worn only at home. A cobbler can repair a worn heel. As for shoe polish, your shoes needn't be mirrorlike, but they shouldn't be noticeably scuffed or dirty either. Keep a simple polishing kit at home and use as necessary. Treat yourself to a professional polish once in a while at an airport, train station, or hotel lobby.

IRONED CLOTHES. The wrinkled look at the office makes you look unprofessional. A touch-up with an iron before work will take a coat hanger crease out of slacks and make any less-than-smooth shirts more presentable. No-iron clothing has made wrinkles a thing of the past.

JEANS

The issue of jeans: Wearing jeans or not is determined by the workplace. At some places, jeans are fine; at others, they are not. However, it is never acceptable to wear jeans that are torn, have holes, are stained, are too tight, and/or are worn out. This applies to men and women. The same guidelines apply to T-shirts where in some companies the company shirt with a logo is perfectly acceptable. On the other hand, good-quality jeans have become a travel attire staple for working professionals of both genders.

CLEAN CLOTHES. Don't be tempted to wear that shirt, tie, or pair of pants with the grease spot, thinking that no one will notice. If it turns out you have to meet with clients, they'll notice. Wearing clean clothes is as essential as combing your hair. Also be careful of clothing that has sat too long in your closet or drawer without being aired out. It can develop an "old" odor that you want to watch out for.

Your Cologne

No element of the businessman's wardrobe requires more subtlety than cologne. If some scents for men are meant to conjure up a woody glade or a citrus grove, they should merely hint at those places—not plop you down in the middle of them. Filling a meeting room with the smell of citrus, balsam, or musk is the job of an air freshener, not you. Wearing too much cologne is even worse at an interview, where the "all things in moderation" approach is key.

Q. What really counts as business casual? When are sandals and sleeveless dresses or blouses acceptable in the workplace?

A. As with all dress codes, casual dress can mean different things at different companies. One standard that helps define appropriateness of clothing is asking yourself, "If I have to meet with the CEO, am I appropriately dressed?" If you are dressing casually, a meeting with the CEO may require that you include a jacket, even if wearing one is usually optional. Typically, shorts are not acceptable. Similarly casual dress for women is company specific. When dressing casually be wary of wearing flip-flops, spaghetti straps, spandex, short skirts, shorts and showing a bare midriff.

Not only do dress codes vary markedly from workplace to workplace, they also can vary according to the time of year or even which day of the week it is: regular-dress day or a casual Friday. In general, sandals and sleeveless dresses and blouses are casual dress that is more often acceptable on a dress-down day or as part of a company's summer attire policy. Most important of all, the appropriateness rests with the decision makers at the company. And the responsibility for establishing a clear dress code also rests with them.

BUSINESS CLOTHES FOR WOMEN

While today's businesswoman has more choices available to her than her predecessors of a generation or two ago did, the principles underlying the traditional dress code are still in place in most professional fields—namely, that good taste is never showy, whether in color, fabric, style, accessories, hairstyle, or makeup. Yes, style and customs change rapidly, but the smart woman in business will ground herself in the traditional styles and then branch out from there.

Here's a basic wardrobe for almost any businesswoman to start with:

- A three-piece suit (jacket, slacks, and interchangeable skirt) or two suits (one with jacket and skirt, one with jacket and slacks)

- A white, cream-colored or solid conservative-colored blouse (not sleeveless)

- A sweater set suitable for the workplace

- A fine silk scarf, conservative and in good condition for the workplace

- A microfiber all-weather coat

- A good-quality handbag

- A pair of one-and-a-half- to three-inch black-leather heels

- A pair of good-quality flat shoes, loafer-style or similar

- Panty hose, knee-high stockings, or trouser socks

- An umbrella

PROFESSIONAL AND CASUAL BUSINESS CLOTHES FOR WOMEN

Women—Professional / Formal

ACCEPTABLE

Dress, with or without jacket

Three-piece suits: jackets, trousers, and
    interchangeable skirts

Separates: Jacket, skirt, slacks

Coordinating belt

White or cream-colored blouses

Coordinating colored blouses

Sweater sets

Silk scarves (standard size, thirty-four inches)

Quality all-weather coats—wool, twill, or microfiber

Good-quality handbags

One-and-a-half- to three-inch black leather heels

Good-quality loafer-style shoes or flats

Tights and/or panty hose

Umbrellas (arriving for a meeting soaking wet is
    not impressive)

NOT ACCEPTABLE

Jewelry that dangles, jangles, sparkles, or is gaudy

Athletic shoes

Fur coats (depends on locale)

Metallic, glittery, or sheer fabrics

Cleavage-revealing tops

Skirts or dresses more than three inches above the
    top of the knee

Women—Casual

ACCEPTABLE

Casual blazers

Tailored pants, skinny pants, capris, pencil pants,
    or long shorts (depends on locale)

Skirts

Dresses (long or short)

Khaki pants

Washable linen pants

Sweater twin sets

Tunic-style sweaters

Plain knit blouses

Loafers or flats

Open-toed pumps

NOT ACCEPTABLE

T-shirts with slogans, sayings, or cartoon characters

Tattered jeans

Spandex miniskirts

Strapless, stretchy bandeau tops

Exercise clothing, sweatpants, or sweat suits

Tank tops

Spaghetti straps

Bare midriffs

Flip-flops

To these you can add garments and accessories that will individualize your look without taking it outside of your workplace norm.

Color Considerations

When it comes to color, what is considered appropriate varies by region as much as by professional field. As always, the smart dresser starts by observing the conventions in her area and her workplace, taking her cues from those around her. But she also knows something about the general perception of various colors.

- Navy blue, burgundy, black, charcoal gray, and taupe are the traditional colors of the businesswoman's wardrobe, with the darker hues worn through the winter. Neutral colors, or tonals, are preferable to pure colors—sea green over kelly green, for example, or peach over orange.

- As for other colors, red is strong and assertive—the reason it's known as a power color. Bright orange, magenta, and other loud colors can cross the line into tackiness in conservative businesses if not worn with care; these bright colors may be worn, but when in doubt, tone them down with a dark color, such as a navy suit.

Coordinate and Accent

Coordinating color in an outfit is equally important. For the more traditional look, start with basic business colors for the major garments and then accent them with brighter colors in small amounts, which will create an eye-catching ensemble. A classic example is the patterned scarf used with a gray or camel suit. A brighter-colored blouse with complementary earrings, necklaces, or bracelets serves the same purpose and balances the overall look. But do be careful of matching colors and accessories too much as they will look forced rather than stylish.

Fabrics

The enduring preference for natural fabrics is rooted in the fact that cotton, wool, silk, and linen breathe while keeping the wearer cool or warm. The new microfibers are synthetics reborn, providing breathability, comfort, and ease of care.

The acceptance of synthetics and knits is particularly good news for businesswomen. These fabrics that were once thought of as suitable only for casual wear can now go into the workplace depending on how they're styled. It's even better news for businesswomen who travel. A garment that blends a natural fiber with a synthetic is more flexible, easier to care for, and less seasonal, not to mention wrinkle-free, making it perfect for wearing on a trip that goes from chilly Boston to steamy Houston.

Accessories

The wide range of accessories that you're able to select from gives you more leeway to achieve a look of authority and style. Choose them to reflect both your own attitude and that of your organization. Remember that accessories, conventional or not, project an image, and you want that image to be positive.

HANDBAGS

A quality handbag is a valuable accessory that need not break the bank. Focus first on neatness and functionality, making sure the bag is large enough to hold all the items you carry with you—a touch-up makeup case, day planner, tablet, cell phone, and wallet for example.

BRIEFCASES

The traditional briefcase is giving way to the protective laptop computer case, the purchase of which demands the same attention to good design and quality as you would devote to a briefcase.

DEVICE COVERS

Choose your tablet, smartphone, and laptop cases and covers with an eye to business, if that's where you will use them most. Save the bejeweled phone case for weekends.

BELTS

When a woman's outfit requires a belt, the classic style is one-half- to three-quarter-inch-wide leather. Buckles can be metal or leather in any simple, quiet shape; if metal, coordinate it to other metal—earrings, necklaces, watchbands, buttons, and bracelets you may be wearing. The belt's color should harmonize with shoe and garment colors. Wear belts loose enough to ride with the waistband of your pants or skirt, not above it.

SCARVES

A scarf can heighten focus on the face or provide visual relief to a monochromatic outfit. Scarves can also dress up a casual outfit or soften a tailored look. Coordinate a multicolored scarf to your ensemble by making sure it picks up a color in the outfit and works with your skin tone.

JEWELRY

If you have a passion for jewelry, curb it during the workday—at traditional offices, at least. Keep in mind that jewelry should accent, not take center stage. Beware jewelry that's noisy—charm and bangle bracelets, particularly—that could be distracting or annoying to others. (See also the box "Tattoos and Piercings," page 24.)

EARRINGS. Simple button-style earrings in silver, gold, or pearl are classic because they harmonize well with jacket outfits. Diamond, pearl, or gold studs or small drops are also always appropriate.

NECKLACES. Two necklace styles are traditional for business wear—pendants with small-scale silver or gold chains or small to medium-size classic pearls. Let the neckline of the garment decide the shape: V-shaped neckline, V-shaped necklace; rounded neckline, rounded necklace. To coordinate a colored necklace with your outfit, make sure its color is repeated somewhere—in a print, the belt, or the skirt or blouse color.

RINGS. With simplicity as the guiding principle, the maximum number of rings for traditional business wear is one per hand (wedding and engagement count as one ring).

WATCHES. Two kinds of bands are preferred in conservative offices: leather in black or brown; and metal in matte stainless steel, silver, or gold. (Match the metal of your watch to that of your other jewelry.) Large-face watches are fine. Remember to turn off any electronic noises the watch makes.

At what time of year, exactly, are you not supposed to wear white? Was it Easter or Memorial Day? A few taboos and customs hold fast, but most others have either relaxed or fallen by the wayside on the road to sartorial correctness.

SEASONAL COLORS

The seasonal injunction against the color white no longer applies. The determinant applies only to white fabrics and materials—and loosely, at that. White suede pumps in November? Sure, if they go with your outfit. The white gabardine skirt is fine for winter, too. Thin white cotton slacks in Minnesota in January? No, for obvious reasons. Also take note whether your white is summer white (which is much more of a bleached, fresh white) or winter white (which has a bit more of a creamy color to it).

Lighter colors are more acceptable at all times of year and are not limited to spring and summer, especially in seasonless fabrics. And vice versa: Forest green, for example, was considered a fall and winter color but is now perfectly fine for a springtime garment.

FABRICS

Objections to certain fabrics for business clothing have largely disappeared, with style a more important issue than "natural versus synthetic" or "woven versus knit."

Knitwear was once perceived as too casual for the traditional business look. But after top designers put knit suits on the map, this attitude changed. Knits have also gained favor because they don't wrinkle, making them ideal for business travel.

For shoes and handbags, patent leather is no longer a spring-and-summer-only choice. Black and dark browns and other earth colors are the conservative's favorites, but patent leather in all colors for shoes and handbags provide a wide range of options for a finished look.

Footwear

The traditional taboos against open-toed shoes, backless shoes, sling backs, and other informal styles still exist in conservative workplaces but have disappeared in most others. Most offices consider the following shoes undesirable: clogs; hiking boots; boat shoes; flip-flops; and chunky, thick-soled shoes. Knowing what's appropriate anywhere is equally easy: the pump. Beyond that, take cues from your peers and your bosses.

PUMPS

The classic business pump has a one- to one-and-a-half-inch-high heel (and the wider the heel, the more comfortable), but any becoming height can be appropriate depending on the workplace. In all but the most formal workplaces, you'll now see a range between three-inch heels and flats. Shoe color is also less of an issue than it once was and most women coordinate their shoes to the color of their outfits, but the traditional business colors remain black, navy, chocolate brown, and taupe. Whatever the color, under no circumstances should you wear shoes that are dirty or scuffed or have worn-down heels.

BOOTS

New boot styles designed with commuters in mind are cross-functional: The upper portion is more formal, while the rubber soles grip the pavement securely. These new styles make it possible to wear boots to the office without having to change to heels. That said, many polished looks accommodate both knee-high or ankle-high boots, acceptable in all but very conservative offices.

ATHLETIC SHOES

Never wear athletic shoes at work, unless it is the norm at a casual dress company or when approved for dress-down days. To wear them to or from the office is fine, however, especially in cities where heels become a problem when negotiating sidewalks and public transportation. Many women keep a pair of shoes at the office or carry them in a tote bag to change into at the office.

HOSIERY

While panty hose or stockings are still the norm with dresses and skirts in the business office, many companies are relaxing or eliminating the panty-hose rules in summer. Before you leave yours home in your bureau, check your office policy, and be sure that the bare-leg look works for you. Knee-high stockings or opaque knee socks are appropriate with slacks. Nude, beige, and black are the basic choices for sheer stockings. In less formal offices, opaque tights are fine, especially in the winter, and should coordinate with your outfit.

THE "DON'T LEAVE HOME WITHOUT IT" EMERGENCY KIT

The smart businesswoman keeps a stash of emergency items in her office or desk. It's wise to have a change of professional clothes on hand for use as needed: a jacket, as well as an extra ironed shirt or blouse and a skirt or pair of slacks. Here's a checklist of other emergency items:

- ☐ Wash-and-dry towelettes
- ☐ Marker for touching up shoe scuffs
- ☐ Lint roller
- ☐ Fashion tape to hold up hems
- ☐ Safety pins
- ☐ Small sewing kit
- ☐ Brushes for hair, clothes, shoes
- ☐ Spot remover
- ☐ Eyeglasses
- ☐ Dental floss, toothbrush, and toothpaste
- ☐ Extra pair of hose
- ☐ Static guard
- ☐ Nail polish—clear for panty-hose runs, your current nail color to repair chips
- ☐ Nail file
- ☐ Lipstick and compact

STAYING WELL GROOMED

Grooming is every bit as important as what you wear. Hair has proved its potential to make a statement as well as or more strongly than clothes do. The amount of makeup sends a message, too—and in most workplaces, understatement in both is key.

Hair

A woman will attract attention with her hair when she has a flattering cut or healthy, shiny hair that simply begs to be admired. What about length? There's no longer a rule, but on the job, keep hair out of the eyes: Tuck it behind your ears, pull it back or up, or aside with a barrette. Clips that create an instant upswept twist are also popular and make for a nice professional look.

Makeup

As a rule, use a light touch—makeup should enhance, not dominate. Extreme eye makeup, very unusual lip color, a lot of lip liner that is in obvious contrast to the lipstick—these are poor choices in most workplaces.

Nails

The best length for nails in most business environments is just over the tip of the finger. The appropriateness of extreme length or colors (black, blue, purple, neon) and fake nails decorated with designs or pictures is in direct proportion to the conservatism of your workplace. Clear nail polish is the best choice if you're uncertain. In conservative offices, a classic red, an understated pink, or clear polish are all fine.

Perfume

Like it or not, the perfume you wear to the office may be offending someone's nose. There has been an appreciable jump in the number of people who claim they are "allergic" to most scents in general, especially manufactured ones. Unless you work in an office with a "no scent" policy, you don't have to go to work scent-free. Just make sure the scent is light and clean, not one of the more exotic or "romantic" blends more appropriate for evening. And use it sparingly: If your scent still lingers in the room after you leave someone's office, you're wearing too much.

After Dark

Evening business functions may call for a dressier wardrobe. On occasion you might need a cocktail dress and possibly even a long formal gown.

PART TWO

THE JOB APPLICANT

CHAPTER 3
THE JOB SEARCH

So what does etiquette have to do with a job search? A great deal indeed. Your stops along the path to employment include meeting new people, communicating your abilities, and proving that you not only have what it takes but would also be nice to have around. Etiquette gives you confidence as you move through this process, letting you focus on the tasks at hand instead of worrying about how to comport yourself.

This chapter takes you on a quick tour through job-hunting territory, with pointers on how to navigate it with self-assurance and civility. Forming the framework are the ins and outs of networking, managing a LinkedIn profile, setting up informational interviews, choosing the right communication strategy, and consulting an employment agency. Advice is slanted toward how you should act in the process and applies to job hunters of all kinds: the new college graduate seeking her first job, the worker looking for a change, the unlucky person who suddenly finds himself out of a job. (For more on the last two cases, see "Leaving Your Job," page 109.) Even though on the surface job hunters may appear to be very different in attitude and style—compare the ponytail-sporting computer genius in the Hawaiian shirt to the budding stockbroker in the expensive bespoke suit—their concerns and course of actions are more or less the same because basically job hunting is about building and managing relationships.

THE RIGHT TOOLS

Finding a job is, first and foremost, an exercise in communication: oral, visual, written, and digital. Assembling the communication tools you'll need is the first step in a successful job search. Computers are gateways to employment. Most companies expect job applicants to have access to the Internet and have an email address as well as having a phone and postal address. Many employers require applications to be emailed, sent as attachments, or even filed online, but that doesn't mean that a letter or printed résumé is a thing of the past. Correspondence on high-quality paper, when done right, can make an especially good impression—particularly when the inclusion of your email address shows that you could have taken the easier but less formal route.

Voice Mail/Answering Machine

Make it easy for people to reach you over the telephone by having an answering machine or a voice mail service. Leave a professional-sounding message. (See "Recording a Greeting," page 246.)

Personal Business Stationery

For all job-search letters sent by regular mail, buy the best-quality 8½ × 11-inch personal business stationery you can afford; the favorable impression made by a 24-pound 100 percent cotton paper is worth the cost. Have it printed (black ink is the fail-safe choice) with your name, address, preferred telephone number, email address, and fax number (if you have one). If having it preprinted is not an affordable option, make sure that your document includes this information prominently in the header. (See also "The Stationery Drawer," page 267.) Never use company letterhead to conduct personal business—especially when looking for a job.

Correspondence Cards

A handwritten note makes an indelible impression in the electronic era, especially in more traditional fields. While cover letters and other formal correspondence should be word-processed on your personal business stationery letter sheets, thank-you notes and personal notes to business associates can be written on a correspondence card. (See also "The Stationery Drawer," page 267.)

Personal "Business" Cards

All job seekers should have a printed personal card of some kind—it's the most efficient way to give someone you meet enough information to reach you in the future. Make sure the card is of high-quality stock and printed with a readable font. Include your full name, home address, preferred phone number(s), email address, and fax number, if applicable. Once you've had cards printed, put a few in each coat or suit pocket, handbag, briefcase, wallet, or card case so that you'll have one handy when needed.

LINKEDIN

LinkedIn is a social media network for professionals. Many people set up their profile as a searchable online résumé. At its simplest, a LinkedIn profile is a place to gather and display professional skills and experience, but it is also more than that. The social aspect of LinkedIn allows users to connect or link with each other. The network of connections around your profile works to verify and substantiate what is in the profile. Every job hunter should have a LinkedIn profile and use the network to research positions and industries as well as to develop connections, leads, and referrals. Keep these tips in mind as you set up and use your account to gain the best advantage.

- LinkedIn is searchable using Google, so build your profile using keywords that you want people to identify with you and your job hunt.

- Use a professional headshot to brand yourself and your profile. It will create the first impression many people have of you.

- Be honest. This is a public profile and the people you have already worked with are as likely to see it as those who may work with you in the future. Be sure to describe all that you have done, but don't embellish or stretch the truth.

- Connect or link with people you know and have worked with. Ask them for recommendations. Their recommendation will become part of your personal profile.

- Recommend others. Share news and work-related information. Stay active on the network and play your part in growing and supporting the community—it shows that you are a self-aware team player.

- Keep up with new features and privacy settings. LinkedIn is growing fast, and as the community changes, the ways that people use it are likely to change as well. It is up to you to stay abreast of both changes to the system itself as well as changes in community norms.

- Don't post personal or nonwork-related content.

THE SAVVY NETWORKER

Networking is a way of "making friends" in the business world. When we get along with people at school, the coffee shop, or a local sports league, we call them friends. When we meet people we get along with in business, it is often called networking.

The smart networker respects the opinions (and time) of others, helps other people as much as she is helped, and establishes rapport long before asking a favor or even offering a business or a personal card. A bad networker is a name-dropper who brags about her connections and comes across as being more concerned about what can be done for her than what she can do for someone else. It's not hard to guess which of the two has a greater chance of success.

Staying in Touch

The first rule of networking is to do it all the time, not just while job hunting. Keeping in touch, as well as helping out people on your networking list when-ever possible, ensures that when you actually do need help finding a job, you can easily call for help. When that moment comes, tell everyone you know that you're job seeking and then leave it at that. As eager as you'll be to whip out your résumé, it's up to someone else to ask for it. Also be careful not to come off as a shameless self-promoter, grabbing every chance to spout off your accomplishments. A low-key mention of your job search is all that's needed; anyone who's interested will probably ask questions or offer to help.

Following are some ways to stay in touch with people in your network, even when you're not actively looking for work:

- Meet for a bite to eat.

- Email a helpful or interesting article.

- Keep an active LinkedIn profile.

- Tweet and retweet within your industry/area of interest.

- Send holiday, birthday, congratulatory, and get-well cards when appropriate.

- Invite to a party.

- Invite to a sports event or a concert when you have an extra ticket.

- Share information about job openings.

Accepting Help from Others

It can feel awkward to ask for or accept help from others. This is one of those times when it is not just okay, it is the order of business. Just remember how it feels, and someday when you have the chance to repay the favor or do a turn for someone else that you do so and continue to pay the goodwill forward.

HELP THEM HELP YOU

When anyone, either inside or outside your network, says he'll be happy to help with a job search, graciously accept the offer. Contact him as soon as possible, definitely within twenty-four hours. Note the type of job you're looking for in a handwritten or emailed note to your helper or referral, pointing out whatever qualifications and experiences make you think you can handle it. If the helper says he wants to tell a friend about you, make it easy. Follow through immediately by sending him a résumé along with a brief letter detailing your career goals. If your contact gives you the name of someone to call, do so. Be sure to tell that person you're calling at the suggestion of your contact. If you're lucky, you might have found the first link in a chain that leads to an informational interview (see "The Informational Interview," page 43) or even a job interview.

THANK SINCERELY

Be sure to thank your helping angel, even if the leads they helped generate do not work out. A handwritten note will give your thanks the weight that it deserves, but a genuine and sincere email is a valid second option. How you handle setbacks and disappointments says a great deal about both your character and professionalism. Sometimes a setback like a rejection provides you with an opportunity to shine. Thanking someone for his or her time and effort is important and, besides being the right thing to do, will leave a lasting impression about you.

Keep a list of the people who have helped you (or even expressed interest in your job search) so that as

> **TIP:** Make sure everything about the name is correct.

soon as you're hired you can deliver the good news to all. A note of thanks also lets you say, "Please call on me if I can ever help you in any way."

Writing Notes

Choose the right medium for your message. You could use LinkedIn, email, a text, an instant message, a tweet, or a handwritten note to send someone a quick thought or thanks.

If, for example, you chat with someone at a cocktail party who says she thinks she'll mention you to her boss, your note will serve as a reminder. Just remember never to assume the favor has already been performed. Notes like this one can set the stage for things to come:

Dear Jane:

I enjoyed meeting you at Sharon Stewart's party last weekend—especially since I never dreamed of crossing paths with a Braves fan in Pittsburgh. Of course, I also really appreciate your offer to mention me to your boss. Your company sounds like the kind of place I'd be interested in knowing more about. Thanks!

Sincerely,
[Signature]
Chris Cavanaugh

If you're using stationery or a correspondence card and it isn't printed with your address and phone number, write them under your signature and include your personal card. Even if you exchanged cards with the recipient, she may have lost or misplaced yours.

HANDWRITTEN NOTES

The power of the handwritten note has never been greater! In a world of ephemeral digital communication, disposable data, and junk mail, a handwritten note says "I am taking the time to reach you in a different and significant way." The medium itself becomes a part of the message and it says, "I care."

EMAIL

Email is the most common type of written business communication. Your note will fit right in with most of the other business communication that someone is dealing with. Just be sure to write a subject line that gets your message read and not skipped over or relegated to a spam folder.

LINKEDIN

LinkedIn is a great and professional way to open an exchange with someone. Don't overdo it with repeat messages or link requests to someone who has not responded. Different people use different criteria to decide how much and how often they communicate and whom they will link with. Increase your chances by personalizing your link request. Don't use the default request language or you'll start to look like a networking robot.

ONLINE JOB HUNTING FAVORITES

www.careerbuilder.com—This is one of the biggest online job listing sites. With over a million listings there are jobs here for just about everyone.

www.monster.com—More than just listings, this industry leader provides other services and information useful to job seekers.

www.craigslist.org—The Wild West of the online classifieds world. Listings come and go very quickly so check this site several times a day for best results.

www.hound.com—You might find jobs here that are not on other big classifieds sites.

TWITTER

Tweets can be a great way to reach out and touch someone very lightly. It is a courtesy to promote others on Twitter by retweeting and including @yourperson in tweets that would be of interest to them. Again don't overdo it. One or two of these tweets each week is plenty.

LETTERS AND PHONE CALLS

Your first contact with a potential employer may result from successful networking, in which case you'll probably have a referral. A letter or phone call to your contact—mentioning who referred you, of course—is appropriate. Alternatively, you may be starting out cold. If that's the case, you'll be writing an unsolicited letter or phoning a potential employer who has never heard of you. A well-composed letter on paper may give you a leg up, and a better chance of getting through than starting out with a cold call.

Cold Calls

After preparing for your call, take the plunge. Don't worry too much about having to make repeated efforts to reach someone: Polite, positive persistence is an admirable quality in the business world. At the same time, listen for signs of exasperation from the assistant when he realizes that it's you yet again. If you sense any irritation, make your next contact a letter.

Once you've been put through to the person in charge of hiring, keep it simple and go one step at a time:

1. Introduce yourself, give the name of the person who suggested you contact the firm (if applicable), offer a brief description of your relevant professional experience and your current job (if any), and say that you're interested in learning about potential openings.

2. If the person seems receptive, ask if you may send a cover letter and résumé (and check to see whether email or paper is preferred). Don't bring up meeting in person unless you perceive some genuine interest.

3. Before hanging up, thank the person, saying, "I know how busy you must be, and I really appreciate you took the time to talk with me." Personalizing your call and finishing on a friendly note leaves your contact with a positive impression.

Q. What would you suggest is the appropriate way to follow up a cover letter and résumé sent via email? Generally when these are sent in response to a classified type ad, the ad stipulates "No phone calls, please." However, the norm for firms seems to be never to respond to applicants at all. I find this trend very inconsiderate although understandable in the current economic climate. Is there any way to get past the email wall and find out whether the firm is still hiring or not?

A. You're trapped in a catch-22: You've got a problem if you act and you've got a problem if you don't act. If an employer says "No phone calls, please" and you don't comply, what does your calling say about your ability to follow directions?

Therefore, let's take making a phone call off the table right away. An alternative is to do some sleuthing and find out the name of a person in the HR department whom you can contact by email.

One way to get the name is to go on the company's website and see if personnel are listed. Another is to call the department and ask who you can contact and what that person's email address is. A third option is to work your network to see if anyone you know can help you get a name to contact.

Companies that don't respond to job seekers when they are answering a job posting ad are inconsiderate, rude, and hurting themselves. Their reputation is tarnished by the bad feelings they're creating among job seekers. That bad image can and will reflect poorly on the company. In addition, the job seekers may one day be clients or prospects with good memories who may choose to take their business elsewhere.

Companies have a responsibility to communicate with all their constituencies and that includes job seekers. If a company tells you not to call and then doesn't follow up itself, ask yourself, "Is this a company I really want to work for?"

CLASSIFIEDS AND WANT ADS

Whether you find a job posting on a company's website, a website that specializes in job postings, or in a newspaper ad, make sure you follow the instructions in the ad.

Some companies give post office box addresses to respond to; others, fax numbers and email addresses.

Be sure to read a job advertisement carefully to try to figure out what kind of employee the company wants, and then use your cover letter to sell yourself accordingly—noting, when possible, experience and accomplishments that meet the firm's needs.

Such careful attention to detail will make your letter stand out among the potentially hundreds of responses. (*Note:* Packages from FedEx and other private express-mail companies cannot be sent to U.S. Postal Service boxes.)

SIGNING UP WITH EMPLOYMENT AGENCIES

Most private agencies represent companies that are looking for employees, not the job seeker. In these cases, you do not pay a private employment agency

> **TIP:** Never sign up with a private employment agency without doing a little detective work. Ask for recommendations for agencies from any friends who have experience with them or even from a friendly interviewer who isn't able to offer you a job. On your own, find out something about the agency's history: how long they've been in business and the professions they specialize in. Also make a call to the Better Business Bureau, who will tell you if any complaints have been filed against the firm.

to help find you a job; the tab is paid by the companies enlisting the agency's help. Companies looking for employees generally list job opportunities and look for prospects in the open market, so you'll be missing out if you rely too heavily on openings provided by an agency. Consider agencies as only a part of, not the totality, of a job search.

Meeting the Recruiter

Try to meet in person with an employment agency recruiter before she presents you as a candidate to an employer. This meeting is as important as a job interview, so dress the part; arrive on time; bring a résumé and list of references; and be prepared to speak succinctly about your goals, accomplishments, and skills. Also, do everything you can to show respect for the recruiter's expertise and time. Courteous behavior will reap benefits; like a potential employer, a recruiter is looking for strong social skills as part of the package.

One explicit difference between an employment agency interview and a job interview is how forth-

coming you are about unfavorable information in your personal or job history. While you would never actually lie during a job interview, you wouldn't necessarily bring up being fired, for example, unless you were asked the question. Not so with a recruiter. Present yourself in a positive light, but avoid unwelcome surprises by telling the recruiter anything about your employment or personal history that could be construed as negative. Because recruiters are answering to the employer, they don't want to be caught unaware after giving a glowing recommendation. Similarly, if your radar tells you that a former supervisor might give you a less-than-flattering recommendation, prepare the recruiter for this possibility.

Remember that the recruiter's job is finding the perfect employee for the employer, not the perfect job for you. With this in mind, be as specific as possible when describing your needs so that you aren't seen as fitting a job that doesn't appeal to you. And remember, the recruiter is not a job counselor. Expect an agency to represent you positively to companies, to keep your job search confidential, and to tell you why a particular employer isn't offering a job—but not to provide career advice.

Temporary Employment Agencies

Approach an interview at a temp agency just as you would any job interview; the more impressed they are, the better the assignments you'll be offered. An agency will need copies of your résumé, so have them ready before calling. Then be specific about what kind of job you're looking for and in what field. If, for example, your goal is to work as a paralegal at a law firm, you could shoot for any job (administrative assistant, for example, or receptionist) at any law firm. Working as a temp is a way to get your foot in the door and meet the people who can hire you permanently, assuming they're going to recognize your skills and talents. Once inside, you'll be privy to job openings in other departments and able to apply for positions as they become available.

ABOUT SALARY

When working through a temp agency, you'll be paid an hourly wage consistent with the industry standard for your geographic location and level of experience. (It is the agency that determines your salary, not the company.) Salaries aren't set in stone, and it's acceptable to try to negotiate an hourly rate with the temp agency that meets your needs and expectations.

THE INFORMATIONAL INTERVIEW

The purpose of the so-called informational interview is to learn about a person's career, company, or industry, with the ultimate aim of advancing your job search. (This kind of meeting is not—repeat, not—an opportunity to flash a résumé or ask for a job.) Through your networking contacts or your own research, identify several successful people within your field of choice or an influential person within a company that you'd like to learn more about. Then begin the process of requesting a brief meeting:

- Send a short letter of introduction (or, in fields that don't stand on tradition, do it via email) stating your background, your career goals, and your reason for wanting to meet.

- End the letter with a promise to call.

- Follow through later in the week, phoning to ask about scheduling a meeting.

Getting In

The easiest way to get an appointment is to already know someone or be referred by a mutual friend. If you're making a cold call, you'll have to work much harder, since getting a response may require writing more than one letter and making several phone calls to an assistant. With each call, strike a balance of politeness, deference, charm, and self-confidence, but be careful not to become a pest. Use your intuition to gauge whether the person you're calling is rolling his or her eyes at yet another call. While persistence with charm often pays off, with the wrong person it can backfire.

Preparing

Once a meeting is scheduled, make the most of it by preparing thoroughly; scour the Internet and appropriate publications. Learn as much as you can about both the company and the field and be ready to state what you hope the meeting will accomplish and to talk about your career goals.

Call the morning of the meeting to confirm the start time, and then arrive five minutes early. Dress professionally, giving as much attention to looking spiffy and well groomed as you would for an actual job interview. Bring a résumé in a folder or briefcase, but don't offer it unless it is asked for. Also bring paper and a pen or a tablet to take notes. Wear a watch, or keep an eye on the time on your tablet since you'll want to be the one to end the meeting when the allotted time is up.

Meeting

During the course of the meeting, play up the pupil–teacher relationship, particularly if you're a recent graduate. Without seeming to pry, ask the person what she learned along the way before succeeding in her career. Take note of any career moves she says were beneficial, plus any that were not. If you can convince the person that you want her advice because you admire her accomplishments, you may well gain a mentor and an ally—a contact who knows just the people who can open doors for you.

Thanking

Follow up an informational interview with a thank-you note. (Send it on the same day of the meeting or, at the latest, the morning after.) Thanking the person for her time—and for sharing insights into her career or company—reinforces the positive impression you hope you made.

CHAPTER 4
TRADITIONAL RÉSUMÉS AND APPLICATION LETTERS

There are many ways to get your information to a potential employer. Choosing the right one depends on you, your industry, the position sought, and the company hiring.

As you prepare to send, fax, email, and post your résumé to points near and far, face up to a blunt reality: The person who receives your résumé is under no obligation to actually read it or respond—and is all the less likely to if it's not well presented or contains misspellings or grammatical errors. To lessen the chance of your résumé's being directed toward the wastebasket or deleted with the click of a mouse, make it easy to read, to-the-point, and error-free. Remember: The care with which it's done announces your professional abilities loud and clear.

For all the attention that goes into creating a résumé (ideally, it should be tailored to the desired job), the end product should be short and sweet—one page or, if you have extensive work experience, two. A "quick take" shows consideration of the reader's time, a fundamental of business etiquette. This is true whether you're applying cold for any job opening within a particular company or for a specific job opening you found in an ad, or you're sending your résumé and cover letter to someone to whom you've been referred.

The cover letter you send along with your résumé should also be limited to a single page. This cover letter is actually a letter of application—and it needs to be a well-crafted piece of salesmanship that separates you from the pack. While your résumé effectively telegraphs the bare bones of who you are and what you are seeking, the letter allows you to expand on how your background projects you as a good fit for a specific company or job.

THE BASICS

Paring down your résumé and letter means taking the trouble to organize and present information so that it's readily accessible; likewise, making sure that it's free of any grammatical and spelling errors shows you as not only meticulous but also respectful—the compositional equivalent of not slouching in your chair. Your dictionary, a brush-up on grammar, and perhaps one of the myriad résumé- and cover-letter-writing guides on the market (each with a somewhat different theory of what's best) will be your tools. No matter which style or format you choose, be mindful of these four basics:

- Make certain your résumé and cover letter are completely accurate and a true reflection of your experiences.

- Illustrate your skills and abilities by relating your specific accomplishments instead of merely listing the jobs you held.

- If you are mailing your résumé and cover letter, use 8½ × 11-inch sheets of good-quality high-cotton-fiber paper in white, off-white, or a muted neutral color. Résumé paper is sold as such and often has a watermark.

- Use a readable typeface like Times New Roman or Cambria. Steer clear of trendy or unusual fonts, and keep the size between 11 and 12 points. Margins should be at least 1.25 inches from the sides and 1 inch from the top and bottom.

Proofreading Your Work

Any mistake in your letter or résumé can cost you the job. There is no excuse for misspelling, poor grammar, or bad punctuation. Unless you're very secure with your writing skills, have someone else proofread your résumé and all cover letters. Another person with an objective pair of eyes can find mistakes and offer suggestions for rewording or deleting information. Another trick is for you to read the letter from right to left, one line at a time; this forces you to look at each word separately. Move a piece of paper down the page to track each line. If possible, wait at least one day between creating a document and proofreading it, so that you bring a fresh perspective to the task.

CHRONOLOGICAL AND FUNCTIONAL RÉSUMÉS

The two classic résumé styles (see next page) are the reverse chronological résumé, which lists the jobs you've had going backward in time, from the current one to your first, and the functional résumé, which describes your skills, abilities, and accomplishments as they relate to the job you seek. Employers are most accustomed to the chronological style, but if you have little work experience or some gaps in employment, a functional résumé may show your skills and talents in the best light.

CONCERNING REFERENCES

It's a good idea to have four or five references who can speak to your capabilities and accomplishments. Remember not to incorporate these references into your résumé or cover letter. Instead, list them on a separate page, after double-checking the addresses and phone numbers. Keep this list current in case you are asked for it. If you're ever caught without it, have it delivered by the next business day.

Asking Someone to Serve as a Reference

Choose your references carefully: Go with people who know your professional skills and capabilities but aren't threatened by your success. Though it's tempting to include relatives and friends, they are never suitable as references unless you've actually worked for them. If you are a recent graduate, you might include professors who can confirm your academic accomplishments and contributions in the classroom.

Once you've made up a list, call potential references and ask if they are willing to be named. If they

---

TWO ADDITIONAL SOURCES OF HELP

There are a number of websites available to help you craft a traditional résumé that represents you well. Far from simply posting your content online, these sites will help you identify a traditional résumé structure that highlights your skills and achievements and adhere to it:

- www.gcflearnfree.org/resumewriting
- jobsearch.about.com/od/resumes/Resumes.htm
- www.theladders.com/resume (site requires log in)

If your design skills on the computer end with word processing, consider hiring a résumé service to help prepare and print your résumé. But be aware that there are two schools of thought on the wisdom of pursuing this route: Proponents say that besides adding technical finesse, a résumé service can take your list of previous jobs and wordsmith it into a maximum-impact marketing tool. Skeptics counter that your résumé will end up looking like it came off the assembly line.

Before you begin, be sure to suggest that your participation in the creative process would be a condition of signing up.

---

are, show concern for their time constraints by asking how they would like to be contacted. If you receive anything less than an enthusiastic response, reevaluate your decision to include that person and consider finding someone else.

After the initial call, offer to get together for a cup of coffee or lunch (your treat, of course) so that

Theresa Montalvo
211 Elmwood Dr.
Houston, TX 77110
(713) 555–1212

OBJECTIVE

Entry-level position in accounting, where exceptional math skills, mastery of applicable software, attention to detail, a willingness to work hard, and a positive attitude are required.

EDUCATION

Currently enrolled in night classes at University of Houston, working toward degree in accounting that will enable me to reach my goal of becoming a CPA. Graduated in 2002 from Hillsboro Junior College, Hillsboro, MA, in top 15 percent of class.

EXPERIENCE

2013 to present: Assistant Bookkeeper, Moonbeam Computers, Katy, TX

• Created linked spreadsheets to track travel and entertainment using Excel

• Maintained an Access database to record additions to fixed assets

• Downloaded mainframe queries to Excel for account analysis

• Designed an information systems improvement that made cost reports available 20 percent sooner

SUMMARY

Creative problem solver who works well with people. Fluent in Spanish. In junior college, awarded Moore Math Medal two years in a row.

Using the functional résumé style, this aspiring accountant shows she's serious by including her eventual goal in her résumé—to become a CPA. Because her experience is thin, she first details her education, then specifies her duties in bulleted entries, with the last showing her as the kind of person who does more than is required. The inclusion of her math award backs up her claim to superior math skills.

SAMPLE CHRONOLOGICAL RÉSUMÉ

Michael Collins
4620 Carroll St.
Laramie, WY 82002
(307) 555-1212

OBJECTIVE

Join a leading company in the HVAC industry in a key sales-management position, with responsibility for sales and service administration in both domestic and international markets.

SUMMARY

Over 8 years of customer service and inside sales experience in the HVAC industry, with emphasis on hydroponic systems and mechanical components. Advance training in the application of chillers, boilers, pumps, and related equipment.

EXPERIENCE

2013–present: Manager of Customer Service, Cool Breeze, Inc., Laramie, WY

Key responsibilities include processing of all orders, dealing with representatives on technical issues, coordinating deliveries with production, and reviewing all purchase orders and other legal documents. Initiated regular weekly meetings with purchasing and production departments to reduce lead time on orders. Recognized as employee of the year, 2014.

2010–2013: Manager of Warranty, Cool Breeze, Inc., Laramie, WY

Reviewed all incoming claims under the standard warranty policy. Approved payments or arranged for appropriate action. Reported to senior management on a weekly basis a summary of all claims and reported any critical areas of concern or developing trends to the Engineering and Corporate Safety Coordinator. Reduced the cost of warranty claims by 35% compared to budget for 3 years running.

KEY SKILLS

Experience in telephone sales
Good working knowledge of order entry
Proficient in use of Internet and Excel, Word, and PowerPoint

EDUCATION

Bachelor of Business Administration, University of Wyoming (2010)
Associate Degree in HVAC systems design and operations, Holbein Institute (2006)
Certificate in advanced air-conditioning repair, Vo-Tech of Laramie (2005)

Summer intern, Hot Stuff Pump Company, Cheyenne, WY (2004). Worked with Chief Engineer on the development of a new heat exchanger. Prepared drawings using AutoCAD 13. Earned 60% of funds needed for college expenses.

Using the chronological résumé style (opposite), this manager in the heating, ventilation, and air-conditioning (HVAC) business is looking for a higher position in another company. Because he is experienced, he focuses his résumé on his work and then lists his educational background at the end. His track record shows him to be a self-reliant person who continues to advance.

you can personally hand over your résumé. If the invitation is accepted, be as aware of your clothing and personal image as you would for a job interview (see "Dress One Notch Up," page 56). Think of meeting with a reference as an exercise in networking; he may be able to give you a job referral as well.

If a face-to-face meeting isn't possible, find out the best way to get your résumé to your reference and do it in a timely fashion. In a separate note, include examples of your work so that the person will be prepared to speak about your capabilities in specifics: "She doubled her sales quota every month" will have more impact than "She's a real go-getter."

Thanking References

Thank all of your references twice, first when they accept the role of reference and again when you accept a job. A typed letter is appropriate, but a handwritten note on your best stationery is more personal. By all means, keep your references up-to-date on your job search, especially when you've had success. Even if references weren't called, thank them for offering their assistance; your diligence will pay off in the future if you need to call on them again. Mention in your correspondence (and in person, when possible) your eagerness to return the favor in some way whenever you can.

WHAT TO LEAVE OUT

As important as knowing what to put in your résumé is knowing what to leave out. Just as you want your writing to be concise, the style and content of your résumé should also follow the classic dictum "less is more."

THE WORD *RÉSUMÉ*. Putting this at the top of the page is not only unnecessary but also takes up precious space. The same applies to the line "References available upon request," which is generally understood.

REFERENCES. Don't add these to the résumé (or cover letter) itself. List them on a separate page and hold on to it until references are requested.

A PHOTO. You want to be hired for your mind, experience, and accomplishments—not your looks. Of course, your photo on social networking sites makes adding a photo moot.

PERSONAL STATISTICS. Don't list strictly personal information that is not related to the job, such as age, height, weight, marital status, or health.

YOUR GPA. At some point, usually five years after your graduation, leave off your college accomplishments and your GPA, even if it was a 4.0. Use your own discretion: A forty-year-old would seem foolish noting that he served as president of his social fraternity, but a twenty-one-year-old with limited job experience should include such an accomplishment because it demonstrates leadership skills.

SALARY NEEDS. Avoid including salary needs unless the advertisement you're responding to specifically asks for them. In that case, include them in the cover letter. Your résumé is never the place to broach the subject of salary.

THE APPLICATION OR COVER LETTER

The goal of your cover letter—technically an employment application letter—is to successfully apply for an interview. A good application letter, supported by a concise résumé, should make the reader want to meet the writer in person. (See also "Effective Business Letters," page 258.) It is not, however, going to get the job for you.

Key Components of a Great Application Letter

As you compose your application letter, keep what you're selling firmly in mind—your abilities, your skills, your experience, and your education as they relate to the employment needs of the company. There will be many things about you that a potential employer does not want to know. Your family, hobbies, politics, religion, and personal traits are of interest only if they bear directly on the job. You have to convince the reader that you are the best person for the position; do this by stating what you can do for the company, not what the company can do for you. (An employer, for example, doesn't want to hear that an applicant regards a job as "an opportunity to improve my financial management skills.") Consider the following tips to make your letter shine.

QUALITY MATERIALS

First of all, use personal stationery and your personal address. Quality writing paper and envelopes reflect directly on you, so make the effort to purchase the best stationery possible. Writing on the letterhead of a current employer is deceptive—and will make a potential employer question your common sense.

MAKE EVERY LETTER AN ORIGINAL

You may be sending out dozens of résumés, but each cover letter should be individualized. You can use your computer to develop a basic format for application letters, but use this format only as a starting point—not as a tool for churning out duplicate letters.

GET THE NAME AND ADDRESS RIGHT

Getting the correct spelling of an unusual name is expected and while it may not gain you extra points, getting it wrong will count against you. If "M. J. Jones, Human Relations Director" is Mary Jane and your salutation is "Dear Mr. Jones," your carefully written letter may hit the recycling bin. If you do not know the correct person to address (as often happens when you respond to a blind ad), call the company and ask. If you can't pin down a contact name, then it's appropriate to address the company or a specific department or position.

A GOOD START

Make your opening sentence and paragraph dynamic. What can you say in your first sentence that will compel the recipient to read on? An example: "For the past year, I have been honing my sales skills in my position as right-hand person to GHI's top salesperson. I would like to put those skills to work for you." Aim for a grabber lead, and avoid openings that are predictable, dry, or hackneyed. If you are writing as the result of a personal referral or recommendation, say so in the first sentence. Include any titles or information that will immediately identify your referral: "Our friend Dr. Robert 'Bob' Johnston, who is still the best physician ever to care for us Western College football players, recommended that I contact you about the sports reporting position with your newspaper." This opening not only identifies the referral by name and title but also establishes a connection between the writer and the reader, provides a key piece of information about the writer, and clearly states the purpose of the letter.

KEEP IT SHORT

Never write more than one page. Use your cover letter to point out and expand on information that is directly applicable to the job you're seeking. You'll also want to briefly explain specific experiences or capabilities you bring to the table, such as overseas service and fluency in a foreign language as long as they are relevant.

NO APOLOGIES NECESSARY

Your cover letters should reflect self-confidence and competence. You don't have to humble yourself or plead—and never apologize.

BRINGING UP SALARY

In general, address the issue of salary in an initial letter *only* when the employer asks for your salary requirements or when the amount of your compensation is your first consideration. If you have to make $60,000 a year, you might as well say so in the letter. Many potential employers use salary figures as a means to cull applications, and frankly, it's pointless to pursue a job that can't meet your financial needs. If an employer asks for salary requirements, you may give either the actual amount of your present salary or a range. It is also perfectly acceptable, however, to say that your current salary is "consistent with industry standards" or that your needs are negotiable.

CLOSING THE LETTER

Notice that the sample application letter on page 53 closes with a commitment to act. Make your follow-up calls on schedule. Your letter also should include a personal telephone number to call you. If you're available only at certain times, give that information as well. Be sure that your answering message or voice mail message is clearly audible and professional and includes your name.

END WITH GRACIOUS BUT NOT EFFUSIVE THANKS

Concluding sentences such as "Thank you for your time and consideration" and "Thank you for considering my application for the position" are always correct.

AN EXEMPLARY COVER LETTER

This is an example of a professional and attention-getting application letter. It is written on the recommendation of a supervisor. It is also an unsolicited letter and must consider the fact that no position may be available. Note that the writer cites a number of concrete, proven skills that she brings to the table—focusing on her account work rather than her lengthy experience as a traffic director, since account service is the area in which she desires employment. She also cites specific, though not confidential, numbers to demonstrate the success of the project she has managed. The writer's one personal remark—about returning to her hometown—is relevant to the job because it establishes her roots in (and knowledge of) the recipient's territory.

Winston R. Smith
Vice President, Account Services
Big Bang Advertising Agency
4321 Creative Blvd.
Chicago, IL 60000

Dear Mr. Smith:

Meredith Gregory, a colleague at Flotsam, Jetsam & Associates, has recommended that I contact you about an account service position with Big Bang. During six years as Flotsam's traffic director, I have had behind-the-scenes involvement in virtually every aspect of the business. But direct client contact is what I do best.

Two years ago, in addition to my normal duties, I became the account manager for Fido Dog Food, then a small division of the Big Cheese Food Products account. The work has been long, hard, and always satisfying, and now I plan to move into account service full-time.

I am very proud of what I've accomplished on the Fido account, especially my direction of the repositioning campaign that has raised the brand from near-generic status to a major regional name. In two years, Fido has expanded distribution, enlarged its product line, and seen a remarkable 73 percent growth in sales. Flotsam has benefited as well, with a fourfold increase in billings, from $500,000 to $2 million.

Why do I want to leave such a booming account? I am known at Flotsam as "the traffic director who does account work," and a full-scale transfer to the account side would be difficult to achieve here. I can bring Big Bang a broad-based knowledge of product and service accounts. I am also a great admirer of Big Bang's strategic planning and implementation as well as the creative work that you consistently provide. And, on a personal note, I would like to return to Chicago, my hometown.

Ms. Gregory tells me that she is looking forward to appearing with you on the research panel at the marketing convention next week. As I know how involved these events can be, I will call you in two weeks to see if we can arrange a meeting. (My daytime number, should you want to reach me, is 212-555-1212.) I realize that you may have no immediate openings, but I would like to discuss future opportunities with Big Bang.

Thank you very much for your consideration.

Sincerely,
[SIGNATURE]
Dorothy B. Gale

CHAPTER 5

THE JOB INTERVIEW

Congratulations! Your job skills—all those abilities and all that experience that you wrote about in your résumé and application letter—have gotten you in the door. Now it's time to stand out from the other interviewees and sell yourself. This is when your people skills bear fruit. Your expertise and experience are vital, but your attitude, your appearance, and how you handle yourself can either clinch or ruin your chances. Remember: The interview is your opportunity to start building the best relationship possible with the interviewer. And that is what etiquette really is all about—building great relationships.

INTERVIEW TOP FIVE

Sometimes the amount of information thrown at you to prepare for an interview can literally be overwhelming. Pay attention to these five potential deal breakers, and you can significantly increase your chances to get the job.

1. Don't be late.

2. Be prepared.

3. Dress one notch up.

4. Smile, speak clearly, and look your interviewer in the eye.

5. Thank your interviewer(s) twice.

1. Don't Be Late

No choice here. Late means late, even if you're just one minute late. Your best bet is to travel to the site of the interview the day before to be sure you know how long it takes to get there. Then add an extra ten to twenty minutes to your schedule as margin for error. Once there, visit a coffee shop or wait outside so you can enter five minutes early. Perfect.

While waiting, be cordial and friendly as well as professional (in other words, not overly familiar) with everyone you meet. You never know how much influence the receptionist or assistant might have.

2. Be Prepared

Some interview questions you can anticipate, others you can't. The best way to stay calm is to recognize what you can control and prepare for that. Improve your odds with some research and self-examination.

Q. I would like your perspective on what I perceive to be a frustrating trend: job applicants showing up too early for interviews. In my current position, I'm required to interview candidates and have noticed they're showing up earlier and earlier. Often I get a call from the reception desk that my candidate has arrived as much as thirty minutes ahead of the appointment. I have a full calendar and cannot take time out to go and greet them, even though it makes me feel uncomfortable keeping somebody waiting idly in reception. Curious of your thoughts.

A. Our number one piece of advice for job seekers, and perhaps the most important, is to be on time: not too early and not too late. Being late, even just a couple of minutes late, is a surefire way not to get the job. You're starting off on the wrong foot, and you're making the interviewer wonder if that's the way you'll treat clients, prospects, and fellow employees.

Being on time also means not arriving too early. Not only does it create an awkward situation for the interviewer, who feels responsible for your comfort during the wait time, but it also can create difficulty for other interviewees, who may not want to be seen interviewing. Often, interviews are staggered so that candidates don't meet in the waiting area.

For the interviewer, instruct your receptionist/administrative assistant to ask an interviewee who arrives too early to wait perhaps in an empty conference room if necessary. Their early arrival is their problem, not yours. Have the receptionist wait to announce the interviewee until the usual five to ten minutes before the scheduled appointment. For the interviewee, avoid creating a difficult situation for your interviewer. If you arrive more than ten minutes early, find a place to wait: your car, a local diner, or a shop where you can browse for a few minutes, and then show up on time.

KNOW THYSELF

Because you'll be asked about your strengths, aptitudes, and experience, it's essential to have a concrete idea of what they are before articulating them to your interviewer. Spend some time reviewing your résumé, refreshing your memory on dates of employment and exact job titles and, if necessary, revising it to highlight the most relevant areas of your experience. During the interview, having it firmly in your head enables you to point out or discuss certain parts of it without consulting a hard copy. Be prepared to talk about something that you have struggled with or found challenging as well as how you dealt with it or overcame it. Knowing your limitations as well as strengths shows self-awareness.

READ UP ON THE COMPANY

Beyond consulting the company's website, resources such as the company's annual report will fill you in on the company's profile as well as its general attitude and position in the marketplace. Google, Facebook, and Twitter will also reveal a lot about a company and its reputation. Collecting information not only helps you anticipate the qualities your interviewer is looking for but also gives you ideas for questions to ask the interviewer (see "Asking Questions," page 61). Ideally, you'll be able to talk about the company's chief products, prime markets, and even plans for future growth.

PRACTICE

Ask yourself the questions you're likely to be asked (see "Answering Questions," page 59), and practice answering them aloud. Get out your laptop and record a practice interview and watch yourself perform. Nothing is quite so revealing or as potentially illuminating as watching your performance on camera.

3. Dress One Notch Up

Like it or not, the clothes you wear to your interview invite snap judgments that are hard to overcome, no matter how well you conduct yourself as a conversationalist and thinker. If you can't make a preinterview visit, call and ask a human resources representative, receptionist, or office manager about the office dress code.

Next, when selecting clothes for your interview, dress one notch better than the standard office wear at that company. For example, if the men in the office normally wear slacks and a sport shirt, you should wear slacks, a button-down shirt and tie, and a sport coat. Management may have a different dress style than the office rank and file. In that case, your clothes should be a conservative version of what employees wear one level up from the job for which you are applying. For example, if those at your level wear a coat and tie, and those at the next level up wear a suit, then opt for the suit.

Avoid items that draw attention. Large ear plugs or facial piercings alone may screen out an applicant before a word is spoken. Yes, dressing and body decoration is personal and a way of expressing yourself, but clothing yourself for a job interview often requires a measure of compromise, especially in traditional fields. Your clothes are one expression of how you see yourself fitting into a company and are an indicator of how you relate to others.

Remember to plan for all of your wardrobe; any coat, umbrella, handbag, or briefcase should be as presentable as the rest of your outfit. Try to carry as little as possible, so you don't find yourself loaded down as you walk into your appointment. Do bring a small leather notebook, planner, tablet, or phone. You shouldn't take notes or use your phone during the interview, but it's smart to have something on hand in case you need to take down phone numbers at the close of the interview or make notes to yourself afterward. You should also carry several copies of your résumé—clean, smudge free, and ready to make a good impression on whoever receives it.

The particular attire advice that follows is slanted toward businesses on the conservative side and will usually put you on safe ground. However, dressing too traditionally could hurt your chances in fields such as information technology, music, and fashion. Either way, having some idea about the attire norms in the industry is important. Again, tailor your wardrobe to the expectations of the company as well as your personal taste.

INTERVIEW CLOTHES FOR MEN

Following are the best interview clothing choices at most companies. (See also "Business Clothes for Men," page 20.)

SUITS. Unless you're interviewing in a field where a suit would look out of place, wear one. It must be perfectly clean and pressed; spots and wrinkles leave a poor impression.

SHIRTS. As a rule, the simpler the better in conservative environments—no bright colors, no wild patterns, no monograms. Light blue or white shirts are common, safe choices.

TIES. In general, now is not the time to use your tie as an expression of your individuality. To play it safe, choose the traditional silk tie in relatively muted colors and patterns (foulard, stripes, paisley, or solid). It may also be wise to avoid ties with large images and designer logos. Learn to tie a basic Windsor or half Windsor.

SOCKS. These are easy: Choose a color that coordinates with your suit (usually black, dark gray, dark brown, or dark blue), and make sure they're long enough not to expose bare skin when you're sitting or crossing your legs. Knee-length socks are a safe bet.

SHOES. Wing tips or slip-on dress shoes in black or brown leather are the classics. As important as the style is the condition: Shoes should be newly polished, and heels shouldn't be visibly worn down.

BELT. Be sure your belt color matches your shoe color. Avoid large, showy buckles.

BRIEFCASE OR LAPTOP CASE. A slim leather attaché or portfolio is the best choice. Make sure the contents are orderly in case you have to open it. If you use a laptop bag or canvas case, be sure it is in good condition and organizes your materials in a neat way.

COLOGNE. Here less is more if you use it at all. Splashing on too much can be the kiss of death. Keep any scent to a subtle aftershave or cologne. It is a good idea to put on extra deodorant, just in case.

THE EXTRAS. Limiting jewelry to a single ring and a watch is the safest choice, although conservative tie clips and cuff links are also appropriate. Remove or choose smaller piercings, and cover tattoos where possible.

INTERVIEW CLOTHES FOR WOMEN

Women have more clothing options than men, but when it comes to an interview, try to put together a simple wardrobe that accommodates a suit with elements that can be repurposed for an interview at a less formal company. (See also "Business Clothes for Women," page 26.)

SKIRT SUIT OR PANTSUIT. This is the risk-free choice for an interview. While natural fabrics were once the only way to go, today knits and natural-synthetic blends are perfectly acceptable.

BLOUSES. Choose a long-sleeved blouse that shows a little cuff beyond the jacket sleeve. Short-sleeved blouses may be fine for work in summer, but not for your interview. A sleeveless blouse? Never—at least in conservative fields. For an interview, a cotton or silk blouse in a neutral color is still the safest choice.

SCARVES. A classic thirty-four-inch square silk scarf that complements your suit in color and pattern can be an elegant touch to your outfit.

SHOES. Pumps with a one-and-a-half-inch heel (and in perfect condition) are standard, as are heels up to three inches, if you can walk in them easily. Choose a color that complements your suit and handbag—black, brown, burgundy, or navy. Avoid open-toed shoes.

STOCKINGS. Choose a shade that approximates your skin color or is a bit darker. Sheer black is also an option if it coordinates with your suit, skirt, or dress.

BRIEFCASE. A briefcase or attaché case is preferable to a purse for an interview, conveying more authority. A small purse kept inside the case will hold your lipstick and other grooming essentials. If you instead use a laptop case, be sure it is in excellent condition.

JEWELRY. Keep jewelry simple, classic, and limited to no more than one of each kind: rings (except for wedding and engagement rings worn together), earrings, suit pin, necklace, watch, bracelet. Skip the charm bracelet or any other jewelry that might jangle or make noise. Again, less is more; you want the interviewer to focus on the total package you present, not your jewelry. Consider removing piercings, other than earrings, and covering tattoos.

PERFUME. Minimalism is the rule for perfume as well: Choose a light, not romantic, scent—and wear it very sparingly. Given the controversy over scent in the workplace, it may be wise to skip the perfume altogether. Deodorant is your first priority—you may want to consider wearing a little extra, just in case.

MAKEUP. Subtle makeup is usually best. Keep your makeup simple—it will mean less chance for smudging and makes for easier touch-ups. One less thing to worry about!

GROOMING AND HYGIENE

While you want to be seen to your best advantage during an interview, you never want to be smelled, except for perhaps the slightest hint of perfume or cologne. Shower or bathe, wash your hair, and use deodorant. And don't forget your breath: Try not to eat before the interview—nothing should come between it and your last tooth-brushing (especially alcohol, which will "loosen you up" right out of a job). Avoid eating garlic or onions even the night before; in some people, the odor of both can emanate from the pores for eighteen hours or more. The same applies to liquor, beer, and cigarettes. If you've overindulged the night before, your interviewer's nose may tell him so—and he'll mark you as undisciplined or worse. Don't rely on breath mints to mask such a serious lapse in judgment.

Finally, try to visit a washroom just before going to the interview for a final check of your clothing, face, hands, and hair.

4. Smile, Speak Clearly, and Look Your Interviewer in the Eye

Engage the interviewer and let your personality shine through. You are showing her that you will represent her company well and that you are a confident, competent/capable person.

ANSWERING QUESTIONS

Answer questions in a clear and confident manner, but be careful not to come off as a know-it-all. Start your statements with "I think . . ." or "I imagine . . ." or "As far as I can tell . . ." instead of "There's no doubt that . . ." or "Everyone knows that . . ." or "It's clear that . . ."

Here are three questions that are usually asked, either directly or in a roundabout way:

WHAT ARE YOUR STRENGTHS? This question can be answered in two ways: (1) with a list of your virtues or (2) with concrete examples of your good points at work. The latter is far more effective in making a lasting impression. Recounting how you took charge of the office when your supervisor was ill is more likely to get the interviewer's attention than something on the order of "I'm good at assuming responsibility when I see a job that needs doing."

WHY DO YOU WANT A NEW JOB, AND WHY WITH US? Put a positive spin on this one. For example, if you're currently employed, avoid saying you feel your talents aren't sufficiently appreciated, you dis-

like your boss, or anything else negative. Instead, say you've gained enough experience in your current job to make you ready to tackle new challenges and you believe this new position could give you the chance. Back this up with your knowledge of how the company operates (something you've learned in your earlier research). Woe to the interviewee who is asked "What do you know about us?" and finds himself at a loss for words.

WHAT WAS THE HARDEST THING YOU EVER FACED IN A JOB? This question demands prior preparation. The idea is not to recount the story of a disastrous situation but rather to talk about a problem that you were instrumental in solving. This shows that you are ready and able to cope with challenges that may come your way. "One week before a major project was due to be completed, my boss had a heart attack. Not only was I coping with my concern for him and his family, I also had to do both our jobs to get the project completed. I was proud that it got done and pleased with the praise I received when my boss returned to work after a couple of weeks."

FIELDING INAPPROPRIATE QUESTIONS

The Equal Employment Opportunity Act outlaws job-interview questions about age, race, color, gender, birthplace, national origins, marital status, parental or family status, sexuality, disabilities, and religion. Most interviewers know the law and won't ask. You'll have to decide if the interviewer is deliberately asking an illegal question or the situation is more of an error on the interviewer's part. In some cases, the interviewer is just plain inexperienced, or legitimate small talk may stray into forbidden territory.

Before you answer, consider carefully what you reveal about yourself on social networking sites. Many of these "illegal" questions may already have been answered by you.

Generally, you'll want to use some tact and either answer briefly or deflect the question. Let's use "How old are you?" as an example. You could answer "I'm in my twenties, thank you." Or deflect with "I'm surprised by your question. I'm not sure how that relates to my potential employment." By questioning the question, not the questioner, you signal that the interviewer is on dangerous ground while giving him a chance to back off or reexamine the appropriateness of the question.

Your other choice is to refuse to answer and point out that the question is illegal. "I'm sorry, but I'm not required by law to answer that question." Realize, however, that acting offended or invoking the law will probably sink your chances of getting the job, even though you're within your rights.

If a question truly offends you, you could thank the interviewer for his or her time and indicate that based on the question this is not the kind of company you're interested in.

However you respond, ask yourself whether you want to work for a company that not only asks interviewees questions that are personally invasive but also flouts the law in the process.

ASKING QUESTIONS

At the end of the interview, you'll more than likely be asked whether you have any questions of your own. This is not merely a courtesy but also a continuation of the interviewer's investigation. Make your questions specific to the company or the job; they should

---

YOU'RE OVERQUALIFIED?

It may seem like an oxymoron, but being overqualified is a concern to some employers. If you are interested in a job that you're overqualified for, your interviewer will doubtless want to know why you're willing to take a step down and, in most cases, accept a lower salary. You can explain that you'll simply be happier with a less demanding position or that you want to spend more time with your family or do more volunteer work—whatever the case may be. But realize that employers are wary of hiring overqualified candidates, seeing them as less likely to be satisfied and therefore more likely to leave. For this reason, convey a message of real dedication to the job, along with a valid reason for wanting it.

You may also want to change the format of your résumé from the traditional chronological form, which stresses the upward direction your career has taken in the past and highlights the fact that the new position would be a step down. Instead, organize your employment history by areas of experience, which shows your qualifications without pointing out the downward move. (See "Chronological and Functional Résumés," page 47.)

---

also reflect your respect for the interviewer and your seriousness about your job search. Rely on the interviewer to have insights about the company and its employees, but don't ask for the kind of information that could easily be found in the company's annual report; otherwise, you'll reveal that you haven't done your homework. Here's a sampling of pertinent things you might ask about:

THE HOLE IN THE RÉSUMÉ OR THE BLOTCH ON YOUR RECORD

Everyone has a past. The really important question is how it affects your future. Be ready to speak candidly about episodes in your past that you might prefer were never mentioned again. The ability to own a mistake and talk about the lessons you learned from it could afford you the opportunity to speak to some of your greatest strengths if you handle it correctly. Denials, obfuscation, and superficial excuses can all make something appear to be still affecting you or even worse than it was.

If you have a gap in employment of more than a year, you may be asked why. The reasons for dropping out of the workforce range from matters of choice (taking time off to raise kids or earn an advanced degree) to the unavoidable (being injured, downsized, or fired).

If you chose to stop working, dwell less on justifying why you thought it a good idea than on how your time off improved you—juggling a houseful of kids honed your organizational skills, for example. You should also use the functional-style résumé (see "Sample Functional Résumé," page 48), which won't emphasize the obvious hole in employment the way a chronological résumé would.

It's only when you've been fired for misbehavior or poor performance that you have your work cut out for you when you're asked, "You weren't employed in 2008 and 2009? Why?" Rather than replying evasively, answer that you and your boss were having differences and couldn't resolve them (which is true)—so you were let go. The worst thing you can do is say anything negative about your former employer or claim that you were wronged. Approach it from the positive side, saying you've grown from the experience and have corrected any shortcomings and that you're eager to put your newfound knowledge to work.

COULD WE TAKE A FEW MINUTES TO REVIEW MY RÉSUMÉ? This question allows you to make sure the interviewer has read your résumé without embarrassing her. It also gives you an opportunity to verbally recap your qualifications, highlighting your assets that best fit the job.

WHICH OF THE JOB'S RESPONSIBILITIES ARE MOST IMPORTANT? You may have read a job description for the position you're applying for, but a boilerplate outline often fails to reflect which of the duties take priority. The interviewer's elaboration on the written description will help you tailor your discussion of your skills to fit the job's most significant aspects.

HOW WILL MY PERFORMANCE BE JUDGED? This question gives you insight into what factors your prospective employer considers most important to completion of the work you are interviewing for.

WHAT ARE THE COMPANY'S STRENGTHS? Ask the interviewer his or her opinion of the company's strong points. This allows you the chance to demonstrate your knowledge of the business, which you gained in your preparation stage.

DISCUSSING SALARY AND BENEFITS

Be ready to talk money if the subject comes up. That means doing your homework. You should research what the average salary is for the job you are going after and how that fits with your salary needs.

Let the interviewer bring up salary. If he does, it won't necessarily mean you have the job, but it's a good sign. The rationale for waiting: If you broach the subject, the interviewer may not have had time to decide that you're a prime possibility for the job, and he therefore may quote the lower end of the range.

It's fine to respond to the interviewer's salary question with a question: "Could you give me an idea of the range?" Once you have an idea of your market value and the company's resources, offer a range of about $5,000 to $10,000 within which you're willing to negotiate. Wait until you've discussed other benefits and compensation before you make your decision on what you would accept. And remember that you don't have to answer on the spot: It's perfectly fine to ask for more time to consider the offer. Do be sure to establish a time frame in which they can expect an answer from you and reply within it.

5. Thank Your Interviewer Twice

The first thank-you comes at the end of the job interview, along with a firm handshake and a clear statement of your appreciation for the time the interviewer took to meet you. Then, that night at home, word-process your second thank-you on your per-

---

INTERVIEW FAUX PAS

As important as the dos that apply to an interview are the don'ts, both in dress and behavior. You may be partial to chewing gum and wearing very bright-colored clothes, but doing either is a major faux pas in all but the most unconventional companies. Here are some things to avoid:

- Arriving late
- Letting your phone interrupt
- Bringing shopping bags or boxes
- Loud colors in your outfit
- Plopping into a chair before the interviewer offers you one
- Using first names unless asked to
- Chattering on and on
- Interrupting or not listening
- Jiggling your knee
- Yawning (you control your other bodily functions, so get control of this one, too)
- Playing with your hair
- Fidgeting in general
- Chewing gum

---

sonal business stationery or write a handwritten note on a correspondence card.

This second thank-you doesn't have to be lengthy: Five or six sentences in two or three paragraphs should do the trick. There's no reason to restate your qualifications, although you may want to address any specific requirement that came up in the interview. (If, for example, you learned that the position involves some contact with trade press, you would want to mention that you were editor of your college newspaper and are familiar with the fundamentals of press releases and interviews.)

Use your thank-you letter to recall strong points from the interview, to answer any questions that may have arisen, and to provide information you have promised: "I was very impressed during my tour of your facilities, and my conversation with Dr. Mitchell was particularly helpful. I am enclosing a copy of my paper on cell phone safety issues that we discussed."

End on an upbeat note by thanking the interviewer and expressing your hope for a positive outcome: "Thank you for your time and interest. I look forward to the possibility of joining your staff." Or "Thank you again for meeting with me. I look forward to hearing your decision about the position."

Put it aside and reread the note the next morning to be sure it is error-free. Then put it in an envelope and mail it, or if you're applying for an internal job, send it via interoffice mail.

If the company is making a decision very soon, you can send an email thank-you right away. Following up that note with a mailed note is the icing on the cake and is not overkill.

WAITING TO HEAR

Waiting to hear whether you've been accepted for the job is one of the most stressful parts of the job search. But face up to the fact that you must do just that: Wait, and be patient. Sending in still more samples of your work or yet another reference can make you look pushy. No matter how important the job is

to you, remember that you're only one of the hiring manager's many concerns. Your best course of action is at the end of the interview to ask when you can expect to hear back. That gives you a date after which it is reasonable for you to contact them. If you haven't heard from anyone within the time frame the interviewer specified, make a brief call saying that you're just checking in to see if there's anything else you should send. Unfortunately, many companies fail to notify the unsuccessful candidates.

RESPONDING TO AN OFFER

All your preparation has paid off; you've landed a job offer. No matter how thrilled you may be about it, however, don't succumb to pressure to give an answer right away. Instead, say something to the effect of "Thank you for the offer. This is very exciting! I'd like some time to consider it. Can I have a couple of days to respond?"

If you have contacts at the company, now is the time to talk to them to learn more about the culture of the company, your immediate supervisor, and the team of people who will be your workmates. Also use this time to consider carefully your salary range and benefits needs.

When you meet again with your prospective employer or call to give your response, be aware this is the time when you have maximum leverage. Be sure to hammer out the details of your benefits package and salary before formally accepting the job. Now is also the time to ask about the potential for upward mobility and growth. If you're currently employed elsewhere, seek agreement from your potential employer to start at least two weeks after your accep-

Q. I recently accepted a job offer. My start date is next week. I was in the process of interviewing with another company, which just invited me to a second interview. I am more interested in the other company and would be thrilled if they offered me the position. How can I gracefully back out of the offer I already accepted?

A. Gracefully? Probably not. You're between a rock and a hard place, and there's no easy way out.

Put the shoe on the other foot: What if the company offered you the job and you accepted. Then they called you a couple of days later to inform you that they had a better candidate who had just walked in the door. "Thanks, but no thanks," they say to you. They're going to hire that person, and you no longer have a job with them. Once a commitment has been made, it's up to both parties to honor that commitment.

You've made a commitment to your new employer. They've acted in good faith and offered you a job that you were willing to accept. Reneging on the offer puts them into a very difficult position. Once you accepted, they began contacting the candidates they rejected when you accepted the job offer. Now they're in the awkward position of having to recontact those people and reopen the job search. It will be an embarrassment and a headache for them, not to mention costly.

Can you back out? Yes, you can, but there are consequences. You'll be burning a bridge behind you. Your reputation with the company that you're leaving in the lurch will suffer. You most certainly will not be able to go back there to seek employment again. Five or ten years in the future you may be applying for a job somewhere else and discover that the person who hired you is now the hiring person at that company. It's not likely you'll be successful with that person this time.

Finally, you are risking a guaranteed job for one that you might or might not get. You may end up with no job at all.

There is a way to avoid this situation. One of the first steps a successful job seeker should take is to contact the other places considering him for employment to let them know he has accepted a position and is withdrawing his application. No bridges get burned and no tempting opportunities suddenly develop to put him in the position you now find yourself.

tance so that you can give your present employer adequate notice. Then, if everything is satisfactory to you, accept the offer with enthusiasm.

RESPONDING TO A REJECTION

The way you handle rejection and disappointment says a lot about you as a professional. Employers know this. They also know how important the right job is and how hard it is to find it. The moment you are turned down is not the moment to disengage; it is the time to take the next step in building your professional network.

So it didn't work out this time? Sending a brief note acknowledging that you've been rejected is far better than just slinking off and acting as if you'd never had personal contact with a company. Thanking the company for considering you will show that you are a person of substance and good manners. And who knows? There's always the chance that you missed being hired by a hair and could be considered for a job in the future.

If the interview thank-you note is one opportunity for distinction, the rejection thank-you note is a glowing golden opportunity. You have done so much work to establish this relationship; now is your chance to secure that work as your search continues.

PART THREE

AT THE
WORKPLACE

CHAPTER 6
YOU AND YOUR COWORKERS

Whether you're starting a new job or have been settled into one for years, you probably find yourself occasionally asking the question: "So just who are these people, anyway?" Here you are for forty-odd hours a week, sharing your time and space with a group of individuals whom you had no part in choosing. The fact that you work in the same field should give you at least one interest in common, but that's not necessarily so—not in an age when more and more people regard their jobs as a means to a wholly unrelated end. The office secretary may be taking dictation only until her screenplay is sold. The accountant in the next cubicle may be crunching numbers but thinking about his plan to win the New York City Marathon. How do you get to know these people? What are the secrets to getting along with them?

Those questions aside, in some quarters of the workaday world there is a cynical outlook about coworkers: "My job is terrific—it's the people I can't stand." Besides being self-centered, this sort of attitude is also self-defeating. Even the evolution toward less formal work styles—flex-time, temporary employment, and electronic commuting—doesn't free employees from the obligation to make the best

of things with their fellow workers and work toward a harmonious atmosphere. Nowhere is the Golden Rule more important than in the workplace. By treating your coworkers with consideration, respect, and honesty, whatever their title or level of responsibility, you'll gain their trust and respect—and establish yourself as a valuable and cohesive part of the team.

WHEN YOUR COWORKER BECOMES YOUR BOSS

Paula was frustrated by her manager because whenever they were having a conversation and the manager's cell phone would ring, the manager would answer it. This went on for months. And then, one day, Paula was promoted, and she became her manager's manager.

Interestingly, as soon as their roles were reversed, Paula's now subordinate no longer answered her cell phone if it rang while they were having a conversation. Paula wasn't impressed by what she perceived as the two-faced attitude of her former boss, that it was important to be respectful to a higher-up but not to an underling.

GRASPING COMPANY CULTURE

A culture is broadly defined as a group that shares beliefs, interests, values, goals, and living styles. Applied to businesses, culture refers to the common characteristics that set one workplace apart from another, including everything from the way major decisions are made and communicated to how the lowliest cubicle is decorated. Cultural differences can exist within a company either between locations, or even between different areas within a building. Employees in the marketing department on the fifth floor of a large business in New York City may have different norms and expectations than the employees in the C-Suite on the twenty-fifth floor. All new employees not only have to learn a new job but also have to adapt to a new workplace culture.

Every company's culture, no matter how formal or informal, is governed by two realities:

- In business, culture is hierarchical—the rules of the game come from the top down. Even those companies that tout their participatory management and flattened pyramidal structures are not exactly democracies.

- Good intentions notwithstanding, business cultures develop over time, become ingrained, and are slow to change. In fact, CEOs who attempt to radically alter a well-established corporate culture will find themselves frustrated and sometimes tossed out of the C-Suite.

Your success in any new job depends on how quickly and thoroughly you master the company culture. Fortunately, you've got plenty of teachers. Along with taking your cues from your bosses, interacting with coworkers will give you all the role models you need. Your coworkers are all individuals—people from diverse backgrounds and with diverse ambitions and objectives. Some you will like; others you won't. But you can learn something from each one of them about how to get along inside the company and in the business world in general—lessons that only work to your advantage.

COMMUNICATING EFFECTIVELY

Success in building relationships with coworkers starts with how you communicate and how you treat everyone in your office. Even if, personally, you don't like a person, professionally you need to be considerate, respectful, and honest with him. Over time you may even discover skills and capabilities in that person that help you build a positive, professional relationship with him.

Face-to-Face

Positive interactions with your coworkers are founded on considerations as basic as respecting their personal space, understanding rank, and giving thought to the way you handle everything from small talk to humor to disagreements.

When you engage in conversation—whether it's chitchat or strictly business—one of the quickest ways to alienate others is to violate their physical space.

- Instead of crowding the people you talk to, step back. About eighteen inches is a reasonable distance.

- If someone is very soft-spoken, you may have to lean in to catch his or her words, but back away when it's your turn to speak.

- Make solid eye contact. An open and interested expression, which begins with the eyes, is far more engaging than an in-your-face stance or posture.

- Be conscious of height differences: Stand sufficiently far away so that the person doesn't get uncomfortable having to look up or down at you.

- Be considerate of persons with disabilities—such as a person in a wheelchair or with a hearing impairment.

- If you're dealing with international coworkers, be sure that you are aware of their conversational customs and taboos.

Respecting Rank

In business, rank is power, so be conscious of the position of the person with whom you're talking. Maintain a respectful conversational distance: no backslapping, nudging, hugging, elbowing, or other touching that implies nonexistent intimacy. And just because you're chatting with your supervisor about the Super Bowl, don't assume that the casual nature of the conversation allows you to dispense with the common courtesies: Don't prop your feet on the desk, drop down on the couch without an invitation, or fidget with the bric-a-brac on the coffee table.

When talking with workers in subordinate positions, don't abuse your rank. Use of courtesy titles is often dictated by company culture, but it is always polite to address people who are considerably older as "Mr." or "Mrs." or "Ms.," whatever their jobs may be (unless they insist you do otherwise). A twenty-five-year-old junior executive may get a power rush from addressing his sixty-year-old secretary by her first name, but in a very conservative organization the rush could be short-lived if his boss doesn't approve.

However, modern workplaces are more relaxed when it comes to addressing bosses by first name. A recent survey conducted by Survey Monkey and The Emily Post Institute found that 91 percent of employees refer to their immediate boss or manager by his or her first name. Interestingly, if the boss is two levels above the employee then 74 percent say they refer to the boss by his or her first name. When the boss is three levels his or her superior, the percentage calling a boss by his or her first name drops to 56 percent. Not surprisingly, bosses refer to their subordinates by first name 92 percent of the time.

Requesting and Offering Help

The best way to get help is to give it. For instance, if you see an office mate working through lunch to collate a large client packet and you pitch in to help, your generosity will likely be returned in kind. Be mindful that a voluntary act is not overtime; your reward is a coworker's gratitude, not extra pay. Don't store your own good deeds away in your mental favor bank, awaiting repayment, or remind everyone of what a good person you are.

When you receive a helping hand, a thank-you is always necessary, no matter how small the favor. If a coworker gave up his lunch hour to help you, then a funny card, a little gift, or an invitation to lunch may be in order. When possible, you might also compliment helpful coworkers to their superiors.

Help for the Newcomer

Be particularly conscious of newcomers. New employees may have crackerjack skills, but they will have a lot to learn about how your business works—names to remember, places to locate, policies to master, reporting relationships to understand. Be helpful and forgiving within reason. Try to recollect how you felt when you were first employed and what information you needed. Volunteer answers, even if the questions haven't been asked yet: "Ms. Hernandez wants those weekly reports in a folder, but Mr. Wilson prefers a memo." Or "If you have a doctor's or dentist's appointment, tell Mrs. Shipman, and she'll clear your schedule." Just remember that help doesn't include office gossip; leave it to the newcomer to make his or her own judgments about coworkers and bosses.

GIVING AND ACCEPTING COMPLIMENTS

You and everyone you work with need occasional pats on the back. The real key is to be an empathetic person, capable of feeling with and for others. This is no touchy-feely exercise. Paying compliments when and where compliments are due is a kind of day-to-day justice. Saying "Well done" or "Good job" to coworkers raises their spirits a notch or two; it also communicates that you are a thoughtful and observant person, capable of giving and sharing credit where it is deserved. Just don't overdo it; handing out compliments too freely and too frequently devalues both your words and your sincerity.

"Aw, Shucks!"

Some people are unsure how to respond to a compliment. They may ignore it. Or they may go into detail about why it isn't deserved.

Two simple words are the perfect response to a compliment: "Thank you."

PASSIVE-AGGRESSIVE NOTES

The passive-aggressive note has become such a presence in today's office that it warrants a bit of discussion. Ironically, most passive-aggressive notes are in fact aggressive-aggressive notes, which directly call out the offenders on the issue at hand. A true passive-aggressive note makes an attempt to be a sweet reminder but comes across as obnoxious. Whole websites, such as www.passiveaggressivenotes.com, are devoted to the phenomenon. A passive-aggressive note might look something like this: "Remember, we all use the kitchen, so please clean up after yourself!" Whereas some take it a step further: "Is this a postapocalyptic world where the blacks and whites of morality have blurred into a hazy gray and every man takes care of himself and only himself? No? Then CLEAN THE MICROWAVE AFTER YOU USE IT!"

Some notes aren't passive-aggressive at all but are simple reminders: "Grayscale copies 5 cents; color copies 9 cents."

Some notes, aggressive or not, are just inappropriate: "Use air freshener after stinking up the bathroom!"

And sometimes it's more about who is posting the note than if a note is posted. After working for two weeks an intern's leaving a sticky note on the water filter saying, "If you use me, refill me!" is inappropriate because this person is new to the environment and should not be making requests like this of others in the office.

Instead of posting your own passive-aggressive note, ask that at the next staff meeting the organizer reserve a little time for housekeeping topics to be discussed: changing paper in the copier, the cleanliness of the kitchen, or refilling the filtered water pitcher. Some suggestions might even become office policy: no strong perfume, no smelly foods, no personal use of the copier. You'll have a better chance of effecting change than with an annoying note.

WHAT TO SAY WHEN . . .

Hearing news of one kind or another about your coworkers' personal lives is inevitable. In some cases, you will want to congratulate; in others, commiserate. If the person is a close friend, you'll probably have no trouble coming up with something to say; for those you know less well, a simple acknowledgment will usually do. (See also "Marking Milestones," page 171.) Following are guidelines on what to say when various circumstances arise:

SOMEONE BECOMES ENGAGED OR MARRIED. "Congratulations," "Best wishes," or "All happiness" are all appropriate responses. Genuinely wish your coworker well. Don't be too inquisitive about his or her choice of spouse, and avoid marriage advice.

SOMEONE IS PREGNANT. Be happy for your coworker, but don't pry. Do not ask if she has a partner. Also refrain from sharing labor and childbirth stories. And never offer your congratulations or ask if a person is pregnant until the person acknowledges it to you. It is impossible to recover from such an error.

The same magic words you learned when you were a child remain magic today. They are among the most useful tools you have in your vocabulary when it comes to navigating the business world with grace and poise.

Please	Softens a request by asking rather than demanding
Thank you	Shows appreciation rather than expectation
You're welcome	Acknowledges a thank-you
I'm sorry	Indicates regret and shows remorse
Excuse me	Asks for forgiveness
Pardon me	Acknowledges a mistake or precedes an interruption

SOMEONE MISCARRIES. A miscarriage is a death, and like any other it will involve grieving. Be sympathetic by recognizing the depth of the loss. Never offer up phrases such as "It was for the best" or "It was just God's will." And never, under any circumstances, imply that the miscarriage may have resulted from something your coworker did or did not do. "I am so sorry for your loss" or "I wanted to express my sincere condolences for your loss" are appropriate offerings of sympathy.

SOMEONE DIVORCES. Divorce is another kind of death. It's better to listen than to talk, although you might offer practical advice (such as how to find child care or file income tax as a head of household) when needed. (See also "Your Divorce," page 80.)

SOMEONE IS ILL. If a coworker or a coworker's relative is seriously or terminally ill, your actions will speak louder than words. Show sympathy by helping the person on the job. Don't complain about absences from the office. Be alert should anyone else try to undermine your coworker's position during an illness or appropriate his or her office or files. (It happens.) Keep the person informed about business happenings.

SOMEONE DIES. When a coworker loses a loved one, write and speak your condolences. If you are close, attending prefuneral and funeral services will be comforting. But merely working with someone is not a reason to take a funeral day off. Never make comments such as "It was really a blessing" or "Be thankful his suffering is over." Offer practical assistance where you can, and be understanding. The death of a loved one will change your coworker, so don't expect him to bounce back in the space of a few weeks to become the person you used to know.

SOMEONE IS FIRED OR DOWNSIZED. Be sympathetic, but don't prolong the agony by talking it into the ground. Accept your coworker's official explanation for a firing, and don't engage in speculation. If you can give practical assistance, do so—a recommendation, help with a résumé update, information on other job openings. But don't let sympathy lure you into encouraging or participating in destructive behaviors such as binge drinking or firing off threatening letters. Finally, don't be surprised if a former coworker drifts out of your life; he needs to move on, and because you are still part of the old workplace and old hurts, you may be left behind.

TAKING RESPONSIBILITY

Everyone makes mistakes. What matters is how you handle the situation once the mistake has been made.

Consider the case of Brad, who was editing the alumni newsletter at a small college in upstate New York. He discovered he had misspelled a word in a prominent headline he had written. The word was not just wrong—it had an embarrassing connotation. After collecting his wits, Brad immediately called the printer, found out how fast the newsletter could be reprinted, and got a price for the job. He then went to the college's president, explained the error, took responsibility for it, told the president how he proposed to fix it, and gave the costs. Quickly weighing the facts, the president approved the reprint and nothing more was ever said about Brad's slipup.

Brad did two things right and saved himself a lot of grief. First, he took responsibility and apologized for his mistake. Second, he worked out a solution to resolve the problem before he went to his boss. Instead of putting a problem on the boss's back, Brad presented him with a solution.

In today's high-stakes business games, not all errors are forgiven and forgotten, of course. Some may even cost a person his or her job. But in many cases, by taking responsibility and by solving the problem, you may navigate the troubled waters with little if any negative effect on your career. To deny that responsibility—to reflexively say, "That's not my fault!"—is almost guaranteed to infuriate everybody.

ENGLISH AS A SECOND LANGUAGE

Q. Should individuals standing around the workplace watercooler who share a common foreign heritage speak in their native language in the presence of nearby English-speaking individuals?

A. First, let's differentiate between a business conversation and a general conversation. Business talk should be conducted in a language that everyone can understand.

Watercooler talk is a different matter. From the perspective of the people speaking another language, it may be as innocent as a few minutes' respite from having to speak a language with which they're not totally familiar or comfortable. Unfortunately, what may be a totally innocent conversation ("How was your weekend?") can seem exclusionary to others who don't speak that language. It's similar to watching two compatriots whispering nearby. True or not, the impression is that they're gossiping, and it can create an atmosphere of mistrust.

If people wish to speak in another language or talk about something privately, it's best to move that conversation to a private location. Around the watercooler, it's considerate to speak in a language everyone can understand.

WATERCOOLER TALK TIPS

Watercooler conversations are an important part of building relationships at work. It is when you and your coworkers let down your guard while sitting at a cafeteria lunch table, waiting for a meeting to begin, or hanging out in the copier room that your personality and real interests come to the fore. Almost any topic is up for grabs as long as it's not malicious, derogatory, inflammatory, or indiscreet.

By being open to opportunities for watercooler chats, you'll discover who the resident expert on opera or NASCAR is as well as who the movie buff, gourmet cook, and night-school scholar are. Your coworkers also get a chance to become better acquainted with you and find out if you're sociable and easy to talk to—a trait that works to your advantage in the workplace. (See also Chapter 22 and the box "How to Be an Expert at Small Talk," page 205.)

- When initiating small talk, be attuned to the other person's receptiveness. If he seems distracted or unresponsive, take the hint and back off.

- Even when the person is willing to chat, don't overstay your welcome.

- Ask for the other person's opinions and show genuine interest in his ideas. Don't try to dominate the conversation.

- If other people come along, make an effort to include them in the conversation. You may need to switch topics to something that everyone can discuss.

- Avoid subjects that are too personal: opinions on politics, sex, personal money, religion.

- It's fine to disagree with someone, but phrase your comments politely. "You're wrong!" is hostile and combative, whereas "Actually, I just don't agree with you about that, but I respect your opinion" is tactful.

- Keep up on current events. Read the daily newspaper, a weekly newsmagazine, blogs. Watch the entertainment shows on television once in a while. Listen to your kids' music station on the radio. Watch the latest, hottest show at least once so you know what people are talking about.

- After making an effort to be informed, think up some questions to ask others when you join a conversation.

- To end small talk, excuse yourself after you, not the other person, has made a concluding statement. Finish with "Well, I think it's time I got back to work" or "This was really interesting. We'll have to talk again."

- If a coworker who just wants to chat interrupts you while you're working, suggest another time. "You've caught me at a bad moment. Can we touch base after I've finished these letters?" If you do the interrupting, be sensitive to the other person's reaction. If your coworker says she can't stop, take no for an answer and don't take offense or feel rejected.

FOUL LANGUAGE

Foul language is a major issue in the workplace. The Ladders website (www.theladders.com) surveyed executives about what etiquette issues could get an employee fired. The number one issue: foul language. Interestingly, both employers and employees see foul language as a frustration. Eighty-one percent of senior executives found that working alongside a foul-mouthed employee was unacceptable, and 80 percent of employees say that workplace swearing is unacceptable. Companies are addressing the issue by creating rules prohibiting foul language and including these rules in employee manuals.

In company cultures where obscenity and profanity are permitted, their use tends to be widespread, and you can't correct everyone. If foul language makes you uncomfortable, signal your distaste by never using these words yourself and by excusing yourself politely from office gatherings whenever the language becomes too raw. Some people will label you a prude, but you may be pleasantly surprised by others who welcome your attitude and even imitate your behavior.

HANDLING PROFESSIONAL DIFFERENCES OF OPINION

You and your coworker have different ideas about how to proceed on a new joint assignment. How do you resolve the situation without ruffling feathers?

When differences of opinion arise on the job, the first rule is to speak up if you feel strongly about an issue. If you have honestly and critically reached a position that is contrary to your coworker's, you have an ethical obligation to state your case as strongly as you can. Remember, it's wise to pick your battles with care. If it doesn't really matter all that much to you whether the office soda machine stocks Coke or Pepsi, leave that debate to others.

Ideally, disagreements between coworkers should be handled in private, but there are times when conflict is integral to the work process—during a brainstorming session, for example, or a policy meeting. In these situations, be considerate of bystanders. State your case clearly and engage in debate if necessary, but don't be mulish. Pay attention to the reaction of others: As soon as you pick up signals of resentment or annoyance, bring the conversation to a close for the time being; otherwise, it could degenerate into personal attacks. "Actually, I think it would be better if we talked about this later" is one way of defusing the situation. Or you could try "Let's take this up when we can get [the supervisor] to help us figure out the direction the company wants to go."

Don't get drawn into other people's disagreements, but at the same time don't feign ignorance if you can really help find a resolution. If, for example, you have factual information that can settle an argument, speak up. Remember, telling what you know or offering reasonable compromises is not the same as taking sides. You might be attacked, but maintain your objective role even if the parties to the disagreement unite against you.

Don't Make It Personal

Never allow a professional disagreement to become personal. Apart from being rude, name-calling and personalizing weaken your case in any argument. The instant you call Joe an idiot for preferring to file alphabetically rather than by invoice number, or make a snide reference during a lunchtime political discussion to Marcia's lack of higher education, guess what happens? Joe or Marcia just won the war, even if you won the battle. If someone calls you a name or challenges your competence, chalk it up to their frustration in the heat of conflict and try your best not to hold grudges.

A few more bits of advice:

STICK TO THE SUBJECT. Don't allow a disagreement to wander into nongermane issues. Be especially careful to avoid referring back to old conflicts. Remember that even if you were proved right in the last argument, you may be wrong in this one. And beware when others try to sidetrack an issue: Diversion, deflection, and tossing red herrings onto the trail are classic tactics of those with the weaker side of an argument. If you fall for this trick, learn from your mistake and listen more closely next time.

BE OPEN TO COMPROMISE. Although you may not get everything you want, resolution is usually better than continual hard feelings. Be sure to document the outcome of the disagreement; if it is business-related, you should also confirm the final resolution with a memo to your "opponent." Documentation and confirmation are important if it becomes necessary to take the matter to a higher level of authority.

DON'T GLOAT. Avoid the temptation to gloat or say "I told you so." If everyone recognizes that you were right, you will only undermine yourself by engaging in petty smirking and arrogance. (You want your colleagues to say, "Josh really knows his stuff," not "Josh knows his stuff, but he's still a jerk.")

When Conflict Gets Personal

It is going to happen. Sooner or later you'll find yourself at loggerheads with a coworker, or you'll be dragged into somebody else's quarrel. You'll hear gossip or, worse yet, become the target of gossip. Or you may find yourself subjected to language, a dirty joke, or offensive comments that disturb you.

How should you respond when a coworker makes blatantly sexist or racist remarks, calls you (or someone you know who is trustworthy) a "liar" or a "cheat," or treats coworkers and subordinates with arrogant disrespect? You must rely on your wits.

For starters, you have an obligation to yourself and your company to confront or report verbal offenders, just as you would a thief or a person trading

---

IN THE OPEN

Some remarks require immediate and public response. Be direct, but remember to confront the remark rather than the speaker. However great the temptation, control your anger and avoid patronizing the person. For example, if a coworker's subject is racial politics run rampant, try something on the order of "People are treated fairly here, Ralph, and I know that your boss got his job because of his ability, not because of his race." If you can (it isn't always easy), give the person a graceful way to retreat from his or her offensive remarks: "I think we talk too much about people's race, don't you, Ralph?"

Whatever you do, don't become involved in a shouting match. You simply cannot out-shout a dedicated bigot or snob. If the offending remarks are habitual, it's time to take the matter to a superior, human resources manager, or ethics officer. If you fear retaliation, make your complaint in confidence.

---

on insider information. If you merely sit back and listen, you become a collaborator—passive but nonetheless guilty. Also, your company can be held liable for the hateful remarks of employees, and while you are in their employ, you owe loyalty to the greater good.

If you find yourself in a situation that you feel demands to be addressed, there are some basic strategies you can employ to help resolve the conflict and build relationships rather than brick walls.

GET CONTROL OF YOURSELF

Trying to engage a person in a debate, especially about a behavior or action of theirs that you think is egregious, is hard enough. Trying to do it while your blood pressure is elevated and you're seething is a sure way to fail. The perpetrator is far more likely to react to your anger than to your criticism of the behavior. So disengage for a time and then, later, ask to speak to the person in private.

While you're collecting yourself, spend a few minutes asking yourself what you want to see as an outcome of any conversation you have with the other person. In most cases, the best outcome would be a combination of changing the behavior of the perpetrator and maintaining or building a constructive working relationship with him.

DISCUSS THE SITUATION ONE-ON-ONE IN PRIVATE

If you can talk with the other person in private, do so. Frame your statements as criticism of the behavior, not the person, and be specific: "You probably didn't realize it, but that comment you made about Leslie's short skirts really was sexist, and I could see that she

was offended and hurt." People who repeatedly offend or degrade others are rarely subtle and usually don't take hints. But they may respond if you address them directly and indicate that your concern is for their own welfare and reputation.

OFFER A RESOLUTION

Stating the problem is just the first part of the solution process. Remember, your goal is to both change a behavior and hopefully avoid creating an enemy. Before you meet with the other person, develop what you think is a reasonable strategy for resolving the situation and moving forward. Then, once you've made your statement and the other person has responded, check to make sure that your strategy still sounds reasonable. If it does, suggest your solution and ask the other person for his or her buy-in. It's not enough simply to state your demand and walk away. In order to reach a resolution, you need to be prepared to work with the other person to refine your solution until it works for both of you.

YOUR PERSONAL LIFE

When it comes to talking about personal matters, employees can be their own worst enemies. How (and how much) you talk about personal issues—dating, marriage, children, divorce, sexual preference, death, personal finances—is up to you. Proceed at your own risk when discussing:

YOUR FAMILY. Some people will be genuinely interested in your background but beware of imposing any family problems on your workmates. People you work with will be concerned that someone close to you is suffering a serious illness, but they neither expect nor want daily updates on the medical details.

YOUR LOVE LIFE. Discussing the details of your love life, especially with coworkers you don't know well, can be obnoxious. Also, don't expect your workmates or supervisors to be your romance counselors or to keep your deep, dark secrets confidential.

YOUR MARRIAGE AND CHILDREN. Marital and parental status are usually the first two pieces of personal information that circulate about a new employee. It's up to you how much or how little you decide to share but avoid imposing your family on others. Don't expect your colleagues to buy your daughter's Girl Scout cookies by the dozens or sponsor your son's soccer team. Don't bring your children to work unless it's allowed; even then, be sure that your youngsters are quiet and respectful of your coworkers' need to get their work done.

YOUR DIVORCE. A divorce is one of the most difficult emotional issues anyone can face, but if you're in the process of one, don't use your coworkers as therapists. Turn to friends, family, and professionals outside the office for support and guidance. You should talk with your supervisor if the divorce process is likely to affect you on the job—requiring time off for meetings with lawyers, court appearances, the sale of house and property, the care of children. There's no need to go into details about the cause of the divorce—and never berate or demean your ex- or soon-to-be-ex-spouse to colleagues or bosses. Simply state the facts and any problems you have or anticipate having.

DIVORCE IN THE SAME COMPANY. When a divorce happens between two employees of the same firm, the stress can affect everyone. The worst circumstance is when a divorcing couple expect their coworkers to take sides, thus turning a private matter into a company-wide tangle. Hard as it may be, divorcing couples have an obligation to keep their personal lives private, except for appropriate notification of supervisors. If the acrimony can't be contained and threatens to infect an entire office, it may be necessary to consider a change of job or transfer for one or both parties.

YOUR SEXUAL ORIENTATION. Revealing sexual orientation or preference to an employer is tricky. Although many states and localities have enacted laws that protect gay and lesbian workers against employment discrimination, not all jurisdictions recognize them as a protected class. Legal status and fairness aside, homosexual employees must take a hard look at their individual workplaces and corporate cultures when deciding whether to disclose their orientation. It is not easy to leave a life partner at home when the company hosts its annual family day, or to be denied insurance coverage for a person who is your true dependent. Fortunately, many enlightened employers realize that sexual orientation, whether heterosexual or homosexual, is irrelevant to job performance.

HANDLING HARMFUL GOSSIP AND RUMORS

What can you do to avoid becoming the subject of office gossip? Simple: Keep personal information to yourself on the job—and don't invite inquiries. Even seemingly innocuous questions about your age, income, personal relationships, sexuality, and politics can set you up for gossip and innuendo.

If you become the subject of malicious gossip or a false rumor, you'll want to uncover the source. Begin your detective work by talking to the person who clued you in; explain to him that the story is untrue and you want to stop it. If you promise confidentiality, there's a good chance you will learn the name of the initial source of the falsehood.

You should then confront the gossip—but stage your confrontation in private. Adopt an attitude of concern rather than anger: "Sally, I hear you told a couple of people that I'm looking for a new job and I've been meeting with a headhunter. The truth is that I had lunch last week with my old college roommate, and he happens to work for an employment firm. But I am not looking for a job, and I'd appreciate it if you would set the record straight." Even if the gossip denies spreading the tale, she'll be on notice because she has been caught, and she'll think twice before gossiping about you again.

Remember that it takes two to tango; a person who is eager to hear the latest gossip is an active participant and hardly blameless, even if he doesn't spread the story. Gossiping, whether you are on the giving or receiving end, can be hazardous to your professional reputation. You never know who's chummy with whom, and you could wind up covered in mud if you dish dirt about the wrong person. If you're faced with gossip from your colleagues, be tactful but firm: "I honestly don't want to hear the details of anybody's private life." If the gossiper pushes ahead anyway, you can politely refuse to listen—"Oh, that sounds interesting, but I'd just rather not know"—and quickly excuse yourself.

GET OFF THE GOSSIP TRAIN

Q. How do you deal with not-so-nice comments, told in a joking manner, about a coworker who is not so popular or well liked or any coworker in general when he is not present?

A. Gossip is insidious and destructive to the work environment. Combat it by refusing to take part. When a conversation turns to gossip, excuse yourself: "I'm uncomfortable talking about Tom this way. I think I'll just head back to my desk." Or consider sticking up for Tom: "Hold on a minute. Tom doesn't deserve to have us talking about him behind his back." Sticking up for Tom and raising your coworkers' awareness about gossip is the best way to avoid it.

Companies recognize that gossip is bad for the workplace, that it causes stress and conflict, which can directly affect productivity and morale. Consequently, companies are starting to institute no-gossip policies with sanctions as severe as dismissal.

DEALING WITH PETTY ANNOYANCES

What should you do when a coworker has an annoying little idiosyncrasy that is threatening to drive you up a wall? The first thing you'll have to decide is whether to deal with the situation or to ignore it. Because you work with people you might not choose to associate with on a purely social basis, you may find yourself putting up with behaviors you might not accept in your friends. Still, while you're obligated to grin and bear most of your coworkers' foibles, you can try, with courtesy, to correct problems that literally affect your work.

Smoking

Smokers are the literal outcasts of most businesses these days—banished to the outdoors in rain, sleet, snow, and hail for periodic puffing. Yet despite (or perhaps because of) this arrangement, tension still persists among smokers and nonsmokers, which means that consideration on the part of both groups is necessary.

If you're a smoker, understand that some people's "smoker's breath" is more powerful than others'—and yours may be on the high side. Breath mints may help, but a good tooth brushing and a dose of mouthwash is better. There's also the problem of smoke-permeated clothing. Try to smoke in ventilated places, and consider taking a stroll in the fresh air before you reenter a smoke-free space.

If you are a nonsmoker, on the other hand, show a little tolerance. Don't comment on how you hate the smell of smoke, for example.

Sidewalk Smoking

Now that smoking has been banned in most offices, front sidewalks have become salons of sorts for smok-

ers, who puff and hang out on intermittent breaks. If you're a sidewalk smoker, be mindful of those who aren't. If, for example, your building entrance is recessed from the street and has an overhang, stand out near the curb so that a curtain of smoke won't collect in the space. In fact, you should stand away from any doorways, no matter what the layout of your building. If there's no out-of-the-way spot to indulge, consider taking a walk around the block or into the parking lot. Always be sure to put the cigarette butt into a proper receptacle.

A Note of Caution. Don't think people don't notice when you're outside having a cigarette several times a day. Someone who's seen standing outside virtually every time anyone walks in or out of the building is going to gain a reputation not only as a smoker but as a slacker. This is one time when a smoker's behavior can reflect on him and his company: "If this guy's allowed to spend most of the day on the sidewalk," people might be thinking, "what does that say about the way things are run inside?"

Bad Odors

A coworker's body odor, smelly feet, or bad breath is an extremely sensitive issue. We are all loath to tell a person about body odor, yet every time we ask our business seminar participants which they would prefer—not to be told about an offensive odor or to be told about it by a friend or a manager—invariably, 100 percent say they'd want to be clued in by a friend. So the next time you have a friend who has body odor, consider what you would want him to do if the roles were reversed. Be a friend: Enlighten him.

Here's how. Do it privately, and start out with something like this: "Bill, because I'm your friend,

I'm going to say something that is really difficult. But I know if the roles were reversed, I would want you to say something to me. So here it goes. I don't think you are aware of it, but you have a problem, and it has to do with body odor. Some of us have noticed it and we're worried that it may have an effect on your advancement in the company. I'm telling you this only to help."

Be warned: Your colleague's response may surprise you. You may discover that your colleague's body odor is the result of a medical condition, medications, or dietary deficiencies.

If you simply cannot do the deed yourself and the problem becomes unbearable, you can discuss the situation with a sympathetic supervisor or human resources manager, either alone or with other coworkers. (This is an instance when a group of concerned employees is more impressive to a boss than an individual complainer.)

Too Much Scent

Perfumes, aftershaves, colognes, and other cosmetics are meant to be pleasant but can quickly become oppressive in a crowded office. Meanwhile, you can help by not overdoing your own toilette. Don't spritz in the office, and don't test any new scent before wearing it to work; body chemistry affects the power of fragrances and can intensify it. Finally, save the heavier scents for nights out. (See also "Your Cologne," page 25; and "Perfume," page 32.)

Many companies are adopting policies regulating the use of scents based on health grounds. Before arriving at work on your first day, be sure to check for your company's policy.

THOSE EMBARRASSING MOMENTS

Spinach stuck in the front teeth, an open fly, an unbuttoned blouse—while these are the staples of situation comedy, they are also very real embarrassing moments. When they happen to you, all you can do is laugh and fix the problem. When you realize they are happening to others, don't laugh. Instead, step in and help. Discreetly tell the person (in private if possible), and if need be, help resolve the problem. If you are a woman and are too shy to tell a male colleague that his zipper is undone, quietly ask another male to do it. When a coworker alerts you to the fact that there's a blob of mustard on your tie or a poppy seed in your teeth, don't take offense. Be grateful; a friend has just saved you from an embarrassing moment.

Some problems, on the other hand, should just be left alone. Someone's dandruff, a hairpiece that looks like a shag rug, or overly applied makeup does not affect the workplace in any serious way and is really nobody else's business. It's up to the person with the problem to realize that it may be jeopardizing his chances for advancement. Only if you're close to the person should you gently suggest that his appearance, hygiene, or an annoying personal habit might be hurting his career.

Chewing Gum

There's nothing inherently wrong with chewing gum; the problem with doing it at work is that you run a constant risk of annoying people who think your gum chewing is socially graceless or simply a disgusting habit. Chewing gum when you're alone is fine, of course, so long as your smacking or bubble popping can't be heard in the next cubicle. But chewing gum in business meetings or with clients and associates is a little like eating with your mouth open: It feels better to you than it looks to everyone else. It's also not a good idea to chew gum while you are on the phone. Your client or colleague may not be able to see you, but she will certainly hear you.

WORKING WITH TEMPS

Welcome temporary employees graciously, and be ready to offer your assistance as they settle into the job. Assume that the temp worker is both skilled and ready to learn, and treat him with the same professional courtesies you would extend to a permanent employee. Be aware that temp workers may well expect a chilly reception, and that it is largely the responsibility of the staff to bring them into the team, show them the ropes, and introduce them in a positive way to the company culture.

If it is your workplace custom to take a new employee to lunch in the first week, do the same for the temp worker who is there on an extended assignment. Get to know the temp and include him in normal office socializing.

Finally, just as coworkers should avoid blaming temps for company hiring policies, you should be careful not to draw temps into office debates about company policies. Don't subject them to your complaints and insecurities or try to elicit their sympathy and support.

If You're a Temp

Temporary employees should do their best to adapt to the customs and culture of a new office as quickly as possible. If you are a temp, your agency should provide you with basic information about your new assignment. Sometimes, though, your assignment may come too quickly for a thorough orientation and your agency may be unfamiliar with the atmosphere of the workplace they are sending you to. Until you get the lay of the land, dress conservatively and behave appropriately. You'll quickly learn whether the office style is casual or formal.

Try not to judge your new coworkers too harshly if they are cold or stiff with you. You may have dropped unwittingly into a major downsizing or a shift in company employment policies. A thick skin can help, but you don't want to be so aloof that coworkers avoid you or, worse, undermine your job. Keep your antennae up, and respond when someone makes a friendly overture. It can't hurt to accept offers of assistance, even when you don't really need the help; doing so shows collegiality and respect for the knowledge and experience of long-timers.

As for socializing with coworkers, be guided by the policies of your agency and explain your situation to the people you're working with. Never discuss salary or benefits, because comparisons will inevitably be drawn. Because you have two bosses—the service employing you and the company contracting with your agency—keeping confidentiality is doubly important.

COURTESIES FOR PEOPLE WITH DISABILITIES

People with disabilities make up the largest minority group in the United States—some 19 percent of the population according to the 2010 census. Behind this statistic are more than 56.7 million individuals who are human beings first and who have special needs second. So when you work with someone who has a disability, put aside any anxiety you might feel ("Am I saying the wrong thing?") and be yourself. Act just as you would with anyone else; if the disability is brought up, it should be the person with the disability who does it, not you.

The Department of Labor's Office of Disability Employment Policy has an excellent web page with advice for interacting with people with disabilities: http://www.dol.gov/odep/pubs/fact/comucate.htm.

Sensitivity in Language

Language matters. How we refer to each other matters. It matters in ethnicity. It matters in religion. And it matters when writing or speaking about people with disabilities. Positive language is inclusive and respectful, whereas negative language singles individuals out in a hurtful way. Avoid words and phrases such as *retarded, handicapped, confined to a wheelchair, dumb, afflicted with,* or *a victim of.* These phrases don't respect the individuality of the person. Instead, affirmative phrases reference the individual: *a person who is blind, a person who is deaf, a person who is in a wheelchair,* or *a person with cerebral palsy.*

Be Inclusive

Never leave a person with disabilities out of a conversation because you feel uncomfortable or because you assume she will be uncomfortable. Include her as you would anyone else, and leave it up to her to decide whether to participate or not.

To Offer Help?

It is always courteous to ask if a coworker with a disability would like assistance, but don't automatically provide help that may be unwanted. Follow the person's cues, and don't be offended if your offer of aid is refused: It is everyone's choice to be as independent as he wants to be.

With the Deaf or Hard of Hearing

Face the person, maintaining eye contact throughout your conversation, since many people with hearing loss can get a lot of information from both listening and reading lips. If the person is hard of hearing, it's helpful to speak up and to speak slowly and clearly, but never shout or exaggerate your lip movements. If speech alone isn't working, it is perfectly acceptable to gesture or write notes.

If you are talking with a deaf person who has an interpreter, always direct your attention to the deaf person rather than the interpreter. (This can feel uncomfortable because the courteous worker doesn't want to exclude anyone from the conversation, but don't worry: Trained interpreters, including those for non-English speakers, understand their role and won't expect to participate.) Speak at your normal rate, being sure the interpreter can hear you clearly.

With Wheelchair Users

Under the Americans with Disabilities Act, most businesses are legally required to accommodate the physical needs of people who use wheelchairs. When you meet, offer a handshake as you would normally (eyes as close to eye level if possible), unless it is clear that the person does not have the use of his or her arms. Don't hesitate to offer your help if you spot someone in a tight situation. Don't push someone's wheelchair unless you are asked. But do offer to push if the two of you are approaching a steep ramp or an obstacle.

The Blind or Visually Impaired

When you greet a blind coworker in the early days of his or her employment, identify yourself by name; your voice will be recognized before long. Whenever necessary, offer to read written information, such as the latest office memo or the cafeteria menu. It's appropriate to offer your assistance in selecting food from a buffet or in getting coffee when every-

one is gathered around the conference table. But be an observant friend, and follow your blind or sight-impaired coworker's lead as to how far to go. Don't pet guide dogs or try out equipment that the person may be using. But do feel comfortable asking a blind person if she would like to take your arm when navigating an unfamiliar area.

With the Speech Impaired

Listen patiently and carefully to someone with a speech impediment. Your understanding of her speech (or of any device used by the person) will improve as you continue to listen. Remain attentive to the conversation even if there are delays. Phrase your questions so they will require a short answer. Don't complete the person's sentences unless she looks to you for help. If you don't understand something, ask a question to help the person clarify the part you missed.

BUILDING PERSONNEL

Naturally, the people who maintain your building—doormen, front-desk personnel, cleaners, security guards—deserve the same cordiality as anyone else

> **TIP:** If you're in the habit of working late, be courteous to the regular cleaning person by saying hello or asking his or her name and introducing yourself. You're not obliged to get involved in a conversation, but being respectful will make the cleaner feel less anxious about intruding on your space and interrupting your work.

you see on a daily basis: a morning hello (or at least a smile and a nod) and a thank-you when they've helped you in any way. You may never actually have been introduced to them, but that's no reason to treat them as if they were part of the lobby furniture.

Post-9/11 Building Security

One of the most visible changes that occurred after 9/11 is the increase in security at office buildings, especially in major metropolitan areas. Often you are required to sign in; show ID; send laptops, purses, and briefcases through a scanner; and wait for an escort to take you to your destination. Treat the security personnel with the same respect you show to others in the building and in your office. Don't ask them to break the rules for you—they're the ones who will get in trouble. If they ask to inspect or scan your briefcase, give it to them politely.

If you go in and out several times during the day, expect to have your briefcase or laptop case inspected each time. Don't be frustrated. It's part of their job to check no matter how often you go in and out.

Also, if you're expecting visitors, make sure to contact security ahead of time so that passes for your guests will be ready when they arrive.

CHAPTER 7
YOU AND YOUR WORK SPACE

The world you inhabit at work encompasses the actual location you work in—your office, your desk, or your cubicle. But you also share communal spaces. How you behave in those spaces will say a lot about you.

- Are you approachable or standoffish?

- Are you organized or cluttered?

- Are you at your desk or a wanderer?

Answers to these questions affect how not only your colleagues perceive you, but they affect the image clients, prospects, and suppliers have of you as well.

This chapter tackles the practical issues of you and your office, including: What messages does your office decor send? How proprietary should you feel about your space? What does your attitude toward your cubicle/office say about you? What rules of behavior apply when a workmate or visitor enters your space?

YOUR OFFICE— A MATTER OF ATTITUDE

Not everyone has an office. If you are fortunate enough to have one, one of the first issues you will face is whether or not to stand to greet people who enter your office and for which people you will choose to do so. Male or female, a well-mannered person rises when either a superior or someone elderly enters their work space. Of course, you also rise for clients and prospects. It's even nice to stand to greet any workmate who hasn't dropped by your office or cubicle for a while. Rising is not an empty gesture done merely for the sake of etiquette but is rather a way of showing respect.

Standing doesn't simply mean rising from your chair and then reaching across your desk to shake hands. Instead, move around your desk to greet your visitor. Then offer her a chair. If you remain standing or looming over a seated person, it puts you in an overtly dominant position. Either sit next to her in another chair or lean or perch yourself on the edge of your desk; this deemphasizes the inequities, if only subliminally.

No matter who the visitor is or what the situation is, anytime you come around from behind your desk and sit near someone, you set up a friendly climate for a more relaxed discussion. (See also "Your Meeting," page 94). The behind-the-desk position is formal and signifies that this is your turf. Bosses, too, will do well by occasionally moving from behind the desk and democratizing the scene.

Closing Your Door

Keep in mind that a closed door is a stark reminder to cubicle dwellers that you have a door and they don't; for this reason, close yours only when there's a legitimate reason to do so. As a rule, privacy is warranted when

- You need quiet to concentrate

- You're meeting with a visitor

- You're discussing a confidential matter with your boss, your reports, or a coworker

Don't abuse the privilege of having a door. A closed door doesn't give you the license to make personal calls all day long or to complete personal tasks. As much as it feels like your home away from home, your office is still the property of your employer—and you're there to do the business you were hired to do. Unless you have a specific reason for doing otherwise, keep your door open.

YOUR CUBICLE— A MATTER OF ATTITUDE

Let's face it. The office cubicle was designed to pack the greatest number of desk workers into the smallest amount of space, not to provide an ideally private and personal work environment.

If you find yourself assigned to a cubicle, the ease with which you handle working in one says much about your resiliency. You won't help your situation by harboring resentment toward your immediate superiors. Decisions on office design are probably beyond their control. Making your desire for an office known to your supervisor is perfectly okay as long as you don't bring it up repeatedly and, at the same time, make it clear that you understand the possibility is contingent on other factors. Stay upbeat, as if you know she'll do what she can when and if the opportunity arises. When the time comes for raises and promotions, the person who accepts his condition with good grace has the edge over the perennial whiner. Regardless of how you really feel, rolling with the punches doesn't mean you're a weakling; it demonstrates a firm grasp of the realities of life in business.

Territorial Imperatives and Privacy

Because the worker in a cubicle is so visible (and all the more so in the half-wall design), there is a subconscious assumption on the part of passersby that he is automatically available. This notion couldn't be further off the mark. However compact or noisy your cubicle domain might be, you still have the right to expect visitors to respect your time and space. The cubicle is your office territory and should be treated as such. Just as visitors refrain from barging into an office or opening a closed door, they shouldn't sashay into your cubicle without knocking lightly and asking permission to enter.

The same applies to your next-door neighbors. Hanging over cubicle walls to communicate can quickly become annoying and invasive. Here plain common sense is called for. It may seem when you are intensely involved with coworkers in a team project that the best and most efficient way to communicate quickly is over the cubicle wall. But it's not. It's an interruption and people generally do not appreciate being interrupted.

If you need to discourage the culprit who leans over the cubicle wall to talk with you, choose your words with care as you speak to him about it: "Bruce, I know it's easiest for you to talk over the wall, but would you do me a favor and come around? Thanks."

Chats, Phone Calls, and Eavesdropping

An unfortunate by-product of the proliferation of cubicle office environments is that those around you can hear everything you say—and vice versa. It takes a very strong-willed individual to tune out the voices around him; in fact, many cubicle workers find this possible only with the help of earplugs, earbuds, or earphones. But remember, too, that the ability to hear and be heard cuts both ways:

- When entertaining visitors, go to a common area so as not to disturb your neighbors.

- Try to dissuade people from loitering or socializing around your cubicle. (A polite "Larry, I'm working on something right now that demands my full concentration" should do the trick.)
- Be discreet—a cubicle is not the place to talk about sensitive matters; discuss anything confidential in a private place.
- If you walk up to someone in a cubicle and find he's on the phone, don't hover there waiting for him to hang up. Leave and try again later.

Whenever you don't want a phone call to be overheard, find an empty office, a private space, or take your call in the lobby on your smartphone or make the call after hours.

Staring vs. Looking

As you walk around your office area, be careful where and how you direct your gaze. There's a world of difference between staring at a person and looking at a person. When you look at something or at a person as you glance around, your focus stays with you and what you are doing. When you stop thinking about what you are doing and your eyes and your conscious mind focus like a laser beam on the person you are looking at, your look becomes a stare. And the other person? She realizes she is the object of your stare. And that's when you've crossed the line.

More Unwelcome Sounds

One of the stickier wickets in the culture of cubicles is the office mate who makes inappropriate or offensive sounds. Burping, the slurping of soup or coffee, loud yawning, smacking of gum, and worse are all amplified in close quarters.

> **TIP:** Be thoughtful of neighbors by maintaining some decorum at your desk. The restroom, of course, is the place to relieve yourself of any physical discomforts. A quick nose blow is one thing, but any major honking should be done where it won't disturb others.

Creative Adjustments

Many cubicle residents have found smart ways to both achieve some level of privacy and mute some of the noises around them. Plants or corkboards placed strategically can help muffle outside sounds and create a sense of privacy at the same time. Before moving panels or putting up makeshift sound buffers, be sure to get permission from your employer or office manager.

Pinups

Cubicle walls often become billboards and are a great way to share a cartoon, a joke, or an article that's particularly apropos. But be careful with your choices: Never put up materials that cross the line to gross or obscene. Anything with racist or sexist undertones is equally out of the question. Even items that may seem a little bit risqué but acceptable to you may be unacceptable to others. Their opinion of you matters, so be extra careful about what you display that others can see.

A Further Note of Caution. It would be impolitic to put up anticorporate articles from magazines or newspapers on your cubicle wall, whether they are written about your own company or the corporate world in general. Anyone passing may perceive them as a direct affront to management.

Work Space Decor

The decoration of your work space depends on a number of things, with the type of work and the amount of customer interaction conducted there being among the most important. If you deal face-to-face with clients and customers on a daily basis, the decor will generally be customer driven. In a service industry such as banking, for example, the environment is often homogeneous, with personal effects kept to a minimum. In an office where creative work is done, such as a graphic design studio, decor is often more personalized. Know the expectations of your company before you start to personalize your work space.

MORE WORK SPACE MANNERS

There are some things that apply to work space etiquette in general, without regard to walls and doors. This grab bag of concerns includes whether you should stand when someone enters, how to play the good host to visitors, and the more mundane (though no less potentially annoying) matters of using a speakerphone and lunching at your desk.

Eating at Your Desk

Eating at your desk is often unavoidable, particularly in busy offices or those without cafeterias. While eating and working at the same time may allow you to leave work a little earlier, taking a break from work and clearing your head (even going for a short walk) may actually make you more productive in the afternoon.

If you are going to eat at your desk (and your company doesn't have a rule against doing so), besides eating quietly (especially in a cubicle), think "smell." It is also a courtesy to throw your lunch trash in the kitchen waste bin. Leftovers in your office trash can quickly become offensive if your wastebasket isn't emptied on a regular basis. Be sure to clean your desk of spills and crumbs. (See also "One

Rule About Food in the Refrigerator," page 96; and "Cooking and Microwaving," page 96.)

Using a Speakerphone

For some people, the effort of picking up the phone receiver is too great; they rely instead on talking or listening to messages by speakerphone. This forces everyone around to suffer the noise, especially those who work in an open-plan office or have thin walls. A speakerphone should be used only in closed offices.

If possible, make conference calls using speakerphones from a conference room. Even closed doors can't always muffle voices, since people tend to talk more loudly on a speakerphone to be heard. (See also "Speakerphone," page 247.)

Saying "Good Morning"

Creating a workplace where courtesy reigns doesn't mean feeling obligated to say hello every time you pass someone in the hall. Being preoccupied with what you're doing is only natural when you're busy and shouldn't be taken as an affront. Of course, you'll want to greet coworkers the first time you see them with "Good morning" or "How's it going?" but after that a quick smile or nod will do. More important is what not to do when passing people in the hall, like staring straight down at the floor with a sour look on your face. Even though it's unlikely to be taken personally, ignoring people does little toward creating the kind of atmosphere that makes the day go better.

Hallway Schmoozing

When chatting in the halls, stand to the side so as not to block traffic—an obvious courtesy, but one that a surprising number of people ignore. If that includes

---

KNOCK KNOCK

Q. I work in a department with over fifty desk cubicles, no walls. When approaching someone to speak to her, is it proper to stand behind/beside her until she notices me, or is it proper to gently knock to alert her that I am standing there?

A. The gentle knock is the appropriate answer. Simply standing there waiting for your coworker to acknowledge you doesn't work. She may not respond, especially if she is on the phone or deeply involved in work, and that would be awkward for you. On the other end of the spectrum, speaking to her without getting her attention first could startle her, interrupt a phone conversation, or cause her to lose her concentration.

Impersonal and public though they appear, a person's cube is as much a personal work space as an office with four walls and a door. It's important to respect the invisible boundaries. Gently knocking announces your presence without causing a rude interruption. Even in an open floor plan, respect the person you are visiting by asking if this is a good time before just launching into a question or comment.

---

you, remember that making busy coworkers detour around you a couple of times isn't a big deal, but after three or four repetitions, it can start to get annoying. Less obvious is what people might be thinking when your conversation goes on for more than ten minutes or so; besides disturbing people in nearby offices, you could be seen as a slacker if you make a regular habit of gabbing away in the corridors.

APPOINTMENTS AND MEETINGS

Meetings around your desk can be highly productive if you observe a few courtesies, but you'll need to evaluate your private space first:

- Is your space really conducive to discussion with a colleague or with a prospect?

- Is it comfortable physically and psychologically?

- Does it provide a level of privacy the visitor will be comfortable with?

If not, reserve a meeting room for appointments.

EARLY ARRIVALS. If a visitor arrives more than ten minutes early and you are not ready, try to keep him from feeling awkward. If there is a receptionist, ask her to make the visitor comfortable and tell him you'll be out as soon as possible. If you work in a small office without a receptionist, come out of your work space and greet the visitor. Accept his apologies for arriving early, offer him an available chair, ask him if there is anything you can get him, and tell him you'll be with him in just a few minutes.

LATE ARRIVALS. If a visitor arrives so late you won't be able to squeeze him into your schedule, accept his apologies and arrange another meeting. Or, should he arrive after you are already indisposed, ask the receptionist or an assistant to tell him you waited as long as you could and that you would like to schedule another date and time to meet.

KEEPING SOMEONE WAITING. Never keep a visitor waiting more than five or six minutes past the appointed time. If you have no choice but to do so,

TIP: When the receptionist calls and says your visitor has arrived, go out to greet him. If you have an assistant, you can ask her to escort the visitor in, but it's even more impressive if you greet him yourself.

walk out and apologize in person. An offer of a cup of coffee and a magazine is also a nice gesture. If something has come up that is going to delay your meeting for more than fifteen minutes, apologize for taking up your visitor's time and ask if he prefers to reschedule on another day.

Your Meeting

In addition to extending a greeting, there are three things you should always do when a business associate from outside enters your work space:

1. Offer to hang up his coat if he has one.

2. Ask him to be seated.

3. Offer him a beverage.

Remember that sitting behind a desk is less personable than taking a chair next to your visitor. If you want the meeting to remain private, close your door; if you're in a cubicle, go to a common area or meeting room, which you should have reserved in advance.

Be sure to have all the necessary materials at hand so that you don't have to navigate through piles of files to find them. If coworkers are participating in the meeting, arrange for them to be present in your office when the guest arrives and then make introductions if necessary.

If a visitor overstays his or her welcome, you can politely end the meeting by stating that you have another appointment or duty.

Seeing Visitors Out

Walk your visitor back to the reception area. Do this even if it's a straight shot and she won't have to make her way through a maze of corridors. Exchange a few pleasantries when saying good-bye; if she shows signs of chatting at length, you can simply explain that you have to get back to work.

COMMUNAL EQUIPMENT

Communal office equipment, which has a way of needing maintenance more regularly than it should, is a lightning rod for the "it's not my job" attitude among workers. Keeping the office technology in good working order is assumed to be the responsibility of someone else, and frequently it is. (In many offices you probably don't have access to toner cartridges and such.) Still, even if it's technically not your responsibility, you should take care of things if you know how. If the signal lights show that a fax machine, printer, or copier needs toner or has a paper jam, either do the job yourself or call the person in charge of machine maintenance right away. This applies doubly in a small business, where in the spirit of team play everyone—including the boss—should pitch in.

Copiers

Copying machines run at different speeds, with some processing thirty pages in half the time that an older machine might take. Those that are on the slow side are ticking bombs, just waiting to create frustrations

> **TIP:** Make arrangements so your desk and cell phones won't ring during a meeting. If you have a Do Not Disturb button on your phone, use it. If you have an assistant or receptionist who receives calls and forwards them, ask him to hold all calls. Establish with the assistant ahead of time what call or situation constitutes an emergency for which he should interrupt your meeting. (See also the box "Phone Call Faux Pas," page 241.)

and even conflicts. But even the use of state-of-the-art copiers requires consideration of the needs of others.

The most obvious courtesy is for someone who has a large copying job to let someone who has a small job go first. It's another matter if you've set the machine for finishing (sorting, stapling, enlarging, or the like) and you need four copies of a twenty-page document. In this case, give anyone who comes to use the machine an estimate of how long your job will take. After any large job, check the paper drawer and top it off as necessary.

Printers

If a coworker hasn't picked up a printing job, don't just toss it aside. Place it face up where it can be clearly seen, or put it in a space designated for finished jobs. It's a nice gesture to drop off a job if it's obvious whose it is.

When the printers are down, don't take out your frustration on the technical support staff, who are undoubtedly doing all they can. Alert them at the first sign of trouble (or call the help desk if you have one), and then turn your attention to something else until the problem is solved.

Furniture

Treat any tables in the reception room, conference rooms, or the kitchen as you would treat your furniture at home. That means putting a sweating glass or soda can on a napkin or coaster to avoid leaving a ring on a wooden table. The same goes for your office furniture, which may be expensive and will more than likely be inherited by someone else one day. Don't wipe greasy fingers on a fabric-covered chair, and don't let the crumbs of your morning muffin fall on the floor where it can be ground into the carpet. Both acts can leave unsightly oil stains.

IN THE KITCHEN

The kitchen has the potential for being the messiest room on the floor, so it's only fair that everyone does his or her part to keep it clean.

- If you spill something—on the counter, in the fridge, on the floor—wipe it up.

- Don't leave your dirty dishes in the sink. Wipe down appliances after you use them.
- If your fridge doesn't have an icemaker, refill the ice cube trays when you empty them.
- If there's a communal coffeemaker, refill it and start a new pot when you take the last cup.
- Report any problems with the vending machine; if management hasn't made it clear who to tell when it goes on the fritz, find out from whoever is responsible for general maintenance and then report the problem and post the information near the machine for the future benefit of others.

One Rule About Food in the Refrigerator

When it comes to the refrigerator, one rule is paramount: It's your responsibility to dispose of food and drinks you placed in it before they start to go bad, rot, or smell.

Cooking and Microwaving

Just as you're responsible for washing your own dishes, you're responsible for cleaning up any appliances you use. If anything you've placed in the microwave or conventional oven or on a stovetop burner boils over or splatters, clean it up immediately with a wet paper towel before it becomes baked on and much more difficult to clean.

Washing Dishes

Don't leave dirty coffee mugs in the sink or food scraps in the garbage disposal. It's each person's responsibility to wash his own dishes as soon as he has finished his meal. Remember, nobody wants to clean up your mess. Be aware, too, that a messy kitchen may lead management to deal with the situation by simply closing the kitchen.

Communal Lunches

Lunch is a great time to get to know your coworkers. More important, it's a great time for them to get to know you. Both the quality of your small talk and decent table manners will help contribute to your reputation as someone who is a pleasure to be around.

Having a regular group to lunch with is only natural, but you should occasionally mix your lunch partners so that you don't become too isolated from your workmates as a whole. Either invite workers from another department or try going at different hours so that you'll encounter a different group of people.

If you bring your lunch and always eat at your desk, be aware that you may appear unsociable. If a coworker who eats in the cafeteria (especially if she is your boss) sometimes drops by and asks if you want to go get a bite, think seriously about taking up the offer and leaving your sandwich in the fridge for tomorrow.

Table Conversation to Avoid

Avoid discussing sensitive work topics over lunch, since people at other tables may overhear. Things that are too personal—the hot date you had last night, the trouble you're having with a child—are also not a good idea. For the benefit of your lunch partners, don't talk about your or anyone else's skin conditions, stomach problems, or operations; these subjects are not exactly appetizing at the best of times. Lunch is a time for relaxing and taking a break—not the place for conversation that would be better conducted after work, if at all.

IN THE RESTROOMS

Depending on the frequency of maintenance, the office restrooms can be more disorderly than the kitchen. Do your part by always using the trash can, wiping up water that splashed out of the sink, and replacing toilet paper rolls as necessary.

Your Toilette

A woman putting on her makeup, a man shaving, or anyone brushing their teeth in a workplace restroom should remember that they are not at home. The important thing is to go about things discreetly, clean up afterward, and not take over the space.

The Toilet

Some people are uncomfortable about talking while they are in a toilet stall, so be cautious about initiating a conversation between stalls. More disturbing in the smartphone era is the person who gabs away on a phone while using the bathroom. Smartphones up the ante of this inappropriate behavior because they have cameras on them. No one wants to have to worry that his or her private moment in the restroom is being captured for anyone to see. Leave the smartphones unused while in the restroom.

The position of the toilet seat can also be a major issue in offices with unisex bathrooms. The best practice is for everyone to agree to put the lid and seat in the down position before flushing. If there is no lid, men should make the effort to put the seat back down after they're done. This is simply not an issue that is worth fighting over.

If you prefer to use one of the disposable sanitary covers or arrange sheets of toilet paper on the seat before sitting down, make sure to flush the paper when you leave, instead of letting it litter the floor.

Finally, there's the inescapable but rarely acknowledged problem of a more delicate nature: odor. Use any air freshener that is kept there.

ELEVATOR ETIQUETTE

The old-style elevator operator, smartly attired in a jacket with gold braid, has gone the way of the pay phone in most office buildings. If you do encounter an elevator operator, however casually he is clothed, any operator is due a "please" and "thank you" whenever you request a floor or disembark. That's not all you need to remember as you ride, however.

Getting On

The rules for entering an elevator are much the same as those for going through a door—gender is not the issue; communication is. Remember, the elderly or incapacitated go first. After pushing your floor button, move back if possible, leaving room for others. (A woman alone in an elevator may choose to stay near the floor-button panel as she may feel safer standing in proximity to the emergency call button.) If you're unable to reach the floor button to push it, ask someone closer to do it for you.

If the elevator is already jammed with people before you get on, don't squeeze your way inside, even if you work in a building where the elevators seem to take forever to arrive. Step back and wait for the next car.

Likewise, patience is a virtue when you find the door closing as you approach. Although it's a nice gesture for a passenger to hold the door for you or push the Door Open button, it's equally thoughtful of you to allow the passengers already aboard to go ahead and get to their floors.

Also, mind your manners. Don't stare at other people, smack your gum (which you should hesitate to chew in public anyway), or sing along with your iPod. If there's a mirror or reflective wall in the elevator, women and men alike would do well to leave their primping for later.

> **TIP:** The subject of your conversation is as important as its volume. If you need to talk about personal matters or exchange trade secrets with someone you see on the ride up or down, wait until you can have your discussion in private.

Chats in Transit

If you're on the elevator and you see someone you know, it's polite to say "Hello" or "How are you?" but be careful about going further, unless you're the only two people aboard. A quiet chat is fine, but talking and laughing loudly may annoy fellow passengers, trapped as they are for the length of the ride.

Getting Off

When the elevator door opens, common sense prevails: Those nearest the front exit first. If several people need to exit on a floor, the first person out should pause just outside the elevator and hold his or her arm across the open door to prevent it from closing while others exit. Alternatively, the other passengers still in the elevator should press the "Door Open" button so everyone can exit as easily as possible.

RIDING ESCALATORS AND MOVING SIDEWALKS

Escalators and moving sidewalks manners are more obvious: Keep to one side so that other people are able to continue walking up or down. If you're the one in a hurry to get off, don't be surprised to find that most people are standing square in the middle. Unless the escalator is so clogged that it's useless to make the attempt, politely say "Excuse me, please" to every person you want to move past. Generally, stand right and pass left. In countries where people drive on the left side of the road you may find people on

---

DOORS, DOORS, DOORS

Doors are the most common spot for close encounters. At busy times of day, people rushing through doors tend to think of the meeting that's starting, the lunch date they're late for—anything but the person coming the other way or following right behind them. Preoccupation could lead to injury if your unknown partner in transit happens to be disabled, elderly, or just inattentive. Be considerate: Open doors slowly and take a moment to look behind you before just letting go of the door.

When two people approach a door together—whether they are a man and a woman or two people of the same gender—the best policy is communication. "Here, let me get that for you" or "Please, go ahead," said by either person, avoids confusion. And here are two other pieces of door etiquette to be mindful of:

- Never squeeze into a revolving-door compartment that is already occupied.
- Stand away from entryways and elevator doors whenever you're biding time in the lobby. If you're waiting for someone, stand against a wall so as not to impede traffic.

---

escalators and moving sidewalks stand on the left and pass on the right.

As you exit the escalator or moving sidewalk, be sure to keep moving so you clear the way for the people behind you.

CHAPTER 8
BOSSES ARE PEOPLE, TOO

As Shakespeare might have said, prick them and they bleed the same as everyone else. In fact, whatever name he goes by (boss, supervisor, employer, manager, middle manager, executive), there's not a boss in the world who doesn't have a boss. The CEO must report to the board of directors; the board of directors to the shareholders. Even the highest-flying entrepreneur must answer to his or her customers, lenders, and the market.

What separates you from your boss is power and responsibility. He has the power to direct and demand your performance; your boss is then also responsible for your performance to everyone above him in the chain of command.

THREE STEPS TO COMPATIBILITY

Over a lifetime of work, most of us will experience good bosses, mediocre bosses, and a few truly atrocious bosses. In every case, three straightforward actions on your part will set the stage for getting the relationship off on the right foot:

- Understand that your boss is a human being.
- Accept the reality that your supervisor is in charge.
- Do your job, and do it on time.

WHEN YOU'RE NEW TO THE JOB

When you take a new job or a new position within your company, your primary challenge is to master your own duties. But to be fully effective, you must also uncover your new supervisor's modus operandi. Different bosses may have widely differing ways of operating: Your old boss required written project reports delivered punctually at the end of each week; your new boss prefers verbal updates and only occasionally asks for written reports.

Your old boss got a kick out of the rubber crocodile collection on your desk; your new boss frowns on cluttered cubicles. When you step into a new job, be open to your new boss's ideas. Stay flexible and remember that there's no absolute right way to run an office.

You can quickly pick up on the most obvious characteristics of your new boss's style by observing your coworkers and their interactions with him. Don't hesitate to ask questions, because your job description will tell you only what is expected of you—not how to do it. If the boss isn't available, it's fine to talk with your fellow workers about office procedures. Just be sure that your questions don't carry any implied criticisms. In particular, avoid the "At my last job, my boss would never . . ." approach.

Here are four tips when starting a new job:

1. **Open your eyes and close your mouth.** You're new; the other people have been there and have established ways of doing things. Experience the procedures and culture that are in place for a period of time before offering your suggestions on how to better the workplace.

2. **Arrive early; stay late.** You'll start the process of building a strong image of yourself in your boss's eyes by being there on time and putting in a full day from day one.

3. **Ask questions judiciously.** Procedures and approaches to work may differ from your previous job, so don't hesitate to ask for guidance.

4. **Be extra careful not to bend the rules or push limits.** This is a time for toeing the line. Learn the rules and customs of your workplace and work within them. At this point your goal is to be a team player.

GETTING ALONG WITH YOUR BOSS

People join companies; they leave managers. You'll see this maxim in numerous surveys about employee satisfaction. And it makes sense. We repeatedly receive letters from people who love their job, hate their boss, and don't know what to do about it. Frankly, how you get along with supervisors is

---

YOU'RE FIFTY AND YOUR BOSS IS THIRTY

Age doesn't matter. Bosses can be much younger than their employees, yet they still deserve the same respect you would accord a boss who is older than you. As you look at that boss who may be younger than your son or daughter, remember that he has that position because someone saw value in his skills or because he started or owns the business. He is your boss. If you are going to have a real problem with that, you may want to consider not taking the job and avoid putting yourself into a situation which gnaws at you every day as that thirty-year-old is telling you what to do. (See also Chapter 10, page 119.)

---

more your responsibility than theirs. Their job is to get the company's work done in the most productive and profitable manner. Your ambitions and goals are your own concern. The challenge facing all workers is how to get the most out of their relationships with their bosses. Here are some suggestions:

SPEAK UP AND OFFER IDEAS. Bosses generally welcome fresh thinking from the people they supervise. Schedule an appointment with him so you can do it at a time and in a place where the boss can focus on what you have to say.

BE PREPARED. Bosses appreciate the difference between those who shoot from the hip and those who do their homework before speaking.

DON'T WASTE YOUR BOSS'S TIME. Be concise and clear. Have your materials and support documents ready, as well as copies of any pertinent papers. You'll not only save your boss's time, but you'll also show yourself to be organized.

LOOK FOR PROBLEMS YOU CAN SOLVE. Bosses look favorably on employees who show initiative.

ASK FOR HELP WHEN YOU NEED IT. Most bosses enjoy teaching and guiding their employees. Asking your superior for help is not a sign of weakness; it is an appropriate recognition of the boss's broader knowledge and experience.

BE A TEAM PLAYER. It may be a cliché, but bosses prefer directing a cohesive group rather than a hodgepodge of self-centered individualists. Prima donnas may be high achievers, but many bosses believe that a group of steady workers is ultimately more productive.

SHOW ACCEPTANCE. Accept your boss's final decisions graciously even when they are contrary to your thinking.

Do Not Undermine

Never try to undermine your supervisor's position. There are a few legitimate situations when you must go above or around your boss (see "Going Over Your Boss's Head," page 107), but otherwise it is an extremely dangerous move. Keep in mind that a company has a large investment in its supervisors and department heads. In a conflict between boss and worker, the boss will almost always win—and the loser will gain only a reputation for underhandedness.

THE ART OF COMPLAINING

There are times when you may have to go to your supervisor and complain, whether it's as minor an issue as grumbling about a messy restroom or as major as being sexually harassed. You may have a personal gripe or your dissatisfaction may be shared by others. In any case, the boss is almost always the person to talk with. To complain effectively is something of an art form. By asking yourself the following questions ahead of time, you can avoid some common pitfalls:

IS YOUR COMPLAINT WORTHWHILE? Does it affect the quality of your work or overall productivity? Is it worth the boss's time, or will you be perceived as a whiner?

HAVE YOU DOCUMENTED THE PROBLEM? It is extremely important that you be able to support your complaint, both to show your seriousness and to validate your claims.

ARE YOU THE RIGHT PERSON TO MAKE THE COMPLAINT? If you lack the credibility to make the complaint, see if there's someone else who can do it.

WHAT RESULTS DO YOU WANT? Be clear about how you would like to see the situation resolved. Your boss may ask you for your opinion. You will want to have a well-thought-out solution ready.

WHAT'S THE BEST APPROACH? Decide if your boss prefers to read or to listen. Then either prepare a memo detailing the situation or ask for a private meeting.

WHAT'S THE RIGHT TIME? By respecting your boss's other obligations, you greatly improve your chances of being listened to.

HOW LONG SHOULD YOU WAIT FOR A RESPONSE? Don't expect immediate action on a complaint. You may not see results for a long time, especially if your complaint involves changing a company policy. A good boss will eventually tell you what came of your complaint, but understand that there may well have been consequences that she cannot discuss, such as the disciplining of a colleague.

If a problem persists after you've registered your dissatisfaction, carefully weigh the pros and cons of further complaints. What seems like reasonable follow-up to you may quickly be perceived as pestering to a boss. There are times when it is better to back off, face reality, and let the issue drop.

Complaining About Conditions

Complaints about workplace conditions can involve anything from poor janitorial service to excessive overtime. If you belong to a union, many working conditions are covered by your union agreement, and you will report problems to your steward or union representative. Otherwise, go to your boss, his or her assistant, or the office manager. Minor problems with the physical environment (you need a new chair or the photocopier consistently malfunctions) can usually be covered in a brief memo or email. More serious or physically threatening problems (loss of a security card, locked fire doors, the presence of unauthorized persons) should be reported as quickly as possible by the fastest means available. Don't hesitate to call the boss directly if the situation is potentially dangerous.

Overtime and Workloads

Problems such as excess overtime and short-staffing are a bit trickier. Don't jump to the conclusion that your boss is at fault. She may already be working to get relief. If your boss is unaware of the problem, it's wise to inform her in a polite manner. The employees may decide it is best to choose a representative to bring the complaint to the boss. Make sure that person has adequate documentation of the problem. (No angry mobs at the castle gate, please!) You stand the best chance of getting the results you want if you frame the complaint in terms of productivity: For example, show your boss how the lack of staff is causing missed deadlines and increased work errors.

The Group Complaint

If conditions don't improve, it may be time to gather your troops and meet with your supervisor as a group. The advantage of a group (made up of department representatives or the whole department) is that numbers can impress even the most insensitive supervisor; most bosses want to avoid serious and widespread morale problems.

The Big Next Step

If group complaining doesn't work, you and your colleagues will have to consider very carefully what your next step will be. Openly taking your complaints to your boss's boss could create an untenable situation. You may find out that the company values your boss's efforts and style and that suddenly you are in a very difficult situation. Instead, you may want to approach your boss's boss or someone in human resources on a confidential basis without naming names to get a sense of how valid your complaint is and to discuss how you can best approach the problem to resolve it. If you choose to openly go over your boss's head, it's preferable to let your boss know what you are doing. Copy him on all letters and memos to higher-ups. Document the problem, and keep the tone of all communications professional. Remember, once the dust settles, your boss may still be the boss.

Serious Complaints About Coworkers

Sometimes you'll need your boss to step in directly on a problem, especially if it is serious or has legal implications. Sexual harassment, racist remarks, religious proselytizing, theft, lying, bullying, threatening behavior—these are all examples of serious problems that can affect the entire company. Your direct supervisor needs to know about them immediately. If you become aware of a serious problem, go straight to your supervisor. Be precise; don't elaborate beyond what you actually know; don't feel obliged to cover for coworkers or explain their behavior. Then leave it to the supervisor to manage the situation.

Is It Worth It?

As for run-of-the-mill irritating, obnoxious, or difficult coworkers, you'll have to decide whether complaining about them is worth the effort. Rachel is driving everyone crazy with her bad moods. Ben's divorce is really affecting the quality of his work.

Assess the validity of your complaint and the value of bringing it up by answering the following questions:

- Is your complaint merely a personal issue?
- Does the behavior affect the way the person or other workers do their jobs?
- Is the problem persistent or short term?
- Is there an underlying condition, such as alcoholism or drug use, that may be the cause?
- Can you talk to the person and work things out, or is the boss's intervention necessary?

Like it or not, sometimes you must simply grin and bear it, tolerating difficult people whose value to the business outweighs their quirks. The egomaniacal salesman who is always the top producer, the temperamental art director who wins all the prestigious awards, the sharp-tongued secretary who is a genius with complex computer programs—they may irritate your boss even more than they bother you. But bosses have the responsibility to balance the general good against the feelings of individual employees.

Taking Action

If you decide to complain about a colleague, arrange a private meeting with your boss instead of writing a memo. (Never complain via email unless you're prepared for your words to become public property.) In your meeting, be calm and focus on the troubling behavior, not the person: "Roger leaves a half hour early at least three days a week, and we're having a problem getting his time sheets" is far better than "Roger is totally irresponsible and deceitful." Be as objective as you can, and don't be tempted to express moral judgments.

OWNING UP TO THE GOOD AND THE BAD

Occasionally, you may find yourself on the receiving end of a heartfelt compliment from your manager. When this happens, the most important thing you can do is to accept it graciously, with, for example, a simple, "Thank you. I really appreciate that you recognize my efforts on that proposal." If others were involved, make sure you point out that the proposal was really a team effort. Don't take all the glory for yourself.

On the other side of the coin, there will inevitably come a time when you screw up. Don't deny your culpability. When you find yourself in the hot seat, rule number one is to take responsibility for your actions. First and foremost, don't wait for your supervisor to come to you. Instead, go to her, explain the situation, apologize, and then offer a solution. As frustrating as your mistake may be for your supervisor, having a problem you caused suddenly land on her desk is even worse. By providing a solution, you not only exhibit responsibility, but you also show consideration for the impact your mistake could have on your supervisor and others.

When you screw up, these three steps will get you back on the right track:

1. **Take responsibility.** A problem occurred. You caused it. Own up to it. When something goes wrong and the boss knows it was you, the most frustrating phrase she can hear is "It wasn't my fault."

2. **Apologize.** A sincere "I'm sorry" should be the first words out of your mouth. They acknowledge you accept responsibility and they indicate you understand that you have caused a problem.

3. **Have a solution.** Problems require solutions. If you cause a problem and then dump it in your boss's lap to fix, she won't be very understanding. But if you accept responsibility, apologize, and then offer a way you can fix the problem, then the boss is much more likely to be understanding. Every boss knows mistakes happen. It's how they are dealt with that matters.

DEALING WITH CRITICISM

In order to learn and profit from criticism, it may be necessary to grow a little armor over that thin skin.

- Learn to listen to what the boss is really saying, without inferring hidden meanings.

- Learn not to react until you have fully digested the criticism.

- Control the instinct to become defensive.

- Count to ten or mentally recite the preamble to the Constitution before launching a counteroffensive.

- It also helps to hone your sense of humor; don't take the boss's favorite joke about "the bumbling junior executive" as suggesting something negative about you.

It's not easy to learn to value criticism, but doing so is a triumph of intellect over raw emotion. In fact, knowing how to offer criticism well—understanding that criticism is an opportunity to learn and improve—is a classic characteristic of good or excellent bosses, and it no doubt helped them to rise through the ranks.

> **TIP:** You can learn from all valid criticism, even criticism directed at others. But sooner or later, there's a good chance you'll have a boss who is just plain mean and abusive. In this case, your options are limited; you can stay and take it, or you can get out. If you stay in the job, you'll have to work hard not to become a victim of the boss's harsh tongue. Be your own critic, and don't take his or her complaints to heart.

Responding to Criticism

If the boss is sensitive or if you need to discuss his criticism in some depth, arrange a private meeting, preferably at a time when the boss is at ease. Try not to be confrontational. Even if the criticism was totally unjustified, phrase your response in terms of what you can do to remedy the situation: "When you were criticizing the Alpha project yesterday, I know you forgot that I didn't work on it. But you've said often enough that these short deadlines hurt everybody. It could be my group next time, and I want to get your ideas for avoiding the problem." You have corrected the boss, but you've also given him an out and moved the discussion forward to a more productive area.

DEALING WITH DIFFICULT BOSSES

Tough bosses are different from difficult bosses. There are tough, demanding bosses who drive you to perform above and beyond anything you thought yourself capable of. A difficult boss, on the other hand, is one whose demands hurt your performance more than they help.

Difficult bosses may be control freaks, credit hoggers, or pass-the-buck types, and their personalities can range from merely hard to get along with to near abusive. But difficult bosses are not, as a rule, out to get you, and they are generally unaware of how their behavior affects their employees.

Discussing the Problem

It can help to talk with a difficult boss in a non-confrontational meeting. You may want to include several office representatives in the meeting to demonstrate that the problem is widespread. Be specific about your complaints and show the boss how the problem is affecting overall productivity and morale. Try not to blame; instead, offer to help and have possible solutions in hand. Be aware that defensiveness may be the boss's first reaction and that change may come more slowly than you'd like. But if your boss shows a willingness to make adjustments in his behavior, be ready to meet him with cooperation.

Going Over Your Boss's Head

If you have to go over or around a difficult boss, keep the boss informed of your actions if possible. If your business has an experienced human resources staff, they may be able to help you decide on the strategy that is most likely to achieve the results you want within the unique structure and culture of your business. Keep in mind that your objective is positive change for everyone, including your difficult boss—not a bloody palace revolution.

Abusive Bosses

Abusive bosses are neither tough nor merely difficult; they are mean and unpredictable. They pick their victims for no apparent or logical reason. They inflict physical and emotional tortures, from ulcers

> **TIP:** The best defense when you can't leave your job is to identify your boss as an abuser and to understand in your heart and mind that you are not the cause of the problem.

and migraines to failures of self-confidence, on their workers. Abusive bosses are deliberately harmful to the people around them.

Before you personally tackle an abusive boss, it's always wise to gauge his role in the company. Remember, not only are people who are rude and uncivil in the workplace three times as likely to be superiors, but they're also likely to be valued employees in the eyes of senior management.

For employees with abusive bosses, there may be no totally happy solution other than escape. But it is not always possible or desirable to transfer or find a new job. Normal complaint and reconciliation mechanisms don't often work with abusive bosses; heart-to-heart talks are rarely helpful either and may even be counterproductive if the boss labels you as the enemy.

Employees may be able to combat abusers through group action. (If you have a union, try taking your issues there.) Documentation and unity are powerful weapons, but you'll need to face up to the fact that even they may not solve the problem.

YOUR CAREER PATH

Your supervisor will have a major impact on your career. She has the power to satisfy your immediate objectives and influence your long-range goals. But when you deal with the boss on issues that affect your career, remember that her primary concern is not your future or your personal situation but rather things that are happening here and now. And that's where you should focus any career discussions with your supervisor as well.

Asking for a Raise or Promotion

If ever a meeting needs to be conducted professionally, it is the salary or promotion discussion. Here are some tips on how to be as successful as possible in the meeting:

MORE MONEY MEANS MORE RESPONSIBILITY. When you are seeking a promotion, be ready to tell the boss what you can bring to the job. Know what the new position entails and how you plan to manage it.

NEVER, EVER BRING UP PERSONAL ISSUES. The boss doesn't care about your second mortgage, your kid's orthodontia, or your grandmother's nursing-home bills.

KNOW WHAT THE MARKET IS FOR YOUR SKILLS. You may want to provide information about the general market standards for a person with your responsibilities. Be careful not to bring up other offers as a threatening or coercive tactic; threats can blow up in your face. If you choose to mention an offer from another company or a headhunter, carefully present it as a means of helping the boss to evaluate your position relative to comparable companies. If you're genuine in your representation, the boss will not be riled—and if she senses that you may be in demand elsewhere, so much the better.

Refusing Offers

What do you do when the boss makes you an offer you have to refuse?

Think about it very hard. Weigh all the pros and cons. Talk with the people who mean the most to you. If you really cannot take on the added hours or excessive travel, turn down the offer. No matter how reasonable your grounds and how sympathetic the boss, your refusal of an offer may well stall your career ambitions for a time. You may face a period of repair work as you rebuild your image with the boss.

LEAVING YOUR JOB

If you're leaving your job by choice, don't signal your intention too early or to the wrong people. If you are looking for a new position, be discreet. Don't, for instance, get your secretary to type your application letters. Ask headhunters to phone you at home, not during work hours on your cell or office phone. Don't schedule a luncheon interview with a potential new employer at your current boss's favorite bistro. People love to gossip about who is planning to head for the door, and your boss will soon get wind of your plans.

When you do have a firm commitment for a new job, the polite move is to schedule a private meeting with your boss right away. While you don't have to go into detail about why you're leaving, it doesn't hurt to leave on a high note—express some positive but sincere words about the value of the time you spent at the company or under his management. Moving on doesn't have to mean letting go of contacts who may be valuable to you in the future.

When You Resign

If you're resigning, be courteous and appreciative in your meeting with (or letter to) the boss. You may want to sound off about every rotten moment you've

THE EXIT STATEMENT

Whether you are resigning or have been fired, you should work with your boss on an appropriate exit statement. It is important for you to participate in composing it, whether the statement is for in-office circulation only or is intended for wider distribution, including news releases. By working with your supervisor on the exit statement, you'll make certain that you and your former employer are telling the same story. Naturally, it's a good idea for the statement to include something about your achievements. If you've been fired, it is unnecessary to explain why. A generic statement is adequate: "Jerry will be leaving Acme this Friday to pursue new career opportunities." An exit statement for a person moving to a new job can be more specific: "All of us at Acme will miss Rebecca, but we know she will be a great success in her new position as human resources director of Manderley Enterprises."

endured and every idiot you've had to work with (the "take this job and shove it" syndrome). Don't do it. You never know when you might need your boss's help down the line, and old employers have a way of becoming new customers if you haven't alienated them. You might even want to return to the company in the future. So make sure you leave on a graceful note, no matter how you truly feel.

CHAPTER 9
THE SMART MANAGER

One key measure of a manager's success is how adeptly he earns and keeps respect in the workplace—from clients as well as from everyone top to bottom in his department and company. Why is respect so important? Because being respectful means understanding how your actions will affect other managers, employees, suppliers, clients, and prospects. Actions that tear others down will hurt productivity, profits, and retention; actions that build will do just the opposite.

Respect hinges on trust. And trust is earned, not given. It is earned by treating people consistently and making decisions honestly. Trust is lost by being less than honest, by not following through on promises, by employing a double standard. Once trust is lost, getting it back again is very difficult.

Smart managers not only know when to lead and when to get out of the way but also respect their employees as people. They use praise when they mean it—and usually get better results in the bargain. They can also be enforcers when necessary but are aware that managing by fear and threats is counterproductive.

Much of the secret of successful management is simply keeping your eye on the company's targets while applying common courtesy, respecting other people, communicating clearly, and keeping

calm under pressure. But when the pressure starts to build—whether from your boss, your staff, or your inner voice—all that is easier said than done.

A POSITIVE CLIMATE

"Creating a positive climate in my office is so important to me," says the head of an advertising agency, "that when I hire people, I tell them that one of the nonnegotiable requirements for working at my company is being able to get along with their coworkers. If they can't, that is grounds for dismissal. Work is already pressure-packed enough. No one should have to tolerate the additional pressure of a negative atmosphere created by people who can't get along."

The way a manager manages directly affects the atmosphere of the workplace. Manage in a positive manner, and the atmosphere will be positive. Manage with fear and threats, and the atmosphere quickly becomes pressure-charged and negative. Although the relationship between employee morale and productivity is always shifting and difficult to pinpoint exactly, there is little doubt that the psychological environment of the workplace directly affects the productivity of employees. A negatively charged atmosphere will sooner or later lead to reduced performance. Efficiency, quality, and productivity all go down the drain.

MANIPULATION'S MANY FACES

The smart manager will avoid manipulative behavior at all costs—no matter how tempted she might be to use such behavior as a motivational club. Not all manipulative managers use fear and threats. Some use more subtle kinds of pressure. Certain phrases can imply pressure, such as:

Everybody is saying that:

- You don't seem to be a team player
- You don't seem to respond well to criticism
- You seem less interested in manufacturing than marketing

Another common ploy is preceded by the apparently gentle question "Don't you think/agree that . . . ?" which implies that if you really don't happen to agree with or think what follows is true, you are in the minority. Subtle and crass manipulation both originate from the same source: a person who wants his or her own way more than anything else—a control freak.

Being Accountable

Every good manager should have the courage to be accountable for his own actions. Owning up to your staff that you made a mistake—say, by admitting that you misread the deadline for a project, causing you and several of them to work late into the night—is the mark of strength, not weakness. Making the occasional mistake is only human; taking blame for

> ### THE EUPHEMISM SCOURGE
>
> Many employees are ready to distrust any "official" statements that come out of the company head office. Why? One reason is that companies tend to speak in a convoluted, self-protective way, employing euphemisms by the dozens. Corporations use euphemisms for basically two reasons: to sugarcoat bad news and to spare feelings. Used in moderation, euphemisms can amount to simple good manners. Most people would probably rather hear "We are eliminating your position" than "You're fired," even though both mean you're out of work. But is it really necessary or helpful for companies to talk about "right sizing" and "reengineering" when what they mean is mass firings?
>
> Many management experts attribute worker cynicism to the fact that most employees see right through the euphemisms and conclude that the company thinks it can pull the wool over their eyes. If a manager faces such a climate of distrust, perhaps the best he can do is tell his staff the unadorned facts as he understands them and ask them to ignore the irritation they feel about opaque company pronouncements.

an error—and immediately setting about correcting it—shows you to be an effective problem solver, not a dodger. Blaming another person, another department, or "circumstances beyond my control," on the other hand, marks you as a whiner and buck passer—and raises a serious question about your integrity. Respect is too valuable an asset for you to risk just to save some embarrassment or pretend that you're infallible.

The smart manager is also willing to admit that she's not all-knowing, whether in regard to the business at hand or otherwise. When she doesn't have the answer to a question that has been posed in a meeting—the approximate quarterly sales figures of a competitor, perhaps—a straightforward "Let me find out" is perfectly acceptable. At the same time, she acknowledges that she's accountable for finding the answer: "I'll find out and let you know by five o'clock today."

Taking Credit

While it is important to own up to your mistakes, you should also take credit for your successes—bringing a project in under budget, for instance, or delivering on a promise to step up monthly production. Don't be so modest that you undersell your achievements. Just remember to recognize other people's contributions and acknowledge them quickly, openly, and generously.

"Try the Truth"

A top executive in a public relations firm has a favorite saying for clients who are at a loss about what to reveal: "When all else fails, try the truth." In business, as in life, telling the truth—no matter what

the short-term consequences—is far more beneficial than getting caught in a deception. People are generally forgiving, almost to a fault. But deceive them and they will remember it for a long, long time. "Try the truth" applies to everyone in the workplace: the boss, the manager, the new employee, the client, the contractor.

INSPIRING AND MOTIVATING

The smart manager doesn't leave it to the human resources department to inspire employees to do their best, to remain loyal to the company, and to maintain high standards. Making yourself available to answer questions and concerns, along with giving frequent feedback about job performance, is really the best kind of motivation, and it keeps the employee headed consistently in the right direction. The old-style taskmaster, who treats employees as little more than cogs in a wheel, is asking for low morale and low productivity.

FOCUS ON NEW EMPLOYEES

Two common mistakes made by managers are (1) assuming that employees know exactly what their jobs are and (2) failing to provide adequate training and feedback. A new worker must be given a job description that includes every duty that is expected of him. No one, neither the boss nor the employee, should suppose that certain tasks "come with the territory" but others do not. Even an employee who has been doing the same job at another company is going to need direction, since expectations vary from workplace to workplace.

Investing time up front in training an employee will pay off in fewer hassles later, ultimately saving time and effort. A manager should check in, if only briefly, with the employee every day for the first couple of weeks if possible (or at least three times a week) to review the work he is responsible for, assess progress, identify difficulties, and provide any encouragement. Make sure the employee understands why each activity is important, how you want it handled, and what level of proficiency you expect of him—now and six months from now. After the first two weeks, continue to review his progress in less frequent weekly meetings. These meetings afford an opportunity for one-on-one training and allow you to reinforce desired approaches and skills. While the employee is learning exactly what you want, you're discovering his strong points and weaknesses. Keep your advice practical, specific, and to the point.

Just be sure that you never renege on a promise to give feedback. If you do, you show the employee that follow-through is not important to you. That sets a bad example, and it could come back to haunt you.

EXPECTATIONS AND RULES APPLY TO YOU, TOO

Nothing is more frustrating to an employee than a manager whose attitude is "the rules apply to you, but they don't apply to me." For instance, the following rules apply just as much to a manager as to an employee:

- Meeting deadlines

COMMUNICATING DOWNWARD

In the executive suite, being available also means communicating downward as well as sideways and upward. Many managers are most comfortable talking with their organizational peers about shared interests and common concerns. And few want to miss a chance of schmoozing with their bosses. That leaves people below them last in line. Be that as it may, every manager should make an effort—at least once a day—to hear what's on the minds of employees further down the corporate food chain.

Communicating downward is not only good for office morale; it's also very good for the business. Those frontline employees who rarely see the inside of an executive office—salespeople, customer service reps, telemarketing personnel—are usually the first to know what's going right and what's going wrong. A smart company makes them feel they have access to the planners and decision makers—a chance to tell the unvarnished truth as they see and hear it every day, unfiltered by middle managers who might try to tone down bad news before it reaches the top.

- Arriving at work on time and staying until closing time
- Cleaning dishes in the kitchen
- Respecting expectations for attire and language
- Returning calls and messages within twenty-four hours (or less, depending on your company's standard)

Q. We have a communal kitchen that all staff, including managers, utilize. The employees are required to take turns cleaning the kitchen. However, the managers are exempt from this task. Should managers be required to "take a turn" if they use the area as well?

A. Unfortunately, we don't make the rules in your workplace. If we did, managers wouldn't be exempt from taking their turns cleaning the kitchen. If they use it, they should take part in taking care of it. However, each company has the privilege of making its own rules. And as long as that is the rule at your company, that's the way it is.

The only way the situation will change is if the employees can convince management to change it. This is not something to take on alone. Before sticking your neck out, you and any other employees who are frustrated with the current situation need to ask yourselves if this is an issue you really want to spend political capital on. If you decide to move forward, don't simply complain; work to change the policy. As a group ask to meet with your manager about the kitchen. Seek her input as to the rationale behind the policy and be prepared to explain why you think changing it would be beneficial to the company.

When you don't follow the rules and expectations of your company, the employees under you are likely to wonder why they should be held to a different standard than you and they will lose confidence and trust in you.

RECOGNIZE AND COMPLIMENT

If a job is truly well done, give it all the praise it deserves. Mentioning one or two specific things that especially impressed you makes your praise all the more convincing. It shows that you understand the difficulties the job posed. And don't delay. Leaving your compliment for a few days keeps the worker in suspense about your opinion of the job done, and you may risk forgetting to deliver it.

If a job is done well enough, but parts of it would benefit from a little constructive criticism, save the latter for later. Allow the recipient to bask in the praise until the next time the subject comes up; then say something like "As great as that proposal was, I think it could've used a few more examples of outside competition. Do you think you could find a few and add them?"

The Power of Compliments

The power of a compliment is greater than you might realize. It makes people feel good—and people who feel good generally are better, more productive employees. That means, of course, that giving compliments is good business as well as the nice thing to do. For the owner of a small business on a tight budget, praise is often the only reward he can afford. In that case, it becomes just that much more important to recognize and compliment a job well done, an effort that went above and beyond, or a great idea.

Make your compliments count. Just as important as giving them is not giving one for every little thing any employee does, which will cheapen the value of your praise. For the giver and the receiver, compliments are best when they are not only sincere but also well deserved.

What's Your Style?

Sometimes the medium amplifies the message. Many managers like to deliver their highest praise face-to-face. Others prefer to put it in writing. It's a matter of personal style—and usually employees know which style their manager uses when he is most pleased. For managers of the terse kind, this could be a brief phone call or email or even just a handshake and a "Nice job" when passing in the hall. Others go further. One executive, when extremely pleased, composes a handwritten message, seals it in an envelope, and then delivers it in person. She gives the compliment verbally and then hands over the written note as well. Employees can hold on to those notes as part of their official record.

BE AVAILABLE

Remember that your first priority as a manager is to get results, and the way to get results is through managing people, not paper. Instead of hiding behind a closed door and your desk, surrounded by a defensive barricade of paperwork, keep your door open—and especially your eyes and ears. You'll learn much about employee attitudes and morale simply by being alert.

There is no better way of finding out who's feeling overlooked or overwhelmed than watching the passing parade and tuning in to the office chatter—and you can ask unhappy workers in for a chat on the spot. That way, their frustrations have less chance of spreading to the rest of the staff.

The telephone can be just as effective a barrier to people management as paperwork. So can email. (Try talking to a manager's back as she sits hunched in front of a computer screen!) The best managers learn to take control of their telephone and email time rather than having it control them. This leaves time for face-to-face meetings and spontaneous conversations—the source of almost all the good ideas that arise in a corporation.

One energy company manager tries to allocate no more than one hour per day to the telephone and email. She gives her email a half hour in the morning and makes her telephone calls in a half-hour slot in the afternoon. People she deals with inside and outside the company know she's a paragon of organization, and if they don't hear from her today, they'll hear from her tomorrow. Some days her calls and email take a little longer, but other days she's done in minutes. It evens out, she says—and the discipline makes her a better manager.

THE POWER OF "PLEASE" AND "THANK YOU"

More often than not the small courtesies get lost in the shuffle of the do-it-now, faster-better-cheaper business world. But saying "please" and "thank you" is not just an empty gesture. Adding "please," for example, before "Come to a meeting in my office at ten o'clock" or "Scan and send this to Bob Johnston" turns a demand into a request. People respond much more positively when something is asked of them rather than demanded.

The same goes for "thank you." When you say "Thank you," you are showing appreciation. When you don't say "Thank you," you are showing that you expected someone to do something. People much prefer to be appreciated.

Manners project a kind of easy confidence. They say, "No matter how crazy our jobs get, let's not forget the social niceties that hold our lives together. Let's not let a bad day destroy our mutual respect. If we keep our heads, things always work out." One manager on the news desk of a national newspaper makes a habit, no matter how harried or exhausted he feels, of greeting everyone he passes in the corridor with a smile and his or her name. If he knows an employee's relative has been in the hospital, he asks, "How's your mother doing?" He has a reputation as one of the most demanding managers on the paper—but he is also one of the most respected and admired. By using "please" and "thank you" yourself, you are setting an example for your staff by making it clear that these common courtesies are part of your team or company culture. Model the behavior, and your employees are likely to follow suit.

LANGUAGE MATTERS

Part of most executives' daily routine is to spend time with an assistant going over projects, reviewing schedules and deadlines, and discussing appointments to be made. It's easy to forget the basic courtesies that make your interaction more pleasant. Shouting "David, come in here!" or running through the litany of things to do without a smile seems demanding if not overbearing. "David, when you're finished with that email, would you please come in?" shows recognition that he is busy and turns an order into a request.

Likewise, saying "you" rather than "I" when making requests implies that David has a participatory place in the process. "I want you to work on the Welt

Most managers have found, some through bitter experience, that it is best not to form close friendships with subordinates. Here are the perspectives of three executives who have faced the situation:

"PROFESSIONAL ONLY." The thoughts of the president of a design firm: "As my firm has grown, I've found relationships with my employees have become more professional and less personal. When it was three of us, we worked closely together in one big open space and we knew everything about each other. Now, with nine people and doors and offices, the relationship between me and the employees is much more 'professional only.' I do care about each of them, but I also care about the business. And no matter how hard I might try, the business would be part of any outside-the-office friendship we might have. So I don't seek or encourage close office friendships. In some ways, that's a little sad. But it keeps things simple."

AWKWARD VS. REWARDING. From the president of a bank: "Any manager has to be extremely careful about becoming too friendly with an employee. For starters, if you're trying to socialize with your subordinates, they could feel obligated to socialize even if they don't want to—and you've put them in an awkward position. Any socializing should be for the purpose of learning things from employees that will help you do your own job better. That's not the same as socializing with people for the fun of it. Just as you don't want to be your child's friend instead of his parent, you want to be a boss first and a friend second."

FUN, BUT WITH LIMITS. From the president and CEO of a real estate development company: "I'm a people person, so personal contact with my employees is very important. It's how I learn about what's really happening in the company, because the information isn't filtered through other levels. In-house lunches, special outings, and an occasional office party are fine—and I saw nothing wrong with taking a bunch of my accounting people recently for drinks at my house and then out to dinner, since they were getting ready for a very tough time with long hours. But even though I get to know my people in a personal way, I usually don't socialize outside the office, with the exception of a few senior managers."

project this afternoon" is better phrased as "David, the Welt project needs some attention—would you please fit it into your schedule this afternoon?"

SOCIAL NETWORKING WITH EMPLOYEES

The reality is that seeking to form bonds of personal friendship with employees can be difficult. Many managers consciously work to keep relationships with their employees on a professional level.

That doesn't mean you can't show concern for personal problems and be supportive. (See "Buddy or Boss?," above.)

The operative word in the manager–employees relationship is *professional*. One of the best examples of the difference between personal and professional is making a friend request to an employee on a social networking platform. (See the box "Usually Your Boss Is Not Your Friend," page 104.) The difficulty comes when you choose a social network like Facebook, which is based on personal relationships, rather than a professional-oriented social network like LinkedIn. A friend request to an employee on Facebook can be uncomfortable and awkward for the employee. Does he accept your request even though he really doesn't want you as a "friend"? Does he ignore your request, which leaves him wondering how you'll feel about not receiving a response to his request? Or does he turn down your request outright?

Save your employees the stress by respecting your professional relationship and stick to professional social networking sites for creating relationships with your employees.

CHAPTER 10
GENDER AND GENERATIONS IN THE WORKPLACE

Business is built on relationships. Building relationships is hard enough with people similar to you. But when people come from different generations—and as many as four generations may be currently working side by side in the workplace—finding common ground on which to build relationships is complicated by different attitudes toward work, the importance of work, and the importance of life outside of work. Gender also plays an important role in building relationships. Being aware of the differences between you and your coworkers, clients, prospects, and suppliers gives you a leg up on building bridges both between men and women and between people in different generations.

GENDER

There are still places in today's world for gendered roles, such as men opening car doors and holding chairs or coats for women. While some women welcome and appreciate these courtesies in the workplace, others strongly prefer not to be singled out by their gender. In business, it's best to take a gender-neutral approach and treat coworkers and employees equally. This doesn't mean that courtesy is gone; instead, think of it as people doing considerate things for people rather than men doing nice things for women.

This leaves men who have been raised strictly to adhere to these courtesies in a tough spot. In business, don't assume you know what the woman you're with would prefer; instead, ask: "May I hold your chair?" "May I help you with your coat?" The question is just as courteous as the gesture, and it allows women who would rather not be treated differently to decline. For women, a simple "Yes, thank you" or "No, thank

---

A DELICATE SUBJECT

Think twice before making a comment on a person's weight, especially if that person is of the opposite sex. Even a compliment about weight loss may be taken the wrong way.

And never, never comment on a woman's pregnancy without first being absolutely sure that she is pregnant.

Language

At no time is it appropriate to speak to someone in terms that use gendered words to belittle or diminish. *Sweetie*, *babe*, *honey*—these have all (it is hoped) left the workplace for good, as have sexual comments about physical appearance. Compliments are still fine, but know that "You look nice today" or "That's a good color on you" is a far cry from "You look hot in that dress" or "Those pants make your butt look great." Tone of voice is equally important; even "You look nice today" can have a new and inappropriate meaning if said in a sexy or suggestive tone.

Titles

Use the title "Ms." at all times when addressing women formally, either in person or in email or business letters, unless you are certain a woman uses "Mrs." for her title. (If writing socially to a couple with the same last name, it is fine to use "Mrs.") Don't use "Miss," either, as it is reserved for very young women, unless you know it is her preferred title.

Gender-Neutral Names

Many men and women with names such as Alex or Jamie find themselves in the awkward position of receiving an email or letter that gets their gender wrong. The best way to respond is to add a simple postscript to the note: "PS: By the way, I just wanted you to know I'm a female Jamie." This is one case in which a smiley face could go a long way to assuring the recipient there are no hard feelings. You could also reply by phone, allowing your voice to be all the clue you need.

Equally awkward is writing to someone and being unsure of whether to use "Mr." or "Ms." When

you" is an appropriate and appreciated reply. Don't take offense at a question born out of courtesy.

Some women will find fault with this and say that men should continue to treat women differently, out of respect. Socially, there is still room for men to open doors on dates and help a woman with her coat; but in business, it is best to keep the focus on a respectful interaction that keeps the emphasis on business.

writing to an Alex or Jamie you haven't met, be careful not to make assumptions. Do a little detective work. Check the company website for a reference to the person. Check social media, especially LinkedIn to see if the person is listed there. If sleuthing doesn't work, try calling his or her office and ask, "I'm writing a business letter; is Alex Samuelsson a man or a woman?" If all these options fail, you have two ways to proceed:

1. Use their first name only, avoiding the issue.

2. If writing formally, address them with no title but use their first and last name, or use the highly impersonal (and potentially standoffish) "To whom it may concern."

Your best bet, really, is to sleuth it out.

Transgender Identification

Many times you will know what pronouns to use when speaking to a transgendered colleague based on how your other colleagues refer to them. When meeting someone who is transgender for the first time, use gendered pronouns that reflect the gender the person presents to the world; attire and/or name are good places to start. If a man is wearing a dress or is introduced as Karen, then use feminine pronouns and the title "Ms." If their name isn't a clue and you remain unsure of their gender preference and need to know how to address them, it's better to ask, "What pronoun would you like me to use?" than to assume and be wrong.

Shaking Hands

It used to be that a man would not extend his hand to shake with a woman unless she had first extended hers to him. This is an old courtesy, meant to allow her to control the exchange or not have her personal space invaded. Generally speaking, there is no need for it in the United States business world, especially in the workplace. (For information on handshaking in other parts of the world, see "Greetings," page 317.) The greatest rudeness would be to fail to shake hands entirely. So men, in a business context feel confident extending your hand to a woman.

WOMEN WHO DON'T SHAKE HANDS

For some women, religion prevents them from shaking hands with men. The best way to handle the situation with men who may not be aware and who extend their hand to shake is to nod your head in acknowledgment and use words to express what the handshake would have signified. "It's a pleasure to see you again. Please excuse me for not shaking hands" or "I'm pleased to meet you, but I don't shake hands." This is not an apology, but an acknowledgment that you are not doing something that would otherwise be expected. In fact, this is not a reinvention of the wheel. This is what anyone who is unable to shake hands owing to illness, injury, or the loss of a hand or arm would do. Whether or not you explain that you don't shake hands because of your religion is entirely up to you. As always, even more important than the manner—shaking hands—is the principle or idea the manner expresses—a friendly, welcoming, respectful greeting that acknowledges the introduction or hello.

STANDING UP

Women, stand up! Stand to shake hands when someone who isn't a regular visitor enters your office or when someone approaches your table to say hello at a restaurant during a business meal or at a business function. Socially, women used to remain seated, but this custom has fallen by the wayside. In business you should always greet colleagues, bosses, and clients at eye level.

Money

Many women find themselves in the position of expecting to pay the bill, only to have the waiter hand it to a man at the table or to have a man at the table literally pick up the bill to pay before she can take it. Either way, the answer is clear. Simply say, "Mark, let me. I invited you." If the man continues to argue, an "I insist" or "No, allow me" is fine, but don't argue further. It places too much emphasis on the bill, even though he should have allowed her to pay.

If your intention is to pick up the tab, there are a few strategies you can employ to ensure that the waiter hands the check to you:

- As you are led to your table, quietly ask the waitperson, maître d', or host to bring the check to you at the end of the meal.

- After the meal, as the waiter approaches your table with the check, extend your hand to signal that the bill should go to you.

- Discreetly give your card to the waiter when you arrive and ask that the bill be prepared and a 20 percent tip added.

- Excuse yourself from the table toward the end of the meal and settle the bill away from the table.

The latter two options are nice as there is no question of payment at all—it is simply handled—and that allows you to keep the focus on the conversation at hand without distraction. (Bear in mind that if you give your card at the beginning or at some point during the meal, you will be presented with a check to sign without having had an opportunity to review the bill first.)

ROMANCE IN THE WORKPLACE

Statistics tell the story: Roughly half of all married couples first met at work. While it is true that romances are a fixture in office life, there is also a heightened awareness of discrimination and harassment, along with the issues of conflicts of interest, distraction from work, and the unpleasant ramifications of a fling's sour ending.

It goes without saying that not all relationships are fraught with danger or even trouble, but entering into a romantic involvement at the office requires no small measure of thought and care.

A Secret to Keep?

If your company has no policy on dating office mates, respect the company's trust in you by proving that your work remains your only focus during the day. It's in poor taste—not to mention unprofessional—to subject coworkers to displays of affection.

If your office bans romances between workers at different levels, consider the options: You could continue the affair in secret, at the risk someone will discover the truth and spread the news; you could ask to bc transferred to another department; you could end the relationship; or you could find a new job.

Even if office romance is permissible, there are couples who prefer to keep it to themselves. If you feel uncomfortable revealing your relationship to co-workers, remember that you have no obligation to do so.

Romances Between Manager and Employee

No matter how professionally you behave during the workday, a relationship between two people of un-equal standing in the office will raise suspicions of unfair treatment or questionable motives, especially if one person supervises or reviews the other's perfor-mance. Inherent here are issues of power, preferential treatment, and manipulation, which don't necessarily play a part in a romance between equals.

If the relationship is serious, one of you (almost certainly the partner of lower rank) should consider requesting a transfer. If this seems like overkill, look at the alternatives: If the relationship were to con-tinue for any length of time, the more junior em-ployee could never be promoted without the risk of people crying unfair advantage. On the other hand, if the relationship were to end badly, there could be issues of harassment or misuse of power that would be traumatizing to both parties.

Romances with Associates from Outside

If you work closely with someone from another com-pany, you face a difficult situation if a romantic rela-tionship results. If the relationship becomes serious, consider removing yourself as the company contact; otherwise, there could be charges of preferential treat-ment. Also bear in mind that if the relationship doesn't last, it may cause tension or even the loss of an account.

WHAT IS SEXUAL HARASSMENT?

Because sexual harassment is often in the eye of the beholder, the government and the courts go to some lengths to define it. According to Title VII of the Civil Rights Act of 1964, sexual harassment occurs in two forms:

QUID PRO QUO. This translates as "this for that" ha-rassment, in which (1) a supervisor offers a job, pro-motion, or raise in return for a date or sexual favors, or (2) a supervisor threatens negative consequences if his or her advances are not accepted.

HOSTILE ENVIRONMENT CLAIMS. More of a catch-all, this section of the law refers to cases that include but are not limited to unwanted flirting, touching, unwanted email, offensive pinups, inappropriate comments, lewd gestures, foul language, sexual innu-endos, repeated requests for sexual favors, demeaning sexual inquiries, and inappropriate comments on a person's dress or appearance.

It is particularly important for workers to remem-ber that what they consider funny may be insulting to someone else. For instance, telling dirty jokes or describing the previous night's sexual activity may seem innocent and natural to the person doing the talking—but appalling and offensive to others. The smartphone and Internet have opened new avenues for harassment through sexting or sending offensive material via email.

Responding to Harassment

Given the open-ended nature of the law as stated, it is important to understand more about the nature of the behavior in question before deciding to make a claim. According to the Equal Employment Opportunity Commission, sexual harassment is defined as "Unwelcome sexual advances, requests for sexual favors, and other verbal or physical conduct of a sexual nature . . . when submission to or rejection of this conduct explicitly or implicitly affects an individual's employment, unreasonably interferes with an individual's work performance or creates an intimidating, hostile or offensive work environment."

The EEOC also notes that:

- Both victim and harasser may be either a woman or man.

- The victim may be the opposite or the same sex as the harasser.

- The victim of harassment doesn't necessarily have to be the person being directly harassed, but could be anyone affected by the harasser's offensive behavior.

If these criteria are met, you need to decide what action to take next.

1. Depending on the seriousness of the situation and your comfort, you may choose to discuss the problem directly with the person doing the harassing. Tell the person to cease, and state in no uncertain terms that you don't condone his or her advances or comments. Depending on the response, you may choose to give an additional warning or two, but make it clear that if the behavior continues, you will report him or her.

2. Check your employee handbook and follow the instructions for combating sexual harassment outlined there. You should speak to a supervisor or a member of the human resources staff to put your employer on notice about your situation. Representatives of the company should take steps to investigate and discipline the perpetrator.

3. If the company doesn't take your complaint seriously, consider contacting an outside agency and/or an attorney who concentrates in the area of employment law as a step toward ending the harassment. One organization offering help is the Equal Employment Opportunity Commission (EEOC). In most states, your first recourse is through a state agency or division that handles sexual harassment claims often related to the attorney general's office. In most cases, depending on the nature of the claim, the state agency will conduct an independent investigation of the claim.

Whatever action you choose to take, keep a record of the encounters you've had with the person who is harassing you and with any contacts in the company from whom you have sought help. It may seem paranoid to jot down the nature of every communication you have with the offending person and to keep copies of any written communications, which may include examples of the harassment, such as emails, and of your discussions with human resources or your supervisor, but if the harassment continues you will need to have accurate and detailed examples: what was said and done; who might have been a witness; and what your employer said and did in response to your complaints. It's also wise to keep copies of your performance reviews at home for safekeeping; if your harasser tries to discredit your work, your documentation of good performance will speak for itself.

MULTIPLE GENERATIONS IN THE WORKPLACE

The current American workforce has four distinct generations that are working together. That togetherness is shattered sometimes by differences in work habits, expectations, capabilities, training, and schooling. Here's how these generations are broken down:

TRADITIONALISTS. Typically, they are defined as born before 1945. You may find them in the senior management positions and/or in the last years of their working life. They tend to be rules-bound, respect hierarchies, and have concrete expectations of their employer's responsibility toward them. Traditionalists used landline office phones for much of their work life and believed personal calls at work were completely against the rules. At one time, they dictated memos and letters for secretaries to prepare. They were thrifty: Long-distance calls cost money; overseas calls cost even more money.

BABY BOOMERS. They were born after 1945 and until the mid-1960s. Having been in the workforce for up to forty-five years, they now fill management and senior management positions. They have a strong work ethic and have learned how to be team players. Baby boomers experienced the first bag phones and wireless technology in its infancy. The landline office

Q. While leaving a business meeting and getting into a minivan with coworkers, I realized I was going to have to climb into the way back of the van to go to lunch. I am the oldest of the group, a fifty-one-year-old female. I tapped a twenty-three-year-old male on the shoulder and said, "Listen, I am pulling the trump card. You are sitting in the back, and I am taking the front seat."

My boss got in the back of the van, as did the others. I don't want to seem like a snotty princess, which I am not; I just expect decent behavior. I also do not want to act like their mother. What would be the proper protocol?

A. The "how" is what matters. There's a difference between slapping them upside the head and gently suggesting a course of action. You shouldn't have to climb into the backseat when there are younger males for whom it would be easier. But your approach was lacking in consideration because you demanded rather than asked and because you expected them to do the wrong thing rather than giving them the opportunity to do the right thing.

As you approached the van, you could have turned to the others and said, "If you guys don't mind, it would be a lot easier for me if I could sit in the front seat. Thanks." Same result—you sit in the front seat—but you don't come across as a snotty princess or anyone's mother.

phone still ruled the office, and written communications primarily took the form of memos and letters. The first PC computers showed up in the workplace in the early 1980s but without Internet social networking. The fax machine was the first change in the speed of communication, paving the way for the adoption of email.

GEN XERS. They were born in the fifteen-year period from the mid-1960s to 1980, so they have been in the workforce between ten and thirty years. They have a more independent streak and have an interest in creating a balance between work life and nonwork life. Email evolved as Gen Xers entered the workplace and began their careers. While office phones were still part of the communications equipment, cell phone use became widespread and started to impact the office environment. The communications technology revolution goes hand in hand with their work experience.

MILLENNIALS. Born between 1980 and 1995, they have been in the workforce the shortest time, from just starting out to no more than ten years in. They grew up with the technology prior generations had to learn as adults, so they seem more adept at multitasking. They thrive on and expect feedback and praise. For millennials, email is the standard written communications vehicle. Social networking evolved along with the millennials, so they are totally adept at it and spend considerable time at it. Texting is second nature.

Stereotyping vs. Generalizing

As easy as it is to ascribe characteristics, it is equally dangerous to assume that all baby boomers or millen-

nials are the same. Not all baby boomers work best in teams; not all millennials expect instant recognition of tasks completed or even effort made; not all traditionalists have the same respect for authority or adhere to rules; and not all Gen Xers are entrepreneurs or eschew being team players.

Regardless of which generational group you may be a part of, it's important to acknowledge and understand the differing perspectives on expected behaviors, ways of showing respect, and social norms that each group has. Since manners are a set of shared social expectations, and those manners and expectations change naturally over time, it makes sense that different generations would have different expectations—and those differences often lead to friction. With four generations sharing the workplace right now, that only multiplies the opportunity for misunderstanding.

It's pointless to try to argue the subjective merits of different generations' expectations for behavior in the workplace (or anywhere). Rather, this is the time to step outside your point of view and ask, "What does the other person expect?" You don't need to agree with that expectation, but you do need to be aware of it and understand how to work with it.

Dealing with Generational Differences

Awareness and *respect* are the keys to how people in different generations can work together successfully. Another area that causes friction between people of different generations is the way they communicate. Traditionalists entered the workforce talking to one another in person; baby boomers communicated over the telephone; Gen-Xers use email; and millennials favor texting.

For example, as a millennial prepares to ask for important information from a baby boomer he may want to think twice before shooting off a text or email and instead consider picking up the phone to make the request. As you prepare to interact with people from a different generation at work, consider the different attitudes and approaches each generation has.

Generational Sticking Points

In addition to commonplace differences regarding language and attire, here are some other areas in which differing expectations can cause friction between the generations. If these are problems in your work environment, apply *awareness* and *respect* as you strive for better working relationships.

PRIVACY. Senior generations expect a high level of privacy about personal matters as well as business matters. They are not likely to share personal information at the office and would consider it unethical to talk about internal company matters to outsiders. Younger generations, on the other hand, value sharing information and see nothing wrong with posting details about their private and work lives on social networking sites.

OFFICE STRUCTURE. Hierarchies, teams, telecommuters—there's a good chance that the modern office will be trying to accommodate all three. Senior workers are used to regular face-to-face meetings, whereas younger workers rely on email and technology to meet in cyberspace.

MULTITASKING. There is no question that the texting generation has grown up doing at least two things at once, which, to those of an older generation, appears distracted, disorganized, and depending on the context, rude.

FEEDBACK. Senior generations expect an annual review from their boss or perhaps their team. They tend to be direct in criticism and don't sugarcoat dissatisfaction. Younger generations expect feedback along the way and want to be praised for the completion of interim steps as well as the final work.

CHAPTER 11
GOOD INTRODUCTIONS

Although the ways of going about an introduction are less rigid than they once were—a reflection of the casualness that has entered all segments of American life—the act itself remains as important as ever. Effective introductions put people at ease and serve to draw new acquaintances into a smoothly flowing, cohesive conversation. Learning how to do introductions effectively and then performing them expertly will make you look confident and professional to co-workers, bosses, prospects, and clients. On the other hand, failing to introduce a newcomer or a stranger, whether a business associate at a meeting, a visitor to the office, or a guest at a party, is a serious social and business error.

THE ALL-IMPORTANT HANDSHAKE

Most people are sizing you up as they shake your hand. As straightforward as this everyday gesture may seem, take into account the following:

WHEN TO DO IT. A handshake is in order not only when you're being introduced but also when you welcome people into your office, when you run into someone you know outside of work, when you say good-bye, when you are offering congratulations, and whenever another person offers his or her hand.

THE GENDER QUESTION. Until recently, it was considered polite for a man to wait for a woman to extend her hand before extending his own, but this is no longer customary—especially in business. A handshake is usually expected, regardless of one's gender.

THE PROPER GRIP. Your grip speaks volumes: A limp one suggests hesitance or timidity, and a bone-cruncher can come across as aggressive or domineering—not to mention painful. A medium-firm grip—the amount of pressure you would apply to grip a doorknob as you open a door—conveys confidence and authority. Also make sure your shake is palm-to-palm (not fingers-to-fingers), and keep your hand perpendicular to the ground. An upturned palm may subconsciously signal submissiveness; a downward palm, dominance.

THE TWO-HANDED HANDSHAKE. This involves clasping the outside of the greeter's hand with your free hand. While this kind of handshake signals warmth, it can seem presumptuous or insincere when used in a first meeting. Take care: Some people consider the two-hand shake too intimate for business, and others may see it as a "power" move, intended to subtly intimidate the recipient.

GLOVED HANDSHAKES. When winter gloves are worn outdoors, common sense prevails: You needn't take them off to shake someone's hand. A woman attending an event that calls for formal attire leaves her gloves on when shaking hands, but she takes them off when it comes time to eat.

The Four Essentials of a Handshake

Whether introducing yourself or being introduced by others, stay relaxed. Always do the following:

STAND UP. In the modern business world, this rule applies to men and women alike. If there's no room to stand—you're wedged behind a table at a restaurant, for instance—briefly lift yourself out of your chair, extend your hand, and then say, "Please excuse me for not standing. I'm pleased to meet you."

SMILE AND MAKE EYE CONTACT. Your smile conveys warmth, openness, and interest in the person you're meeting. Making eye contact shows that you're focused on the person you are greeting.

TIP: When shaking hands with an elderly person, take your cue from their grip and respond with equal or slightly less pressure.

THE FIST BUMP

We've seen it, we've done it—the fist bump. After a putt rolls in for a birdie or a slap shot catches the upper corner. In fact, most anytime congratulations are in order, people bump fists. Or they high-five.

But in business, you still shake hands. As you sign a contract for a new piece of business, you shake hands with the client; you don't offer a fist bump. When the human resources VP offers you the job or promotion, you shake hands; you don't high-five.

Leave the high fives and fist bumps for your personal life. In business, congratulations are demonstrated by shaking hands.

STATE YOUR GREETING. The direct "How do you do?" or "Hello" or "It's so nice [great] to meet you" are excellent openers. Repeating the person's name—"How do you do, Ms. Dowd?"—not only is flattering but also helps you remember the person's name.

SHAKE HANDS. A proper handshake lasts about three seconds; the clasped hands are pumped two or three times, after which you let go and step back.

The Non–Hand Shaker

From time to time, you may meet someone who doesn't offer his or her hand to be shaken. This may be due to a fear of germs, or the person may be from another culture with different customs. If you are faced with a nonshaker, withdraw your hand as unobtrusively as possible and move on.

If you are concerned yourself about coming into contact with another person's germs, take this far less rude approach: After introductions are made and handshakes exchanged, keep your fingers and hands away from your mouth, nose, and eyes. Then, as soon as you can politely excuse yourself, make a trip to the restroom to wash your hands. Not shaking is a quick way to sour a potentially valuable relationship. Once you start off on the wrong foot, it is very hard to recover.

When You're the Introducer

When it falls to you to make an introduction, remember two things: (1) State the parties' names in full, and (2) offer snippets of information about them (their professions, perhaps, or where they're from), "Ms. Dawson, this is Scott Bernstein, our marketing assistant. Scott, meet Carol Dawson, from Wilde and Wooley." Information about the person (in this case, the client) puts her into a context and provides an opening for conversation: "Wilde and Wooley? They've been going great lately, I hear." Or "Do you know Karen Nelson? I used to work with her before she joined your firm."

TIP: When you are introducing people of unequal rank or age, use professional titles if they are called for. For example, a young salesman meeting a physician would be introduced to Dr. Michael Yamaguchi. An official title such as governor, congressman, or one of the various military ranks is retained even if the position is no longer held.

Your choice of words when making an introduction is flexible. "I'd like you to meet . . ." or "May I introduce . . . ?" or any other reasonably gracious phrase you feel comfortable with is fine.

Who Is Introduced to Whom?

The question of who to introduce to whom is solved by following one simple rule: Talk to the more important person first.

- If you're talking to a client and your boss approaches you, say to the client, "Mr. Client, I would like to introduce you to my boss, Mr. Manager." Then, turning to your boss, you say, "Mr. Manager, I would like you to meet Mr. Client. Mr. Client is CEO of . . ."

- If you are talking to your boss and a client approaches you, say to your boss, "Excuse me." Then turn to the approaching client and say, "Mr. Client, how nice to see you. I would like to introduce you to my supervisor, Mr. Manager." Then turn back to your boss and say, "Mr. Manager, I would like you to meet Mr. Client. Mr. Client is CEO of . . ."

Importance can be defined in many ways: by job level, age, experience, and degree of public recognition. A client or prospect is always considered more important than a supervisor or boss. If you're not sure who takes precedence, make an arbitrary choice and forge ahead with the introduction. A slight error in protocol is much less of a misstep than failing to make the introduction at all. When introducing peers of equal status, it doesn't matter who you talk to first—again, what matters is that you make the introduction.

HUGS AND KISSES

Hugs and kisses in greetings usually take these five forms:

1. THE KISS. Kisses on the cheek are better left to social situations. In business, men and women executives should refrain from kissing in public, since even a peck on the cheek might be misconstrued. The occasional peck on the cheek is the exception when the parties know each other well, especially when they greet each other at a quasi-social event like a convention.

2. THE AIR-KISS. What began as a way of avoiding lipstick traces and smudged makeup is now an accepted form of greeting. The cheek is put alongside the other person's cheek; a full-fledged air-kiss repeats the gesture on the other cheek. The habit of air-kissing often looks artificial in a business setting: To the person watching, it looks insincere; to the recipient, it may seem all the more artificial.

3. THE BEAR HUG. Save this two-armed hug for old friends or for business associates with whom you're especially close and haven't seen for a long time.

4. THE SEMI-HUG. Engaging in a momentary clutch (each person placing his or her arms briefly around the other person's shoulders) is sometimes appropriate among businesspeople of the same sex, but only if they have a close personal friendship as well.

5. THE SHOULDER CLUTCH. This involves grabbing each other's right upper arm or shoulder with the free hand while shaking hands. It is best used by business associates of the same sex who haven't seen each other for a long time but maintain a warm relationship.

No matter what profession you're in, avoid close contact with another person when you are ill. It's perfectly polite to offer an excuse for not shaking, "Please excuse me for not shaking hands, but I have a cold. It's very nice to meet you." It's more welcoming to tell someone you have a cold and keep your distance than to risk infecting him or her.

Introducing Someone to a Group

If you find yourself introducing someone to a group—a circle of friends at a cocktail party, for example—wait for a conversational opening to present itself, then grab your chance: "Hi, everybody. I'd like to introduce you to Sandy Vail, who's in from Tennessee." Next, introduce the people standing near Sandy by name. Others can introduce themselves later. If, however, the person you are introducing is one of your clients and the group is made up of colleagues, then the client is the "important" one to whom the others are presented: "Linda Ambrose, I'd like you to meet our sales staff."

When You Are Introduced

When you are the one being introduced, be sure to follow the four essentials for an introduction—beginning with standing up. If the person making the introduction is having trouble remembering your name, rescue the situation by offering your name to the introducer or extending your hand and saying your name directly to the other person.

If an introducer gets your name wrong, mispronounces it, or relays inaccurate information about your job or background, politely make the correction without embarrassing him or her. "Actually, it's June, not Joan." Getting your name straight matters most when (1) you expect to see the person you're being introduced to again or (2) the person will be introducing you to others. If you're not likely to meet again, it's best to let the error slide.

Introducing Yourself

If you're attending a business meeting or social gathering and no one introduces you, jump right in. Just step up and say, "I don't believe we've met. I'm Mary Buchwald from Hill and Dale." Be sure to state your first and last names, and if necessary, ask others to state both of theirs.

Refrain from putting a courtesy title or honorific before your name when introducing yourself: "Hi, I'm Mary Buchwald"—not Ms. Mary Buchwald. A doctor, clergyperson, or someone holding political office or in military service would use his or her professional or official title depending on the context of the meeting.

Concerning Names

Etiquette says you shouldn't use a person's first name until he asks you to do so; at the same time, rigid adherence to this custom can make you look stuffy.

Take your cue from the person you're greeting. If he immediately calls you Jack, there may be an unspoken understanding that you're on a first-name basis. When in doubt—if, for example, the person

---

YES, MA'AM; NO, MA'AM

Q. Is it appropriate to say "Thank you, ma'am," or "Yes, ma'am," and so forth in a work environment?

A. In some areas of the country, notably the South, it is both traditional and respectful to address women as "ma'am" and men as "sir." However, in business, whenever you are unsure of a person's preference, the best course of action is to address a woman by title and surname: "Yes, Ms. Jones" rather than "Yes, ma'am." Unfortunately, "ma'am" is one of those titles that's considered respectful by some and offensive by others.

---

is older than you, a top-level executive, or a public figure—test the waters before taking the plunge. One use of "Mr. Quinby" will usually give you the answer. Unless he says, "Please call me Roy," keep using "Mr." or the appropriate honorific.

REMEMBERING NAMES

For many people, names go in one ear and out the other during introductions. Their minds suddenly go blank and nervousness sets in the moment they have to shake hands. If they concentrate on anything, it's themselves—the impression they're making and whether they're saying the right thing—rather than on mentally registering the other person's name.

Overcome this problem by putting the focus on the other person as you're being introduced. When someone offers her hand, make a point of listening to her name, repeating it in your greeting, and then imprinting it in your mind by visualizing how it would look written down—or even emblazoned across a billboard.

FORGOTTEN NAMES

If you suffer a memory lapse when greeting or introducing someone you've met before, don't be ashamed to admit it. Be honest: "I remember meeting you, but I simply can't recall your name." Instead of concentrating on your own embarrassment, try to put the other person at ease. It's much better to admit your memory lapse than not to do the introduction.

Try to avoid bluntly saying, "What did you say your name is?" Better excuses are "I've just drawn a blank" or "My memory gets worse by the day," which puts the blame on you. If you recall anything at all about the person, bring it up: "I clearly remember the conversation we had about Fiji, but your name seems to have slipped my mind. What is it again, please?"

DIFFICULT NAMES

If the name of someone to whom you're being introduced is highly unusual or misheard, ask for it again: "I'm sorry, I didn't quite catch your name." Making sure that you pronounce a name correctly shows respect and consideration. If the name is especially complicated and you expect to see the person again, ask him or her to give you a business card.

When Introductions Are Unnecessary

If you're walking with a group and meet someone you know coming in the opposite direction, etiquette says you're not required to pause and make introductions. If you stop to chat briefly, the group should continue on while you finish your conversation and catch up. Likewise, if you're dining with a group and someone you know walks by your table, you're not obliged to introduce them to your assembled friends. If you want to exchange a few words with the person, step away from the table. On the other hand, if there is any question in your mind as to whether you should make introductions, then by all means make them.

YOUR TRUSTY BUSINESS CARD

The business card serves a few functions:

- It invites a new business acquaintance to get in touch with you.

- It defines your position and responsibilities (e.g., Vice President, Sales).

- It provides a number of ways to reach you: mailing address, telephone, fax, email address, and possibly your assistant's telephone number and alternate phone numbers for you.

The smart businessperson should never be without at least a few cards in a jacket pocket, wallet, pocketbook, or briefcase. You never know when you might need a card (at a dinner in a restaurant, say, or sitting next to someone in the bleachers at a stadium). They should be in perfect condition when you present them. The best way to protect them and the cards you receive as well is to keep them in a business card holder. They are widely available at stationery, office supply, and department stores.

How to hand out business cards, and to whom:

- When you meet someone for the first time and you think you might want to contact the person again, offer your card and ask for one in turn. Probably the one exception is when you encounter a top executive who clearly outranks you; if such a senior person wants your card, she will ask you for it, or she will give you her card if she wants you to have it.

- When given a card, don't just snatch it and jam it into your pocket. Hold it carefully and take a moment to look at it, perhaps complimenting its design. "Great logo!" Then slip it into your wallet, card case, or date book.

- When giving cards to more than one person, offer each person a card rather than presenting a fistful.

- Offering your card privately to someone at a social event is perfectly fine—but hold off on detailed business talk until another day. Don't pop out your card in the middle of a dinner that has nothing to do with business; if you want to present one, wait until you've left the table and are saying your good-byes.

CHAPTER 12

HOSTING, ATTENDING, AND SPEAKING AT THE PERFECT MEETING

You may love meetings, hate them, or fall somewhere in the middle. But take a moment to reflect: Business meetings give you, the participant, a chance to display your skills and talents—to show off in a positive way—and to take the measure of your colleagues. Consider this, too: More than a few advancement-minded workers have undercut their own interests by failing to demonstrate the most basic meeting etiquette.

MANAGING A MEETING

Managing a meeting successfully is an art, not a science. A science is a set of rules for doing things; an art form draws on the ability to adapt creatively and appropriately to each new situation. This explains why some people put on great meetings, whereas others consistently botch the job. Artfully adapting requires that you are willing to do things differently, to embrace change, to be observant, be yourself, be firm in your willingness to lead and control, and be respectful of individuals and the group as a whole.

A Question of Purpose

Unfortunately, far too many meetings end up being unproductive time wasters—a discourtesy that falls directly on the shoulders of the people who call them. They don't have a clear goal in mind at the start. They wander from concept to concept and go off on tangents. They don't start on time and/or they don't end on time.

By contrast, a good business meeting has a legitimate business purpose. Know exactly

- Why you want to have a meeting and what outcome you want to see from it

- What you want to accomplish. Do you want to inform your participants about an issue and get their feedback? Brainstorm ideas? Assign tasks?

- How many issues you plan to consider

- Whether decision making is involved

At the same time, be careful that your stated purpose isn't overly ambitious or unrealistic. For example, a

Let the nature of your meeting decide how you issue the invitations. If you're calling a small, informal meeting, a telephone invitation may be just fine, but a written notice (memo, letter, or email) is even better. Always send written invitations for formal meetings. Only gatherings such as corporate shareholders' meetings and annual board meetings require formal, printed invitations.

Try to give your invitees as much advance notice as possible—at least forty-eight hours for in-house meetings, one to three weeks for formal meetings. Remember, too, that the longer the meeting, the more schedule-shifting it will require for participants. If your invitees will be coming from distant locations and travel arrangements need to be made, as much as four to six weeks' notice may be needed.

For all but the most informal meetings, you'll want to include the agenda with your invitation. You may also want to include a list of all participants. (Advance lists of attendees are normally provided for large, professional conferences and international meetings.)

Be sure to provide some kind of response mechanism—your name and phone number for an informal notice, RSVP information or a reply card for formal invitations. It's a good idea to ask for a response by a certain date so that you can reschedule the meeting if too many invitees are unable to attend. To guarantee good attendance, you or your assistant should give your invitees confirmation calls on the day before the meeting and remind participants of time, location, and any materials they need to bring.

Calendar-scheduling software programs simplify the scheduling of meetings. After inputting the participants' names, the time, the date, and the duration, the software tells you if anyone has a scheduling conflict. Invitations and responses are also made through the software, establishing an electronic trail that makes it hard for anyone to claim that they didn't know the meeting was being held.

---

meeting in which a wholly new problem is presented may not accomplish your goals if you also rush your attendees into making decisions based on the new information. They need time to mull over the issues privately. Remember, meetings are designed for discussion, not thoughtful reflection.

Once you're clear on the purpose of the meeting—the what—you can then proceed to fill in the who, where, when, and how. When it comes to planning a successful session, the devil, as the saying goes, is in the details. You'll want to be certain that you've prepared for every aspect of the meet-

ing. Remember, it's your meeting and your responsibility.

The Who—Whom Should You Invite?

When developing your list of invitees (whether all in-house, all clients or customers, or a mix of both), decide who will help accomplish your purpose. Resist the temptation to include anyone else, but also consider the list carefully so that you won't inadvertently leave out a key player. In short, the size of a meeting depends entirely on its purpose. When the meeting objective is clear, the participants almost choose themselves; you invite the people who can help achieve your goal.

PART-TIME ATTENDEES

You may want to plan for certain people to attend only part of the meeting. Example: An advertising executive calls a morning-long meeting to discuss creative planning for a new client; she asks representatives from the media department to attend for the first hour only and then thoughtfully plans a break at the hour mark for coffee and snacks, allowing the media buyers to make a gracious getaway. Segmenting like this allows busy people to participate only when they are needed, without feeling obliged to remain once their involvement is done.

The How—What's the Agenda?

Your agenda establishes how you will achieve your goal for the meeting. Even for informal weekly staff meetings, you'll want to have some sort of agenda. Depending on the purpose of the meeting and the company culture, this can range from a list of topics the leader has jotted down on a pad to printed copies for all attendees that lay out the agenda in detail.

> **TIP:** As the meeting leader, keep a private agenda that lists the items that absolutely must be acted on. As the meeting progresses, make sure you steer the proceedings to accomplish your must-dos before a key player has to excuse herself from the meeting. As you organize your agenda, you'll be able to estimate closely the amount of time needed for each agenda item.

Some planners recommend scheduling action items (decision making and problem solving) first, as a way to motivate prompt attendance. Others prefer scheduling discussion first and then proceeding to decisions. However you decide to organize your meeting, include adequate time at the end for wrapping up—summarizing discussion points, clarifying assignments, reviewing decisions, setting deadlines, and (only if necessary) scheduling a subsequent meeting.

WHEN AND WHERE?

When you set the meeting time, think of your invitees' schedules. Friday afternoon, for example, is usually disastrous because participants' minds have already left for the weekend, even though their bodies are still in their chairs. Also be attuned to the rhythm of your workplace: Are your coworkers busiest in the morning? Then meet in the afternoon. Try to avoid Monday mornings and Friday afternoons for obvious reasons. The more people invited to your meeting, the more difficult scheduling will be. While you may not always be able to clear your starting time with everyone, you should at least check with key participants (including any guest speakers) before settling on your schedule, to avoid locking in an inconvenient time.

With the list of invitees and the agenda determined, you have the tools to decide on time and location. The number of participants, format, and style of the meeting (casual or formal, in-house or with clients) will tell you what size room you'll need and how it should be furnished. If it's a simple announcement meeting for employees, you can jam a lot of people into a small room for five or ten minutes and ask them to stand without any discomfort. If you're planning an all-day seminar, you'll need a room with comfortable tables and chairs and plenty of elbow room. Be sure to book and confirm your meeting space well in advance; many a meeting has had an embarrassing start because the proposed meeting site was already in use.

PREMEETING PREPARATION

The last step in planning your business meeting is to walk yourself through the actual process of the meeting. Consider your meeting subject, your participants, and your own past experiences. Try to visualize everyone together in your meeting room: How are they interacting? What is being done? Is your vision of the meeting accomplishing what you want? What would make it more effective? You might want to employ techniques you've learned elsewhere to engage your participants: A role-playing session, for example, may help salespeople identify hidden customer service problems.

Is that lengthy statistical presentation really necessary, or can it be handled with handouts and a short summary? Review your agenda to be sure you haven't planned too much; you can always revise the agenda before the meeting if need be.

What materials do you need to provide? Always bring sufficient copies of the agenda to the meeting. Be sure, too, that you have copies of any necessary background information, reports of previous meetings, and research reports for all participants. For the participants' convenience, consider preparing labeled file folders. It's also a good idea to email these materials ahead of time so that participants can prepare themselves as well. If your attendees need to bring materials, be sure to let them know well in advance.

Try to know something about each person you're inviting to the meeting—especially if you have included people who don't know one another or with whom you have never worked. Meetings often begin with a meet-and-greet period, in which case you will have to be the spark to get things moving. Be prepared to make friendly, courteous introductions, including names, titles, company or department.

Try to anticipate technical problems that are likely to bog down the meeting if you haven't cleared them ahead of time:

- Have you checked the equipment in the room to make sure it is working?

- Does your computer connect to the projector and display your presentation?

- Is the Internet connection working and do you know the use name and password?

- Does the video conference equipment connect to the remote sites?

- Does the conference telephone have a dial tone, and do you know the telephone number you are calling into?

- If you are connecting into an offsite presentation vendor like GoToMeeting, have you checked your login information ahead of time and done a practice run-through?

Off and Running

The biggest mistake a meeting organizer can make is to assume that a well-planned meeting will run itself. That's like assuming that if you peel the vegetables and cube the beef, the stew will make itself. Managing a meeting is analogous to a chef cooking a great meal: Following a recipe, you prepare the raw ingredients, set the temperatures, mix and blend the

ingredients, juggle pots and pans, time everything to
perfection, and finally bring the finished elements together on a plate. Four essential actions will ensure
that your meeting runs smoothly:

1. **Start on time.** A late start sets a negative tone,
   signaling to participants that you are not in control and that you're not altogether respectful of
   their schedules.

2. **Keep things on track.** Every meeting is rife
   with opportunities to run off onto interesting
   but irrelevant tangents. Your job is to keep the
   proceedings focused on your agenda points. Be
   polite but firm. "That's an interesting point,

Sarah, and I'd like to discuss it with you after the
meeting. But right now, I want to stay with the
problem of . . ."

3. **Encourage full participation.** Be alert to who is
   speaking and who isn't. Some people simply reserve their comments until they have a full grasp
   of the issues, and you don't want to pressure them.
   But others—especially junior-level employees or
   attendees who are new to your group—may need
   to be drawn into the discussion.

4. **End on time.** If you can consistently accomplish
   this simple but elusive goal, your colleagues
   will be grateful. It shows you are organized, in
   charge, and respectful of the attendee's time.

Wrapping Up

Leave enough time near the end of the meeting for a
purposeful summing up. Your wrap-up gives you the
chance to delineate what has been accomplished in
the meeting in an organized manner and to clarify
assignments and responsibilities. It also allows you to
use your conclusion to smooth any ruffled feathers if
the meeting has been heated or rancorous. Even the
smallest, most casual meetings need a summing up so
that the participants leave with a clear understanding
of future expectations.

Following Up

It is always smart to follow up your meeting within a
day or two with a thorough recap memo or letter to
all of the participants.

ACTION PLANS. Your memo should elaborate on
the details of your summary assignments and sched-

DEALING WITH PROBLEM PARTICIPANTS

Every meeting has them—the manager who is happy only when he is dominating the discussion, the department head who can't stick to the subject, the know-it-all who always displays her superior grasp of the facts, the devil's advocate who feels compelled to shoot down every new idea, the constant interrupter, the chronic latecomer. You can't change them, so you'll have to deal with them as best you can.

The Dominator, the Know-It-All, and the Devil's Advocate usually thrive in open discussions, but you can thwart them by either directing questions to others or, if necessary, politely cutting them off. You can stop the Interrupter with comments such as "Can you save that thought until the Q-and-A?" or "I think Mrs. Rodriguez was getting to that point.

Let's let her finish." For the Shooter-Downer, a simple reminder will do: "Tom, let's get the ideas on the table first and look at the pros and cons before we dismiss any possibility, no matter how out there it seems. Thanks." As for the Latecomer, she'll usually slip in and apologize later, but if she enters armed with elaborate excuses, signal her to be quiet and hope she gets your message.

The point is that you can't fully control everyone's bad habits. You do, however, want to make a polite but firm effort to deal directly with problem people and difficult situations in order to keep the meeting moving forward smoothly. Even if you ultimately don't succeed, your other participants will see that you recognize the problem and are willing to try to correct it within the bounds of common courtesy.

---

ules and include confirmations of any formal decisions or votes.

THANK-YOUS. In most cases, the memo itself is a sufficient thank-you to participants, but you will want to write formal thank-you notes to speakers, special guests, and anyone else who has contributed to the success of the event.

EVALUATION. Set aside some personal time to evaluate your meeting (and be ruthlessly honest):

- Did the meeting accomplish what you wanted? If not, why not?

- Was the agenda flawed?

- Did you lose control at any point?

- Did you invite the right people for your purpose?

- Was your organization too rigid or too loose?

- Did a problem crop up that you should have anticipated but didn't?

TIP: Change your thinking about the difficult participant from being a problem to being an opportunity. How you deal with the situation shows a lot about your ability to work under stress and to handle a difficult situation. These qualities will reflect well on you from your manager's point of view.

Too many managers become wedded to a meeting format instead of learning from their mistakes. But by analyzing each meeting you hold—good, bad, or indifferent—and doing it while the particulars are still fresh in your memory, you open the door to on-going improvement.

ATTENDING A MEETING

People attending a business meeting have their own responsibilities for helping to ensure that the meeting is a success.

The Invitation

Meetings start with an invitation that may be as simple as a phone call or text message or as formal as a written or printed invitation sent in the mail. Regardless of how it is delivered and its formality, every invitation requires a response. Your first mannerly step is to respond to all meeting invitations, whether your attendance is compulsory or not.

RSVP

As soon as you receive a notice for a meeting, check your schedule to make sure there's no conflict and then make your reply. Even if your invitation doesn't specifically ask for a response, do it; a quick phone call will usually suffice. If you're unable to attend an optional meeting, it's a good idea to explain why, particularly if you have a business-related conflict. This tells the person calling the meeting that your absence is justified; it may also prompt him or her to reschedule the meeting at a more convenient time.

If you're not sure if you can attend, you still owe it to the inviter to respond right away. In this case a simple, "Hi, Tom. I got your invitation. I have a possible conflict I want to check on first. I can let you know by tomorrow. Is that okay for you?"

IF YOU'RE ATTENDING

If you're able to go to the meeting, prepare in advance. Study the agenda and determine what you can do to be ready to join in the discussion. If you don't receive an agenda or your invitation doesn't include particulars of the meeting, ask the meeting organizer what you can do to prepare and whether there are any materials you should bring. To avoid implying the organizer has been remiss by not including an agenda, couch your questions in terms of seeking direction: "I just want to be sure that I'm up to speed for the meeting."

IF YOU CAN'T ATTEND

If you can't attend, let the organizer know immediately. You may want to send a surrogate to the meeting, but

---

YOU'RE NOT INVITED

Try not to interpret exclusion as an affront. It may simply be that the organizer believes your time is better spent at something else or that decisions will be made that are above your level. If you have a close relationship with your supervisor, you may want to ask why you weren't invited; if the exclusion was a mistake, your supervisor is in the best position to correct it. But whatever the cause, take it in stride, and never try to force or wangle your way into a meeting. Being excluded is a temporary disappointment, but a reputation for manipulation and bad temper has longer-lasting consequences.

BACK-TO-BACK MEETINGS

Q. I had back-to-back meetings scheduled today. With ten minutes left in the first one, it was still going strong. I didn't know what to do, so I sat there and ended up being fifteen minutes late to the second meeting. That didn't go over well. What should I have done?

A. Ouch! You were stuck between the proverbial rock and hard place. Stay at your first meeting and you risk being late for or miss the second one. Leave the first meeting before it is over and you risk dissing the people there. Doing nothing and just sitting there didn't resolve the situation as you clearly left the people in the second meeting hanging and felt your own anxiety level rise with every second that ticked by. What can you do or say to resolve the situation without angering either group?

You had two choices. At that ten-minute mark you could have decided to be at your second meeting on time and announced, "I notice it's ten of the hour, and this meeting was scheduled to end at 11:00. I'm due at another meeting at 11:00, so could we schedule a follow-up to continue the discussion?" Or you could have decided to stay at the first meeting but explain to the participants, "This discussion is really important, and it looks like it will go past the hour. I need to let the people at my 11:00 meeting know that I'm going to be delayed. I'll be right back."

Which of these two options you use depends on the answer to a simple question: Which meeting is more important? For instance, you might be meeting with your CEO in the first meeting. In that case, it's not likely you'll announce at 10:50 that you'll have to end your meeting with her to meet with your team. Conversely, if your second meeting is with your CEO, you need to wrap up the first meeting so you can be sure you'll meet with the CEO on time.

The best way to deal with back-to-back meetings is to prevent them from happening in the first place. Keep a fifteen- to twenty-minute buffer zone between meetings. And remember to allow for travel time to get from one meeting to the next. At the very least, before the start of your first meeting talk to the person running it to let him know you have a tight schedule and will need to leave when the meeting is scheduled to end. That keeps you on schedule, with no announcement necessary.

always check with the meeting organizer first. Follow up on meetings you miss: Find out what happened and if you have any assigned tasks. If possible, make an effort to get a detailed report of the proceedings.

The Importance of Punctuality

When you are on time you are demonstrating that you are organized and respectful. Conversely, if you are late, people may think of you as disorganized and disrespectful. Therefore, arrive on time, not too early—no more than five minutes—but not late.

THE EARLY BIRD

Most meeting specialists warn strongly against arriving more than a few minutes early. The person holding the meeting may be involved in last-minute preparations or may be trying to clear away other business before the meeting's start, and he or she will feel compelled to stop and greet early arrivals.

COMING IN LATE

Arriving late is sometimes unavoidable, whether the meeting is in-house or elsewhere. If you know you're going to be tardy, tell the meeting organizer as soon as you can; he or she may want to adjust the agenda if your participation is needed at a certain point. With advance notice, the organizer can also save a chair for you in a spot least likely to cause disruption. If you're delayed on the way to a meeting, this is a perfect time to make use of your cell phone. At least by calling or texting you are being respectful of your host and the other guests. Not calling and just showing up late certainly starts you off on the wrong foot.

When entering a meeting in progress, be as unobtrusive as possible. Walk in, and take your seat. If the situation allows it and you won't be interrupting, you can offer a brief apology. Regardless, it helps to have everything you need, such as pen and pad, at hand when you enter the room. Don't disturb the meeting by rattling papers, snapping a briefcase open and shut, shedding a coat or jacket, getting coffee, or whispering to your neighbors. Use your printed agenda to get up to speed with what is going on.

If a formal presentation is in progress when you arrive, you may want to delay your entrance until there is a natural break and you can slip inside the meeting room. Late arrivals are the bane of speakers because they inevitably distract the audience and break the flow of the presentation.

> **TIP:** When adding a meeting to your schedule, remember to factor in enough time to get to it, especially if the meeting is in a different building.

OTHER TIMING ISSUES

Even the best-planned meetings can run overtime, so as an attendee it's wise to pad your schedule a bit to accommodate late endings. For short meetings allow an extra five or ten minutes while for a longer meeting allow an extra fifteen to twenty minutes to cover most situations.

If you must leave a meeting early or right on schedule, tell the leader in advance. Seating can be arranged so that you can depart without disturbing others.

The Politics of Meeting Seating

If seating isn't assigned, let the key participants take their places first and then fill in around them. Don't head for the top or bottom of a conference table unless you're the leader. A good organizer will tell everyone where to sit, but if the seating order is unclear, ask the leader where he or she would like you to be. Even if you're an important guest (the client rep at a business presentation, for instance), check with the meeting leader about seating; there may be a reason, such as vision line, to seat you somewhere other than the head of the table. In a seminar or open seating arrangement, find a place where you can see and hear clearly.

As the organizer/host of the meeting, it's your responsibility to decide where people should sit. With a small group, you can easily do it on the fly, but with a larger group take a few minutes before the meeting to consider a seating plan. Here are five points to consider:

1. The most important seat is at the head of the table and is typically reserved for the host, chairperson, or most senior individual at the meeting. At a rectangular table, the head of the table is at the end that looks toward the entrance as opposed to the end next to the entrance. Interestingly, this seat commands a direct view of everyone at the table as well as everyone entering the room, making it a position of strength in conducting and participating in the meeting.

2. The second most important seat is the position at the opposite end of the table. Likewise, this person has a view of everyone at the table. Sometimes there is no seat available at this position, which only enhances the position of the head of the table.

3. The seat to the right of the head of the table is, also, a premium position. In social situations, it is the position given to the guest of honor. In business meetings, it is considered valuable because the occupant has the ear of the person sitting at the head of the table. The person seated here may be a key confidant or adviser to the person at the head of the table. Similarly, the person to the left of the head of the table is in a strong position.

4. People seated to either side of the person at the opposite end of the table are in positions of strength as well.

THE BRAINSTORMING SESSION

Many companies have meetings to brainstorm ideas, and these lively sessions have an etiquette all their own. The meetings can range from four people wheeling extra chairs into someone's office to three-day, off-site meetings where groups keep to a tight schedule and then either record or make presentations of ideas.

Some things to remember:

• The notion that "nothing is off-limits" applies to ideas, not manners. Although brainstorming is supposed to be free-form, talking over one another and interrupting will most likely neither contribute to the freshness of the concepts nor spark any new ones. If you're bursting to get an idea out, jot it down on paper and wait until there's an opening to speak.

• Don't shoot other people's ideas down with "We've tried that before." Also, never disparage an idea, no matter how bizarre it may be. Remember that brainstorming is the forum for off-the-wall concepts that will eventually be reshaped into marketable ones. Even if someone's idea is so ill conceived that it's ludicrous, don't say so flatly. When you point out its shortcomings, start with the positive things about it and then come up with ways it could be made stronger.

• When a group has to work individually at a communal table to get their ideas on paper or disk for a presentation, keep distractions to a minimum.

• Save food for scheduled breaks. Snacks (especially the crunchy kind) can be distracting.

5. People who fill the seats along the side are in the less favorable seats. They cannot see the other people at the table as easily and their influence with the key decision makers is diminished by not being near them.

Do Your Part

Whether the organizational skills of the meeting manager are brilliant or nonexistent, you have not been invited to a meeting to sit on your hands or surf the Internet on your phone. Your participation is needed. When you've prepared well and followed the proceedings attentively, participating should be no problem.

- If your opinion is requested, give it.

- If you have an idea, state it.

- If you need more information or clarification, ask for it.

There are times, of course, to remain quiet. Example: Your department is making a new business pitch to a prospective client. Although the mood of the meeting is casual, every step has been carefully choreographed and rehearsed. You and the other members of your team have been assigned specific roles in the presentation. This is not the occasion to speak out of turn or propose an untested idea.

Avoid Interruptions

Turn off your cell phone, watch timer, and anything else that tends to "beep" or ring unexpectedly. (Another hint is to eat something before a meeting to avoid a grumbling stomach.) If you have an assistant, inform him (or the office receptionist, if necessary) that you will be in a meeting until such-and-such

time and under what circumstances, if any, you are to be disturbed.

During Breaks

Plan breaks if the meeting will be lengthy; no one should be expected to sit for longer than an hour and a half. In addition to bathroom visits, breaks also offer participants the opportunity to check messages and return calls. By scheduling regular breaks you encourage people not to use their communication devices during the meeting.

Breaks are also a valuable point in a meeting to get to know participants on a more personal level and to build relationships. Instead of talking with your colleague, use the ten or fifteen minutes to chat with someone you don't know. (See the box "How to Be an Expert at Small Talk," page 205.)

At Meeting's End

Wait until the meeting is over to gather your things and then leave. Naturally, you'll want to thank the leader politely, but unless a postmeeting event has been scheduled, it's best to depart promptly. You have other business to attend to, and so does everyone else. If you want to have a word with a guest speaker, be extremely conscious of the person's time constraints and of other people who might need to speak with him or her. If you have questions that weren't answered during a presentation, it's preferable to write any speakers, telling them where and when you met and asking for a response at their convenience.

What's Next?

For participants, following up a meeting generally means doing what you were assigned to do. You may need to clarify assignments with the meeting leader, although you should receive a postmeeting confirmation or summary memo. Thank-you notes are not appropriate for the majority of meetings, but it's always nice to compliment the meeting organizer at the first opportunity. Thank-you notes or letters may be written for large conferences, seminars, and formal meetings that involve social activities, as well as for some informal meetings, such as lunch at the invitation of a client.

WHEN YOU'RE A GUEST SPEAKER

Should you ever be called on to speak at a meeting, you won't necessarily be taking part in the meeting itself but instead imparting your wisdom from a podium. Unless you're an old hand at public speaking, you'll learn that there's more to the assignment than the content of your speech, regardless of the size of the meeting you're asked to address.

First of all, understand the assignment thoroughly. What is the subject? Are you the only speaker or one of several? Are there particular issues you need to address? Are there problems or situations you should be aware of?

There's a story about a well-known chef who was invited (and handsomely paid) to address the spring luncheon of a prominent Jewish women's organization. He duly spoke to the group, delivering a fulsome presentation on the planning of Easter activities and preparation of the perfect Easter ham! This is an extreme example of poor preparation, but it illustrates some of the common pitfalls of public speaking.

Getting Things Straight

A speaker should always research the group that invited him and the location of the event: Who will comprise the audience? How many? What are their interests? What are the unique characteristics of the business or organization and its location? An attentive speaker can be more engaging and successful by customizing even a canned speech with local references.

At the same time, you should provide all necessary information regarding your needs to the organizers. Will you need equipment such as microphones, easels, and a projector and projection screen? Also relay any other special requirements such as transportation or dietary needs. Once prepared, you may proceed as follows:

APPRECIATE THE AGENDA. Arrive on time, stick to the program, and don't run over your allotted time. Clarify in advance whether your presentation is to include a Q&A session. Be alert to time cues from the organizer.

MEET AND GREET. Plan to arrive early if you can. Check out the environment. Test your equipment to be sure it synchronizes with the equipment the venue is providing. Get a sense of the audience and mingle if possible. Speakers can learn a great deal from a relatively few minutes of pre-event chitchat with some of the audience members.

BE PROFESSIONAL. When something goes awry—a glitch in the microphone or a last-minute change of room—take it in stride.

SAY THANK YOU. Highly paid speakers are sometimes all too aware that they are not speaking from the goodness of their hearts. But all speakers should be grateful for the opportunity and the platform to express themselves. Thank-you notes to organizers are a must.

ELECTRONIC MEETINGS

Conference calls—calls where more than two parties are talking with each other—have evolved from meetings organized by dialing into a conference call center with a meeting code and password to calls that are easily organized on your phone. Similarly, video conference calls have also evolved from events that had to be organized at a video conference center that was either a room in your company or a space you rented by the hour to events that can be initiated from your phone as well. With Skype, Google Talk, Google Chat, FaceTime, or similar smartphone services you can run a conference call or video conference call from your computer or right from the palm of your hand. At The Emily Post Institute we conduct our weekly staff meeting as a video conference call with participants joining in from a variety of locations.

While conference calls may be simple to initiate, they also pose challenges. Here are ten ways to make your conference calls successful:

1. **Be mindful of time.** Attendees can be anywhere, and time zone differences can be a real challenge. Be especially careful when a person is halfway around the world. Depending on where they are relative to you and the international dateline, your Monday may be their Sunday, Monday, or Tuesday. Many a conference call has been missed because people weren't very clear with establishing the exact time and day for everyone involved. For instance, we once had a call scheduled for 8:00 A.M. Singapore time on a Monday, and we mistakenly planned to be on the call at 8:00 P.M. Monday. Big mistake. At 8:00 A.M. Monday, Singapore is a whole day ahead of Eastern Standard Time. We were meant to be ready for the call at 8:00 P.M. Sunday.

2. **Make sure everyone is aware of who will be on the call.** If you have several people within a location, try to have them in the same room. Don't have someone listening in whom you haven't introduced to everyone on the call.

3. **Limit interruption from external noises.** Close your conference room or office door. It's a courtesy to the other people on the call as well as to the people in your office who aren't on the call. Also, be aware if external noises, such as a regular garbage truck pickup, that could make it difficult to conduct the call.

4. **Ready your equipment.** Check your equipment ahead of time, especially in a conference center where you may not be familiar with the equipment.

5. **Establish your agenda.** Have an agenda prepared and distributed ahead of time so people know what is to be accomplished and how much time is available.

6. **Make introductions.** At the start of the call introduce everyone and have each person say hello so other participants can begin to identify people by the sound of their voice. Doing this also allows each location to check sound quality and volume.

7. **Monitor your Mute button.** Watch out for mistakenly thinking the Mute button on your phone is on when in fact it's not. You never want to hear someone saying, "We can still hear you."

8. **Avoid disturbing noises.** Rustling of papers, tapping of pens, drumming of fingers on a tabletop, eating food—these are all examples of noises that are easily heard and can be disruptive for other participants.

9. **Wrap it up.** Ten minutes before the end of the call, let people know you are arriving at the end of the meeting. Use that time for any summation and for reiterating any to-dos that have been assigned or volunteered for during the call.

10. **Follow up.** Send out a meeting summary after the meeting.

(See also "Using a Speakerphone," page 93, and "Speakerphone," page 247.)

CHAPTER 13

TELECOMMUTING AND THE HOME OFFICE

Working at home: What a great concept. Whether you're self-employed or you telecommute instead of going into your office every day, working out of a home office has real benefits. Not having to commute is a big one. Being more independent and in charge of your schedule is another.

Whether you work for yourself or someone else you are responsible for getting your work done. Goof off, and it will catch up with you: Either you'll stop getting a paycheck from your employer or your own billings will quickly dry up.

Success, in other words, depends very much on your own initiative. Fortunately, there are a number of things you can do to help motivate yourself and stay focused on the job while at home.

SETTING YOUR PARAMETERS

For many home-based workers, the chief advantage of the home office is that it lets them achieve a more equitable balance between work and family. The key word here is *balance*. One of your most difficult tasks will be to convince loved ones that you really are working.

Unless you lay down specific ground rules and communicate these clearly, you will defeat the purpose of working at home. The same goes for friends and neighbors, who require a special set of considerations. You'll want to make things run as smoothly in your relations with them as you do with your business associates.

When you explain your working rules to family and friends, you don't need to be apologetic. Even the most considerate family and friends may suffer from the common misconceptions about home-based work—you're available any time and you can drop whatever you are doing. Make it clear that you are earning your livelihood, not indulging in a hobby.

"Oh, Those Kids!"

Children have different levels of understanding depending on their ages, and whatever your children's ages, they will need constant reminders of your rules. Provide the information appropriate to the child's understanding, repeat it often, and update it when needed. While a three-year-old should be able to grasp the basic concept that Daddy is working, a discussion about the importance of advance scheduling for school activities or trips to the mall should be reserved for a preteen or teenager.

Here are some guidelines for helping you and your children adapt to a home-based work situation. Ask other family members to reinforce any rules you lay down. Spouses, grandparents, and older siblings—many adults serve as models of behavior for children. When the other adults in the family show support for your work and respect for your rules, your kids will probably follow suit.

MAKE A SCHEDULE. Since you are no longer on a strict nine-to-five schedule, you can arrange your busy times to suit your family's needs. But being flexible doesn't mean being totally free-form; you need structure in your workday. If two parents work at home, try to schedule work hours so that family responsibilities can be alternated. Make it absolutely clear that your work hours must be honored.

BE HONEST. Don't make promises to children that may not be kept. Spurred by love and guilt, all working parents are quick to promise to do things "later" or "tomorrow" in order to get through the moment peacefully. Unless you're certain you can

KNOWING WHEN TO STOP

Long hours are not a reliable measure of productivity, so it's important to know when to call it a day. If you are working at home in order to see more of your family, don't stay cooped up in your home office all hours of the day and night. Even if you live alone, you still need time for yourself. All work and no play makes you just as dull as the corporate drone. You need R&R if you are to be effective at your work. There's no need to give up your regular vacation, weekly round of golf or tennis, or lunching with friends; clients will come to respect your time off, knowing you'll give them more in return if you come back relaxed and fresh.

TIP: Don't promise yourself a future vacation while you fail to take daily breaks, don't work when you are truly sick, and don't give up on housework. (Your home is an extension of your office and an important part of a positive work environment, as well as a positive image for visiting clients.)

keep your word, resist the temptation. Don't, for example, promise to attend the school play when you have an important deadline on the same day. Children will be disappointed when you must say no, but they will be resentful when you say yes and then fail to meet your commitment.

DRESS THE PART. Although one of the perks of a home office is the end of everyday formal office wear, you may find that a businesslike appearance helps younger children distinguish between work time and playtime. If children see you in your bath-

robe when they leave for school and you're still in your bathrobe when they return, they will logically conclude that you haven't been doing much business during the day. You can assemble a work "uniform" as casual as jeans and a sweater that nevertheless signals to children that your workday has begun.

DEFINE "EMERGENCIES." Of course, you want your children to interrupt your work when a real problem occurs. But don't expect them instinctively to know what constitutes an emergency. A fall from the swing set does require your immediate attention—but a lost Barbie or a dirty soccer uniform does not. Be patient and explain repeatedly, especially during the early stages of your business when children are making their own adjustments to your new lifestyle.

NO TRESPASSING. Your office is an office, not a playroom. Until children are sufficiently responsible, they should probably not be allowed to enter your office unless you're present.

DO NOT TOUCH. As a rule, do not allow children to use your business computer for homework or surfing the Internet. It's always possible they could erase an important document or download a file that introduces a virus with disastrous results. Also put your work supplies and materials off-limits. Just about every home-based worker with children has at least one horror story of the critical meeting notes or the message with the client's private phone number that turned up months later, glued to an art project or crumpled in a toy box.

To Take Them Along?

Include your children when appropriate. It is perfectly acceptable to take your child when you make drop-off deliveries or do routine errands. It is unprofessional to bring your children to meetings with your clients or employer. And never expect busy secretaries to mind your kids while you are meeting with the boss.

When your children are mature enough, it's fine to introduce them to clients or colleagues who are meeting at your home office. Then they should excuse themselves so you can meet in private.

PHONE HOURS

Make it clear to the people you do business with what hours you keep—you don't want to be on call at virtually any time of day and night. By the same token, find out from individual clients what their set business hours are. If they have none, ask them to give you a time frame for calling so that you don't risk waking them up or calling when they have something regularly scheduled.

> **TIP:** Be sure your business number is listed in the business section of your telephone directory under your business name. Keep your residential number separate.

Children Answering the Phone

It's important to teach your children good telephone etiquette early especially if you have a landline for your business that they can answer, too, because you

---

> ### " . . . AND THIS IS ROVER"
>
> Pets are not usually a problem for the home-based worker unless you receive clients or customers in your home. Pet owners can be a myopic bunch when it comes to their beloved Fluffy or Spot. But not everyone loves pets, and some of your important guests may have genuine aversions to them. Allergies to pets are relatively common, and your meeting will not go well if your client is sneezing and teary.
>
> Inform any visitors of your pet situation ahead of time, and vacuum away all pet hair before they arrive. If your dog is likely to pounce on strangers who knock at your door, keep it leashed or penned during meetings. Even better, contain the family pet outside or in the garage when clients are expected. Clients who don't enjoy being licked, pawed, or even cuddled may be too well mannered to say so—and all too anxious to take their business elsewhere.
>
> Pets, dogs especially, don't have to be seen to be a nuisance. Many home-based workers conduct business via phone, conference, or video calls. A barking or yapping dog will be a disruptive and annoying intrusion to virtual meetings as well.

never know who's calling. Your stodgiest client will be mightily impressed when your youngster replies with a polite "Yes, sir" or "Thank you, ma'am." Develop a simple response for your children to use when they answer your business phone: "Hello, this is Brown's Custom Draperies. May I help you?" or "Hello, this is Richard Mazurek's office. May I help you?"

Your biggest challenge will probably be training your children not to scream for you; kids are kids, after all, and inclined to follow the shortest route between A (the phone receiver) and B (you). For those times when you're away from the office, older children can be taught to take careful message notes, and they will usually be flattered to be trusted with this important job.

FRIENDS AND NEIGHBORS

Even the most supportive adults may find it difficult to accept the proposition that you are "at home but unavailable." People who would never arrive unannounced at your office building will unthinkingly expect you to be ready for long chats whenever they drop by your home office. You will have to be polite but firm—very firm. Make it clear that, except for emergencies, you are not to be disturbed between such-and-such hours. Your fax machine and photocopier are not neighborhood resources. Another suggestion: Don't answer the home phone while you're "at the office." Let the home answering machine be your secretary.

"Would You Mind . . . ?"

One problem common to home-based workers is coping with requests for free services. The graphic designer who sets up at home is suddenly a prime target for everyone who wants "a little help with the church newsletter" or "a nice-looking flyer for the yard sale." The accountant who works at home has friends and neighbors who want him to "look over" their 1040 forms at tax time. You may decide to refuse everyone because you may fear that a well-intended exception or two will cause resentment among those you turned down. The best practice is to identify the groups and people you are willing to help at the beginning of the year. You can explain to the others that you already have commitments, but you would be willing to consider their request another year. Another effective strategy is to meet such requests with a cost estimate. Put a dollar value on your time. People who are serious about using your services will pay while others will stop asking you.

From a humanitarian and business standpoint, charitable work is good for you and your community—but nonprofit clients can also be the most demanding of all, with little understanding of your need to be profitable. If you take an assignment from a charity, be clear from the start if it is gratis or if you expect payment. Regardless, draw up a contract specifying the work you will do and what, if any, compensation will be received. If you are willing to donate your time or work for cost, set reasonable goals and deadlines. If a nonprofit (or anyone else) wants your work for free *and* in a rush, say no immediately. Your paying clients are your primary focus and responsibility.

Still another option is to choose a group that you really care about and limit your "donations" to that organization. (You may want to select a charity that is not the traditional beneficiary of large donor funding.) The advantage of selecting only one or two charities is that you can get to know them well, become familiar with their needs and goals, and establish long-lasting relationships.

Be a Good Neighbor

Inform your near neighbors that you're working from home at the very start and then go about your business as unobtrusively as possible. They'll want honest assurances that your business will not disrupt their lives, put them at risk, or impact their property values.

Be a good neighbor by doing the following:

- Consider the aesthetics of the neighborhood. Be sure to abide by all town regulations, especially those concerning signage, noise, and parking.

- Hold meetings or receive customers at home during standard business hours. Traffic before 9:00 A.M. and after 5:00 P.M. should be kept to a minimum.

- Never hog the available parking. If you share a driveway with neighbors, be sure their access and egress is never blocked.

- Don't expect a neighbor to sign for your deliveries on a regular basis.

CHAPTER 14

BUSINESS IS BUILT ON RELATIONSHIPS

You or your company can have all the skills needed to get the job done, but if you don't build a better relationship with your client than your competitor does, you'll lose that client to the competitor. At Peter's advertising agency, he had one test to determine if a client relationship was strong or faltering: "As long as a client wants to call me when she has a need or when she wants advice or as long as she takes my calls when I contact her, then I know we have a strong relationship that ensures ongoing business. But the moment she stops calling me or doesn't take my calls, that's when I know we are either in danger of losing her as a client or we have already lost her." The agency's goal was to never lose a client because a relationship soured.

TRUST IS AT THE CORE OF EVERY RELATIONSHIP

If your clients are comfortable with you and have confidence in you then they will trust you. And trust is at the core of how you maintain and grow your relationship with your clients. The opposite also is true: Lose a client's trust and his confidence in you and it won't be long before he is no longer your client.

Right from the very first contact, you are in the process of earning trust and engendering confidence by the way you interact with a prospect or client. What are some of the most basic steps you can take to earn that trust?

- Be on time for every meeting—both in person or on the phone.

- Return phone calls promptly.

- Answer emails immediately even if it is simply to signal you received it.

- Meet your deadlines.

- Listen attentively.

- Follow through on any promises or commitments you make.

- Deliver work for the price you said you would do the job.

Who Are Your Customers?

Certainly customers or clients are the people who engage you to do work on their behalf. However, there are other people you interact with every day who you should treat just as though they are a client or customer.

AREN'T SUPPLIERS CUSTOMERS AS WELL? Vendors and suppliers deserve to be treated just as you would treat a client. You should deliver your work to them on time, treat them positively and in a friendly manner, and pay them on time. (See "Six Steps for Keeping Contractors Happy," page 162.)

AREN'T YOUR FELLOW WORKERS CLIENTS AS WELL? One company had a policy that if a meeting with a client interfered with an internal meeting, canceling or changing the internal meeting was the accepted practice. Unfortunately, some of the people at the company didn't interact with clients, they only dealt with people inside the company. The result: They were frustrated that they were always treated as second best. Those canceled meetings caused them difficulty in doing their work.

> **TIP:** Use your computer calendar to set reminders for contacting your client over the next six months or year. You can vary the type of contact from short phone calls to invitations to lunch or dinner. By preprogramming them into your computer, you reduce the possibility of too many of these business-social contacts in too short a time or, conversely, forgetting to do them at all.

> ### THE CLIENT AS PART OF YOUR NETWORK
>
> Once you've established a relationship and a track record with a client, then you can consider asking her to be a part of your network or you can send her an invitation to join you on LinkedIn. Just be sure to wait until the relationship has been established and the client has experienced your ability to get the job done. That way she has concrete information on which to base any recommendation she may make on your behalf.

AREN'T SUBORDINATES CUSTOMERS, TOO? The people who perform tasks to support your work should be treated in the same way you would treat a customer. The mail delivery person, the tech person, the administrative assistant—they, too, deserve to be treated positively and in a friendly manner.

MAINTAINING THE RELATIONSHIP

If your new business contact blossoms into an ongoing, productive association, then the process of doing business will automatically give you plenty of opportunities to develop that relationship further, both at formal meetings and at more casual business meals and business-social events. Still, use consideration and your common sense in gauging how often to call or schedule a get-together with a client: You want to be a receptive and available business colleague, not a pest.

In cases where there's no active business relationship, but you still want to keep up with a potential

The Client as Friend

One of the benefits of doing business is that you get to meet all kinds of people. Sometimes you'll meet people who end up becoming good personal friends as well as customers. Having a client who is also a close friend can help cement a long-term relationship. But each person also has to maintain a careful balance between friendship and business. Don't let your friendship get in the way of the following:

DEADLINES. Deadlines affect more than just the two of you. Other people's jobs and livelihoods depend on the work being done on time. Using a friendship to allow a deadline to slip is a fast way to abusing the friendship and losing it altogether.

BIDS. It is especially important when doing business with friends to spell out clearly what you are doing for the friend and how much it will cost. Approach this part of your work just as you would with any client. If someone is doing work for you, insist on an upfront bid in order to ensure that there is no problem when the work is done.

PAYMENT. It's amazing how fast money can come between good friends. If you're the person providing the service, it's your responsibility to prepare and send an invoice in a timely manner and to spell out the particulars, just as you would for any client. If you're the client, it's your responsibility to pay your bills in your next regular cycle of payment. Don't use your friendship as an excuse for dragging out payment.

COMMITMENTS. Finally, don't make any promises motivated by feelings of friendship that you can't keep.

client on the chance that future business opportunities may materialize, an occasional phone call or lunch invitation is a good way to stay in touch without going overboard. Sending holiday or birthday greetings is another excellent way of maintaining ties; you can enter your contacts' birth dates on your computer calendar and set a reminder for a week ahead of time to mail a card that will arrive on time. You don't have to send a gift—a card is plenty. Indeed, a gift could be seen as excessive.

Handling Difficult or Demanding People

Handling an angry or difficult customer is never pleasant, but it doesn't have to be complicated. Many books try to break down difficult people into various personality types and then tell you how to tailor your response accordingly. But all you really have to do is listen very carefully to what a customer with a complaint or a client with an attitude is saying and how he is saying it, while at the same time keeping your own emotions in check. Once you do this, difficult people will actually tell you how to respond. Simply set aside any general or nonconstructive criticism, and focus on the customer's specific complaints—then work toward resolving them. You'll find this approach works equally well over the phone or in person.

If you can, identify something specific in the complaint that you can fix right away. The immediate resolution of at least part of the situation will help give you time to deal with the whole complaint later.

WHEN YOUR COMPANY IS IN THE WRONG

Unfortunately, things do go wrong. And when they do, how your company handles the problem affects your future relationship with the client or customer. Often, a complaining customer will have a legitimate gripe regarding a slipup on the part of your own organization. There are three steps involved in effectively accepting responsibility for a problem or error.

1. **Apologize to the person.** "Mr. Smith, I'm really sorry that the person you were talking to didn't follow through. I can understand your frustration fully. I'm going to . . ."

2. **Offer whatever solution or action you feel you're capable of providing.** This solution may simply be a promise to look into the matter and then report back. You don't have to admit liability or culpability—but you do need to show that you're willing to pursue the matter and to try to find a resolution that will be satisfactory to everyone.

3. **Follow through.** Whatever you do offer as a remedy, be sure to follow through. Your first job at this point is to be sure to get back to the person when you said you would. Reliability instills confidence and that is the first step in rebuilding trust.

Unfortunately, problems or mistakes often lead to frustration on a customer's part. And that frustration can, in turn, manifest itself in anger, either in-person or on the phone. Either way it will take patience, skill, and diplomacy on your part to resolve the situation and, hopefully, reestablish a positive relationship.

Dealing with an Angry Customer Face-to-Face

When you are face-to-face with an angry customer, your biggest challenge is to immediately guard against letting yourself get angry in response. Anger feeds on anger; if you get hot under the collar as well, you are more likely to exacerbate the situation than defuse it. Instead, let the customer vent. His venting may go on for several minutes or longer, so just be patient and listen carefully to what he is actually saying. Separate the anger from the problem, and focus on the problem. Possible outcomes include the following:

- You may be able to solve the problem on the spot.

- You may need to ask the customer to wait while you look into it.

- If you can't solve the situation then and there, set a time when you can get back to him, and give him your contact information so he can get in touch with you if necessary. Be sure to follow up when you say you will.

- If it is a problem that you can't resolve, get a supervisor, let her know the situation, and introduce her to the customer.

Dealing with Angry Callers

Everyone gets them occasionally: calls from customers who have some sort of bone to pick. Luckily, most customers with a problem are neither out of control nor insulting. They realize that mistakes and oversights occur from time to time and that you're not the one to blame. If you sound genuinely interested in helping them, they'll usually keep their cool. Focus on the problem and look for a solution that is within your means to accomplish but also provides them with satisfaction.

Of course, there are the firecrackers with short fuses—the ones who literally explode in your ear. With these folks, it's essential that you try to keep from taking any remarks personally, even though you may in fact be under personal attack. If you reach a point where you've had enough ranting, personal abuse, or profanity, you are fully justified in saying good-bye and hanging up. If this does happen, report the incident in detail to your boss, quoting the abusive caller verbatim if possible. Most companies have policies articulating when a caller has become abusive enough that it is okay to end the call. If your company does not have such a policy, work with your manager to adopt one.

Fortunately, it's rare that callers behave so badly and most angry callers will calm down. Here are some tips on getting past a customer's (or anyone's) anger as quickly as possible:

- Let the angry caller rant for a minute or two. That usually relieves the rage he has built up.

- Don't interrupt—even if he pauses or says something that sounds like the beginning of an apology, such as "I don't like to get this mad, but . . ." A comment by you at this point may set off another round of explosions.

- As the caller is venting, try to detach yourself from the emotional context of what he is saying, and almost like a scientist, objectively consider and remember the words he uses.

> **TIP:** A particularly effective tactic, and good manners to boot, is to tell an irate customer that if for some unforeseen reason you can't call her back at the specified time, she should call you collect or at an 800 number. Though this courteous act may seem as if it's letting you in for trouble you could avoid, it is the kind of graciousness you would expect from a friend in the business—and that's exactly what an irate customer is afraid she doesn't have.

DON'T TAKE IT PERSONALLY

At a busy passport office in a major southern city, the US government has decided that one employee is enough. There are times when the waiting line snakes out of the cavernous main hall and spills into the long main corridor of the vast old post office building. "Disgruntled" is a mild description of most of the waiting people. Meanwhile, behind the passport window, Polly, the one employee, is also responsible for answering telephone inquiries—and the line never stops ringing. Yet when she answers the phone, she is unfailingly courteous and helpful. Incredibly, she maintains the same calm pleasantness when passport applicants, some of whom are ready to explode, finally reach her window.

How does she do it? "I keep telling myself not to take it personally," Polly explains. "Being the only one here is not my fault. It's not under my control. I think these people have a right to be mad, but all I can do is be as quick, careful, and helpful as I can." Once in a while, after standing in line for an hour or more, a passport applicant gets to her window so hot under the collar he can't stop venting. When that happens, Polly says, "I ask him to go talk to my supervisor down the hall and to tell her that I need help. That often makes people feel better, though it really doesn't get me any more help. I'm lucky because my supervisor does have a nice manner."

This harried but even-tempered worker's experience illustrates the two most important rules of dealing with unhappy customers or clients (in fact, almost any peeved person):

- Don't ever take a customer's anger or criticism personally. If you do, you will probably lash back in kind—and that makes everything worse.
- Always remember that you are not alone—you have coworkers and supervisors you can turn to for support when you need it.

- When you sense the caller's anger has run its course, make a brief comment that demonstrates that you've listened closely and that you understand how important the problem is to him.

- If that goes well, introduce yourself (if you haven't already), spelling out your name, giving your title and offering a callback number in case they get disconnected. Then state that you want to help solve the problem. This may pleasantly surprise the caller, whose fury is likely due in part to his anticipation of a hostile reaction to his plight.

- If the caller explodes again, ask for his number and say you'll call back in a couple of hours or at a specified time the next day. Use this breather to collect your thoughts and to talk to your coworkers or supervisor about how you should proceed with this tough case.

- When you've decided how to resolve the situation, always emphasize to the caller the actions you will take (even if they don't fully meet his demands), rather than the actions you can't take. Never promise to do something you can't deliver on.

- If the problem turns out to be the customer's fault—a failure to follow a basic instruction, for example—never adopt a superior tone. Doing so implies that if only he'd been smarter, he could have saved you both a lot of turmoil. Instead, patiently walk the customer through the required steps.

Sometimes, despite your best efforts and extraordinary self-control, nothing you say satisfies an angry caller, and your company loses a customer. This happens to everybody. Don't let it eat away at you, because you've done your best.

Making Promises

When dealing with an aggressive, angry, or puzzled customer, it is essential to tell the truth (without revealing company secrets) and to follow through on any offer or promise you make. Not to do so is almost as bad as losing your temper and yelling or slamming down the phone.

- If you can't promise an immediate solution, stress the urgency you feel about the customer's problem by responding, "I'll look into it immediately" or "I'll ask my supervisor the minute I hang up" or "I'll ask our technical staff what could have happened."

- If you promise you'll ask someone else about the customer's problem, then do so as soon as possible.

- If you have to explain why you can't do what the customer wants done, be sure your facts are accurate.

- If you offer to call back and report what you've found out, before ending the call ask the customer for her number and the best time to reach her—and then be sure to phone at the appointed time.

DEALING WITH CONTRACTORS AND VENDORS

The importance of treating customers with respect goes without saying. Some firms, however, make the mistake of turning around and treating their contractors and vendors as if they were lower down in the pecking order. In view of the fact that your contractors and vendors can make or break your relationships with your customers, giving them anything less than the same consideration you would show to a customer or client is a serious blunder for the smart businessperson—as well as bad etiquette.

Six Steps for Keeping Contractors Happy

Treating your contractors well can pay major dividends, especially when you need their extra effort on a project. Here are six simple steps you can take to ensure extra service from any contractors with whom you do business:

1. Treat the contractor courteously at all times.

2. Be reasonable with deadlines. Don't ask for the impossible. (When you do ask for the impossible, make sure the contractor knows how grateful you are for the extra effort he or she is giving you.)

3. Don't ask for a rush job when you don't need it.

4. Let the contractor know when the job isn't time sensitive.

5. Pay promptly.

6. If you ask for a favor, be ready to return the favor in the future.

WHEN DEADLINES AREN'T MET

A brochure for a conference delivered the day after the conference ends really does no good. Missed deadlines and ignored delivery dates can bring a company to its knees—and lose you customers. If the holdup is internal, you can apply several kinds of pressure to the tardy individual or group, from gentle nagging and prodding (don't be afraid to ruffle feathers, the stakes are too high), to a company's ultimate weapon—the threat of firing. If you are a manager, you may also be able to reallocate people and other resources to get the job done.

With an outside contractor or vendor, you have less control—and all the more reason to be extremely alert to deadline slippage. Of course, there may be times when you have to hold a contractor's or vendor's feet to the fire in order to meet your obligations to your own customers. As you do with an internal project, set a schedule up front with deadlines that must be met. Have everyone concerned buy into and sign off on the schedule. A paper trail is essential so that nobody down the line can claim they "weren't consulted" or "weren't informed" about a deadline. (It's also a good idea to insert stiff penalty clauses into all contracts, though these can be difficult to

> **TIP:** If, despite all your watchfulness, a critical deadline is missed, don't make the often-fatal mistake of trying to keep it a secret between you and your contractor. You should tell your direct superior, and if he or she agrees, you should bring in the lawyers. Keeping quiet about a lagging project could cost your company millions, and cost you your job.

enforce—and may be small consolation if the project fails to meet its final deadline.)

A good manager is sufficiently on top of things to know when a contractor's work is falling behind. At the first sign of danger, you should meet with the project team and ask what it needs to get back on schedule. At this point, you betray no lack of confidence that the project will go smoothly after a few minor adjustments. In fact, let it be perfectly clear that there is simply no alternative—because, you remind the group, "everybody here knows the consequences of not bringing this project in on time."

At the same time, if deadline problems still seem to be cropping up, be doubly sure that you are holding up your end of the bargain. Ask yourself whether you and your subordinates are meeting all of your own deadlines and getting all necessary materials or information to your contractors in a timely and effective way.

Soft Speech, Big Stick

As long as the contractor demonstrates the ability to meet the schedule (or get back on it quickly if there is a slipup), you can be Mr. Nice Guy. But remember Teddy Roosevelt's remark about speaking softly and carrying a big stick. Your big stick is the schedule and any upcoming payments linked to it. No matter how pleased you are with the creativity of the team and the quality of its work, always keep the schedule at the forefront of discussions. Not-so-subtle remarks like this are not out of line: "I'm very pleased with progress so far, Mr. Henry. I see we have a delivery of prototypes due nine days from today, on the fifteenth, and a review session on the twenty-second. I'm assuming you have no problem with those dates. We're very tight on this one, as you know."

PART FOUR

RISING TO THE OCCASION

CHAPTER 15
BUSINESS GIFTS

The giving of gifts is a time-honored and thoughtful way of building business relationships. Whether the exchange takes place with someone outside or inside your own firm, a thoughtful present to mark a holiday, an occasion, or to say "Thank you" can be the perfect way to say "Our relationship is important to me." But gift giving has its risks as well: If you choose a present that's inappropriate, too personal, or in the wrong price range, even the best of intentions can quickly backfire. This is a time when the use of careful consideration and tact becomes especially important.

GIFT CHOICES

Whether you're giving to a coworker or a business associate from outside, your choice of gift depends on the occasion, your relationship to the recipient, and your position in the company. Whether you know the recipient well or not, keep the gift professional. The best approach is to select a gift that can be used in the workplace—perhaps a reference book, a nice calendar, a pen-and-pencil set, or a picture frame.

Temporary Gifts

Flowers, foodstuffs, candy, and beverages fall into the temporary, or perishable, gift category. These are appropriate for most occasions—but especially when a more enduring gift could become an uncomfortable reminder of an illness, a hospitalization, or the death of a family member.

FLOWERS

A great all-purpose gift, flowers can be sent to anyone at any time, thanks to credit cards, teleflorists, and the Internet. You can also pair cut flowers with another gift (say, a vase or a mug) or attach theater tickets or a gift certificate to the arrangement. But don't choose flowers without thinking: A classic seasonal arrangement is appropriate no matter what, but a delivery of long-stemmed roses will imply romantic sentiments. Similarly, when sending flowers internationally, take care to learn about local customs so that you don't choose flowers with the wrong connotation. At any time, consider the occasion and circumstances before choosing what flowers to send:

- For an office mate, choose either an arrangement or a potted plant.

- A get-well card is usually a sufficient gesture when someone is ill, unless it's someone with whom you have a close relationship. If you choose to send flowers or a potted plant to someone who is hospitalized, check with the hospital first to make sure they are allowed.

- When sending a plant, pick one that's easy to care for; the last thing the patient or worried family members need is a failing plant that needs reviving.

- For a funeral, check the obituary to find out if a donation is requested in lieu of flowers. If flowers are okay, they can be sent to the funeral home or the family's home.

FOOD

This is one gift that can be shared with others and, with a little research, can be personalized. Find out from the recipient's assistant or spouse if there are any particular favorites; at the same time, make sure the person has no food allergies. If time isn't a consideration, scan catalogs and the backs of magazines for mail-order firms, which offer everything from prime steaks to specialty cakes, fruits, smoked salmon, or trout. Or you can keep things economical and impart a special touch by preparing the food yourself—your prized recipe for toffee or brownies, perhaps, or a basket of exotic fruits—and packaging it attractively.

WINE AND LIQUOR

Take care giving wine or liquor as a business gift. There are plenty of other gifts to choose from without the downside of giving alcohol and creating a potentially embarrassing situation with the recipient.

GIFTS TO OUTSIDERS

Gifts from the company or its individual senior employees run the gamut from gifts that recognize standard holidays and personal events sent to customers and clients to more individualized gifts thanking business associates for a favor or entertainment. Gifts may also be sent to congratulate a client on a promotion or an award or to express sympathy for an illness or a death.

From the Company

Clients and customers are the usual recipients of gifts sent by the company as a whole. These may be annual holiday presents, or tokens of appreciation. Consumable gifts like a fruit basket or a box of chocolates are an excellent choice as many in the receiving company can share in the gift. Gifts to individuals or small groups can be as varied as coffee mugs, appointment calendars, paperweights, pen-and-pencil sets, T-shirts, and umbrellas. If gifts of this kind are going to bear your company logo, they should be well made and in tasteful colors, with the logo understated enough not to look like an advertisement.

Some companies prefer to show appreciation at holiday time by giving a donation in the recipient's name. Charitable gifts are a perfect example of a win–win situation: The recipient is glad to be recognized, the company giving the gift makes its appreciation known, and both companies are helping society at large—showing themselves to be good corporate citizens. Corporate giving also engenders pride in the company and sets an example for employees.

BUSINESS GIFT IDEAS

There are two key rules in picking out a business gift: Don't make it too personal, and don't buy something that's inappropriately expensive. Also, be aware of any price limits that have been set by your firm or the recipient's company. Many organizations have a cap on gifts—which is also the maximum amount you're allowed to deduct on your taxes for an individual business gift.

Gifts that are appropriate for business colleagues include the following:

ITEMS FOR THE OFFICE

Attractive wall calendar

Daily calendar featuring a favorite sport, travel destination, or comic strip character

Paperweight

Pen-and-pencil set

Desk caddy

Picture frame

Date book

Leather tablet holder

Plant (one that doesn't need much light or maintenance)

Framed poster of an artwork or featuring a favorite sport or activity

TRAVEL ITEMS

Folding umbrella (a high-quality one)

Leather passport holder

Travel clock

Noise canceling headphones

Foreign dictionary app

Preprinted luggage tags

GENERAL ITEMS

Leather business-card case

Music gift card

Job- or hobby-oriented magazine subscription

Computer case

Movie or theater tickets

Gift certificate to a favorite restaurant

Tickets to a sporting event

Business-related book on history or travel or on a special interest or hobby

Coffee-table book on a favorite sport, activity, or travel destination

Golf or tennis balls or other sporting equipment

Cooking utensils

Subscription to a "food of the month" club (check on preferences first)

Engraved paperweight, pen, or pocketknife

A THANK-YOU
FOR A THANK-YOU

Q. At work, is it proper for my department to send a thank-you card to another department that has provided lunch as a thank-you (to my department) for helping them meet their revenue goals?

A. It is always appropriate to thank someone for a kindness even when that kindness is an expression of thanks itself. The other department went above and beyond simply saying "Thank you" by hosting lunch for your department. Acknowledging that effort with a thank-you card would be a very nice gesture and not at all "over the top."

From Individuals to Customers and Clients

Individuals in the company who give gifts to outsiders are usually at the executive to middle-manager level. If this includes you, it goes without saying that you must abide by your company's policies and follow company traditions. Some firms forbid any gift giving to or from business associates. If your company does allow exchanges with clients, you should still make sure your gifts are in line with the value of those given by your colleagues and that the gift doesn't exceed the financial limits set by either your own company or the recipient's. When in doubt, check with your intended recipient's human resources department; sending a gift to a client who's unable to keep it is awkward for both giver and receiver. (See also "Accepting and Declining Gifts," pages 173.)

Finally, never give a gift of any sort to an outside business associate who is either currently involved in a bidding process with your firm or receiving a bid from you or your company—no matter what time of year it might be.

GIFTS FROM THE OUTSIDE

Rather than setting a ceiling for the cost of gifts received, some companies have a policy that any gifts costing more than a certain amount must be disclosed to management. This is a way of keeping tabs on what's coming in from outside and seeing to it that everything stays aboveboard.

Most companies allow employees to receive token gifts from customers and clients because sending them back could insult the giver, especially during the holidays. Some businesses also require that any foodstuffs received from outside be shared because the usual recipients of such gifts tend to be those employees who have the advantage of dealing face-to-face with customers, whereas the people who work behind the scenes often go unrewarded.

EXCHANGING GIFTS WITH PEOPLE INSIDE YOUR OFFICE

Holiday gift giving is such a long-standing tradition in some workplaces that it can't be ignored. To ease the financial strain of providing every coworker with a gift, many companies have a holiday grab bag or Secret Santa system that ensures everyone gives and receives one gift, with expenditures limited (usually to $10–15). Just be sure to abide by the spending limits. It is fine to give humorous (but not off-color) gifts to coworkers at holiday time, and homemade gifts are a thoughtful and frugal way to spread good cheer.

Coworkers: Yes or No?

If you decide on your own to give gifts to colleagues you're close to, be sure to give gifts to selected individuals in private so that other colleagues' feelings aren't hurt. Something to brighten up his or her work space is usually a good choice, as are books, music, and gift certificates for movies or the local cafe. Tailor gifts to the individual: You probably know what types of items would make someone's office more pleasant or that would be enjoyed outside the office. (See also "Accepting and Declining Gifts," page 173, and the box " 'Thanks!,' " page 174.)

Bosses: Yes or No?

Don't give a gift to your boss that's just from you. Other employees may take exception to what they see as your effort to play up to the boss. Also, resentment is likely if your gift is twice as expensive as another employee's gift. The best solution is for the employees to get together and give a gift jointly to their supervisor. A group gift lacks the hint of currying favor that a personal gift may have.

Your Assistant: Yes or No?

While you should be cautious about giving gifts to individuals inside your office, your assistant is an exception. The gift choice depends on his or her length of service: If it is less than five years, a gift in the $25 range is sufficient; with longer-term assistants, you may want to be a little more generous.

The number one rule for employer-to-assistant gifts, be they for holidays or for birthdays, is to make sure they're not too personal. Perfume, lingerie, jewelry, and even clothing items can be misconstrued and are therefore out of bounds. That doesn't mean picking the most impersonal item you can find, however. Always consider your assistant's likes and interests in choosing what to give him or her.

MARKING MILESTONES

Your business associates from both outside and inside the office may live in different worlds but all share life's major milestones. Acknowledging birthdays, weddings, and other events shows you respect someone's life outside of work. You're not expected to give a gift for every significant day in every client's or colleague's life, of course, but some occasions call for a card at least. While chipping in for a group gift is perfectly fine, you might also want to send a separate card to people with whom you are especially close.

A Birthday

Though you may have ignored a colleague's or client's birthday in previous years, it's a good idea to recognize a significant one—say, forty or fifty. But note that within the office there exists a double standard for birthdays: It's appropriate for a boss to give an employee a gift, but when it's the other way around, a birthday gift might be interpreted as kissing up. Use your judgment to decide whether a card or participation in a group gift is the better gesture.

A Wedding

If you've received a wedding invitation from a coworker or client, send a gift, even if you don't attend. (There are exceptions to this, however, including an invitation from someone you barely know.) Then again, it may be that you know of an associate's wedding but aren't invited. If so, don't be offended; some people prefer to keep their work and personal lives separate. If you still want to send a gift, that's okay. An alternative is to send a card with a personal note of best wishes.

The Birth of a Baby

Unless you're close to the parent(s), a group gift is the best idea. Standard gifts include baby clothing, stuffed animals, toys, picture frames, and receiving blankets—but try for some originality. A hardback edition of a classic children's book has a truly timeless quality; inscribe it with a message that will be appreciated by the parents and understood by the child when he or she reaches reading (or read-to) age.

APPROPRIATE OR NOT?

Besides good taste, two other qualities determine the appropriateness of a business gift: its cost and how personal it is. Cost is mostly an issue when giving to customers and clients, with the overtone of bribery or brown nosing growing in direct proportion to expensiveness. Gifts that are too personal are also out of place in business, including gifts between close colleagues that are exchanged at work. Consider carefully your relationship to the person to whom you're giving and what he or she will think appropriate. If you're unsure, it's always safer to err on the less personal side.

A Death

The standard gifts of condolence when a business associate is dealing with the death of a close relative are (1) flowers with a card, (2) a donation to the deceased's favorite charity or a medical organization, and (3) food, which gives the family one less thing to think about as they grieve. Consult the obituary to see whether it includes instructions on where to send flowers or donations. Remember that when someone is mourning the death of a family member, the most important thing is to offer condolence and support. This can be done effectively through a note or a simple verbal acknowledgment; express your sympathy and your willingness to help as soon as you hear of the person's loss.

THE ART OF PRESENTATION

Even a gift that's thoughtfully chosen, timely, and wonderful in itself can have its effect dulled by a sloppy presentation. Wrap your present carefully; if you're unable to do a professional-looking job, have it wrapped at the store. Two other things to remember:

- Modesty may be an attractive quality in other situations, but never belittle a gift you are giving; be as positive as possible, emphasizing that you thought especially of the recipient when choosing it. Gifts mean more when you're proud to give them.

- Whether a gift is sent or given in person, attach a card—especially if the gift is one of many the person is receiving. Cards serve not only as an expression of your sentiments but also as a useful reminder when thank-you notes are written.

A correspondence card is ideal, but a business card can also be used. With the latter, draw a line through your printed name and write a short, personal note. A mere phrase will do: "Best wishes, Beth Landau."

ACCEPTING AND DECLINING GIFTS

When receiving a gift in the presence of the giver, you may open it as soon as possible; usually, the giver will want to see your reaction and be thanked on the spot. At a shower or retirement party, the opening of presents is often a party in itself. If the occasion for giving is formal, however—a wedding or an official ceremony—gifts are generally put aside, to be opened later.

Act delighted when receiving a gift, regardless of what you actually think of it. Effusing comes naturally if you're thrilled with the gift but not so easily when you're not. Even if the present is the last thing you wanted, thank the giver for his or her thoughtfulness, letting your tact mask any disappointment. Be pleasant but noncommittal: "It's so nice of you to think of me this way!" or "What an imaginative gift!" Do the same in your thank-you note.

Speaking of thank-you notes, the standard is if you open the gift in front of the giver and thank him or her personally, then a note is not required. That said, even though it is not required, think of writing a note in addition to your in-person thanks as an opportunity to reach out to the person one more time. It is an easy gesture for you to make that will create a positive impression of you in the giver's mind.

RETURNING A GIFT

Q. How do I politely return a gift of money to a client?

A. Money is no different than any other type of gift. It is really nice when a client wants to show his appreciation, but company rules often prohibit employees from accepting any monetary gifts. The best course of action is to return the gift right when it is offered or to send it back immediately. Even as you're saying no to the gift, show your appreciation for the thoughtfulness of the giver by what you say as you return the gift, either in person or by a handwritten note. "Tom, thank you so much. I really appreciate the thoughtfulness of this gift, but my company has a strict policy and I'm not allowed to accept it. I hope you'll understand."

Declining Gifts

Having to pretend a little pales in comparison to the discomfort of declining a gift, which may be necessary for either of these reasons: (1) Its cost is over the limit allowed by your company, or (2) it is too personal or sexually suggestive.

In the too-costly case, there is really no need for embarrassment: In effect, it is the company, not you, who is declining. A handwritten note clearly stating this is all that's needed, regardless of the giver's motivation. The note that follows is an example of one that will spare hurt feelings on the part of someone who had good intentions yet at the same time will also dissuade anyone who was trying to curry favor from doing so again.

Dear Mr./Ms. Sharpley, (or Dear [First Name] if you are on a first-name basis)

I found the carved bowl you sent delightful, but I'm afraid the rules here won't let me keep it ($30 or more at Kettle & Black, and it's automatically "return to sender"). I'm sure you understand that I really have no choice. Still, I greatly appreciate your thoughtfulness and look forward to maintaining our productive business relationship.

Sincerely,
Diana

A gift with obvious romantic overtones is more difficult. You don't have to return a dozen long-stemmed red roses, but you could let the sender know (verbally or via a note) that while you know he meant well, sending such gifts are inappropriate in light of your professional relationship.

More serious is something sexually provocative, like lingerie. If you're given such a gift in person by a member of the opposite sex, return it on the spot, making it clear that the gift is improper: "Honestly, I can't accept this, and I think it's obvious why." Then put the same statement in writing and send it. Make a copy of your note and keep it as a record in case any repercussions arise down the line; in an era when legal ramifications are an ever-present possibility, you may need evidence of your reaction.

CHAPTER 16
TABLE MANNERS BASICS

All the rules of table manners are made to avoid ugliness. To let anyone see what you have in your mouth is repulsive, to make a noise is to suggest an animal, to make a mess is disgusting.

—EMILY POST, *ETIQUETTE*
(1ST EDITION, 1922)

Emily Post got it right. In one sentence, she covered the principal reasons why table manners exist. Virtually all of the issues covered in this chapter have to do with avoiding one of these three transgressions. If you bring nothing else away from this discussion, when you think about any action you take at a meal, remember her words and ask yourself, "Does it have the potential to be repulsive, sound like an animal, or make a mess?" If it does, then don't do it. (See also *Emily Post's Etiquette,* 18th edition, and www.emily post.com for more information, illustrations, and videos on table settings, holding utensils, resting and finishing positions of utensils, holding glasses, and pouring wine.)

WHY DINING ETIQUETTE MATTERS

Nobody is going to adopt or change a behavior just because Emily Post says so. But give someone a good reason and then they'll make the effort. So why does dining etiquette matter?

Grossness

The act of eating is, in one word, gross. Think about it: You cut up food on a plate, try to spear it with or balance it on a utensil, lift it to your mouth without spilling or dropping it, and then, once in your mouth, chew it into a pulp before swallowing it. And you do all this while sitting across from a person with whom you are trying to have a conversation, which requires you to open your mouth. What table manners do for you is limit the grossness of the process of getting food to and into your mouth so your interaction with those you are dining with can be as pleasant as possible.

Confidence

In addition, table manners give us confidence by providing guidelines on what to do during this very public and at the same time very personal activity. When you know what to do, you can be focused on the conversation and building relationships instead of worrying about which fork is the right one to use, or how you should eat asparagus, or if you may pick up a lamb-chop bone. Having confidence in your table manners is one of the surest ways to make a positive impact on your dining companions.

Differentiator

Good table manners are critical for another reason as well: People judge other people by their table manners. In a business situation, table manners may well be the key factor that differentiates you from your competition. The businessperson whose dining skills are smooth and easy allows the focus of the others at the table to be on the business conversation and not on how she's holding her fork, or how she didn't know what do with the artichoke, or worse, the awful slurping noise she made with her soup.

GUIDE TO TABLE MANNERS

Many people fear that they won't know what to do or how to behave at the table. After all, no one wants to look foolish or ignorant. Fortunately,

---

ALL ABOUT THE NAPKIN

- When you first sit down, place your napkin in your lap right away.
- If you need to leave the table during the meal, loosely fold the napkin so no soiled area shows and place it to the left of your place setting, not on your chair.
- When you leave at the end of the meal, fold it loosely so no soiled area shows and place it to the left of your place setting.
- Don't tuck the napkin into your shirt below your neck.
- About your tie: Don't flip it over your shoulder to prevent it from getting food stains. Instead, eat carefully so you don't splatter your food on your tie or shirt.

---

there's a simple solution to the problem: Whenever you aren't sure what to do, simply sit back, wait, and watch. Notice how other people are handling the situation, or which utensil they are using, or which glass they are drinking from—and then follow their lead.

With that general guideline in mind, the following is a step-by-step guide to table manners, from first arrival to final thank-you. The more you know about table manners and the more you practice, the more confident you will be. Whereas the advice is geared to a restaurant setting (which is where most business meals take place), it is equally applicable to meals held in a private dining room, someone's home, a club, or other location.

Holding Utensils

How you hold your fork, knife, and spoon is very noticeable to the other diners at your table—or not. When held correctly, you don't draw attention to yourself and instead the focus remains on the conversation. But, if you hold your utensils incorrectly, it's as if you held up a big sign saying, "I don't know what I'm doing." People notice and their opinion of you is diminished, thinking you lack sophistication or that you never bothered learning manners.

HOLDING A FORK OR A SPOON

To use your fork or spoon, hold it like a pencil, not a shovel: Rest it on the middle finger of your dominant hand and let your forefinger and thumb grip the handle. Use either utensil to scoop the food, taking only enough for one, comfortable bite. Taking a heaping amount risks a spill or getting food on your face.

CUTTING FOOD WITH A FORK AND KNIFE

Gripping the handles of your knife and fork in your fists like daggers actually makes the job more difficult. Holding the knife and fork correctly provides you with the most control—and the least chance of sending a piece of meat flying.

- Hold the knife in your dominant hand with the blade down. Place the end of the handle in the palm of your hand. Place your forefinger on the top of the blade where it attaches to the handle. Grasp the handle with the remaining fingers and your thumb.

- Hold the fork in your other hand with the tines facing down. Place the end of the handle in the

> **TIP:** The "tines down" rule is by no means written in stone. But whichever style you choose—American, Continental, up, down—never grip the fork in your fist and use it as a spear or shovel.

palm of your hand. Place your forefinger on the top of the fork where it attaches to the handle. Grasp the handle with the remaining fingers and your thumb, like a pencil.

- Spear the piece of food you want to cut with the fork tines, pressing down on the handle of the fork with your forefinger. Use a sawing motion with the knife to cut a bite-size piece. Try to keep your elbows close to your body as you cut.

Getting Food to Your Mouth

There are two styles for handling the knife and fork while dining: the American style and the Continental (also called European) style, which is used not only by Europeans but also by some Americans who prefer it. Is one more proper than the other? No. In fact, there's no reason not to use both during a meal: You might want to cut and eat the meat in the Continental way, for example, but eat other food using the American style.

THE AMERICAN STYLE. Begin by cutting food with the fork in the left hand and the knife in the right as described above (or reversed if you're left-handed). Then you place (not prop) the knife on the edge of the plate and switch the fork to your right hand before raising it, tines up, to your mouth. The fork should rest on the middle finger of your hand, with your index finger and thumb gripping the handle slightly above.

THE CONTINENTAL STYLE. In the European style, the food is cut in the same way. The knife, however, is kept in the cutting hand while the other hand lifts the fork to the mouth. The fork is held tines down with the index finger touching the neck of the handle or changed in position to tines up with the handle resting on the middle finger, with your index finger and thumb gripping the handle slightly above.

Usually, you see a person eating Continental-style with the fork in the left hand and the knife in the right hand. However, a left-handed person will do the reverse because the knife is in the left-handed person's dominant hand. Again, either way is acceptable.

Some General Table Manners

Throughout the meal, you will encounter a number of situations that can occur during any course, such as passing the salt and pepper or putting your utensils down while eating or when you're finished.

WHAT ABOUT SALTING AND PEPPERING FOOD? Be sure to taste the food before putting salt or pepper on it. That way you'll know if it needs the seasoning. It would be a shame to ruin good food because you salted before you tasted. In addition, you imply that the chef did not know how to properly season the dish.

HOW DO YOU PASS THE SALT AND PEPPER? Always pass them together. If a person asks for just one, pass both anyway. Put them down on the table instead of placing them in the person's hand.

AS A GUEST, WHEN CAN YOU START EATING? In business situations, it's best to wait until everyone is served and the host has started eating or invites you to begin. This is true for all the courses served at the meal.

AS A HOST, WHEN CAN YOU START EATING? You can graciously respect the fact that good food should be eaten while it's hot. Once three people are served, consider giving those guests who have been served permission to start. You might say something like this: "If you've been served your food, please begin and enjoy your meal while it is still hot."

WHY PASS TO THE RIGHT?

It simplifies life at the table if food is passed in just one direction. For instance, if the bread starts out to the right and the butter to the left, at some point halfway around the table a person is going to be faced with the problem of trying to handle both the bread and butter at the same time. It's easier if everyone simply passes in one direction. Thus, for the sake of practicality, the guideline is to pass right rather than left, since most people are right-handed. They receive the plate or basket with their left hand, which leaves their right hand free to easily serve the food to themselves.

TIP: When someone near you on your left asks for something to be passed, it's okay to take the more direct route and pass left.

CAN YOU PUT YOUR ELBOWS ON THE TABLE? Between courses, it's perfectly acceptable to put your elbows on the table slightly—just stay clear of any spills on the tablecloth. In fact, from the perspective of body language, by leaning forward with your elbows on the edge of the table and your hands clasped in front of you, you are projecting an image of being attentive and listening closely to the speaker. While eating, keep your elbows off the table. You should never rest your head in your hands while your elbows are on the table.

WHERE DO YOU PLACE YOUR UTENSILS IF YOU'RE NOT FINISHED EATING? While you are still eating you may want to put your utensils down. Simply place the utensil(s) on the edge of the plate: knife across the top, fork or spoon near the middle. Do not place used utensils on the table or tablecloth.

WHERE DO YOU PLACE YOUR UTENSILS WHEN YOU'RE FINISHED EATING? At the end of a course, the utensils are placed side by side diagonally across the plate. Imagine your plate is a clock face: Place the utensils at roughly the 4:20 position. When servers see utensils set in this position, they recognize it as a sign that they can remove the plate.

IS IT ACCEPTABLE TO BLOW YOUR NOSE AT THE TABLE? Really, it's not. (The one exception is a quick, slight dabbing—not blowing—of the nose.) Any blowing of your nose into a tissue should take place away from the table, preferably in a restroom. Don't even think about sitting at the table and blowing into your napkin.

> ### "KEEP YOUR KNIFE"
>
> What should you do when a server asks you to hold on to your knife as he clears your salad plate? Really you have two options: Explain that you would prefer to have a clean knife for your main course or place your knife on you bread plate. The one thing you shouldn't do is place a used utensil back on the table.

Sometimes sneezes come on very quickly. If you don't have time to cover with your napkin, at least turn into your elbow to cover the sneeze. If you have people sitting close to you on either side, it's better to look down to your lap and sneeze into your hands or napkin than it is to turn to the side and sneeze directly into the face of your neighbor. If necessary, ask for another napkin. Both sneezing and nose blowing should be followed by a quick visit to the restroom to wash your hands and clean up.

WHAT ABOUT PASSING GAS? This is a potentially embarrassing situation, so treat it as such by excusing yourself from the table to take care of the matter in the restroom. If you do pass gas, just say "Excuse me" and carry on with your conversation.

WHAT DO YOU DO WITH A FINGER BOWL? A finger bowl is a bowl of water placed in front of you at some point during the meal. It is not soup so don't start eating it. Instead, you use it to gently clean your fingers. You may encounter a finger bowl after a finger-food appetizer, after eating a hands-on meal such as lobster (in this case there is often a lemon slice in the water), or at a more formal meal, before dessert is served. Dip your fingertips, one hand at a time (not one finger at a time), into the water and then dry them on your napkin.

WHAT SHOULD YOU DO IF YOU HAVE SOMETHING IN YOUR MOUTH YOU WANT TO REMOVE? You have two choices here, but the important thing is to remove the food as unobtrusively as possible. The most appropriate thing to do is to raise the utensil you are using to your lips and gently push the offending article onto the utensil and then place the object on the side of your plate. The alternative is to use your tongue to gently push it onto your lips as you quickly grasp the item between your forefinger and thumb and place it on the edge of your plate. In either case, you can raise your other hand in front of your mouth so others at the table don't see you push the offending article out of your mouth. The exception is when you have a large mouthful of gristle and fat. In this case, excuse yourself to the restroom and remove it. No one will want to look at that on the side of your plate, and it does not belong in your napkin.

WHAT CAN I DO IF I EAT SLOWLY? You're going to feel uncomfortable if everyone else is finished and you still have half your meal to enjoy. You can speed up your eating by

- Preparing the next bite while chewing the food you've just put into your mouth

- Ordering small plates or taking smaller servings

- Limiting your side of the conversation to short answers, asking questions, and being sure to eat while your partner is talking

WHAT CAN I DO IF I EAT TOO FAST? Likewise, if you're constantly finishing way ahead of others, you might want to slow down by

- Putting your utensil(s) down while you are chewing

- Taking smaller bites

- Engaging in conversation rather than taking bite after bite

Working with Your Server

IS THERE ANY SENSE TO HOW SERVERS BRING FOOD AND TAKE AWAY EMPTY PLATES? Actually, there is a protocol for serving and removing: Serve from the left and take away from the right. The server will approach you from the left side to bring your food to you, and he or she will approach from the right side to remove a plate or bowl.

SHOULD YOU PICK UP YOUR FORK IF IT FALLS ON THE FLOOR? No. Leave it there; tell the server and ask for another fork.

WHAT DO YOU DO IF YOU SPILL FOOD OR DRINK ONTO THE TABLE? Quickly pick up the fallen glass and if the spill is going to run off the table, place your napkin over it. Get the server's attention, point out the problem quietly and ask him or her to bring you a fresh napkin, then finish covering the mess. If your spill gets onto another person's clothing, it is very important that you offer to get the affected garment cleaned. Never try to clean the spill off the person, allow them to do it themselves.

HOW SHOULD YOU SIGNAL A SERVER? Make eye contact with the server and quietly say "Excuse me." If he is across the room and you can catch his eye, gently raise your hand to shoulder level and motion to him. At no time is it appropriate to call out to a server or to wave frantically (unless it's an actual emergency, such as choking).

AT THE TABLE

The most important thing to keep in mind when deciding which fork or knife or spoon to use is this: You always use the utensils on the outside of the place setting first. If you don't use a utensil for a particular course, then when the course is removed from the table, the waitperson will remove the utensil for that course as well. Table settings are decoded in full in Chapter 17.

Before the First Course Arrives

Along with the drinks, the arrival of bread marks your first opportunity to deal with food at the same time you are trying to carry on a conversation.

WHAT DO YOU DO WITH THE BREAD BASKET, BUTTER, AND OLIVE OIL? Most often bread is placed on the table in a basket that everyone shares. If the bread is placed in front of you, feel free to pick up the basket and offer it to the person on your left. Then take a piece yourself, place it on your bread plate, and pass the basket to the right. The same goes for the butter or the olive oil for dipping. Be sure to take butter or olive oil from the communal plate and put it on your bread plate. Don't repeatedly take butter from

---

BREAKING BREAD

Q. When at a business dinner at a high-end restaurant that serves a loaf of bread rather than individual pieces, is it proper to break the bread into pieces for the entire table or should a knife be used to cut the bread?

A. We don't like it when restaurants serve whole loaves of bread rather than offering individual rolls or a loaf that has already been sliced. Worse are restaurants that serve whole loaves without providing a napkin or cloth to hold the bread and a knife to cut it. Grasping the bread with a bare hand can be disturbing to others at the table. Tearing off pieces just adds to the offense. If you're served a whole loaf without the cloth or knife, ask the waitperson to bring them. Then it is perfectly appropriate to hold the bread using the napkin and cut several pieces for the table and certainly more considerate than just cutting a piece for yourself.

---

the communal plate to put directly on your bread or dip directly into the communal olive oil.

NOW THAT YOU HAVE BREAD AND BUTTER, WHAT DO YOU DO? You place the bread and butter or olive oil on your butter plate—yours is on your left—then break off a bite-size piece of bread, put a little butter on it or dip it in the olive oil, and eat it. Don't butter the whole piece of bread or dip it in the olive oil and then take bites from it.

Appetizers and Soup

The first course to arrive will be your appetizer or soup, if you ordered one. Appetizers are typically eaten with a fork and knife, though in some cases they may be eaten with your fingers. If you do eat food with your fingers, try to pick up bite-size pieces rather than bringing a big piece of food to your mouth and then tearing a bite off with your teeth.

WHAT ABOUT SHRIMP COCKTAIL? Shrimp cocktail is usually served in a wide glass with a stem, set on a small plate. If the shrimp is bigger than one bite's worth, then either cut it with the edge of the shrimp fork or spear it with your fork and cut it with a knife on the plate on which it's served. When faced with shrimp cocktail and no fork, simply hold the shrimp by the tail, dip it into the sauce—just enough to coat, not so that you have a huge dollop of sauce that could drip or get on your face as you eat it—and take a bite. Fork or no fork, when the shrimp is big and the sauce is yours alone, you are free to double dip. If the sauce is communal, don't double dip.

CLAMS AND OYSTERS. Unless your host gives you permission to slurp the clam or oyster directly from the shell, use the little oyster fork to get the clam or oyster to your mouth.

As the host: If people at your table order clams or oysters on the half shell, you can offer them the alternative of picking up the shell and sliding the clam or oyster into their mouths rather than using the fork. Frankly, there's something unappetizing about a clam or oyster dangling from a fork as a person tries to get it into his mouth, so we suggest you give permission to slurp.

WHAT'S THE PROPER WAY TO EAT SOUP? Dip the spoon into the soup to get a spoonful with a motion that moves the spoon away from you rather than toward you. You can gently brush the bottom of the spoon on the edge of the cup or bowl to catch any drip. The reason for the motion away from you is to avoid inadvertently directing a drip into your lap.

CAN YOU TIP YOUR SOUP BOWL OR CUP? Yes, it is acceptable to tip the bowl—but only for the last drop or two. Again, tip the bowl away from you rather than toward you.

WHAT DO YOU DO WITH THE OYSTER CRACKERS? If oyster crackers come with the soup, you can add them to your soup. Larger crackers, however, should stay out of the soup; eat them with your fingers instead of crumbling them into the bowl.

WHERE DO YOU PUT THE SPOON WHILE YOU'RE EATING? If the soup is served in a cup, it will come on a saucer. When you want to put your spoon down, place it on the saucer. If the soup is served in a shallow bowl, rest the spoon in the bowl, even if it is delivered with a plate underneath.

WHERE DO YOU PUT THE SPOON WHEN YOU ARE FINISHED? When soup is served in a cup, place the spoon on the underplate; when it is served in a shallow bowl, place it in the bowl itself. The only difference is to make sure that the spoon in the bowl has the handle positioned at 4:00 (pointing to the lower right). This position lets the waiter know you're finished with the soup.

All Things Wine

For millennia, the enjoyment of good wine with a meal has been a real social pleasure. Today is no different. However, it is equally important to note that at no time should a person feel compelled to drink wine if she doesn't want it. (See also the box "The One-Drink Rule," page 198.) If you decide you do want to partake of some wine at a business meal, there are guidelines that should be followed.

HOLDING A WINEGLASS

White wine should be enjoyed chilled so hold the glass by the stem not the bowl. Holding by the bowl will cause the heat from your hand to warm the wine. If it is served in a stemless glass, grasp it as gently as you can with your fingers and so as little of your hand touches the glass as possible.

Red wine should be held with your hand cupping the bowl. The warmth of your palm and fingers helps warm the wine and release its flavor.

WHAT SHOULD YOU DO IF YOU DON'T WANT WINE?

Don't turn your glass upside down or put your hand over the glass as the server is about to pour. The easiest thing to do is simply to say to the server, "No, thank you," as she approaches to pour wine for you. If you don't notice the server and she pours you wine, just leave it in the glass and continue with your conversation. That's much more important than whether you have wine in your glass.

"WHY DON'T YOU CHOOSE THE WINE?"

The menus have been perused and the chit-chat is gathering steam, when your host abruptly thrusts a wine list the size of a small book in your direction: "Harry, why don't you choose the wine?" Bewildered, you haven't a clue where to start.

One response is to be honest: "I'd love to, but I know so little about wine I think I should leave it up to you." (Note: Never be embarrassed by your lack of wine savvy; even self-styled "wine experts" are often clueless about pairing wines with food.) An alternative is to ask the other guests for suggestions as you glance over the list: "Which red do you think will go best with the dishes we're having?" What you should never do is fake it; otherwise, you could end up with a wine that overpowers the food and pleases no one—with you as the guilty party. Your safest bet is to order a red and a white for the table.

With this default option in mind, learning a few wine basics will put you on relatively safe ground for the future. If, after reading this, you want to learn more, it's easier than you might think: Numerous apps exist to help choose wines. (But don't haul out your smartphone at the table for a consultation.) In addition, there are a number of excellent small books available on wine appreciation that can take the mystery out of choosing.

HOW DO YOU POUR WINE?

You may be asked to refill your dinner companion's glass. Fill a glass of white wine to about two-thirds full. If pouring red wine, fill the wineglass so it is approximately half full, or to the widest point in the bowl to provide maximum surface area to interact with the air. As you finish pouring, tip the neck of the bottle up to cease the flow and twist the bottle at the end of the movement. This small twisting motion will prevent drips from falling and landing on the tablecloth or, worse, the person you are pouring for.

CAN YOU DRINK BOTH RED AND WHITE?

Yes, although you should finish one before switching to the other. For instance, you may start with white during the appetizer or, at a formal dinner, during the fish course and then switch to red for the main course.

The Salad Course

In most restaurants and homes, the salad course will be served after the appetizer and before the main course. Occasionally, in a more formal setting or at a French restaurant, the salad will be served after the main course. In a home setting, salad may also be passed around the table during the main course.

CAN YOU USE A KNIFE TO CUT YOUR SALAD?

Sometimes it can be hard to cut the lettuce with the edge of your fork. In this case, yes, you can use a knife, particularly if there are large lettuce leaves. If you have two knives to choose from, use the smaller one; otherwise, use your main course knife. In either case, leave your knife on the salad plate when you are finished. If the server starts to place your main course knife back on the table, ask him to bring you a clean knife instead.

HOW DO YOU EAT . . . ?

- **Cherry tomatoes.** Very carefully. Try to spear the tomato with your fork and cut it in half. (This isn't always easy.) The best way to spear a cherry tomato is to use your knife blade to trap the tomato as you push the fork's tines into it. If you put a whole cherry tomato in your mouth, close your lips tightly before biting into it. If you don't, you will likely spray seeds and tomato juice across the table, much to your embarrassment.

- **Olives with pits.** If the olive is part of a salad, you should use your fork to move the olive to your mouth. If it has a pit, you can discreetly remove the pit from your mouth by gently pushing it back onto your fork or gently removing it with your fingers and putting it on the side of the plate. The key is a quick, smooth, unobtrusive motion that doesn't attract the attention of others. Either way you do it, cover your mouth with your free hand.

The Main Course

If you order for yourself, you can avoid any potential difficulties by ordering food that is easy to eat and that you know you enjoy. In some business situations, however, the meal is preordered for you—which means you may be faced with food you either don't like or don't know how to eat.

WHAT DO YOU DO WITH BONES? At a business meal, don't pick up a bone and eat it with your fingers unless you see your host doing it. One exception would be eating foods that are clearly finger foods, such as chicken wings served as an appetizer or spare ribs or possibly fried chicken. (Even with fried chicken, and even in the South, check out how your host is handling it before you pick it up with your fingers.)

As a host: If you notice that someone has ordered rack of lamb or chops, give him permission to pick up the bones: "You know, Tom, I hate leaving those last flavorful bites on the bone. It really is okay if you want to pick them up." With that permission offered, the guest should neatly go ahead and enjoy.

SHOULD YOU CUT OFF ONE BITE OF MEAT AT A TIME OR SEVERAL BITES AT ONCE? You should cut one bite of any food and then eat it before cutting the next.

HOW ABOUT LINGUINE OR SPAGHETTI? When you are at home, practice twirling linguine or spaghetti onto a fork. It's easier to twirl it if you place the tips of the fork against the side of your plate or the bowl of a spoon. If you twirl one or two strands at a time, you shouldn't get an overly large mouthful. Don't use your knife and fork to cut the plate of spaghetti up into small pieces.

DO YOU EAT VEGETABLES SERVED ON A SIDE PLATE DIRECTLY FROM THE PLATE? If the plate of vegetables is just for you, you can eat directly from the side plate. If you are sharing the vegetables with other people, transfer your serving from the side plate

---

ENJOYING FRENCH FRIES

At home or out with friends, your fingers will do very nicely, but at a business meal use your fork instead of your fingers.

---

to your dinner plate. Usually, the dish will come with a serving utensil, but ask for one if it does not.

CAN YOU SHARE A TASTE? Unless you know the person well, avoid sharing food entirely especially in a business setting. If you do know the person well or your host offers to share a bite and you don't want to refuse, either hand your fork to the person, who can spear a bite-size piece from her plate and hand the fork back to you, or (if the person is sitting close by) hold your plate toward her so that she can put a sample on the edge. Don't be tempted to hold a forkful of food to somebody's mouth or reach over and spear something off someone else's plate.

IS IT ACCEPTABLE TO SOP UP SAUCE WITH BREAD? Don't do this at a business meal unless the host says this is acceptable or does it himself—in which case it's okay. Remember, don't hold the bread in your fingers and push it around in the sauce. Instead, break off a piece of the bread spear it with your fork, and then dab the bread in the sauce and eat it.

WHAT IF YOU DON'T LIKE THE FLAVOR? It happens: You're served a beautiful, carefully prepared dish, and you take one bite and don't like it at all. Maybe it has blue cheese in it, and you can't stand blue cheese.

Don't make a fuss or comment. Simply eat the other food on the plate. If the host says something to you, reply that you appreciate the effort that went into making it, but it's not for you. At a restaurant, don't ask the server to bring you something different—you ordered the dish, so now it is yours. (See also, "When the Waitstaff Asks for Food Orders," page 198.)

WHAT IF THE FOOD HAS SOMETHING WRONG WITH IT? In this case, ask the server to take it back. It's perfectly acceptable to expect to get what you ordered. Perhaps you wanted your meat medium-well-done and it came out rare. The kitchen will either fix the problem and then return that food to you or bring you another serving.

Dessert

SHOULD YOU USE A SPOON OR FORK TO EAT PIE WITH ICE CREAM? It's your choice. You can use either a fork or a spoon or both—the fork for the pie, and the spoon for the ice cream.

WHAT ABOUT FRESH FRUIT? While fruits like grapes, cherries, and whole strawberries can be eaten directly with your fingers, don't simply pick up larger fruits like apples or peaches and take a bite out of them. Quarter large fruit with your knife, remove the seeds or pit, then pick up a section and eat it. Generally, fruit will be served ready to eat with a spoon or fork. Use a spoon for fruits such as berries and a fork for fruits that are easily speared, such as melon cubes or banana slices.

WHAT IF YOU DON'T WANT COFFEE? Simply tell the server when he asks. Don't turn your cup upside down on your saucer. At banquets and large events, there are times when different servers will repeatedly ask if you want coffee. The easiest thing may be to let one of them pour a cup and then leave it. That will stop the interruptions.

WHAT DO YOU DO WITH A TEA BAG? If you are served tea in a cup with a saucer, simply place the tea bag on the saucer. If you are served it in a mug, place the tea bag on your dessert plate (or other nearby plate at your place setting). If you don't have a plate available, place the tea bag in the bowl of your spoon. Or you can ask the server for a saucer when she serves you the tea in a mug. Do not, under any circumstances, place the tea bag directly on the tablecloth. You should also forgo winding the string around the tea bag to squeeze the tea bag dry.

CHAPTER 17

DECODING THE TABLE SETTING

While your basic knowledge of table manners (see Chapter 16) is critical to your success at a business meal, knowing how to decode the intricacies of the table setting will help you be a more confident and comfortable dining participant. Instead of worrying about which fork to use or why you have two knives at your place setting, you can be engaging in conversation with the other participants. The confidence you show allows other people to focus on what you have to say rather than what you are doing—increasing the likelihood that they'll feel comfortable doing business with you.

Place settings vary greatly depending on the formality of the event or the locale. Settings can also be traditional or inspired by a local custom. Traditionally, utensils are positioned with forks on the left side of the plate and knives and spoons on the right. Sometimes the waitperson may bring your utensils wrapped in a napkin, however, leaving you to position them yourself.

Regardless of the formality of the event or the place where it's being held, most likely the table will be set with any number of utensils, glasses of different

shapes, and an assortment of other items. The easiest way to become comfortable approaching a table setting is to learn the function of all the different items—and then to learn how those items have been arranged quite thoughtfully for your use. (See also *Emily Post's Etiquette,* 18th edition, and www.emilypost.com for more information, illustrations, and videos on table settings, holding utensils, resting and finishing positions of utensils, holding glasses, and pouring wine.)

THE FORMAL PLACE SETTING

Large business events or high-end restaurants are the most likely places to encounter formal table settings, complete with a full array of drinking glasses and flatware. Even for the table-savvy, a refresher briefing on table settings can be extremely helpful.

Plates

At formal occasions, you'll often have several plates at your place from the very beginning: a service plate, the large plate at the center of the place setting (also known as a charger or a place plate); and a bread plate

The Formal Place Setting

(just above the forks and slightly to the left). Small first-course and salad plates will be brought out by the server as needed and then set on the service plate. Your dinner plate will replace the service plate when the main course is served.

Glassware and Napkins

The most common glasses you're likely to see are the water glass (placed just above the knife) and one or two wineglasses (placed just to the right of the water glass)—the larger one for red wine, the smaller for white. At more formal table settings, there may be additional glasses: the cylindrical champagne flute, which is better at keeping the wine bubbly than the saucer-shaped champagne glass of old and, occasionally, a sherry glass, a small, V-shaped glass.

The napkin, either folded or rolled and inserted into a napkin ring, will be to the left of the forks or in the center of the service plate. Napkins that have been decoratively folded (such as in a fan shape) are sometimes set inside the water glass.

Utensils

Utensils should be limited to what is needed for a meal.

The traditional place setting is managed from the "outside in," meaning you use the utensils at the outside of the setting for the course you are currently eating. Note: If you do not eat a course, when the server removes plates for that course, she will remove your unused utensils. That way you have the utensils for the next course at the outside of the setting.

A Typical Formal Place Setting

Let's take a closer look at a full formal place setting, starting at the outside and working in. On the left of your place setting, you'll find the following:

FISH FORK. This fork appears in a place setting when a first course of fish is served. It is at the outside left of the place setting, since it is the first fork used.

SALAD FORK. This smaller fork is likely to be set to the left of the dinner fork, meaning that the salad will be served *before* the entrée. It will be set to the right of the dinner fork, next to the plate, if salad is served *after* the first course.

DINNER (ENTRÉE, OR PLACE) FORK. This largest of the forks in a place setting is used to eat the entrée and accompanying side dishes.

And on the right side, you'll find these items:

OYSTER (SHELLFISH) FORK. This small utensil is used for oysters, shrimp, clams, and similar first-course shellfish. It is the *only* fork placed on the right side of the place setting, to the right of the spoon(s) and sometimes resting in the bowl of the soupspoon.

SOUPSPOON OR FRUIT SPOON. If soup or fruit is being served as a first course, this spoon is the outside utensil on the right side of the plate.

FISH KNIFE/SALAD KNIFE. This smaller knife is positioned to the left of the soupspoon/fruit spoon and to the right of the dinner knife. The fish knife has a curved blade; the salad knife a straight blade.

DINNER KNIFE. This large knife is used for the entrée and is placed just to the right of the plate.

STEAK KNIFE. If you have ordered beef or game, this knife might be brought out by the waiter as a replacement for the dinner knife.

Here are some other utensils at your formal place setting:

BUTTER KNIFE. This small knife is placed across the edge of the bread plate. It is replaced there after each buttering.

DESSERTSPOON AND DESSERT FORK. At most formal meals, the dessertspoon and dessert fork are brought in just before dessert is served. Sometimes, at a meal hosted at home, they are paired and placed above the dinner plate from the beginning of the meal. The handle of the fork points left and the handle of the spoon points right. The spoon is usually placed above the fork.

A CHALLENGE TO YOUR DINNER PARTNER

Tradition has it that the sharp edge of the knife should always point toward you and not away from you. In times past, knives doubled as weapons and cutlery. Pointing the sharp edge or the sharp tip of the knife at another diner was perceived as a threatening gesture. So, at the table, always have the sharp edge of the blade point in or toward yourself in respect of that tradition.

TEA OR COFFEE SPOON. This small spoon is presented to the diner at the end of the meal, when coffee and tea are served.

DEMITASSE SPOON. This very small spoon is served on the saucer with demitasse coffee or espresso.

THE INFORMAL PLACE SETTING

There's no mystery to setting a proper table—especially an informal one, which calls for fewer utensils. The basic rule: Utensils are placed in the order of use, from the outside in toward the plate. A second rule, although with a few exceptions: Forks go to the left of the plate, and knives and spoons go to the right.

The typical place setting for an informal three-course dinner includes these utensils and dishes:

TWO FORKS. A large one (the dinner fork) for the main course and a smaller one for a salad or appetizer. If the salad is to be served as the first course, the small fork goes to the left of the dinner fork; if the salad is served after the main course, then the smaller (salad) fork is placed to the right of the dinner fork.

DINNER PLATE. Usually there are no dinner plates on the informal table when diners sit down.

ONE KNIFE. The dinner knife is set immediately to the right of the plate, its cutting edge facing inward; it may be a steak knife depending on the main course. If the appetizer or salad requires a knife, a smaller knife should be set either to the left or right of the dinner knife, depending on when the course is served.

SPOON(S). Typically, just one spoon for soup or dessert is set in an informal place setting. It goes to the right of the knife.

GLASSES. A water glass and one wineglass (or two, if two wines are being served) are placed at the top right of the dinner plate. If wine is not a part of the meal, the goblet can be used for water or iced tea or not set at all.

NAPKIN. A folded napkin is placed in the center of the place setting or to the left of the forks. Alternatively, the napkin can be placed under the forks.

Other dishes and utensils are optional, depending on the menu or the style of service, and may include the following:

THE SALTCELLAR

If you encounter a saltcellar (a small open dish) rather than a traditional shaker, use the accompanying small spoon to salt your food. If no spoon comes with the cellar and you are sharing the cellar with others, dip the tip of your unused knife, which has a stainless-steel blade and will not be corroded by the salt, into the salt and deposit a little mound of it on the edge of your dinner plate. Then you can take a pinch of salt between your thumb and forefinger to sprinkle on the food. If you have your own personal cellar at your place setting, taking a pinch of salt with your fingers shouldn't raise any eyebrows.

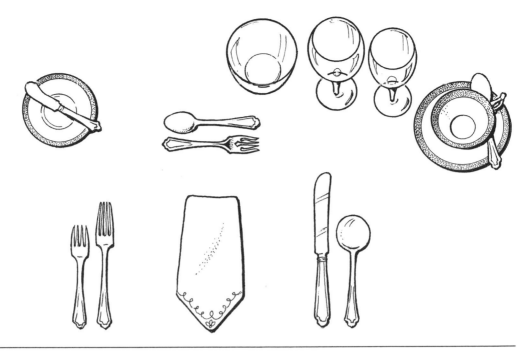

The Informal Place Setting

BREAD PLATE WITH BUTTER KNIFE. The bread plate is placed above the forks, with the butter knife resting across the upper edge.

DESSERTSPOON AND DESSERT FORK. These can be placed either horizontally above the dinner plate (the spoon at the top and its handle to the right; the fork below and its handle to the left) or beside the plate. If beside the plate, the fork goes on the left-hand side, closest to the plate; the spoon goes on the right-hand side of the plate, to the left of the soupspoon.

COFFEE CUP AND SAUCER. If coffee is served during the meal, the cup and saucer go to the right of the knife and spoons. If it is served after dinner, the cups and saucers are brought to the table at that time.

GLASSWARE

Aside from the water goblets and wineglasses on the table, cocktail, liqueur, or punch glasses may be used at various times during the meal, with a server bringing them out as necessary. The following is a guide:

WATER GLASS. It may be a bowl-shaped glass with a stem or a highball glass. The usual capacity is 10 ounces or slightly more.

ALL-PURPOSE WINEGLASS. A straight-sided glass with a capacity of 6 to 9 ounces may be used for both white and red wine. It is filled three-quarters full or less.

RED WINE GLASS. The classic bowl has a slight tulip shape. Although the total capacity is 8 to 10 ounces, the glass should be filled only to the widest point of the bowl.

WHITE WINE GLASS. This differs from the red wine glass by having straight sides and a smaller capacity—5 to 8 ounces. It is filled three-quarters full or less.

CHAMPAGNE GLASS. Called a flute, this cylindrical glass has replaced the traditional saucer-shaped coupe because it keeps the champagne bubblier. It holds 5 to 7 ounces.

PLACE CARDS AND SEATING

You should expect to see place cards at formal dining affairs. If there is a place card for you at your table, do not change the location of your seat so you can have a "better" seat or sit with a friend. In fact, there is a standard protocol regarding who sits where. As with introductions, "importance" comes into play, regardless of gender. Tradition says that a guest of honor (not necessarily someone for whom the party is given but sometimes a person of rank instead) is always seated to the host's right, with those lower in the business hierarchy seated progressively farther down the table.

If this arrangement seems shockingly undemocratic, keep in mind that top executives and foreign visitors often adhere to protocol and expect the same of everyone else. In any event, that some seats at the table are better than others is rarely apparent to other guests.

When there are no place cards, be wary, especially if you are a junior member of the team, of taking the best seat in the house (the ones with the seat back to the wall or next to the host). Wait for the host to indicate where you should sit. If it is truly open seating, try choosing a place next to people you don't know. Make an effort to get to know them rather than safely sitting with a friend. The business meal is an opportunity to broaden your horizons and make new contacts.

CHAPTER 18
HOSTING OR PARTICIPATING AT THE BUSINESS MEAL

The decision whether to meet over breakfast, lunch, or dinner depends mainly on which of these meals best fits the time constraints of the participants. Also, take into account what you wish to accomplish. A breakfast gathering, for example, may be ideal if the aim is a quick, straight-to-the-point meeting—while evening is undoubtedly the best time for a more leisurely paced business meal.

THE BUSINESS BREAKFAST

A breakfast meeting has real benefits: Many people are at their sharpest early in the morning. As with lunch, the timing of a morning meeting helps it stay short and focused. Unlike lunch, it barely interrupts the workday, if at all. Plus, breakfast is less costly than either lunch or dinner.

A business breakfast can be held at any location that is handy to both host and guest: a restaurant or coffee shop, a hotel dining room, or perhaps a private club. If it's convenient for all concerned, guests can even be invited to breakfast in the host's office. Putting out a selection of Danishes or muffins and coffee,

tea, or juice requires little preparation and lends the meeting the affable touch of an away-from-the-office meal. Business is discussed once orders have been taken or as soon as attendees have helped themselves. Let the host or meeting organizer start the discussion.

THE BUSINESS LUNCH

Lunch is the traditional workhorse of business meals. Because the participants have to return to the office, the meeting stays relatively short and focused. There are other advantages as well: Unlike a business dinner, lunch is faster-paced, it doesn't cut into someone's personal time, and it doesn't raise the issue of the inclusion of a spouse or significant other.

The typical business lunch lasts from just over an hour to two hours, but a participant who is on

> **TIP:** At a breakfast or lunch meeting, the business part starts after orders have been taken, and let the host or organizer initiate it.

a tight schedule shouldn't take this for granted. Let the host know at the time of the invitation about any known conflicts or time constraints. If a last-minute conflict arises that could affect how long you can stay, you should say so at the start of the meal. "Before we get busy, I have a meeting at the office at one thirty—bad luck, I know, but it was called at the last minute." (Note: The excuse should be real, not made up.)

THE BUSINESS DINNER

Whether it takes place at a table for two or involves a large group, the business dinner is considered a premier event and is generally oriented toward camaraderie. Because no one has to get back to work, dinner also proceeds at a more leisurely pace. The longer time span also can be an advantage when doing serious business is the goal of the dinner.

Dinner is the most meaningful meal with which to mark special occasions—the retirement of a long-time employee, for instance, or the welcome of a new client into the fold. It is also the more logical choice when entertaining a business associate from out of town who is traveling with his or her spouse.

On occasions such as these, business will doubtless come up as a conversational topic, but the aim is usually the strengthening of relationships, with an eye on mutual rewards to be gained in the future.

THE MOST IMPORTANT THING TO DO: PARTICIPATE

The ultimate reason for getting your table manners down cold is that it leaves you free to concentrate

TIP: It is up to your host to decide if business is discussed. If business is going to be discussed, the host should wait until after the main course has been finished before bringing it up. The time before the main course is completed is for diners to get to know one other and build the relationships.

RESTAURANT PREMEAL PREP FOR THE HOST

When you're hosting a business meal, a little careful preparation will go a long way toward making the occasion a success. Here are some thoughts to keep in mind:

CONSIDER YOUR GUEST'S TASTE. If possible, find out whether your guest(s) especially likes or dislikes certain foods or ethnic cuisines. You can simply ask when extending the invitation; or a call to an assistant might give you the answer. You could also give your guest a choice of two or three restaurants. If you're hosting a group, choose a restaurant with a wide-ranging menu so that everyone invited can find something to his or her taste.

CHOOSE A RESTAURANT YOU KNOW. Even a popular new place with the hottest chef in town may have snail-like service or be so noisy or cramped that it's hard to carry on a conversation. Also keep in mind that if anyone is going to travel fairly far to reach the restaurant, it should be you and not your guest.

INVITE WELL IN ADVANCE. You or your assistant should arrange any business meal at least a week in advance, so that the guest can fit it into his or her schedule and have time to prepare for the meeting.

MAKE IT CLEAR THAT YOU ARE—OR AREN'T— THE HOST. So there is no question about who's footing the bill, ask, "Will you be my guest for lunch?" On the other hand, if you and the other person see each other frequently and have developed a close working relationship, you may want to go take turns paying or split the check. If so, a simple "Do you want to have lunch next Tuesday?" or "How about if we split lunch next week?" is a graceful way to suggest this.

TELL YOUR GUEST WHAT TO EXPECT. So that your meal partner can prepare and bring along any pertinent materials, be specific about business topics you want to discuss and how deeply you'll be delving into them.

RESERVE A TABLE AHEAD OF TIME. Failing to reserve a table risks getting the meal off to a late start—a real problem at lunch or breakfast, where time is at a premium. If you have a preference for seating—a spot that's especially quiet, for example—make your request when you make your reservation.

RECONFIRM WITH YOUR GUEST. This is a must, saving real embarrassment later on. Call on the morning of a lunch or dinner; if you've scheduled breakfast, call the day before.

---

on the most important task of any social or business meal, which is to participate. This means being focused on the conversation. You don't want to dominate the discussion, particularly if you are a junior member of the party, but you do want to make comments and ask questions. When the table isn't involved in a general discussion, it's tempting to talk just to one person next to you. But don't give into that temptation. Instead, be a good conversationalist with the people seated on *both sides* of you.

As the host: It's your job to steer the conversation, to suggest topics for discussion, and to make sure that everyone at the table is given the opportunity to be part of the general conversation.

RSVP

As a guest, the first thing you should do is respond to the invitation. If it's a phone call, you can simply accept, reject, or delay your answer on the spot. But if it's a voice mail or written invitation, you have an obligation to respond in a timely manner

1. To let the person know you received the invitation

2. To let the person know who is coming and who is not as the number of people accepting affects planning for the meal

Best practice is to contact the host within twenty-four hours of receiving an invitation.

ARRIVING FOR THE MEAL

The impression you make on your business meal companions starts when you first arrive at the restaurant. In fact, the very first things you do are critical to the success of the rest of the meal. When you start off on the right foot, you can quickly focus on building a great relationship. Start off on the wrong foot, on the other hand—by being late, for example—and you'll have to spend valuable time trying to recover rather than building rapport.

Preplanning

DON'T BE LATE. It's appropriate that this is the first rule of table etiquette. It may also be the most important. Arriving even five or ten minutes late leaves a bad impression; any later than that sends a clear message of carelessness and thoughtlessness.

DRESS APPROPRIATELY. Show respect for your host or guests by looking sharp. This is a time to dress up a little rather than dress down. Pay attention to grooming as well—clean hands and face, combed hair, fresh breath.

TIP: You can always remove a jacket or tie, but having to put one on, or borrow one from the club or restaurant, does not make a good impression.

When You Arrive at the Restaurant

WAIT. If your host hasn't arrived, wait in the lobby or waiting area for her. Don't go to the table or the bar and wait there. However, when the establishment is filling up and you, as a guest, are advised by the restaurant staff that it is best to sit at the table, it's okay to do so, but don't order anything until your host arrives.

As the host: Wait for your guests in the lobby. If some of your guests have already arrived, you should wait in the lobby only until the time of your reservation. Then proceed to the table and have the maître d' or waiter escort the late guests in when they arrive.

TABLE LOCATION. The host deals with table selection. As a guest, do not check out the table location and then suggest that the waiter or maître d' change it. Your host may have asked for that table for a reason; it's not up to you to second-guess her.

As You Approach the Table

LOOK TO THE HOST FOR SEATING ASSIGNMENTS.
Your host may have a specific seating arrangement in mind, so you should let him point you in the right direction.

As the host: Be prepared to indicate where people should sit. The guest of honor—the client, the talent, the CEO—should sit in the best seat at the table. Usually that is one with the back of the chair to the wall so that the guest of honor won't be sitting in a traffic area with waiters and busboys passing behind him or her. Once the guest of honor's seat is determined, the host should sit to his or her left. Other people are then offered seats around the table. If spouses are with you at a business dinner, the male host has the female guest of honor sit to his right while the female host has the male guest of honor sit to her right.

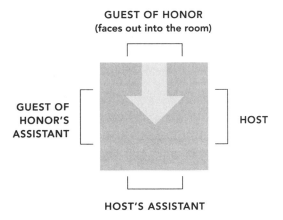

GUEST OF HONOR
(faces out into the room)

GUEST OF HONOR'S ASSISTANT

HOST

HOST'S ASSISTANT

Placing Orders

Once you are settled in your seats, you can expect a waiter to come to the table to take drink orders. The waiter may also bring menus if the food hasn't

SHOULD A MAN HOLD A CHAIR FOR A WOMAN?

When sitting down for a business breakfast, lunch, or dinner, a man can easily make the error of trying to hold a chair when the woman doesn't want him to—or just as easily make the mistake of not holding a chair for a woman who believes such a gesture is an integral part of the man's role, whatever the setting. What to do?

Communication is the answer. As the man and woman approach the table, the man simply says, "May I get the chair for you?" Now she can make the choice: "Why, yes. How thoughtful. Thank you." Or "No, thank you, but it was nice of you to offer." Instead of a confusing, awkward moment, the situation passes without a hitch, and they can focus on building a better relationship—which, after all, is the primary purpose of any business-related encounter.

THE BLACK NAPKIN: WHAT IS IT?

Most restaurants set their tables with white cloth napkins. Unfortunately, sometimes these napkins can leave white lint on people's dark/black clothing. To remedy this situation and not frustrate patrons, many restaurants stock alternative black napkins. If you are wearing dark/black pants, skirt, or dress, you can request a black napkin instead of the white one if you see them employed by other patrons. Some waitpersons will recognize the situation and ask you if you prefer a black napkin before you request one.

A word of caution: Alcohol creeps up on you unexpectedly. Nobody goes out to a business meal thinking that they are going to get drunk and do things for which they will have to apologize the next day.

But it happens. And when it happens, business can be lost, jobs put in jeopardy, and promotions put on hold.

The only way to avoid the problem is to follow the one-drink rule: Limit yourself to one drink during the evening or don't drink at all. The days of the "three-martini lunch" and "keeping up" are over. People choose not to drink for personal, health, or religious reasons, so being a nondrinker or limiting yourself to one drink is readily understood in the business world.

already been ordered for you. Now you are faced with your first decision: Do I order an alcoholic beverage or not? Consider carefully the benefits of the "one-drink rule" and what you'll do if the waitperson asks you for your drink order before asking your host or others at the table.

WHEN THE WAITSTAFF ASKS FOR DRINK ORDERS

WHAT SHOULD YOU ORDER? If you are a junior executive at the table and a waitperson asks you first, err on the side of caution and order something nonalcoholic. As the first person to order, you don't want to be in the situation where you are the only person at the table to order alcohol. If others, including your boss, order an alcoholic drink, you can either quietly change your order before the server leaves the table or opt not to have alcohol before the meal. Either choice is appropriate.

As the host: When the server asks for drink orders, let your guests know your expectations for drinking at the table. By saying, "While John is deciding, I'll order. I'd like an iced tea, please," the host is signaling that this is a working meal where drinking isn't appropriate. Conversely, by saying, "While John's deciding, I think I'd like to order a Pinot Grigio," you've given your guests the signal that they may feel comfortable ordering something alcoholic if they wish. If you don't drink but would like your guests to be comfortable ordering cocktails, you can say, "John, please feel free to enjoy a glass of wine or a drink."

WHEN THE WAITSTAFF ASKS FOR FOOD ORDERS

WHAT SHOULD YOU ORDER? As you look over the menu, keep in mind four important guidelines to ordering:

1. Order medium-price dishes, not the most expensive items on the menu.

2. Know the food you are ordering. This isn't the time to be adventuresome and order something you've never had before. Not only might you not like it, but it also might be difficult to eat. You want your focus to be on the people at the table, not on your food.

3. Order food that is relatively easy to eat. Linguine with clam sauce is very tasty, but eating linguine is a challenge that's nearly certain to leave your tie or blouse spattered with sauce.

WHAT DO YOU DO WHEN . . .

It's the rare restaurant meal during which at least one perplexing question doesn't arise ("Should I ask for a to-go bag?") or a glitch doesn't occur ("Is that something in my water?"). These pointers will help you cope:

THE FOOD ARRIVES AT DIFFERENT TIMES. At a business meal with a colleague or client, if your dining partner's food arrives before yours does, encourage her to eat it before it gets cold. Likewise, if your own food has to be sent back for any reason, urge her to continue eating. If you are at a meal with your boss or other people who rank higher than you, wait for a signal from them that you may begin eating. At a meal with people of similar rank, if three or so people at a large table receive their food and there is a wait for the rest, they may start eating so their meals won't get cold. At a buffet, it is acceptable to start eating once you have returned to the table.

YOUR FORK OR GLASS IS UNCLEAN. If your yet-to-be-filled water goblet seems soiled or any utensil is unclean, don't announce it to everyone at the table—especially the host. The next time a server stops by, discreetly ask for a replacement.

YOU SPOT A HAIR OR A BUG. If there is a speck floating in your water or a hair or a pest of some kind in your food, simply refrain from drinking or put down your fork until you catch the attention of the waiter. While it's probably impossible to keep the rest of the table from knowing something is amiss, try your best not to cause a fuss.

YOUR DINING PARTNER HAS FOOD ON HIS FACE. If you notice a speck of food on someone's face (or, in the case of a man, on his beard), you're doing him a favor by subtly calling attention to it. Do so with a light "Oops, there's something on your cheek." You might signal silently by cocking an eyebrow while using your index finger to lightly tap your chin or whatever part of the face is affected. As prevention for yourself, the occasional dab with your napkin will help ensure no wayward bits of food stay put for long.

YOU HAVE SOMETHING STUCK IN YOUR TEETH. Occasionally running your tongue over your teeth may let you know whether you have food (the usual culprits: spinach or poppy seeds) caught between your teeth. You can try using your tongue to remove it. If the food stays put, it may be better to excuse yourself from the table and go to the restroom to remove it rather than worrying about it for the rest of the meal or rummaging around in your mouth with your finger or napkin.

YOU'RE FINISHED, BUT YOUR PLATE IS STILL HALF FULL. At a business meal, forget the to-go bag unless you're dining with a good friend and the two of you are splitting the check or paying for your own meals. Even then, don't load up the bag with butter, sugar packets, or any other ancillary items.

---

4. Opt for something you can eat with a fork and knife. While a burger might be on the menu, unless you plan to eat it with your fork and knife, it's best to leave "hand food" for a nonbusiness meal.

As the host: Give your guests guidance about ordering. You can let them know what you are ordering. For instance, ordering an appetizer says to the others that it's okay for them to order one, too. Point out items on the menu that you recommend. You're at a steak house and you know the New York strip is fabulous. By mentioning it, you give them permission to order it.

WHAT IF THE MENU IS PREARRANGED AND YOU HAVE A SPECIAL DIETARY NEED? If, for instance, you are a vegetarian, it is perfectly acceptable to quietly ask the waiter whether there is a vegetarian selection available. If there isn't, you can ask him or her to bring you a plate without meat on it. The key is to make your request known without making a big deal out of it.

IS THERE ANYTHING YOU HAVE TO ORDER? As you listen to other people ordering, you realize they are all having an appetizer, a salad, and a main course—while all you want is a main course. There is no requirement for you to order any course you don't want. Simply order the main course and politely say "No, thank you" if you are asked whether you want anything else.

The Meal Is Over

When the meal is through, you still have several things to think about as you prepare to leave the restaurant, mainly taking care of the check.

WHO PAYS? The person who does the inviting does the paying. If someone invites you to lunch and the server places the check on the table, don't make a grab for it. Let the person who invited you have the opportunity to pick up the check and deal with it.

WHAT IF THE SERVER GIVES THE CHECK TO YOUR GUEST? This is an especially common situation when the host is female and the guest is male. In this case, be firm and say, "Jim, I invited you to lunch. Please let me have the check. I'll take care of it." A simple way to prevent this from happening, whether you are male or female, is to let the server or maître d' know in advance that the check should be brought to you. Alternatively, near the end of the meal, excuse yourself to the restroom. On your way there, give your credit card to the waitperson and ask her to prepare the check, add a 20 percent gratuity, and have it ready for you to sign on your way back to the table. It's particularly nice when the check never comes to the table and you can keep your focus on your guests instead of figuring the tip and paying the check.

Whoever is paying the bill should check to see if a gratuity has already been included in the total—something that is standard procedure at some restaurants especially for groups of six or more people. You'll often be tipping not only the waiter but other restaurant staff as well. (See also "How Much to Tip," page 300.) Tip according to these general guidelines:

- **THE WAITER OR WAITRESS.** Twenty percent is the standard tip today.

- **HEADWAITER/CAPTAIN.** You may occasionally have a head waiter or captain take your order while your waiter will bring the food to your table. As tips are pooled you can leave a single tip. Or if you choose to tip the head waiter or captain separately, give the waiter the standard tip and add a 10 percent captain's tip separately on your receipt.

- **THE SOMMELIER, OR WINE STEWARD.** An appropriate tip is 15–20 percent of the cost of the bottle. If you buy more than one bottle, you tip on the total cost of the wine, not just the first bottle. If you tip a sommelier directly, remember to deduct the cost of the wine from the bill before figuring the tip for the waitstaff.

- **THE BARTENDER.** Tip 15–20 percent of the tab or a minimum of $1 per glass of beer or wine and $2 per mixed drink.

- **THE COATROOM ATTENDANT.** A tip of $2 is appropriate for the first coat and $1 more per additional coat.

- **THE PARKING VALET OR GARAGE ATTENDANT.** A $2–$5 tip is paid when your car is returned.

DO YOU WRITE A THANK-YOU NOTE? In addition to saying a gracious "thank you" to the host at the end of the meal, a note sent by the guest serves as a thank-you for the meal and an enjoyable time, as well as a confirmation of any decisions that were made. A follow-up phone call could be made instead, but a note has two advantages: It doesn't interrupt the other person's day, and it comes across as warmer and more gracious. (See "Expressing Thanks," page 202; and "The Thank-You Note," 262.)

As the host: A gracious way to reconnect with your guest is to send him a note the next day thanking him for joining you for lunch. It's an opportunity to reiterate a point or two you made during the meal and to gently let him know you will be contacting him soon.

DO YOU HAVE TO RECIPROCATE WITH AN INVITATION? Does inviting someone to a business lunch, dinner, or breakfast mean they are obligated to reciprocate tit for tat? Not necessarily. The rules governing the reciprocation of invitations vary from situation to situation.

- You are not expected to repay an invitation to a strictly business meal (especially one charged to an expense account), no matter who invited you—a customer, a client, or your boss. But you may certainly do so if you have continuing business together.

- A client who is entertained by a salesperson or supplier is not expected to return the invitation, even if his or her spouse or family was invited.

- Do return social invitations from coworkers and other business associates, whether they've extended the hand of friendship to cement a business relationship or you simply enjoy one another's company away from the office. But you have some leeway in how you reciprocate. For example, you could have your colleague join you for a cookout at your house as your thank-you for a restaurant dinner.

Expressing Thanks

A handwritten thank-you note sent the next day to express your appreciation for being hosted at a business meal accomplishes two things: It sets you apart from your competition, in cases where they don't send notes, and it gives you a reason to make another contact with your host—which keeps you at the top of her mind in a very positive way. (See "Do You Write a Thank-You Note?," page 201.)

CHAPTER 19
BUSINESS EVENTS

Business events can run the gamut from formal business dinners to casual office parties. But no matter what form an event may take, the general purpose remains the same: to connect and spend time with your colleagues and business associates. In order to accomplish this, you need to be able to focus all your attention on the people you're with. Being familiar with the protocol of various business affairs—whether they're held in a restaurant, a club, a private home, or your own offices—leaves you free to partake in and enjoy the event, and be confident in your ability to handle any social or etiquette issue that comes your way.

Business events can take many forms, but what they all have in common is a measure of sociability above and beyond that of an office-bound meeting or appointment. In fact, at some events business matters may not be mentioned or referred to at all. Your own behavior at these events is every bit as important as the fellowship they foster. Remember: These are the particular times when your conversational abilities, your self-assurance, and your table manners are all on display at once. Bear in mind, too, that your manners reflect on the company you represent. Hand-in-hand with your ability to converse and connect with others is knowing how to use the cutlery and eating your food with skill and finesse. (See Chapters 16 and 17.)

THE ART OF MINGLING

Don't be embarrassed to introduce yourself to someone. When another person is standing alone, this ritual poses no problem (see "Introducing Yourself," page 133); introducing yourself into a group conversation is slightly more difficult.

- Try to find a group that has at least one person whom you know.

WELCOME A STRANGER

The next time you are at a business event and a stranger tries to join your group, welcome him. Treat that person just the way you would like to be treated if you were in his shoes. Greet the stranger by offering your hand and introducing yourself first and then the others in your group. "Hi, I'm Jake Wrench. This is Maria Sinclair and Sarah Rodriguez."

- Approach with a smile on your face.

- Nod a greeting as you join the group.

- Introduce yourself at the next small break in the conversation: "Hi, I'm Aaron Sanders from MNO."

> **TIP:** Remember, attendees at business functions expect that strangers will be introducing themselves, so they're likely to be open to meeting you.

What do you do if you don't know anyone in a group and you wish to join? Approach the group, but be careful not to interrupt a person in midsentence. Instead, wait and listen for a break or for the person to finish his or her thought. Then make eye contact with one of the group, reach out your hand, and introduce yourself: "Hi, I'm Erin Shaw from LMN."

Here are some other tips for mingling:

- Put aside any shoptalk of the critical or confidential kind. It can be tempting to relax when you're outside the office, but remember to keep your professional demeanor. A slip of the tongue can come back to haunt you—plus you never know who might overhear.

- Avoid telling off-color jokes and, with strangers, it may be best to avoid telling any jokes at all. What you think is tame or funny, another may think is offensive or fail to see the humor.

- Keep your voice volume to a reasonable level, so as not to add to the din.

- Keep a close rein on drinking. Nothing has as much potential to undermine a good impression as alcohol. Remember that a relatively small amount of alcohol is enough to loosen the tongue. You may be undone to wake up the next morning and realize that you were, in fact, simply blabbering on. (See also the box "The One-Drink Rule," page 198; and the box "One Too Many," page 211.)

EVENT EXPECTATIONS

Regardless of the type of event, there are certain common expectations and protocols of which you should be aware. Certainly, engaging in small talk and "working the room" are vital parts of being successful. But so, too, are responding to invitations, punctuality, toasts, and the thank-you.

RSVP

It is mandatory to respond when you receive an invitation to an event. Too many people fail to adhere to this most common courtesy. Event planners, hosts, and hostesses describe the lack of RSVP as the single most frustrating part of organizing and putting on events.

Be on Time

As a rule, punctuality is stressed more at a business affair than at a purely social one. For a business dinner or event, arriving on time is not only expected—it's also the considerate and smart thing to do. Even if the event is a large reception at which guests' arrival times are fluid, it's still wise to arrive close (within five to fifteen minutes) to the time stated on the invitation.

HOW TO BE AN EXPERT AT SMALL TALK

Some people seem to be natural talkers. They approach total strangers and are immediately able to be completely at ease and conversational. How do they do it? Here are six tips to help you be a great conversationalist:

1. **BECOME FAMILIAR WITH VARIOUS TOPICS.** Read newspapers and newsmagazines to be knowledgeable about world and national events. Read your local paper and tune in to the local news as well. Peruse general-interest magazines and watch television newsmagazine programs to keep up to speed on what's happening in entertainment and the arts. Know which sports teams are succeeding and which aren't. Make it your assignment to be a generalist and to know something about a lot of different things. You don't have to be an expert on all topics, just have enough information to open the door to conversation.

2. **ASK PEOPLE THEIR OPINIONS.** Before you go to an event, list three or four questions you can ask at the start of a conversation, couching these questions in terms of asking a person for her opinion. People love to be asked for their views on any number of subjects. All you have to do is ask a person for her opinion, and you've given her permission to talk away.

3. **STAY AWAY FROM CONTROVERSIAL TOPICS.** Politics, sex, money, religion—don't go there. These are potential argument starters that can backfire on you.

4. **LEARN ABOUT YOUR HOST(S) AND THE OTHER GUESTS.** If possible, find out their interests ahead of time. Do they enjoy skiing, traveling, hiking, collecting stamps? You can ask colleagues or your boss, or if the event is in your host's home or office, take note of pictures and other objects for clues.

5. **LISTEN. LISTEN. LISTEN.** Become a great listener by focusing on the person who is talking and tuning out the other distractions around you. Stand up straight and show your interest by making eye contact, nodding, and occasionally paraphrasing what the other person is saying to show you understand. (See also "The Art of Listening," page 235.)

6. **PRACTICE. PRACTICE. PRACTICE.** Try talking to people who are "safe" (that is, non-business-related) conversational partners: cabdrivers, people at the supermarket checkout counter, your seatmate on a plane. Becoming comfortable with these folks will help you to be comfortable with strangers at company functions, where the small talk may really matter.

Making Toasts

At many large parties, toasting the guest of honor or the host with wine or champagne may be expected. (It's fine to toast with any liquid—even water.) Anyone considering making a toast should prepare beforehand, if only to mentally rehearse what you plan to say so as not to fumble the words. Unless your toast has been designated as the principal one of the evening, keep your remarks short and to the point. The principal toast is a small speech of sorts, and it should be composed in writing and rehearsed by the speaker in advance. A glance at your notes is acceptable, but try to speak as extemporaneously as possible.

The protocol points of toasting:

- The host is the first to toast, attracting the crowd's attention by standing and raising his or her glass; tapping on a glass with a knife should be considered a measure of last resort.

- At formal occasions everyone, except the person being toasted, stands.

- The guests respond to the toast by taking a sip of their drinks—but never draining the glass.

- The person being toasted does not drink to himself.

- After the toast, the person who is being toasted rises, bows in acknowledgment, and says thank you. He may also raise his own glass to propose a toast to the host, the chef, or anyone else he sees fit to so honor.

- At private or small informal dinners, it is acceptable for everyone—toaster and toastee included—to remain seated.

Is a Thank-You Note in Order?

The answer to "Should I write a note?" is that it's never wrong, but it might depend on the type of event or the way the invitation was issued. (See "The Thank-You Note," page 262.)

THE CORPORATE EVENT

Corporate events range from small gatherings to large formal or semiformal events put on by the company, or events attended by company representatives. These can include affairs from company picnics and barbeques (possibly potlucks) to events for which the dress is black tie and no expense is spared. The purpose may be to launch a new product, to garner publicity, or simply to create goodwill among employees, prospects, and/or clients. Large or small parties limited to the company's employees might mark an anniversary or toast the retirement of a prominent executive. These events may be held at traditional off-site venues like the ballroom of a hotel, a full-service party facility, a private club, or the CEO's home. A museum, a park, a historic house, a theater, or a botanical garden are some examples of typical but nontraditional venues.

Invitations

When planning a company-sponsored event, it's important to set the right tone from the start, beginning with your invitations. The employee in charge of drawing up the guest list should start by consulting every department head to make sure no key clients or customers are overlooked. Once the list is compiled, the invitation is written so that recipients are

[corporate logo]
In honor of The Zerfoss Group, Limited
Judith Alexander
CEO of Alexander & Anderson Industries
requests the honor of

Mr. and Mrs. Richard Bailey's

presence at a cocktail buffet
on Wednesday, January twelfth
two thousand eighteen at
six o'clock
The St. Regis Hotel
New York City

RSVP Card Enclosed

Black Tie
Dancing

Formal invitations are set in a traditional serif typeface; the numbers are spelled out. For a more personal touch, the example shown here includes the recipients' names, which are handwritten.

[CORPORATE LOGO]

Gordon & Muse Advertising
James Evans
President
requests the pleasure of your company
in honoring
Molly Collins of Blacklock Products, Inc.
at a Cocktail Buffet
on Tuesday, September 29
6 to 9 P.M
Atlanta Botanical Gardens

RSVP by September 15
Lily Yarborough
Gordon and Muse Advertising
71 Pine Dr.
Atlanta, GA 30305
(404) 555-1212 / l.yarborough@gama.com

Business Dress

An invitation for a more informal event uses numerals for the date and time as well as a less traditional typeface. Information for RSVPs—name, address, and telephone number—is also supplied.

told everything they need to know before accepting and attending. For a large event, invitations should be mailed six to eight weeks in advance; for cocktail parties or less formal events, three to four weeks in advance.

Whether your invitation is formal or fanciful, the envelope addresses can be typed or printed, though for more formal events handwritten is preferred. Use a fountain pen, not a ballpoint. Don't go overboard with showy calligraphy, and never use address labels. The invitation should include the following:

- Who is hosting (usually the senior officer, CEO, board of directors)

- The purpose of the event

- The date, time, and location

- The style of dress

- Whether there will be food and/or dancing

- How to reply

- Other enclosures, such as a map or instructions about transportation routes and the availability of parking; or an admission card, which will note whether the invitation admits one or two.

A formal invitation is traditionally engraved or printed in black on quality white or ecru paper and is usually a double-fold card. But unless the company's image calls for such formality, lighter designs that set the mood are perfectly acceptable.

Is There a Receiving Line?

Because a receiving line speeds introductions, arranging one is a smart choice for functions of more than sixty people. Guests who arrive too late and find the line disbanded must accept not only that they may not meet the host but also that the host may never know they were present.

It's fine for guests to hold a drink while waiting in a receiving line, but they should set their glasses down before it is their turn to go through. Servers may be standing by with trays for that purpose. If you see none, then find a nearby table and deposit your glass. Once the moment arrives, shake hands, introduce yourself if you do not know the host, and briefly exchange a few pleasant words with each member of the line. Be careful to avoid lengthy conversations so as not to hold up those behind you.

Greeting the Host

If the party is large and has no receiving line, the host may appoint two or three people as introducers. Introducers make sure that every person who arrives eventually meets the host at some point during the evening. Do make it a point to locate the host on your own if necessary, so that you're able to briefly say "hello" and thank him or her for the hospitality. At some large, formal functions without a receiving line, an MC or other designated person announces and introduces the host and honored guests to the entire party.

If it's impossible to thank the host—this can happen, particularly at the party's end, when he may be swamped by people trying to do the same—write a note the next day (see "The Thank-You Note," page 262) in which, along with your thanks, you express your regrets that you weren't able to thank him in person.

Drinks and Hors d'Oeuvres

At a business event, predinner drinks and hors d'oeuvres will more than likely be served—from a bar, buffet tables of various kinds, trays carried by waiters who circulate through the room, or any combination thereof.

The Bar

If there is no true bar on the premises, bartenders will serve from a table, mixing drinks or pouring wine or beer as requested. Before ordering, be certain it's your turn. If you're in doubt, ask anyone who arrived at the bar or drinks table before you whether he or she is being served.

Waiters, too, will probably be passing through the room, taking drink orders and serving drinks. Don't make a beeline to a waiter to grab a glass or place your order; either wait patiently until the waiter comes your way or go stand in line at the drinks table or bar. Keep the drink in your left hand so that your right one doesn't get cold or wet from holding a drink and is ready for handshakes. When your glass is empty, look for a sideboard or tables where used glasses and plates are deposited; if you can't find one, ask a waiter or the bartender what to do with your glass and then thank him when he more than likely takes it.

Passed-Tray Food Service

This may be the only food service offered, or it might be combined with self-service at a buffet table or stations. Waiters circulate with trays of hors d'oeuvres, stopping to offer them to guests.

Finger foods and bite-size hors d'oeuvres can usually be taken in your fingers and eaten directly. The server will also have small napkins that you can take to clean your fingers.

What to do with food skewers or toothpicks after you've eaten an hors d'oeuvre? There's usually a small receptacle on the waiter's tray for used ones. If not, hold any items (including drink stirrers) until you find a wastebasket or can give it to a passing waitperson. Don't place used items on the buffet table unless you see a waste receptacle there.

The Buffet Table

Hors d'oeuvres and canapés may be set out on a buffet table, with guests picking up plates and helping themselves to both finger foods and dishes that require a fork. Take small portions, and don't return for plateful after plateful; at this stage of the party, the food takes a backseat to the people around you—not the other way around.

Food Stations

Food stations are smaller tables set up in strategic locations around the room. Each holds a different kind of food—filet, turkey, shrimp, pasta, ethnic specialties, vegetarian dishes. The idea behind this arrangement is to create several shorter lines instead of one long one. Often referred to as "heavy hors d'oeuvres," food stations can take the place of a sit-down dinner or a buffet table. Don't be surprised if there is no other food service than the food stations.

At the Table

At a large sit-down dinner, there is a good chance you'll be seated with strangers—but only momentarily, since making introductions all around is essential. People seated together at a table always introduce themselves to each other as a sign of courtesy and respect, even when they expect to conduct separate conversations. At a small table—six or fewer people—you can shake hands with each person. At a large table—seven or more people—shake hands with the people near you who are easy to reach, and then acknowledge the people farther away with a nod, a smile, and a "Nice to meet you" greeting.

PLACE CARDS AND MENU CARDS

The presence of place cards on the table—or, alternatively, a card given to you listing your table number—means that the host has decided where you are to sit. It is extremely rude to alter the arrangement of the cards or switch them with those from another table as a means of getting closer to the head table, obtaining a better view, or sitting with friends or colleagues. Hosts take great care with seating plans and your seat was chosen with you in mind and your tablemates are people your host would like you to meet.

OPEN SEATING

If no place cards are on the tables, guests may sit wherever they choose. At the same time, they should never seat themselves without asking those already at the table for permission: "Do you mind if I join you?" or "Excuse me—are these chairs taken?" (A chair tilted against the table is the traditional signal that the place is reserved.) If you're given the go-ahead, introduce yourself, along with your spouse or significant other, as you sit down.

When Dinner Is Served

No matter how elaborate the table setting or service may be, remember that the way you treat those around you—not to mention your sparkling wit and tasteful attire—will be remembered far longer than your misuse of a fish fork. Table manners are a vital concern, but they should never be fretted over so much that your anxiety overshadows your comfort, sense of ease, and ability to be a good conversationalist. (See also Chapter 16 and Chapter 17.)

OFFICE PARTIES

Office parties serve to build morale and showcase the company. They, especially the informal variety, also provide employees with the chance to become better acquainted and perhaps to establish real friendships—an important side benefit in a time when the workplace has become the principal venue for social contacts.

Invitations

Whoever in the department is in charge of the party (or, if it's a company-wide affair, the company event planner) will send a memo on paper or by email to each staff member. An example: "The production department will celebrate a good year and the holidays on Friday, December 23, in Meeting Room C. All work stops at 3:30 P.M. sharp for refreshments and a buffet. Will you join us?" When the party is to be held in a restaurant, hotel, or club, more formal invitations may be sent.

Spouses, significant others, and dates may or may not be invited. If spouses and significant others are included, then single employees should be given the opportunity to bring a guest as well. The party invitation should be clearly addressed to invitees by name: "Mr. and Mrs. Brown," "John Brown and Sarah Foster, " or "Ms. Greene and Guest."

Office Party Dress

At a party held after work in the workplace, both men and women can simply show up in the clothes they have worn all day. Or they may opt to change into fancier dress in anticipation of the event.

At an office party held outside the office, both men and women generally change from work clothes into dress clothes. Because this is a business affair, overly dressy or revealing clothing is in poor taste. It's advisable to err on the conservative side. If you're unsure about the proper attire, check with a colleague who has attended these off-site social events in the past or with the event coordinator.

OTHER OFFICE OCCASIONS

Employers and employees often throw parties when someone leaves or retires, when a coworker is going to be married or about to have a baby, or when individual achievements are to be honored. Office sports teams traditionally celebrate with postgame get-togethers. Many businesses also have regular birthday parties for workers.

Special-occasion parties may be given by the boss or by the staff; they should include the entire department and possibly any special friends of the guest of honor who work in other areas of the company. While spouses and significant others of the guests aren't necessarily included in such events, especially

TEN TIPS FOR THE HOLIDAY OFFICE PARTY

Q. I'm new to the workplace and this is my first holiday office party. What should I know?

A. The holiday office party is a time for everyone in the office to kick back and enjoy each other's company. This type of business social event is more social than business. Yet, as fun and party-like as it is, there are situations that can trip you up and cause you to have to apologize the next day. That's something you want to avoid. Here are ten tips for navigating the office party (whether it's your own, a client's, or a vendor's party) and making it an event to remember positively.

1. When the invitation is issued, make sure to RSVP as soon as possible but definitely by the "reply by" date.

2. If the invitation includes a significant other, be sure to ask him first and then let the organizer know if you're attending alone or with him.

3. Give your significant other the heads-up about what to wear so she can plan accordingly.

4. Arrive on time. There's nothing worse than being late and looking like you either don't care or are disorganized.

5. Be sure to introduce your significant other to your boss and to the people you work with, especially if she's never met any of them. It helps her to put a face to the names of the people that you talk about when you come home.

6. Don't abandon your significant other. Make an extra effort to include him in the conversation.

7. Avoid talking about work. This event is a time to get to know your coworkers on a more personal level—discover their hobbies and interests. You may find out the person you haven't connected well with at work shares your interest in movies, cycling, or music.

8. Beware of drinking too much. Often the office party starts right after work. You may not have eaten much all day. Long before you're over the limit, alcohol can cause you to say or do things that you might regret or have to apologize for the next day. Avoid that possibility completely by not drinking at all or by adhering to a one-drink rule for the evening. (See the box "The One-Drink Rule," page 198.)

9. Enjoy the food, but eat in moderation, and most certainly don't ask if you can take a "to-go bag" home.

10. Thank your boss and the organizer of the party twice, once at the end of the party when you find them and say good-bye and the second time when you send a thank-you note to each of them. (See "The Thank-You Note," page 262.)

if the party is given within regular office hours, the spouse or partner of the guest of honor should be invited.

These informal parties may be given in the office, a conference room, or the cafeteria. Alternatively, a lunch or dinner can be held at a nearby restaurant. A staff committee or the boss's executive assistant is usually designated to handle the details, including time, place, menu, entertainment, and gifts. Company sponsored parties should be funded by the company, not with contributions from employees. If you are the party organizer, make sure you have established who is paying. If it is an event for which employees are paying, say a baby shower for a coworker, then it's a good idea to collect party funds before you begin incurring out-of-pocket expenses.

There are several important rules to remember when planning a special-occasion party:

- Clear the event with your superior. Be certain that the scheduled date and time don't conflict with important business.

- Reserve the party space well in advance.

- Don't impose your party planning on people who are trying to work. Be considerate of your coworkers' time and job responsibilities.

- Don't overdo your party privileges; a weekly—or even a monthly—party is simply too much. So is throwing a workplace bridal shower for your coworker's sister's granddaughter.

SHOULD I SEND A THANK-YOU NOTE AFTER A HOLIDAY OFFICE PARTY?

Q. I thought company parties are a way for the employer to say "thanks" and therefore not something the employee should have to send a thank-you for attending. If the parties are hosted and paid for by a boss or colleague out of their own pocket, then a thank-you is expected. How are the attendees to know? It is always okay to send a thank-you if you are not sure and to err on the side of graciousness?

A. A holiday party is a gesture of appreciation. Your question points out that the office party is the boss's way of saying thank you to the employees and as such you wonder if a thank-you really requires a thank-you in return.

One manager told us that following a holiday party the support staff wrote thank-you notes, but that his upper-level reports did not, subtly implying that the company "owed" them the party or dinner. The manager has a decidedly negative opinion of those who didn't write and, conversely, an excellent opinion of the support staff who did show their appreciation. Looked at this way, there is only an upside, and sending a thank-you note becomes the obvious choice. It is an opportunity. Take it.

CHAPTER 20
SOCIALIZING OUTSIDE OF WORK

Not all business events are business activities. There are times when you will be invited by a business associate to accompany her to a nonbusiness event such as a golf outing, a sporting event, the theater, or a social club. Typically, these events do not include business discussions but instead are a great opportunity to get to know your host and to build a relationship on which business can more easily be conducted later.

Most important, even in these situations, remember that how you represent yourself and your company and your actions will affect possible future business, jobs, and promotions. Focus on the relationship and the point of the event. Be a congenial guest, always demonstrating a positive attitude. You can't turn off who you are or who you represent just because it is one minute past five o'clock.

AT COUNTRY CLUBS

The country club is a mainstay of business entertaining—a place where company executives invite clients or customers to enjoy an afternoon in the sun, and their guests return the favor. Country club golf courses, tennis courts, and swimming pools have been the scene of countless friendly competitions between business associates of one kind or another. Indeed, it's long been said, only partly tongue-in-cheek, that more major business decisions are made on the green than in the executive office. In reality, talking business on the course is considered ill mannered and a breach of golf etiquette. Use the on-course time to get to know the other people in your foursome. If you are going to talk business, do it at the nineteenth hole or at a meeting sometime later.

The country club is also an ideal place to entertain even when no sports are involved: The setting is superb, and there is usually only one sitting at lunch and dinner, which means you can linger at your table for as long as you like. When sports are the central

---

TIP: Always send your host a written thank-you note. (See "The Thank-You Note," page 262.)

activity, lunch or after-game cocktails are usually on the agenda to ensure that there is ample time to talk, whether about business or life in general. Lunch may be the climax of a morning spent on the golf links or tennis court, or the prelude to an afternoon game—assuming that no more than a half day is to be devoted to the outing.

Who Pays for What?

Many businesspeople simply take turns paying for everything at their respective clubs. At other times, certain customs are common when a match or event is taking place:

- A one-day golf or tennis tournament typically has an all-inclusive price that includes greens fees and a meal; there is an understanding that the host usually takes care of the cost.

- Clubs have varying policies for charging greens fees and cart or caddie fees to a member's account. In some cases, it is mandatory that all fees be charged to the member's account. In this instance, the polite guest will offer to take care of the tips for the caddies. (Ask the member or the caddie master what an appropriate amount is at that club.) At the time of signing in, the guest should at least offer to cover his or her greens fees. The host will probably decline the offer. The best way to reciprocate is for the guest to extend a return invitation to an event at the guest's home course or club.

- Ahead of time, ask your host about tipping policies for starters, back room boys, locker room attendants, and other club staff.

- Some clubs have a no-cash policy. In this case, your host knows he or she will take care of the expenses. Inviting your host out another time is one way to balance the ledger.

THE SPORTING GUEST

Whenever you're invited to a business associate's country club for a round of golf or a game of tennis, don't automatically accept unless you (1) know the rules of the game and (2) can play well enough not to slow others down. Being honest about your knowledge and abilities will allow the host to decide whether to suggest another sport or to limit the occa-

---

THE CELL PHONE AND THE COUNTRY CLUB

A guest answered a call on his phone at a club with a strict policy against cell phone use. Later, the hosting member was admonished that he was responsible for his guest's failure to follow the rules and he was in danger of being assessed a $100 fine.

Your best course of action when visiting another club is to turn your phone off as you get out of your car. Not put it on vibrate or anything else. Turn it off.

"But I have an app for gauging distances on my phone. May I use it?" you ask. Before you turn on the phone to use the app, check with your host and/or the pro shop to find out if using a phone in this way is acceptable. If it is, be sure to put it on vibrate and turn the volume all the way down.

sion to lunch. Remember, this is a friendly competition: Play your game, don't throw a match, and don't gloat if you win.

If you feel perfectly secure with the sport of choice, accept with enthusiasm. On the day of the game, make a point of arriving early—you don't want to be the person responsible for getting things off to a late start. As a token of your appreciation, you might bring a sleeve of golf balls or a can of tennis balls.

Dress appropriately and even more conservatively and carefully than you might at your own club or course. Be aware of any dress requirements. A tennis facility may require all whites. A golf club may have a strict collared-shirts-only requirement or a no-cargo-shorts rule.

AT MEMBERS-ONLY SOCIAL CLUBS

Members-only social clubs are places where tradition is important: They typically feature dining rooms with a first-class menu and expert staff, a lounge, a library, and various fitness facilities. Unless a private room is rented for the purpose, business is not conducted in the public areas of most of these clubs. Many have bylaws specifying that business-entertainment reimbursements from a member's company are not allowed; all expenses, including dues, must be paid personally. While business may be discussed, using an item of business paraphernalia, be it a smartphone or a folio pad, is usually off-limits.

When a guest is invited to a members-only club, he or she should ask the host what to wear; many have strict dress codes. For the host's part, it's never out of line for him or her to mention the type of

dress expected at the club at the time the invitation is extended. Guests who are unaware of the club's customs will be grateful for the information; showing up badly overdressed or underdressed could end up embarrassing both parties.

Hints for guests:

- Don't strike out on a solo tour of the club. You should enter the library or lounge only if escorted by your host.

- If you have drinks at the bar before dinner, limit yourself to one. Also, remember that confining your drinking to soda or water is perfectly fine. (See also, "The One-Drink Rule," page 198.)

- Don't be stiff, but do behave impeccably. Your actions reflect not only on you and your company but on your host as well.

AT SPECTATOR SPORTS

A host who invites a business associate to a spectator sport of any kind—tennis, hockey, baseball, or basketball—should always order tickets in advance. In addition, if the budget allows, reserving a car for transport to the stadium or arena will prevent any parking problems. During the event, the host should offer to purchase all food or drinks. The guest, on the other hand, will be wise to do the following:

- Take your cues from your host. Ask him what he's wearing before you put on your jeans.

- Have a beer or other alcoholic beverage only if he does.

- Whether you support the same team or not, show your support by cheering, not jeering.

- If you are rooting for different teams, don't gloat if your team wins.

- Volunteer to buy a snack and a drink for your host and any other guests.

- Don't take it on yourself to yell at obnoxious spectators.

- Stay in your seat while play is going on. If you must leave, get up and return when there is a break in the action.

AT THE THEATER

For culturally minded businesspeople, an invitation to a play, a concert, an opera, or a ballet is an excellent choice, particularly when spouses or partners are included. Starting or ending the evening with dinner makes for an even more memorable occasion. Unless you, as the host, are already familiar with your guests' tastes in such things, ask which kind of entertainment they favor; people who love musical comedies might find it hard to stay awake at the ballet. Once you determine what best fits the bill, purchase tickets in advance and ask for the best seats possible; if that means settling for the peanut gallery, try another show of the same type.

Arriving and Being Seated

It is mandatory to arrive on time—even more so if you are picking up the tickets at the box office. Most theaters hold reserved tickets until twenty minutes before curtain time and then sell them on a first-come, first-served basis. Also remember that along with talkers, late arrivals are a major source of aggra-

vation for theatergoers. At most performances, latecomers aren't seated until a scene change occurs—no exceptions.

Traditionally, there is protocol for seating, starting with the host taking the aisle seat after his guests have entered the row. If there are two couples, the spouse/significant other of the guest sits next to the host, and vice versa. When there are several couples, the host's spouse leads the way into the row and the others follow, with women and men alternating. If they have to pass others in the row, they should do so facing the stage and also excuse themselves to each person they move past.

Any able-bodied person who is seated should stand up to let new arrivals into the row.

Noise

Talking or whispering during the show is frustrating for those around you. Watch the show; talk later. Any theatergoer carrying a phone should keep it turned off during the performance. Doctors and other audience members who must be on call are wise to bring a device that signals with a light or a silent vibration. If your watch makes a regular, audible beep, turn it off or leave it at home.

Applause

If you're not sure when to clap, wait to see what everyone else does; little is more embarrassing than breaking out in applause while the rest of the audience stays quiet.

DINING OUT WITH COWORKERS

Since your coworkers may be personal friends as well, it's normal to socialize with them at lunch, after work, or at home. Letting your hair down in a social setting should be done with care. In a relaxed atmosphere—especially if alcohol is present—tongues are loosened and defenses are dropped. Don't make the mistake of believing that off-the-premises conversations are also off the record. If you pass along a rumor, take potshots at an absent coworker or boss, or reveal a workplace confidence, you can be sure that what you said will get back to the office, sometimes faster than you do, even when you are among friends. Also remember that talking shop or even just swapping work stories may be easy and fun for you and your coworker, but the others you are with could feel very left out of the conversation.

When you have lunch or dinner out with coworkers, the big question is generally who will pay and how much. The best way to ensure fair payments is for the group to reach an agreement before placing any orders. Ideally, everyone in the group agrees to split the bill evenly. On the other hand, if Lucy eats like a bird and everyone else is up for the surf 'n' turf, ask your server to bill Lucy separately, and split everyone else's bill even-steven. If the orders look to vary significantly, request separate bills for everybody. Bar bills should be divided among the drinkers only.

It is inappropriate to ask a server for separate checks at the end of the meal or to invite a newcomer to dine without making it clear at the outset that everyone is splitting or responsible for his or her own check. Be conscious of what you order compared to your companions; if you owe substantially more than they do, take the initiative by speaking up and paying the piper. If someone offers to put the whole bill on her credit card in order to save time, be sure to pay her back immediately. People tend to forget small debts, but it is rude and thoughtless to expect a generous coworker to come around with hat in hand when her credit card bill arrives. Finally, if it's the Thursday before payday and you really can't afford a meal out, politely ask your coworkers for a rain check rather than borrowing from someone.

At the Bar

In groups of three or more, the smart course is to agree in advance to split the total bill at the end. When a coworker agrees to be the designated driver for your group, show your appreciation and pay collectively for his or her iced teas, colas, and bar snacks.

CHAPTER 21
BUSINESS ENTERTAINING AT HOME

Inviting people to your home is a more personal way to entertain. Home events can range from the formal sit-down dinner party for your boss or client to a barbecue for coworkers and their families. Though the purpose of a business party is primarily social, as the host you'll want to stay on your toes even more than usual. For better or worse, your spouse or significant other, your home, and your entertaining style all reflect who you are. How well you carry off a social gathering is part of a larger picture. Showing your proficiency in getting the party organized, keeping it running smoothly, and staying cheerful and relaxed will inevitably strike your business associates favorably.

INVITING GUESTS

How formal should your invitations be? This varies according to the situation: If you're inviting, say, a client who's in town for a few days, a simple phone call is sufficient. Try to organize the date before your client arrives in town. The same goes for inviting local clients or customers—although in this case you

should include spouses or partners, too. Depending on the circumstances, you may also want to invite a few nonbusiness friends, whose presence will lessen the likelihood of your company or professional field ending up as the evening's one and only topic.

THE SIGNIFICANT OTHER'S ROLE

It goes without saying that when business-people entertain at home, their spouses or significant others need to do their part to get things organized and make guests feel comfortable. Since there will undoubtedly be a great deal of job-related chat among people they may or may not know, partners should appear interested and make it a point to listen and to ask questions. At the same time, they should also feel free to discuss their own professional or personal interests. It's always helpful for the significant other when names, roles, and relationships of the guests are reviewed before the party.

A written invitation is more appropriate when inviting your boss (or others of high rank), unless the two of you have developed such a close working relationship that it would seem artificial to stand on ceremony. Inviting others with whom you work presents the special challenge of not offending those coworkers or associates who aren't invited. Either keep the invitation private or invite those who weren't on the list the last time you entertained.

Some executives and managers who entertain regularly make a practice of inviting each staff member to their homes once a year, one at a time; others choose to throw parties with small groups; still others may prefer to invite the entire staff at once. Just remember to invite the person's significant other as well.

SETTING THE TABLE

Although a formal dinner calls for a tablecloth, at informal dinners place mats are also an option. A bare table is a modern alternative for an informal meal. (See also "The Formal Place Setting," page 187 and "The Informal Place Setting," page 190.)

China and Flatware

If your good china and flatware won't stretch to meet the number of guests, you have three options. The first is to set a second, smaller table with your everyday dinnerware or even with dishes and place settings borrowed from a relative or friend. Alternatively, you can rent china, glassware, and flatware or purchase a "catering set" of varying sized plates, glassware, and flatware that will serve for all your guests.

The third choice, appropriate for truly casual affairs, is to mix and match. After all, making sure that every piece of china and flatware matches is less important than the conversation and the quality and presentation of the food. Worn or chipped plates, cups, and saucers won't make the grade, but using different patterns or colors is acceptable as long as they're somewhat in keeping with the occasion. For example fine bone china paired with plastic glassware is not a good match. The idea is to create a harmonious whole.

FORKS

Follow the order of the letters in the word FORKS, left to right, to help you remember how to set a table correctly.

- The *F* stands for forks and indicates that the forks in your place setting go on the far left of the setting.
- The shape of the *O* represents the dinner plate which is to the right of the forks.
- The *R* (which is just to the right of the *O*) indicates that all the other utensils go to the right of the dinner plate.
- Next comes *K*, which stands for *knife*, and indicates that the knives are set just to the right of the dinner plate.
- Last comes the *S*, for *spoons*, which are placed to the right of the knife or knives.

That's it: Remember FORKS, left to right, and you'll always place the utensils in the correct position in the place setting.

Centerpieces, Candles, and Other Accoutrements

The centerpiece is just that: flowers or something ornamental placed in the exact center of the table. Fresh flowers are the obvious choice, but an arrangement of silk flowers, bowls of fruit or ornamental vegetables, or a striking antique or contemporary glass ornament are also options. Whatever you choose, make sure the centerpiece doesn't stand so tall that your guests can't see over it.

Candles, generally, are placed symmetrically on either side of the centerpiece. If you want to create a more dramatic mood by using candles as the only source of light, you might want to place one above each place setting so that guests can clearly see their food. While white or ivory is the traditional candle color for a formal dinner, color isn't an issue at informal affairs: Simply choose whatever you think looks best with your china and linens.

> **TIP:** Scented candles should never be used at the dinner table because they will compete with the scent of the food.

Place a set of salt and pepper shakers at each end of the table. At even the most informal meal, these two basics should be a cut above those you use every day. If you are seating eight or more, consider additional pairs of salt and peppers on each side of the table, one for each set of two diners.

HOSTING A SIT-DOWN DINNER

Whatever cuisine or serving style you choose, there are a number of things to consider beforehand—most obviously, your available space and the tastes of your guests. While it's nice to try to accommodate in-

---

YOUR GUEST IS . . . VEGAN, PALEO, ALLERGIC . . .

Catering to your guests' food issues may present enough of a problem to keep you from ever inviting anyone—personal or business—to your home. If you are a vegetarian, you don't have to include meat in your menu for the meat eaters. You'll design a menu full of nutritious, tasty vegetarian dishes so your meat eaters will be okay going without. But if you like to prepare meat or fish, organize your menu so you have several nonmeat dishes to make a pleasant meal for a vegetarian.

If a guest has informed you of an allergy, you can try to accommodate him or her or make sure the person knows if a dish includes something problematic so he can avoid it. Simply say "No, thank you" if you are served something you cannot eat.

If a guest has a strict dietary issue, and you know ahead of time, you can offer to prepare a plate especially for him or her. Or the person can offer to bring his or her own so as not to create a difficulty for you. Some people with severe allergies, dietary restrictions, or strict food preparation constraints just may not be able to accept invitations to meals prepped in a home kitchen. Try not to take offense, and find another way or venue to entertain this guest.

vitees' idiosyncrasies and special food needs, remember that the goal is to offer enough variety to please everyone, without tailoring the meal to any one person's particular needs.

Single Hosts and Hostesses

A single man or woman might consider asking a friend to act as a cohost. This makes sense because some of the guests (the business associates) will already be acquainted, whereas many of the rest (mostly significant others or dates) will not be. With two hosts sharing the duties of refilling drinks, replenishing food trays, and chatting with guests, the flow of the party is likely to be smoother than if one person tries to do everything by him- or herself. The point isn't for you to have a date to your own party but rather to have someone you can turn to for help. Another option would be to hire a caterer and free yourself of the serving duties so you can focus on facilitating conversations and guiding the evening from a social standpoint.

Meeting and Greeting

Your significant other isn't expected to join you as you greet arriving guests at the door. Instead, introduce him as soon as the opportunity arises. After greeting a guest, introduce him to people who have already arrived. Then return to the door to greet the next guests.

Before-Dinner Drinks

When predinner drinks or cocktails are being served, plan for dinner to start about an hour later than the time specified on the invitation. If drinks are not part of the plan, you should still wait twenty to thirty minutes before serving the meal; this allows time for any late arrivals to say their hellos.

Don't forget to provide soda, juices, and mineral water for those who want to forgo alcohol. If you offer snacks or hors d'oeuvres, keep them fairly light so that they don't compete with the meal. At the same time, be sure to replenish hors d'oeuvres as necessary.

Last-minute checklist: Before you call your guests to dinner, the butter and condiments should already be on the table, the water glasses filled, any candles lit, the plates warming in the oven or on a hot tray, and the wine either in a cooler beside the host or within reach of the table.

LATECOMERS

The before-dinner drinks have been enjoyed and the olive pits dispatched to the wastebasket, and the first course is ready and waiting. But a guest (or guests) has yet to show up. What to do? Etiquette says that the host waits for fifteen minutes before serving dinner. That's it. But take note: Tacking on even a brief grace period shows inconsideration to the many for the sake of the few. When the latecomer finally enters the dining room, he should immediately apologize to the group at large for delaying the meal. If the grace period has expired and the meal has begun, the tardy one is served whatever course is being eaten at the time. If this happens to be dessert, the host sees to it that he gets a plate of the main course from the kitchen as well. The gracious host also refrains from making sarcastic or negative comments to the latecomer.

The Call to Dinner

When the time to eat arrives, simply say, "Dinner is ready. Shall we go in?" Suggest to guests who are holding drinks that they bring them to the table, and then lead the way into the dining room.

Plan your seating arrangement ahead of time while you're setting the table. If you're not using place cards, then indicate where people are to sit as you approach the dining area. (See "As You Approach the Table," page 197; and "Place Cards and Seating," page 192.)

When guests are seated at two tables, it's only polite that the host sit at one table and the hostess or cohost at the other. If there are more than two tables, ask a good friend to act as a surrogate host at his or her table, seeing to it that wine is served and plates are refilled.

Serving the Food

As the host, you can let the guests pass the serving platters to one another as they serve themselves. Alternatively, you could place dishes on a sideboard, buffet-style, and let guests serve themselves before being seated. Another option is to hire someone (a few senior high school or college students, for example) to serve dinner and clean up. They could also pass hors d'oeuvres before the meal.

If the meal includes two or more sauces or other condiments, it's smart to serve these in a divided dish or on a small, easily managed tray; this ensures that they are passed together and that the guests see all the choices.

When it comes time for dessert, your pièce de résistance can either be brought to the table on individual dessert plates or served from a plate or bowl set by your place at the table. In the latter case, the filled dishes are then passed to the guests.

Serving the Wine

The simplest way to offer wine at the dinner table is for you, as host, to do the pouring. Place the opened bottle on the table in front of you, preferably on a coaster or in a wine holder to prevent any drops from staining the tablecloth. At a small table, you may remain seated and pour for each person. At a larger table, you may need to stand and walk around the table, pouring for each guest. If you are entertaining a number of guests, a second bottle is placed at the other end of the table, with your spouse, cohost, or a guest doing the pouring and refilling. The person pouring should not ask guests to pass their glasses to him or her.

Clearing the Table

When it comes time to clear the table, never scrape or stack dishes; instead, remove them two at a time.

WHEN TO START EATING AT A BUFFET

At a sit-down dinner you should wait until the host asks you to begin eating or until the host picks up his fork and starts. But a buffet is different. If seating is casual and not at a table, you can start when you take your seat. If there are several tables to eat at, you can begin eating once you're seated as others may be at the end of the line and not returning for several more minutes. If you're all sitting together at one table, wait until several people, say three or four, are seated and then begin eating.

TIP: Regardless of the situation, the kind thing for a host to do is to announce to people as they get their food that they should please begin eating when they sit down.

After the main course, salt and pepper containers, salad and bread plates, condiment dishes, and unused flatware should be removed as well.

For a larger party, you may want to arrange ahead of time for a guest who is a good friend to help you with the clearing. If other guests offer to help, appreciate the offer and then decline it: "No, thank you—really." Your other guests should be just that—guests—and remain at the table.

After-Dinner Coffee

Simply have three choices ready—a pot of brewed coffee, a pot of decaffeinated coffee, and a pot of hot water with a choice of tea bags, including both herbal and regular. Don't forget the milk or cream and sugar.

After-Dinner Drinks

Offering after-dinner drinks can bring an especially cordial touch to the evening's end. If you're serving coffee, a tray holding bottles of liqueurs, brandy, and Cognac—along with the appropriate glasses—may be brought in at the same time. Then ask each guest which he or she would prefer.

PLANNING AND HOSTING A BUFFET

There are several advantages to a buffet: For one thing, it lets hosts accommodate more guests than they can at a traditional sit-down meal. In addition, guests and hosts usually have more time to visit, since the meal can be prepared in advance and guests can serve themselves.

The menu for a buffet will depend partly on whether your guests will be seated at tables or dining

THE BOSS IS COMING TO DINNER

You may want to invite your boss and his spouse simply to introduce them to your family or to repay an invitation previously extended to you. If your boss—or any other guest of high rank from your company—is of the old school, keep the following in mind:

- If you and your boss don't socialize regularly at work, you'll probably feel more relaxed if you include a few other guests. Select people with interests similar to hers.

- Don't put on airs. Act normally, and entertain normally. Don't hire a caterer unless you would ordinarily do so. Don't purchase special tableware just for the occasion. Don't serve a hard-to-carve roast unless you know you can handle it. In other words, be yourself. Being gracious and interested will impress the boss far more

than trying to outdo yourself in a way that she, more than anyone, knows you can't afford.

- If you have small children, by all means introduce them to your guests, who will surely be delighted to meet them. After a few minutes have passed, however, let the children excuse themselves. If possible, hire a babysitter to help look after them so you can focus on your guests.

- If you work in the kind of highly traditional office where workers address a person of higher rank as "Mr." or "Ms.," don't suddenly switch to "Ralph" or "Susan"—either in the invitation or while chatting during the evening. You and your partner should shift to using first names only once you've been asked to.

---

from their laps. If the latter, choose foods that are easy to manage with a fork alone; also, avoid dishes that are soupy.

No matter what the seating arrangements are, steer clear of foods that have to be eaten just after being taken from the oven, such as soufflés. Beyond that, use simple common sense when planning the menu. For example, french fries get soggy over time, while stuffed potatoes do fine at room temperature. Another bit of common sense: When serving cheese, meat, or anything else that needs to be sliced, do all the slicing in advance so that the buffet line doesn't come to a standstill as guests take on this task themselves.

Setting Up

When ready to set out the food, stack the dinner plates at one end of the buffet table, marking the beginning of the line. Next comes the food: the main course, vegetables, salads, bread, and sauces and condiments. It's a good idea to place the main course—the fish or meat—after the side dishes. It's one way to be sure there is enough of the main course for all the guests. The napkins and utensils come at the end, so that guests don't have to juggle them while they're serving themselves their meals.

If your party is fairly large, set up two lines. If the room is spacious enough, place the buffet table in the center of the room with a line on either side. Or you can set up two lines on each end of a long table. Either way, guests will be able to get their food more quickly with two buffet lines.

The Food Is Served

When all the guests have arrived and the allotted time for drinks is over, announce that dinner is served. Your guests, who are always served before the host and hostess, should then form a line around the table, helping themselves to the buffet.

Buffet Beverages

If possible, place beverages and glasses on a separate sideboard or nearby table. If guests are seated at tables, place water glasses on the tables and fill them before guests sit down. Wineglasses should also be at each guest's place but not filled in advance. One or two opened bottles of wine can be placed on each table or on a separate side table and poured by anyone who chooses to. Or, as guests are seated, the host can offer to pour wine for them.

When iced beverages are served, stacks of coasters and cocktail napkins should be set out around the room so that sweating glasses won't leave rings on tabletops.

If coffee has been placed on the sideboard, guests may serve themselves at any time. Otherwise, the host or hostess takes a tray set with cups and saucers, a coffeepot, brewed tea, and cream and sugar into the living room to serve after dinner.

PART FIVE

COMMUNICATION

CHAPTER 22
THE GOOD CONVERSATIONALIST

No matter what field of business you're in, the way you speak is fundamental to how you are perceived. People who use incorrect grammar, who are indifferent listeners, or who talk mostly about themselves are seen in a less-than-positive light. Whether you're making a sales presentation or chatting with your supervisor, the ability to reach and influence a listener with your speaking voice is one of the most valuable assets you have.

Speaking poorly, on the other hand, can have serious consequences: Eighty percent of executives questioned in a study by a midwestern university cited a lack of communication skills—not technical expertise or overall performance—as the main reason employees were held back in their careers.

THE IMPRESSION YOU MAKE

Every time you speak, the listener is subconsciously registering the quality of your voice, your enunciation, your grammar, and your choice of words. Most often, it is only when one of these elements deviates from the norm that it's noticed—for better or worse.

VOLUME. It goes without saying that midway between loudness and softness is most desirable. An overly loud voice almost always annoys or unnerves other people, while a too-soft delivery can make you seem uncertain, vulnerable, or shy as well as difficult to understand.

TONE. A monotone flattens not only your message but also the listener's interest as well. Use inflection to put stress on the word(s) that are most important and add variety to your speech.

SPEED. The rate at which you speak is important. Fast talkers are hard to understand, and they frequently have to repeat themselves. Slow talkers can make the listener impatient.

ENUNCIATION. Don't swallow syllables, slur words together, or drop final letters. Dropping letters—the *g* in words ending with *-ing* being the prime example—should be reserved for informal talks among friends; when speaking over the phone or engaged in a business conversation, enunciate the entire word.

ACCENT. So long as your grammar and word usage are correct, you should never be embarrassed by a regional, ethnic, or foreign accent. Your accent is a drawback only when it's strong enough to hamper communication. With someone from outside your region, speak clearly and more slowly.

Grammar and Word Usage

Some grammatical rules have relaxed in recent years, more so in conversation than in writing. But don't be fooled into thinking that correct grammar no longer matters—it does. Because older generations, including bosses and upper-level executives, have had grammar drilled into them, they are more sensitive to misuse of language. When your message contains spelling, word choice, or grammatical errors, you present a sloppy image of yourself. If you're sloppy with something as basic as a communication, your client, prospect, or boss may wonder if you'll be sloppy with the critical work you are tasked with doing.

TWO COMMON ERRORS

Putting a preposition at the end of a sentence is no longer frowned on. For example, "That's the store I went to" is now preferred over the awkward "That's the store to which I went."

However, misuse of the subject (I, he, she, they) and object (me, him, her, them) is still incorrect. For example, saying, "Frank gave an assignment to Paul and I" is a very common error but still an error. The basic rules still hold fast.

Brushing up on grammar doesn't have to be a chore. Google will tell you the difference between *which* and *that* or *who* and *whom* the next time you face the choice in your writing. The dictionary is a helpful resource for correct usage, too. In addition, there are a number of good, basic references on grammar and writing. (For a list of useful titles, see "Look It Up," page 256.) Use these opportunities and resources to teach yourself the correct usage in a given situation.

Vocabulary

Having a good vocabulary doesn't mean using big or rare words in place of small ones, so avoid overusing the thesaurus; it's the ability to say what you mean clearly that matters. In most conversation, using *endeavor* for *try*, *conclude* for *end*, or *prognosticate* for *predict* sounds unnatural and forced. Strive instead for a vocabulary that's wide-ranging yet direct. Practice using new words to keep expanding your vocabulary, but focus on words that are recognizable to most people. Carefully chosen, descriptive words improve communication and leave the listener with a positive impression in the process.

Pronunciation

If you are unsure how to pronounce a certain word, or you hear someone pronouncing a word differently than you do, look the word up as soon as possible. A good dictionary will always include a written guide to pronouncing each word listed. Or visit the website Howjsay.com or any online dictionary where you can have the word pronounced for you.

Jargon

The world of business has done more than its share to inject jargon into American speech. "Corporate speak" is responsible for enshrining words such as *innovative*, *value-driven*, and *proactive* into everyday speech—while turning nouns like *impact* (as a replacement for *affect*), *transition* (for *change*), and *reference* (for *refer*) into verbs.

While many people think that using jargon makes them appear more professional, jargon tends to muddy language, robbing it of sharpness and power. Stating your thoughts in clear, descriptive terms is usually preferable to couching them in jargon—though not always. If, for example, everyone in your company uses a certain term—*media opportunity* for press conference—it's better to adopt its use.

Similarly, acronyms can cause trouble when readers or listeners aren't familiar with what the letters stand for.

Foul Language

A survey from TheLadders.com showed that use of foul language is one of the etiquette offenses that employers say would be most likely to cause them to fire an employee. While we all know not to walk around the office shouting a string of four-letter words, using inappropriate language is a mistake that many more people make than they realize. Even occasional swearing, say when you become emotional or feel justified,

GET IT RIGHT	
YourDictionary.com identifies one hundred of the most commonly mispronounced words including:	
Right Way	**Wrong Way**
across	acrost
Arctic	Artic
ask	aks
business	bidness
candidate	cannidate
foliage	foilage
jewelry	jewlery
library	liberry
masonry	masonary
mayonnaise	mannaise
percolate	perculate
prerogative	perogative
prescription	perscription
sherbet	sherbert
take for granted	take for granite

can get you into trouble precisely when you should be keeping your cool. Best practice is to swear off profanity completely in professional settings to avoid even the possibility of giving offense or of appearing as if you are out of control.

The question of what is truly bad language has evolved since George Carlin delighted in teaching us the seven words that censors won't allow on network television. It may seem obvious but there is gray area here that can get you into trouble if you are not careful. For one person the word *sucks* is a great descriptor to indicate something was bad. For others, use of the word itself is vulgar and inappropriate. Does

OMG mean "oh my gosh," or is it shorthand for taking the Lord's name in vain? Some people think this is the worst use of language imaginable and find it deeply offensive. For others, it is simply a common texting shorthand for expressing surprise that has caught on in daily speech. Because many people do feel strongly about these two types of language, you should be very careful using either of these terms in a professional context, whatever your personal feelings may be.

THE ART OF CONVERSING

Being a good conversationalist is less a matter of eloquence than of adequately hearing others out and getting your message across—a simple interaction that is vital to conducting business. In the 1937 edition of *Etiquette*, Emily Post wrote, "Ideal conversation must be an exchange of thought, and not, as many . . . believe, an eloquent exhibition of wit or oratory." She held that the secret to effective dialogue with another person was not cleverness but rather learning to "stop, look, and listen." "Stop," wrote Mrs. Post, means "not to rush recklessly forward"— that is, don't start talking merely for the sake of filling dead air. "Look" means to look at the face of the person to whom you are speaking. And "listen" means exactly that; it is, she said, "the best advice possible . . . since the person whom most people love . . . is a sympathetic listener."

Besides observing these timeless fundamentals, the pointers that follow apply equally whether you work in a less conventional workplace or in one that is more formal.

Q. Could you please address the regrettable habit that has sprung up, that of a reply of "No problem" as opposed to "You're welcome?" I am routinely getting this answer, particularly from the younger set, those whom I have just thanked for doing their job—the one they get paid for! "No problem" sounds insincere and insouciant. Of course I am a senior staffer at the company, so perhaps this is a change I should learn to accept. I hope not!

A. When you respond to a "Thank you" with "You're welcome," you are acknowledging the thanks and letting the person know you appreciate it. To say nothing when someone says "Thank you" to you is the equivalent of ignoring the person, and nobody likes to be ignored.

If you really do want to thank someone in return, saying "You're welcome, and thank you, too" is the best solution. Saying "You're welcome" first removes any implication that you are simply dismissing the person's "Thank you" by not acknowledging it.

"No problem" has wormed its way into the normal dialogue we experience with each other. We hear it from all ages of people, not just young people, and we're inclined to accept it as part of our language today. That said, the same advice holds true for a "No problem" or "It's nothing" response to a "Thank you." Precede it with a "You're welcome," and now it works perfectly well as a response.

Three Tiers to a Conversation

TIER 1—SMALL TALK

This is safe territory. You can talk about these topics just about anywhere, with anybody: sports, the weather, music, movies, celebrities. In fact, it is a good idea to cultivate interest in a few of these topics so that you have conversation fodder ready and at your fingertips. Read blogs, scan current headlines, or listen to the news while you make dinner or breakfast to stay abreast of current events, sports, pop culture, even the current forecast.

TIER 2—CONTROVERSIAL TOPICS

Politics, religion, and sex are all potentially controversial topics. People have strong and often differing opinions about them so they are best approached carefully, if at all. Don't assume others hold the same views as you do just because you work on the same team or went to the same college. Venturing too far or expressing your opinion too strongly on any one of these and you risk offending a colleague, boss, client, or prospect. There are plenty of other things to talk about, so why take the risk?

TIER 3—PERSONAL AND FINANCIAL

Family and financial matters are so personal that you should not ask probing questions about these topics or offer too much information about your own circumstances to colleagues or business associates. These are topics reserved for close friends, those you trust to respect your personal information. Avoid these topics unless your business relationship has developed into a true friendship, and even then, save them for outside your business relationship.

Know When to Hold Your Tongue

A conversation isn't about indiscriminately sharing everything that's on your mind. A good outcome can hinge as much on what you don't say as on what you do. Use some discretion. Just by thinking to yourself before you speak, "What am I going to say and why am I going to say it?" will help you avoid the rash and unconsidered statements that can get you into so much trouble. When you find yourself wondering if this is the right moment to say something, remind yourself of the old saying "It is better to keep your mouth shut and appear foolish than open it and remove all doubt."

TALKING BUSINESS

Whenever you are discussing a contract, forging a deal, or doing business of any kind, think of your conversation in terms of three stages: the warm-up, the core, and the wrap-up.

The Warm-Up

Once you and your business companion have said your hellos and taken your seats, engage in a little small talk—chat that can range from the day's top news story to your golf handicap to, yes, the weather. You might devote five minutes or so on this opening segment. The purpose is to break the ice and set the stage for the business that is to follow. This is relationship-building time and far from being an empty gesture it is an important opportunity. (See also the box "How to Be an Expert at Small Talk," page 205.)

The Core

Next the talk turns to the business at hand. In this longer portion of the conversation, make your personal investment clear by sitting erect and making eye contact. As the conversation gets rolling, keep in mind that you are engaged in a dialogue, not a monologue. Even if you're launching into a lengthy explanation of a complicated new technology, draw the other person into the conversation by pausing occasionally to ask questions, such as "What do you think so far?" Also, be careful to say "you" as often as "I"; this conveys a message to your partner that you consider him or her integral, not tangential, to the business being discussed. However, be sure that your "you" questions won't be construed as challenging the person's ability to understand or follow. "Am I going too fast for you?" can sound aggressive and condescending.

Although, for the most part, you should put jokes aside during this stage, it doesn't have to be completely serious, either; leavening the conversation with the occasional funny aside or pertinent anecdote can keep the atmosphere more relaxed and help you get your message across. Hammering your point too aggressively or relentlessly, on the other hand, can have the opposite effect.

The Wrap-Up

End with a brief recap of any decisions made during the conversation to ensure there are no misunderstandings. Once you've wrapped up your business and resumed your small talk, stick with it. Letting go of the business topic and ending the conversation on a purely social note is an implicit acknowledgment of the personal nature of the business relationship. Always conclude a conversation with a personal good-bye and "Good to see you"/ "Good speaking with you"/"Good to talk with you" or something similar.

THE ART OF LISTENING

The ability to listen is one of the most important talents you can bring to business conversations. The following scenario illustrates what it takes to listen well.

A young woman named Leigh was recently hired by a large bank based in Denver. She had been looking forward to taking a vacation day on Friday. But she changed her plans on learning that she and a small group of other employees were invited to a Q&A session with a financier of some note. She was also nervous. "I'm really thrilled to be invited," she confided to a friend, "and you can bet I'll listen as hard as I can. But I just hope I *hear*."

In her own way, Leigh perfectly described the three essentials of active (as opposed to passive) listening. They apply to telephone conversations as well as face-to-face meetings.

BE THERE. If a session where valuable information will be exchanged is scheduled, attend it; even if it's at an inconvenient time, don't enlist a surrogate. You don't want to count on someone else to tell you about what was discussed. And when you do show up, be present mentally and emotionally as well; if your attention wanders, you're not really there.

LISTEN CAREFULLY. Listen not just to the words but to the tone as well. Take notes if the situation permits it. If you're not sure about the propriety of notes (at a lunch, for instance), the simplest thing to do is ask, "Mind if I jot down a couple of your points?"

HEAR. Now apply a higher level of hearing that goes beyond the physical words to their meaning— mulling over and absorbing what the speaker is saying, why he is saying it, and what it means for your future association. With this step, you become an active participant in an exchange of information, even though you may not yet have uttered a word.

Listening Skills

In the corporate world, it's not only discourteous but also unprofessional to be an indifferent listener. Supervisors claim they can easily tell whether a subordinate has been listening by the quality of the questions asked at the end of a discussion, along with the accuracy of his or her summation. Score high as a listener by doing the following:

CONCENTRATE. Pay close attention to what the other person is saying, and resist the temptation to let your mind wander. Also try your best to be patient with someone who's speaking too slowly or faltering in getting their message across.

RECONFIRM. To show you understand, occasionally paraphrase what the speaker is saying. Once you've picked up the rhythm of the other person's speech, you should be able to do this without seeming to interrupt.

WAIT. In conversation, patience is a virtue and interrupting is a sin. There's a fine line between the occasional interruption made to confirm or question a particular point and one that's made because you are bursting to throw in your two cents' worth.

QUESTION. If you don't understand something, ask for an explanation or ask for the information to be rephrased.

RESPOND. Use positive body language to show you're paying attention. Lean slightly toward the speaker, and react to what he says with the occasional nod, smile, or lifted eyebrow. Don't cross your arms.

KEEP STILL. If you're at your desk, don't shuffle papers or make a halfhearted effort to continue whatever you're working on. When standing or seated in an audience, refrain from any distracting gestures, such as rattling the change in your pocket.

Gentle Guidance

The simple technique of seeming interested in what a person has to say can dissolve barriers of suspicion and build feelings of friendship and trust, allowing people to open up. It is a skill long used by successful diplomats, winning politicians, and the best salespeople. If you move the conversation along with gentle, intelligent questions, you'll more than likely gain valuable information, given freely, without seeming nosy or intrusive—information that can make a difference in the outcome of a business transaction. Here are some conversational gambits that will help you get into areas that might be sensitive, and make your partner more likely to be forthcoming:

"I was talking to a colleague the other day and he said the marketing plan looked a little weak, and I don't know if I agree. What do you think?"

"I read an industry report the other day about Behemoth Booksellers that claimed a merger was in the offing. Have you heard anything like that?"

"If you don't think it's a good idea to tell me, please know I completely understand, but I was wondering . . ."

"My boss was interested to hear that I was having lunch with you today. She's really sorry she couldn't join us, and she asked me to ask you if your company still plans to bid on the Epsom and Saltz project."

Note the frequent mention of third parties—"an old friend," "my boss," "an industry report." This helps remove your questions from the realm of personal curiosity to a more general, shared level of interest.

BODY LANGUAGE

At times, the words and tone of the speaker may be enough to gauge the meaning of what is being said. But a person's posture, facial expressions, and gestures also send messages—some of which are open to interpretation, others of which come through loud and clear.

STANCE. Someone who stands with his back straight, shoulders back, and chin up flashes a message of self-confidence and ambition. Also note that standing with your hands clasped behind you or at ease by your side is a more graceful and authoritative pose than sticking your hands in your pockets. Do not stand with your ankles crossed or your arms folded in

THE ART OF QUESTIONING

Asking the right questions can set you on the road to success, whether you're participating in a meeting, dealing with a customer, or evaluating a new client, vendor, or other prospective business partner. Some people mistakenly believe that by asking questions, you're ceding control of the discussion to whoever is responding. Producing answers, they reason, is more impressive than questioning. But in reality, the reverse is true: Using questions creatively is a way of artfully guiding the discussion in the direction you want.

Asking questions has another benefit, as well:

In business, as much as in social situations, most people really enjoy being afforded the chance to talk about themselves—their likes and dislikes, their views and opinions. You may have noticed that anybody with a reputation as a good conversationalist is less likely to be a raconteur than a person who asks thoughtful questions and listens well. When you encourage someone to talk, you will almost always learn things about them that you wouldn't learn if you chose to dominate the conversation—and you'll also leave a much more favorable impression.

---

front of you, nor should you hold on to one of your arms at the elbow; these poses signal shyness and insecurity, or could be interpreted as defensive.

SEATED POSTURE. Slouching in a chair conveys laziness, tiredness, even disrespect. Some body-language experts see crossing one's legs while seated as a defensive gesture, yet many people (men and women alike) simply find this position more comfortable. A less ambiguous signal is jiggling the knee or continuously shifting in your seat, which communicates insecurity or apprehension, especially during an interview.

FACIAL EXPRESSIONS. A smile denotes warmth, openness, and friendliness. But don't overdo it. False smiles and never-ending smiles make you look phony and can invite suspicion. On the other side of the coin, a frown or a furrowed brow suggests anger or worry, even if your words are positive.

EYE CONTACT. Looking into the other person's eyes shows your interest in the conversation. Do not, however, go to the other extreme: Staring can look threatening and strange. The desirable middle ground is reached by shifting your focus to other parts of the face from time to time, especially the lips. Notice if your eyes always tend to look down when you break your gaze, it can give the impression that you lack confidence. If you have trouble making or sustaining eye contact, you can always focus on the bridge of someone's nose.

GESTURING. Go easy on the gestures: Using your hands to emphasize a point is fine, but overdoing it makes you look too excitable.

FIDGETING. Certain habitual actions may seem normal to the person who is doing them, but they can make others uncomfortable. Generally, the fidgeter isn't even aware that he fidgets. Avoid playing with your hair, tie, or jewelry; biting your lip; drumming your fingers; cracking your joints; and jiggling the change or keys in your pocket.

NODDING. Nodding doesn't necessarily mean you agree, but that you understand. Be careful, though: Too much enthusiastic head nodding can make you seem like a kiss-up, literally a "yes man," especially when directed to your boss.

CHAPTER 23
ON THE TELEPHONE

When Alexander Graham Bell made his first call to his assistant in the next room, it was a business call. On March 10, 1876, he rang up his assistant, Thomas Watson, and said, "Mr. Watson, come here. I want to see you." Not even a "please."

For the next hundred-plus years, calls were made with telephones using landlines to connect them. As office phones proliferated, rules for their use evolved. And then in a relatively short few years, the cell phone and now the smartphone have become a critical component of modern business communication devices. While many of the rules for using an office phone apply to using a smartphone for work, those rules have had to be modified to address issues specific to wireless anywhere communications.

PLACING BUSINESS CALLS

Almost all phone calls fall into one of two categories depending on whom you are calling: someone you know (a warm call) or someone you don't know (a cold call often associated with prospecting for new business). Whether you are making a cold call or a warm one, you can take specific steps to make that call as successful as possible.

Prepare Ahead of Time

Before placing your call, prepare by writing down any questions you want to raise, along with the specific topics you want to cover. Even if an item seems minor, jot it down; it's easy to forget something once the conversation starts rolling. Then place these notes by the phone so you can refer to them throughout the call. If your call involves facts and figures, gather together all data sheets or other reference materials you might need.

You'll also want to keep a blank pad and pen handy so you can take notes during the conversation. In addition, be sure to have access to a calendar in case you need to discuss dates and times for meetings, projects, and deadlines.

Identify Yourself

No matter who answers your call—the person you're trying to reach, a receptionist, an assistant, or your contact's voice mail—identify yourself. Unless you're calling someone with whom you regularly do business, identify your company, too: "This is Katherine Bowlin of Sellmore Marketing." Give your full name even if you talk with the person fairly often, since he may not be as familiar with your voice as you think.

Using your first and last names each time you call will also reinforce your name recognition.

Next, quickly explain why you've called and ask if this is a convenient time to talk. (Failing to ask this question is one of the most common of all telephone errors.) If she says talking now is fine, state the purpose and estimated length of the call: "Mrs. Peterson, I have a question about the marketing proposal. It should take about five minutes." Be realistic: If you suspect five minutes is a conservative estimate, say so.

If the person you call says she's busy, ask when you might call back. Try to avoid having her return the call for two reasons: (1) She may not do so, and (2) an unscheduled call may catch you at an awkward time or without your thoughts collected or your notes at hand.

You're Put on Hold

If you reach a receptionist who transfers incoming calls or an assistant who takes calls for his boss, chances are you'll be asked if you mind being put on hold. If pressed for time, tell the person answering that you'd prefer simply to leave a message—then leave your name, your company name, a brief reason for the call, and a time when you'll call back.

It's perfectly proper to hang up and call back later when you are placed on hold for longer than three minutes. Even though you've been treated badly, try not to show your annoyance when you finally connect. Politely say that you were unable to hold, and leave it at that: No explanation is required.

Wrong Numbers

When you've dialed a wrong number, admit it and apologize. Don't just hang up. Instead, simply deliver the line that has done service in the cause of good manners for generations: "I'm sorry. I must have dialed the wrong number." Then give the person the number you were trying to reach, to make sure you don't make the same mistake twice.

ANSWERING BUSINESS CALLS

Never underestimate the importance of how you answer the phone. You never know when it may be the first call from a potential client or customer. Your attitude and demeanor, in turn, will form her initial impression of your company, and you want it to be positive, not poor. Here are three other considerations:

- An incoming call answered by an actual person instead of a machine not only makes a good impression, it also earns the caller's gratitude by not putting her in electronic limbo.

- Your voice should sound pleasant and calm whenever you answer the phone, no matter how overworked, stressed, or rattled you feel at the time. Remember, you're speaking for the company, not yourself.

- Whenever possible, answer the phone promptly—that is, by the third ring.

Identify Yourself

Answering with your full name is an absolute necessity whenever a call is coming from outside. Then what to say? Although "Helen Bonner speaking" is not impolite, "This is Helen Bonner" sounds less abrupt. Then follow with something on the order of "May I help you?" Of course, it is best to begin answering a call by saying hello or good morning or good afternoon. If you work in a company with several departments, state your department after your name: "This is Angela Dixon, Rights and Permissions."

Inconvenient Timing

You're terribly busy? If you don't have an assistant to field incoming calls and a client or customer calls at an inconvenient time, give her precedence over any work you're doing if at all possible. If this is impossible, explain your predicament and tell her you'll

Thirty years ago, who could have dreamed that placing a call to a business or government department would be as frustrating as it is today? Just try finding a customer service number to call on the contact page of a company's website. If you are even able to hunt down a number, you risk being put on hold indefinitely or hearing a recorded voice: "Press 1 for . . ." It can feel like someone slamming an electronic door on our simple desire to connect with a human being. We press and press again, our blood pressure rising, until we finally reach the desired person—recorded, as often as not, asking us to please leave a message.

But here's the bottom line: Whether or not you're ultimately successful in completing a call, any frustration must now be brushed aside. Smart businesspeople treat every communication, even those mediated by a recording device, with courtesy.

phone back when it suits her. Agree on a time, and then keep your word. If you do have an assistant, ask her to take messages or route calls to your voice mail when you're busy; or if your phone system allows, send your calls to voice mail.

PHONE MANAGEMENT SKILLS

Whether you have an assistant or not, be familiar with the way your phone system operates so that you are adept at using the hold and transfer features.

Transferring Calls

If the person you're talking with needs to be transferred to someone else in your company, first give the caller the correct extension in case she is disconnected. Then tell the person to whom the call is being transferred who is on the line and why she is calling; this spares callers from having to repeat themselves.

The Art of the Hold

If not handled properly, the phrase "Hold, please" can turn a polite request into a rude experience. Receptionists, assistants, secretaries, and all others who field incoming calls need to be sympathetic to and respectful of the person on hold. Doing the following will help keep a caller's frustration and annoyance to a minimum:

- Never tell someone to hold; *ask* them instead. More important still, *wait for the answer.* The question "May I please put you on hold?" is doubly irritating when immediately followed by silence or recorded music.

- Give the reason for the hold. "Ms. Tomkins is on another line," for example. Or "She's somewhere nearby; I'll have to page her" or "I'll have to check to see who can handle that."

- When someone is holding, deliver a progress update every sixty seconds: "I thought she was almost done with her call, but she's still on the line." At the second or third check, ask whether the person would like to keep waiting or would rather leave a message.

Screening Calls

Assistants also bear the burden of screening calls for their bosses and others. If every caller identified himself or herself correctly, there would be less of a need for a potentially awkward informational question—"I'm sorry, who is this?"—to identify the mystery caller. This is an area that can get touchy but is really a practical and understandable necessity. For example, a caller is asked his name and put on hold. Then, when he is told the desired person is unavailable, he may feel he has been deemed unimportant. Similarly, a caller who's asked "May I ask what this call concerns?" or "Do you know if they are expecting your call?" might resent having an assistant determine whether his call is worth putting through. However, from the point of view of the gatekeeper, this is important information for trying to decide how to handle the call. If you are asked a question like this, it's your obligation to answer. Even if the matter is a complicated one, the briefest summary—"It has to do with the new banana importing law"—should be satisfactory.

It is up to those whose calls are being screened to furnish their assistants with the language to be used and the criteria for putting a call through. It's then the assistant's job to use that language and apply that criteria.

Returning Calls

A large number of businesspeople hide behind their voice mail. Don't be one of them. If someone leaves a message asking you to call back, do so as soon as possible—or at least on the same day the call was received. Twenty-four hours is as long as a call can go unreturned without violating the standards of good manners.

If it's an especially busy day and you suspect the call will take more time than you can spare, call the person back, explain the situation, and ask if you can set a time to talk later. Or if you have an assistant, ask him or her to call back and explain the delay, and then arrange a callback time that will be convenient for both parties.

If You Share an Extension

When answering a phone shared by others, state the department name before giving your own: "Quality Control, Bill Fryer speaking." If the call is for someone else, say "Just a moment, please" before handing over the receiver. If the person isn't in, tell the caller when he's expected back, if you know, and offer to take a message. Don't volunteer gratuitous information about why someone's not available. If the person is in a meeting or on vacation, say so. Otherwise, don't feel you have to explain his whereabouts.

If you go in search of the person being called, tell the caller how long it will take: "If you can wait two minutes, I'll try to find him." If you haven't located

---

CALLER ID

The positive about caller ID is it allows you to prepare for a call before answering it. The negative: Answering your phone and using the caller's name at the outset may throw him or her off guard; you may come off as being sneaky—plus, the caller may not be the person identified on the screen.

the person within the allotted time, return to the phone with your update. "I'm sorry, but I couldn't find him. If you give me your name and number, I'll leave them on his desk." An alternative is to ask if the caller wants to be routed to the person's voice mail to leave the message himself.

WHILE ON A BUSINESS CALL

Once you do get through to the person you're calling, keep in mind that the impression you make depends entirely on your voice and choice of words, making it all the more important to sound professional and personable. Even when rushed, make an effort to speak slowly and distinctly. The way you hold the receiver matters as well: Tucking it under your chin or holding it below your mouth makes you harder to understand.

Follow cues from the person you're speaking with to establish the call's tone. If someone is all-business and no-nonsense, you should be, too. Others may be informal and chatty. Indulging someone who strays off the business subject may have the benefit of leading to the discovery of common interests or backgrounds, provided the tangent doesn't distract you from the purpose of your call. People who've never met face-to-face sometimes click and establish a kind of rapport. The goodwill that results makes it all the easier for you to keep the business relationship running smoothly.

Call Waiting and Other Interruptions

Being interrupted by a second call is less common than it once was, now that most office phone systems have voice mail, which automatically records a message from a second caller if you're on the phone. If you have a voice mail system, ignore the call waiting signal. If your system has call waiting without voice mail, you don't have much choice except to answer the incoming call. Apologize to the first caller and say you'll return immediately; put him or her on hold and quickly explain to the other caller that you'll have to call back.

When you switch to the incoming caller, try your best to keep a conversation from starting. Your responsibility is to the first caller, who should never be left on hold for more than thirty seconds. Even this brief period can seem like an eternity when a conversation that had been going full steam is interrupted. If the incoming call is extremely urgent, however, explain to your first caller why you must hang up and set the time you'll call back.

When you have to put someone on hold for other reasons—retrieving data sheets from another office, for example—say how long you'll be off the line. Then return when promised, even if you haven't found what you're looking for. If necessary, explain that you'll need a few more minutes and will call back as soon as your search is successful.

When a coworker arrives at your office door and sees you are on the phone, he should have the courtesy to leave. If he hovers and becomes a distraction, stop the conversation at an opportune moment and say, "Will you excuse me for a moment? There's someone at the door." Then quickly determine why the other person is there, or mouth or signal, "I'll see you later."

Technical Glitches for Cell Phones and Landlines

When a disconnection occurs, it is the caller's responsibility to call back. Apologize: "I'm sorry; we got disconnected. I think we left off with the annual report."

> **TIP:** One technique for sounding upbeat is to smile as you speak—the theory being that a smile makes the voice brighter and more pleasant.

And move back to the business at hand. Do this even if the conversation was nearing an end; not calling back is like walking off in the middle of a face-to-face talk.

If you're the one who was dropped, stay available for a few minutes. It is far better to be able to pick the business back up and conclude the call properly than to let it drop.

If a bad connection or static on an old landline makes it difficult to hear, don't be embarrassed to ask the other person to hang up so that you can try again later. A second call often solves the problem and avoids the dangers of miscommunication due to a bad signal.

CLOSING A CALL

When you end a business call, don't leave matters hanging. Wind things down with a conclusive statement: "I'll get the final figures to you by noon Friday" or "I think we agree we need more research. Shall we talk again, maybe tomorrow?" Then sign off on a positive note with a polite acknowledgment: "Thank you for calling" or "It's been nice talking with you."

A few minutes spent discussing things that have nothing to do with the business at hand are perfectly in order after callers have established a friendly relationship. But don't overdo it: Without any visual clues

CHECKLIST FOR TAKING PHONE MESSAGES	from the person with whom you are speaking, it's hard to tell when you're wearing out your welcome.

CHECKLIST FOR TAKING PHONE MESSAGES

When you take a telephone message, both the caller and the person you're taking the message for will appreciate it if you do the following:

- **GET THE NAME AND NUMBER RIGHT.** Ask the caller for her complete name, and then ask for the spelling, since many names can be spelled more than one way—for example, Jean or Jeanne, Allen or Alan, Deborah or Debra, Anderson or Andersen. Also, read the phone number back to the caller to verify it.

- **ASK THE NAME OF THE CALLER'S COMPANY.** This may help the person for whom you're taking the message identify the caller more easily. It also provides an idea of what the call may be about.

- **NOTE THE DATE AND HOUR.** Jot down the time the call came in so the person knows how long the message has been sitting there.

- **ADD YOUR INITIALS OR NAME.** Do this in case the person receiving the message wants to know more about the call.

- **DELIVER YOUR MESSAGE.** All your good efforts to write the information down will be wasted if you don't make sure the message gets to the intended recipient.

from the person with whom you are speaking, it's hard to tell when you're wearing out your welcome.

ANSWERING MACHINES, VOICE MAIL, AND MESSAGES

Whether you use an answering machine in a home office or are connected to a voice mail service at your company, there are certain practicalities and civilities to keep in mind.

Recording a Greeting

On your office phone, a no-nonsense, straightforward greeting is by far the best choice. Short and sweet is the goal—your full name, your company name, and a request that the caller leave a message: "This is Miguel Hernandez at Johnson-Cowles. Please leave your name and information."

You may also want to change your greeting daily to give callers information about a change in your schedule: "On Tuesday, July 12, I'll be out of the office until eleven o'clock, but I'll be available for the rest of the day. If you leave a message, I'll call you back as soon as possible." You might also refer callers to someone who can deal with emergency situations: "If you need to speak with someone immediately, you can call Cassandra Ruiz at extension 7131."

When you're going away on a business trip or vacation, change your greeting before you depart. After identifying yourself, say "I'll be out of the office until Monday, August 17. Please call back then." You should also give the name and number of someone else in your department to contact if an issue needs to be discussed before you return. For safety and security, do not leave this message if you work from home. Instead, simply ask callers to leave their name and number.

Leaving a Message

When leaving a message, state your name and number slowly and clearly at the *start* of the message—after all, someone will be taking it down. Many people ramble on until they realize they're about to be cut off, then recite their number so quickly that it's often unintelligible. Also, keep your message short: Since most people have little tolerance for long messages, you risk getting passed over or deleted if you don't get straight to the point. Worse still, long messages can overwhelm a voice mail system. Finally, repeat your name and number at the end of the message.

Returning Calls

Return all calls left on your answering machine or voice mail within twenty-four hours whenever possible. Even though many people no longer listen to personal messages left on mobile phone voice mail before calling someone back, in business make this a practice when you don't know what the call is about. Listening to your boss's message before returning his call may save you both valuable time if he is just looking for a piece of information and has already left a message telling you what he needs. If you are the one leaving a message, reduce the potential for telephone tag by stating your business clearly as well as where you can be reached and when—and then make it a point to be available at that time.

> **TIP:** Close your office door before making any call using a speakerphone. Even though voices are amplified by a speakerphone, people generally tend to talk louder than usual when using one. The result? Workmates within earshot are disturbed by the noise.

SPEAKERPHONE

The most important rule for using a speakerphone is this: Immediately tell the person on the other end of the line that you are using one. If he or she expresses any hesitation, explain why you are on speaker—because you'd like other people in the room to be included in the conversation, for instance, or because it makes it easier for you to take notes. Most people won't mind as long as they're asked beforehand and they understand the reason for it.

If others are present, identify them at the very start of the conversation: "There are three people from marketing here joining in—Leslie Marshall, Andy Armistead, and Kathy Kincannon." The participants should then introduce themselves so that the person on the other end can begin to link voices to names—sometimes a difficult task, since sound quality isn't always optimal. It is less confusing to the listener if each participant identifies himself when he speaks: "Tom, Andy here." You can also make it clear who's talking by saying, for example, "I agree with what Kathy just said" or "I see Leslie has a question for you."

In an open work environment, it's important to be mindful of coworkers when using a speakerphone. They will be annoyed, and rightly so, if they are subjected to the dial tone, the beeping of the dialing, and the ringing of the call before you bother to pick up the receiver.

VIDEO CALLS AND ONLINE CONFERENCING

The videophone call and online conference are an integral part of business communication, whether you use video calling such as Skype, iChat, Google Chat, or a web conferencing service like GoToMeeting. These services are widely used to connect remote workforces and organize meetings across great distances. However you feel personally about the ability of these tools to effectively replace in-person meetings, they are certainly one of the most sophisticated options for communication in the modern business world. Here are several points to keep in mind to get the most out of these technologies.

Preparation

Before you begin, be sure that you have tested all of your systems and technical capabilities. This means more than just familiarizing yourself with software features and system requirements for a web conferencing service. Computers behave differently when they are connected to new monitors and sound systems. Each piece of equipment needs to be tested in the way it is going to be used before you can rely on it.

If you are setting up your equipment for the first time or are in a remote location, talk to someone who is familiar with the system ahead of time and show up early to troubleshoot any difficulties that may arise. Ask about connector cables, operating system compatibility, and backup systems should something go

wrong. If you are working with a service provider, talk to a representative well ahead of time. Complete any trials or tests that he suggests and make contact with the provider's help and support services so you have someone to call if you need them later on.

Give remote participants correct and detailed instructions for how they can participate. As the host, you might be working with people who may not be as familiar with the technology as you are. Do your part to keep the process as simple and clear as possible to make it easy on everyone.

Best Practices

To ensure a smooth videophone call or online conference, do the following before connecting with others:

- Use a private room or location. An office with a door that closes is best. This will reduce noise and distractions and decrease the likelihood of unplanned interruptions.

- Think about your background. This includes both the sound and the visual field. Minimize background noise and hums, and position yourself so that bright light from a window to the side or directly behind you doesn't obscure your face.

- Many systems use an open microphone and speaker the same way as a conference call does. It is polite to identify everyone who can hear what is going on and, at the same time, to let them know that a live microphone and camera are recording and transmitting.

- In a home office, backgrounds that are clean, uncluttered, and not overly personalized keep the focus on the participants and the content of the call or meeting and look more professional. Barking pets, personal clutter, food, and beverages in the frame diminish a businesslike impression.

- Check that everything is working for all participants before you begin.

TTY

For people who are deaf or hard of hearing text telephones, also called teletypes (TTYs) or telecommunication devices for the deaf (TDDs), are in common use. These devices, which look like small typewriters, permit two people to communicate by typing back and forth in a conversational manner over a phone line.

If your office isn't equipped with a TDD, you can still communicate with a hearing-impaired person by using a relay service. In this case, the hearing caller speaks to a mediator, who relays words to the recipient by typing them into a console; the words then appear in the display window of the recipient's device.

If conversing with a hearing-impaired person over a TDD, address him directly, as if the mediator weren't present. Do not say, "Tell him that . . ."or "Ask him to . . ."

CHAPTER 24
THE SMARTPHONE

Smartphones are great when used properly; they allow us to have a level of access and availability that has never before been possible. They can connect multiple parties to a conference call or video chat, function as a TTY device, send and receive emails and text messages, take pictures, connect us to online spaces, and access important (or just fun) information instantly through millions of apps. Their very utility, however, is also their downfall. Or, more appropriately, our downfall.

Inappropriate use of these phones can do very real damage to business relationships. When a businessperson becomes controlled by his phone rather than maintaining control of it, he will ultimately end up using it inappropriately, offend others, or present a poor business image of himself. Never lose sight of your first priority: building successful relationships. Those aren't just the relationships your phone keeps you connected to; they are also the ones you are face-to-face with or in earshot of. One of the ways we demonstrate our respect for others is by giving them our full attention. Divide your attention between people and a device—even for work-related reasons—and you run the risk of those around you perceiving that you have diminished your respect for

them, too. Rules about smartphones aren't one size fits all. They are about using your judgment to make smart choices about how and when you use—or don't use—your phone.

This chapter is specific to smartphone etiquette; we suggest you also review Chapter 23, as much of the general etiquette advice there applies to making any business call—whether from a landline or mobile phone.

BASIC RULES FOR SMARTPHONE USE

Here are four basic tips every smartphone user should know and use:

1. Don't let your phone ring or sound text or email alerts if the noise will disturb others around you. Meetings, presentations, when you are sharing an office—these are all times when turning the phone off (or at least setting it to silent) is mandatory.

2. Don't take your phone out and start using it if there is any possibility someone around you will be bothered by your use of it. Ask yourself if the

people around you are a captive audience. Examples include those in a car, train, elevator, checkout line, waiting room, airport gate, restroom, restaurant, cafe, theater, or meeting. Also note that texting, emailing, and using social networks or the Web while in a small space with someone can also be considered rude.

3. Absolutely never say anything confidential, personal, or private if others can overhear you. Instead, stop the conversation by telling the other person you'll call back when you can talk privately. Never assume those around you won't listen to or be bothered by your conversation. It's much harder to ignore a conversation when you hear only one side of it than when you can hear both people talking.

4. Speak quietly. At home, in the office, or on the street, most people's phone voices are consistently louder than their regular voices. Even with headphones or a wired or Bluetooth earpiece, you don't get an accurate read on your voice volume.

In Meetings

One of the most client-requested Emily Post Business Etiquette Seminar topics is on inappropriate phone use, especially during meetings. Sometimes it is busy employees who feel that they need to be checking and responding to messages as they arrive. Other times it is a boss who uses the weekly staff meeting to catch up on his email. Whatever the excuse, it is incredibly disruptive and undermining when people are texting, emailing, and instant-messaging while a meeting is going on. When you are meeting with others you should give them your full attention: devices off.

DROPPED CALLS

The person whose phone dropped the call is the one responsible to call back from a stronger signal location as soon as possible. If you are unsure, assume it was you and try the call again.

If you need to confirm a detail from an email or check your calendar for meeting-purposes, say so when you consult your device: "Let me check on that." If digital note taking is not the norm for other meeting attendees, announce in advance what you will be doing so they don't think you are distracted with other work or, worse, nonwork.

You may need to take a call or watch for an incoming email during a meeting. Let the others (or at least the meeting organizer) know at the start of the meeting that you may need to step out discreetly at some point. A planned and explained interruption is much easier for others to understand than one that is abrupt.

When you are a meeting facilitator, help everyone involved by setting expectations clearly at the start.

- Remind participants to silence or put away devices.

- Start your meeting by announcing when you will be taking breaks so participants know when they will be able to check messages and voice mails.

- If screens are allowed but you are concerned participants will use their smartphones, tablets, or laptops for nonmeeting purposes, at the start of the meeting announce, "Please close all screens [or apps] that don't pertain to this meeting."

At Your Desk

In times past when people only had an office phone, rules were generally strict about when and under what circumstances personal phone calls were allowed. Today that dynamic has changed because almost everyone at an office has a personal cell phone. As a result, the control businesses had on personal calls has evaporated. But don't think personal phone use during office hours hasn't been noticed by management.

The amount of time you spend on a personal phone at the office has an impact on your professional image. "My kids use it to reach me in case of an emergency"; "I use it to talk to my parents' doctors and manage their care"; "I make quick calls to handle personal business that would otherwise take me away from my office"—these rationales aren't persuasive to management. According to a survey by TheLadders .com on what etiquette offense can get an employee fired, executives listed "making too many personal calls while at work" in the top five.

Take Your Personal Calls in Private

Someone taking a personal call should move to a private area—a staircase, a conference room, the lobby, or even outside. While this is an appropriate solution once in a while, the person who regularly takes several calls a day will quickly be labeled a slacker. Managers will notice as well, which could lead to unpleasant consequences.

Think, too, about what constitutes a private space. If anyone else is in a hallway, staircase, or especially bathroom, it is no longer private. Move to another spot away from people to finish your call.

Out and About

Smartphones come into their own, for instance, when you're out for a walk, in the airport, or in a cab. In these situations, there is often a very good reason to use one:

- You've left the office and are delayed for an appointment.

- You've forgotten to relay an urgent piece of information to someone.

- You suddenly remember you need another set of figures for a meeting.

But just because you're in a public place doesn't mean you can use your phone without regard for people near you. Just remember:

- Volume matters outside the office as well as in. Don't shout into your phone while walking down the street: It's you, not the person on the other end, who is contending with ambient noise.

- It's not just your volume that matters: If you are running late for a business meal at a restaurant, text, rather than call, your appointment if he is likely to have arrived. This saves him having to find a quiet place to get the message.

- Be aware of your surroundings. Don't get lost in a conversation and forget where you are. Consider substituting a quick email memo or text message for a call the next time your flight lands or a brilliant idea strikes on a bus to save those around you from the details.

- Stand aside to take calls if you need to: Don't block street or sidewalk traffic, doors, Jetways, or entryways.

- Look before crossing the street.

- Don't make calls while others are trying to serve you, say at a checkout or airline counter.

In Restaurants

While cell phones have a place in business, using them in a restaurant is another matter entirely. After all, restaurants are places where people come to relax and dine and to focus on conversation: their conversation, not yours. The rule is simple: Excuse yourself from the table and make or take the call in an anteroom or a lobby, or simply step outside. At business and social meals alike, making or receiving a phone call at the table is clearly both inconsiderate and intrusive, and it takes you away from your goal: building a relationship and doing business with the person in front of you.

When you arrive at the table, turn your phone off or put it on a silent ring mode and then put it in your purse or pocket. Do not place a phone on the table. A phone out on a table is like a ticking time bomb; you and your companions are just waiting for it to go off, and it says to the people you are with that your phone is more important than they are.

Obviously, there are exceptions—for example, a doctor who is on call. Most doctors, perhaps because of the confidential nature of their profession, demonstrate excellent cell phone manners. They ex-cuse themselves from the table and move to a place with privacy to respond to their page or call.

What do you do if the person at the next table is gabbing away on a phone while you're trying to talk business or enjoy a meal with colleagues? If he's rude enough to be on a phone in a restaurant, a dirty look will probably be little more than water off a duck's back. Instead, ask the waiter or manager to talk with the offender. Never approach a stranger and try to correct his behavior. You have no idea how he will react, and the result could be an unpleasant—and unhelpful—confrontation.

In the Car

Calling from moving vehicles brings up the question not only of etiquette but also of safety. Carrying on a phone conversation diverts the driver's attention from the road, and driving with only one hand heightens the danger even more. Many states are making it illegal to use handheld devices while driving—so be aware of the laws in your area and when you travel. While the use of the speakerphone, earbuds with a microphone, or a Bluetooth hands-free device will lessen the risk, you are still a distracted driver, and distracted driving is a major cause of automobile accidents. The smartest choice is to pull over to the side of the road before making a call.

TIP: Let the person on the other end know if there are other people in the car who will be privy to the conversation. And its corollary: Don't subject your carpool to your private or business conversations.

WHAT THE FUTURE HOLDS

Manners for email, smartphones, and social networking might be specific to those technologies, but the ideas that govern those manners—the principles of etiquette—aren't new. While there is no way to know what comes next with digital etiquette until new technologies emerge, we already know the blueprint for any new rules or guidelines. The etiquette for any new technology will stem from these questions: How will using this technology affect any other people, and how can that interaction be a good one?

The answer to those questions, while specific to the new technology in question, will need to demonstrate consideration, respect, and honesty toward anyone affected. How we do what we do will change with new advances, but what we want out of it as a society—to be treated in a way that acknowledges our humanity—won't. (See also "The Three Principles That Govern All Etiquette," page 6.)

CHAPTER 25
THE GOOD WRITER

No skill is more important than the ability to organize and convey information with clarity and coherence. Ultimately, this means being able to write effectively as virtually every type of business requires writing of some kind—emails, letters to clients, memos to co-workers, reports, requests, recommendations, manuals, newsletters, PowerPoint presentations, even notes for the office suggestion box.

THE MECHANICS OF GOOD BUSINESS WRITING

Some types of business writing are highly formalized, such as the financial section of a company's annual report. Others are extremely informal, like interoffice emails or texts, for example. Most of the material businesspeople are expected to write falls into the category of "general writing"—more organized and attentive to correct grammar and construction than spoken conversation but not nearly so rigid and rule-bound as legal or scientific writing. Whatever the format, however, all good writing must meet four basic tests:

- Is it accurate? (Does it correctly describe the situation?)

- Is it clear? (Have you said what you intended to say?)

- Is it coherent? (Will it make sense to the reader?)

- Is it correct? (Are there any misspellings, typos, grammatical mistakes, or structural errors?)

The Importance of Grammar

It is interesting how often we use the language of building when discussing writing. We "construct" sentences. We "structure" paragraphs. Words are the basic building blocks of writing . . . and grammar is the blueprint.

If your grammar is poor, you won't be able to say what you mean; you may even convey messages that you don't intend. Your audience—the reader—may form a negative opinion of your competence or your seriousness. It is not an exaggeration to say that the writer of an ungrammatical letter (a job-application cover letter, for example) may live to regret it.

Organize and Outline

Many people can write a grammatical sentence but are unable to put together a coherent paragraph. Their ideas tumble around like clothes in a dryer, making it impossible to sort the shirts from the socks. Even the most patient reader won't put up with confused, chaotic writing for long.

To avoid this outcome, take time to outline your thoughts before you actually start writing. Begin by jotting down the main points you want to make, and then look over your notes and decide how best to organize them. Here are two ways:

- The step-by-step outline. This works best when you want to explain a process. If a step is out of order, you'll be able to spot the error in your outline and make the correction.

- The cause-and-effect outline. Use this when you want to describe how something happened. Make an outline that clearly relates the cause and the ensuing consequences.

Outlining may seem time-consuming, but word-processing programs make it easy and it will save you much rethinking and rewriting down the line. An outline will also help you stay on track as you write. It's often tempting to follow an interesting tangent, add unnecessary details, or drop in an amusing comment or personal story. But your readers have time constraints, too. They want you to get to the point quickly and make your case clearly; every extraneous bit of information becomes a distraction and a delay.

Be Consistent

Consistency in business writing is essential to clarity and brings an important unity to your writing in terms of point of view, tense, and mood. As you compose your rough draft and then edit it, keep the following factors in mind.

POINT OF VIEW

When you begin a piece of writing, you first have to decide what point of view to use in telling your story—either the first person (I, me, my, mine, we, us, our), the second person (you, your), or the third person (he, she, it, him, her, his, hers, its, they, them, their). Your job is to select a point of view and then stick with it. Readers will find it hard to follow writing that shifts from one perspective to another.

FIRST PERSON. Business writers frequently use the first person point of view, especially in letters, memos, and internal reports. It offers an individualized, personalized perspective. The first person can also be found in formal writing, but it is most often used when the writer wishes to set a friendly, more casual tone.

SECOND PERSON. This point of view is less common because it adopts the viewpoint of the reader rather than the writer. It is most appropriate in writing that instructs (this book, for example). The second person can also be used in letters. Be careful, though: Second-person writing can easily become accusatory, judgmental, and hostile: "You should know that . . ." or "Your duty is to . . ."

THIRD PERSON. This is an objective viewpoint. It allows the writer to maintain a detached perspective—an observer of the action rather than a direct participant. The third person generally sets a more formal tone than the first person. In the language of journalism, it is the reportorial, not editorial, point of view.

TENSE

Tense indicates when an action or event takes place. All verbs have tenses to indicate whether something is happening in the present, happened in the past, or will happen in the future: "I'm eating at the Greasy Spoon"; "I ate at the Greasy Spoon last Tuesday"; "I will eat at the Greasy Spoon next week." Unless there is a clear difference in time ("We received your broken fax machine yesterday, and we will repair it next week"), select the tense that expresses the time frame of your writing and use it consistently.

READ IT ALOUD

If you're stuck on a writing project, take a few minutes to explain to a colleague what you're trying to say—and then write that explanation. If no one is available, visualize such a conversation instead.

Once you've finished a piece of writing, make a point of reading it out loud. You'll quickly hear the spots where your argument sounds forced, your phraseology is clichéd, or your grammar falls short. If you're repeating yourself or taking too long to make your point, that will quickly become apparent as well.

When you receive an important, well-written communication, try reading it out loud. Voicing the words of others literally forces you to slow down and hear the way the words are put together and can be a model to help you organize and improve your own writing.

TONE

A final unifying element in writing is tone. This is the attitude of the writer, reflected in the writing. You may wish to take a serious tone that reflects your knowledge and professionalism when writing a report or proposal. Conversely, you might choose a light one when writing a memo about the annual Christmas party to members of your work team. You will probably want to adopt a conciliatory and polite tone when responding to a customer's complaint, whereas a tougher, no-nonsense tone could be the best choice in a performance review for an employee who constantly procrastinates on assignments.

Once you've decided on the right tone, maintain it throughout. Sudden changes in tone or mood—what might be called manic-depressive writing—disorient the reader and leave the impression that the writer is uncertain or conflicted about the subject.

Proofread

Once you've gone through a series of drafts and arrived at a piece of writing you're happy with, your job still isn't done. No matter how organized you are or how cogent your presentation may be, all your best efforts will go down the drain if you make grammatical errors, misspell words, or misuse punctuation. The minute a mistake is spotted, however, the reader's attention turns to the mistake, distracting attention from the points you're trying to get across.

The bottom line: An ounce of prevention is worth a pound of cure. Proofread everything before sending it out into the world—especially those emails you dash off in a flash. For a formal letter or a report, have a colleague go over it with a fine-tooth comb (and be ready to reciprocate when she asks you to do her the same favor).

BEWARE SPELL-CHECK

Spell-check is great, but don't assume it's foolproof. Peter's ad agency once made the mistake of referring to a certified public accounting firm as a certified pubic accounting firm. Spell-check did not help.

EFFECTIVE BUSINESS LETTERS

The old-fashioned personal business letter—written on pristine, high-quality paper, sealed in an envelope, and delivered by post or by hand—remains the single most impressive written ambassador for your company. A letter has a dignity that cannot be equaled by electronic mail or faxed correspondence. Email and faxes have a spontaneous, off-the-cuff quality akin to a telephone call. A letter, by contrast, says that someone has planned, written or keyed, and edited and revised a message. In other words, the sender has expended time—the most precious commodity—to communicate with the recipient.

It's a shame, then, that so many businesspeople regard the writing of business letters as a chore. But it doesn't have to be that way.

The Standard Form of a Business Letter

In the United States, the standard business letter follows block format or modified block format. Block format is the most common. The entire letter is left justified. In the modified block format the date and the closing begin at a center-point tab, whereas addresses for the sender and recipient, the salutation, and the body of the letter are left justified.

In both styles, the body of the letter is single spaced with double spaces between paragraphs and paragraphs are not indented. Use a single space between each part of the letter, but leave four spaces between the closing and your typed name so that you have room for your signature.

Use a standard, 12-point font such as Times Roman or Cambria; these are professional-looking and easier to read than sans serif typefaces such as

Arial or Verdana. The font for your letter should complement, but does not need to match, the font and type size of the letterhead design. A minimum one-inch margin for sides and one-and-a-half-inch margin for top and bottom is standard; margins adjust to accommodate letterhead and graphics.

The Standard Parts of a Business Letter

The standard business letter includes the following parts.

SENDER'S ADDRESS

If you are not using personal or company letterhead printed with your address, start your letter with your address information: company name, street address, city, state, and ZIP code. Omit your name and title, as they will be included in the closing.

DATELINE

This consists of the month, day, and year the letter was written or completed. The month should be spelled out in full, and all numbers should be written as numerals (January 1, 2018, not Jan. 1 or January 1st). The date is typed flush left or beginning at the center point following a blank line after the recipient's address or two to six lines below the letterhead.

REFERENCE LINE

Some letters require specific reference to file, account, invoice, order, or policy numbers. These references are usually typed below the dateline, but they may also be centered on the page. When the letter runs longer than one page, the reference line should be repeated on each subsequent sheet, flush left as the first line of the page.

AGGRESSIVELY NOT PASSIVE

The goal of business writing is to be clear and direct. Beware of the passive voice, when instead of the subject acting on the verb, the verb acts on the subjects. Using the passive voice can make what should be the object of the sentence rise to the importance of the subject. Here are some examples:

Active: The sales team sold 420 units in the last quarter. (Emphasis: sales team.)

Passive: Four hundred twenty units were sold last quarter by the sales team. (Emphasis: units.)

Active: Management will make all decisions. (Emphasis: management)

Passive: All decisions will be made by management. (Emphasis: decisions)

Your writing will be stronger when your subject takes action.

SPECIAL NOTATIONS

When necessary, letters may include notation of the means of delivery—"certified mail" or "registered mail"—or on-arrival instructions, such as "personal" (to be opened and read by the addressee only) or "confidential" (for the addressee or other authorized personnel). These lines are typed in all capital letters and placed flush left. On-arrival notations are also printed in capital letters on the face side of the envelope.

INSIDE ADDRESS OF THE RECIPIENT

The inside address is usually below the dateline. When a letter is addressed to an individual, the inside address includes the following:

ADDRESSEE'S COURTESY TITLE AND FULL NAME. When writing to a woman you don't know, you can address her as "Ms." For unisex names like Pat, Jan, Leslie, Alex, Hillary, and Lynn, however, a phone inquiry to the recipient's firm to confirm his or her gender will save potential embarrassment. Names from other cultures can also be problematic. If you cannot discover the sex of the person, you should drop the courtesy title in the address and the salutation ("Jan White"; "Dear Jan White"). It's awkward but better than risking an unintended insult. Use titles for elected officials, military personnel, medical doctors, and clergy. If your recipient holds a doctoral degree, you can use either "Dr. Smith" or "John Smith, PhD." For physicians, either "Dr. Smith" or "Jane Smith, MD" is acceptable. In a business context, use professional designations rather than courtesy titles: "Clara Jones, CPA"; "Ralph Bostwick, Esq."

ADDRESSEE'S BUSINESS TITLE, WHEN REQUIRED. When an individual holds more than one position in a company, your decision to use all titles or just one will depend on the purpose of the letter and the recipient's preference. Do not substitute a business title for a courtesy title, however. Address your letter to "Mr. Richard Lambert, President, Alpha Company," not "President Richard Lambert."

NAME OF BUSINESS. It is equally important to write the name of the company or organization exactly. Look for details: Is "Company," "Corporation," or "Incorporated" spelled out or abbreviated? Does the company name include commas, hyphens, periods, or ampersands? Are words run together? Which letters are capitalized? Find out by checking letterhead, corporate publications, the firm's website, or the phone book.

FULL ADDRESS. In the address, numbers are generally written in numeral form unless they are part of the name of a building (One Town Plaza). As a rule, street numbers are written in numerals (123 East 17th Street), though First through Twelfth are often written in full. Also, spell out any number that may cause confusion (One I Street). City names are written in full unless an abbreviation is the accepted spelling (St. Louis). State names can be written out or the two-letter postal service abbreviation can be used—followed by the ZIP code. Foreign addresses should conform to the standards in the country of receipt.

When the letter is to a business or organization, the address line includes the following:

- Full name of the company, firm, or organization

- Department name, if necessary

- Full address

TO THE ATTENTION OF. If you are writing a company or company department, you may also want to include an attention line that directs your letter to a specific individual ("Attention: Mr. Benjamin Hayes" or "Attention: Director of Health Benefits"). The attention line is placed below the address and above the salutation; the salutation itself is directed to the company or department.

SALUTATION

Your salutation is your greeting. In most cases, it is a simple "Dear Mr./Ms. _____ " or "Dear Dr. _____ " followed by a colon. It is a general guideline that you salute a person in a business letter with the same name form you use in person; so a business salutation uses a first name *only* when you know the addressee well or have agreed to correspond on a first-name basis. If in doubt, err on the side of formality. (For a complete chart showing forms of address, see page 269.)

What to write when you are addressing a company rather than an identifiable person? The old-fashioned "Gentlemen" is obviously inappropriate unless the organization includes no females. "Dear Sir/Madam" is the usual form. "To Whom It May Concern" is acceptable but rather formal. Otherwise, you can address the company ("Dear Blue Sky Investments") or department ("Dear Investor Relations") or direct your salutation to a specific position ("Dear Human Resources Director"). A more general salutation such as "Dear Sales Representative" is also acceptable.

BODY

Whether your letter consists of a single paragraph or several, the chief rule here is brevity. Business letters should not go beyond one page unless absolutely necessary. The trick is to be concise and to the point but never discourteous. The standard form is to leave a blank line between paragraphs instead of starting a new paragraph with an indent.

CLOSING

When ending your message, stay friendly and brief. If you know the recipient, it's fine to end on a personal note: "Please give my best to your wife" or "I enjoyed seeing you at the trade show and hope your trip home was as pleasant as you expected." Even if you don't know the person, your closing can be friendly

> **TIP:** Do not thank someone for something they have not yet done: "Thank you in advance" is presumptuous. Simply close with "Thank you."

and helpful. ("I look forward to talking with you soon." Or "Please call me directly at 555-1212 if you need additional copies of the brochure.") It is always polite to say thank you for a service or attention.

COMPLIMENTARY CLOSE. A complimentary close is used on most letters, typed two lines below the last line of your message and positioned flush left in block form or starting in the center in modified block form. In most business letters, you want to end on a friendly but not too familiar note. Use variations of "truly" ("Yours truly," "Yours very truly," "Very truly yours") or "sincerely" ("Most sincerely," "Very sincerely," "Sincerely yours," "Sincerely"). "Cordially" and its variations are proper closings for general business letters, especially when the writer and the recipient know each other. If you are on a first-name basis with your addressee, informal closings are appropriate ("As ever," "Best wishes," "Regards," "Kindest regards," "Kindest personal regards"). Closings such as "Respectfully" and "Respectfully yours" indicate not only respect but also subservience and are usually reserved for diplomatic or ecclesiastic communications.

SIGNATURE. Your handwritten signature will appear aligned below the complimentary close, followed by the typed signature. Your business title and company name may be needed, but don't repeat information that already appears in the corporate letterhead. Your name is typed just as in the handwritten signature. The courtesy title "Mrs.," "Miss," or "Ms." may be added to indicate a female writer's preference. Academic degrees (PhD, LLD) and professional ratings (CPA) may also be included in the typed signature. If more than one writer is signing a letter, the written and typed signature blocks can be placed either side by side or vertically.

FINAL NOTATIONS

If someone else types or keys your letter, the typist's initials may be included two lines below the signature block. Once standard in business letters, the use of initials is now a matter of corporate style.

When you are enclosing materials with your letter, the notation "Enclosure," "Enc.," or "Encl.," sometimes with an indication of the number of enclosed pieces—"Enclosures (2)"—is typed below the

signature block. The notation "Separate mailing" or "Under separate cover" followed by the name of the piece or pieces ("Separate mailing: 2018 Annual Report") appears when materials are being sent separately.

Courtesy copies—notated as "Cc:" or "Copies to"—indicate that your letter is to be distributed to other people. The names of these recipients are listed alphabetically, and you may also include their addresses if this will be helpful to your recipient.

A postscript, or PS, can be added below the last notation and should be initialed by the letter writer. Postscripts are a common tactic in contemporary direct-mail advertising, as if the writer had one last brilliant reason for you to buy the product. With word processing, however, postscripts are rarely necessary and may signal to the reader that you did a poor job of organizing your thoughts if you left important information out of the body of your letter.

THE THANK-YOU NOTE

While it's true that a well-written thank-you note is an art, you don't have to be Shakespeare to be effective with your appreciation. Follow these guideline on when and how to express your gratitude.

When to Send

If you were the guest of honor or hosted to a sit-down meal in a restaurant or someone's home, then a handwritten note is in order. For regularly scheduled events such as chamber of commerce mixers, a written note isn't necessary unless you have a particular reason to thank your hosts. It's always a good idea to send a written note when hosted by your boss or company CEO, no matter the event.

When the invitation was made by phone, a phoned thank-you the next day is appropriate. If the invitation was made via email, then an emailed thank-you is appropriate. If the invitation to a private event (as described above) was written or printed, then a written thank-you note is called for. In any of these cases, as a guest it is always appropriate to write a short thank-you note to your host.

If you're the host and you've invited a prospect or major client to lunch, you may also write a short note to her, thanking her for taking the time to meet with you.

The Fine Points of Thank-You Notes

While your words are the main event, attention to the following details will add polish to your thank-you note:

PAPER. Either a fold-over or correspondence (flat) card is fine—it's a personal choice. Chose stationery or note cards that are businesslike in design.

INK. Use blue or black ink to write your note.

HANDWRITING. It's important to handwrite rather than type and sign your note, even if you don't think your handwriting is particularly good. Write slowly and be as legible as you can if you are concerned. Your handwriting is an important part of what makes the note personal and meaningful. (See also the box "Thank-You Note Services," above.)

DETAILS. Include the date.

BUSINESS CARDS. While it's not wrong to enclose your business card, only do so if you know the recipient does not have your contact information.

What to Say

A thank-you note isn't a chore—it's an opportunity. In business, being thought of as a gracious, "with it" person sets you apart from your competition on both a personal and corporate level. A thank-you note is a quick, easy, and inexpensive way to accomplish this.

Dear Monica,

Thanks so much for the lunch today—and for introducing me to the Café Rouge. I see why it's your favorite restaurant— their Beef Bourguignon was exceptional. I really appreciated your wise counsel about the transfer offer, and I'll be in touch when I'm settled in Seattle.

Yours,
Sarah

Or, in a somewhat more formal tone:

Dear Ms. Jones,

Thank you so much for lunch today. The restaurant was elegant, and the meal was delicious. Most of all, I appreciate your ideas and guidance about my decision to transfer to the Seattle office. Your suggestions really helped me to get my priorities in order. I look forward to entertaining you on your next visit to the Northwest.

Sincerely,
Sarah Dawson

WRITING EMAILS

Email is perhaps the most common form of writing in today's business environment. The average corporate employee receives an avalanche of emails each day, about 110 on average. Simply sorting and reading email is one of the most important skills in a business professional's toolbox. Make sure that yours are emails worth reading. Write clear and concise emails that give information and communicate needs effectively.

State Your Business

State your business succinctly in the subject line and then clearly and concisely in the body of the email. People want to know why you have sent them something. Don't simply forward emails without comment or send people open-ended messages. If you are simply sharing a piece of information, say so. If you are keeping someone informed or up to date, say so. If you are communicating a piece of critical information, indicate it.

Ask for What You Need

Ask for what you need and state clearly how you want your recipient to respond. If the time frame of a reply matters to you, be sure to set one. You cannot force someone to respond in a timely manner, but you can give him or her information to know how to best deal with you.

Don't Email Angry

Beware of trying to convey emotional content or of trying to resolve complex emotional problems via email. It is hard to write clearly about emotional content or resolve complex problems in the body of a business email. If you find yourself rewriting your email several times because you don't think your response is clear, this is an indication that you should pick up the phone or schedule an in-person conversation.

THE "WHO WHAT WHEN WHERE RULE"

One of the clearest ways to determine if an email is the best way to communicate with the recipient is to ask yourself if it focuses on who, what, when, or where. If, however, your email delves into why or opinion, you may want to think twice before sending it. The recipient only has your words on the page to decipher your meaning, intent, and tone. Without visual clues or the sound of your voice your message can easily be misunderstood. When it's more than just the facts, opt for a phone call or an in-person meeting.

If you find you are about to send an angry response or convey upset or displeasure, save the message as a draft and give yourself some time to cool down. Later, either revise your email or ask yourself if the message might be better delivered personally with a call or visit.

Proofread and Review

As with all correspondence, reread what you have written before you send. As we have seen, sloppy writing speaks poorly of you, even in a less formal communication.

- Check for correct spelling, grammar, and punctuation.
- Review for clarity, especially regarding an expected response or time frame.
- Review for tone.

THE PARTS OF AN EMAIL

When you initiate an email with someone, treat it like a little letter: Use salutations, write in complete sentences, and finish with a closing. Once the back and forth of an exchange has gotten under way, it is okay to get more informal and let the salutations and the closings drop away. When you are conversing, you don't keep using someone's formal title after the introduction has been made. An email exchange is like a developing conversation in this way. When you initiate a new exchange start again with proper letter formatting.

TO FIELD. Be sure you are sending to the right person. Use Reply All very sparingly and carefully. Be very careful of auto-fill as you might end up sending that personal email to peter@yourboss.com instead of to peter@yourfriend.com. One trick is to fill this in after you have completed your email to be sure you are communicating the right message to the right person and that you don't inadvertently send it before you want to.

SUBJECT LINE. Construct a descriptive and accurate subject line to get your email read. And be careful that it doesn't have any spelling mistakes in it, either.

SALUTATION. Open with a "Dear _____" and use proper titles when emailing someone for the first time. Less formal salutations include "Greetings," "Hello," and "Good Morning," or the person's name.

BODY TEXT. Keep your writing brief and clear. Use correct spelling and proper grammar to be sure you are well understood.

CLOSING. Close with "Sincerely" and your name on the next line. Less formal closings include "Regards," "With Thanks," and "Warmly."

SIGNATURE. Build and use a signature for your emails that has your current contact information and represents you professionally.

TIP: "Sent from my iPhone" or "Sent from my (fill in device name), please excuse any typos" is not a professional signature.

WRITING MEMORANDA

By definition, a memorandum—memo—is an informal written communication, usually sent within an office or company for quick and concise communication of news, requests and responses, procedures, and some employment-related information. Today the memo is as likely to be sent as an email as posted in the staff room.

The format for memos differs from business letters in address, salutation, content, and close. Memos can be typed on letterhead, but companies often have a standard memo form, printed or as a word-processing template. Memos may be sent as the body of an email or as an attachment. The basic address style is:

TO: Name(s) of primary recipient(s) or group

FROM: Name of sender

DATE: Day of sending

SUBJECT OR RE: A brief but precise title, such as "Thursday's New Business Presentation" or "Changes in Employee Health Insurance"

COPIES: Name(s) of other recipient(s)

List names by order of established management hierarchy—highest to lowest position—or alphabetically. Use an alphabetized listing when the recipients are roughly on the same job level or share responsibility for a project. For memos with wide distribution, you may want to address them to a group ("The Staff," "Purchasing Department," "Birthday Party Planners").

A memo does not have a salutation, and a memo gets to the point in a more direct manner than a typical business letter. The tone is usually casual and friendly, though the rules of good grammar and clear construction are always important. The informality of memos means that the writing is closer to a conversational style. Still, a business memo is not a personal letter, and memos should never include private information or waste the reader's time by straying from the topic into marginal or unrelated issues.

Memos do not include the complimentary closing of business letters and are not signed by the sender, although some writers initial their memos. It never hurts to conclude with thanks or compliments or words of encouragement. ("We all know that this project is our first real shot at national recognition, and I really appreciate your willingness to put in the extra hours and effort to make it our best.")

THE STATIONERY DRAWER

A set of stationery is called a wardrobe. Good stationery is also a representation of your image and should be a part of your professional wardrobe. In an increasingly digital world, correspondence on paper presents a great opportunity for distinction. Think of business stationery as a form of public relations. Whenever a piece of paper goes out, it should look good and suit the occasion, because its appearance reflects on the image and character of the business. To be prepared for most business communications, the effective businessperson's stationery drawer should contain the following:

CORPORATE LETTERHEAD. This is an 8½ × 11-inch sheet of good-quality (high-cotton fiber and usually 24-pound weight) paper that is imprinted with the company name and other pertinent information, including full address and telephone number, fax number, email address, and website URL. Law firms, medical partnerships, and other professional groups may include a complete list of partners on the letterhead. (*Note:* This can be costly, considering that the letterhead must be reprinted whenever a partner joins or leaves.)

Letterhead can be used by anyone in the company for official correspondence, unless it is printed with the name and title of a company officer or a partner. The name and address of the company should be printed on the face side of the matching envelope. If a letter runs to more than a single page (generally, it should not), then use a blank second sheet of the same paper.

MONARCH SHEETS. Also called executive sheets, these measure 7¼ × 10½ inches and are used by individuals for personal business letters. Monarch sheets and their matching envelopes are imprinted with the name of the individual and the address of the business, but not the business name.

Monarch sheets are sometimes used as business letterhead by physicians, lawyers, consultants, and other professionals. In this instance, it is correct to

From time to time, companies send out formal printed announcements—notices of change of address and new office openings, additions to staff, promotions, deaths. Whether these announcements are conservative or creative depends on the company's general graphic standards, its corporate image, and the occasion. Announcements should focus on a single item and, as with all good business writing, should quickly get to the point. Grammatically, a company or business name is always treated as a singular noun and requires a singular verb— "Smythe, Smythe & Jones is pleased to announce . . ."— but when the members of the company are emphasized, then the plural is used—"The Directors and Officers of Jones Company are pleased to announce . . ." Announcement cards and matching envelopes are ordered when needed. A formal announcement would read:

The Board of Trustees of High Q University
is honored to announce that
Michael Kemerling, PhD
has been elected to
The Fortescue Chair of Medieval Literature
and will assume the post
on the first of February,
two thousand eighteen

print the name of the company or firm, address, and telephone and telecommunications numbers on the sheet. Monarch sheets used as corporate letterhead also may require second sheets in the same paper and size.

CORRESPONDENCE CARDS. These are used for short, personal messages, including thank-you notes. The cards are printed with the individual's name only; the name and business address are printed on the matching envelope. Usually $4\frac{1}{2} \times 6\frac{1}{2}$ inches, these cards are made of a heavier weight paper or card stock and do not fold.

ENVELOPES. Envelopes should match your corporate letterhead and other papers in size, quality, color, and printing style. Generally, return names and addresses are printed on the face side of envelopes to meet postal regulations. In fact, before placing any stationery orders, it's a smart idea to check with your local postal authority for the most up-to-date rules. This applies to all mailings you send out, including windowed billing envelopes and response envelopes, as well as prepaid stamped envelopes of any kind.

BUSINESS CARDS. The last basic item in the stationery drawer is the business card, which is customarily presented during business occasions. Although there seems to be no end to the gimmicks offered for these small essentials, the classic is a $3\frac{1}{2} \times 2$-inch card of heavy paper stock in white or ecru, printed in black or gray ink. Alternative sizes and shapes may not fit standard card holders or wallet slots.

The card should include only pertinent information: name and business title, business name, address, telephone (cell and/or landline as pertinent) and fax numbers, and email address. If your name is ambiguous (Marion, for example, or Pat), include your courtesy title (Mr. Marion Brown, Ms. Pat DiBernadino); otherwise, use your full name only. (See also the box "Your Trusty Business Card," page 135 and "Business Cards," page 313.)

A card printed on a special form to fit Rolodex-style address holders can be a real convenience for clients, suppliers, and others who frequently contact you by phone, fax, or email. Naturally, these cards should include the same information as your business card.

Business cards should always be handed out discreetly (never in the first minutes of meeting someone, thrown in a pile on a table, or during a meal) and accepted graciously. The information on your card should also be kept up-to-date, and the card should be clean and not creased, dog-eared, or folded.

WHAT'S IN A NAME?

In business correspondence, getting a person's name and title correct is essential. Not only do name and title identify a person, but they also signify position and rank, achievement, and even self-concept. The person who receives your letter has an ego, and it may be a large one. If you have a history of correspondence, check your file letters from him; the courtesy or business title from the typed signature line will indicate how the person prefers to be addressed. This information may also be found on an executive letterhead or in a company directory or annual report. If necessary, there's nothing wrong with calling your addressee's business and making inquiries; asking for the right name—including spelling—and title shows concern and respect on your part.

FORMS OF ADDRESS

	INSIDE & ENVELOPE	SALUTATION
US Government Officials		
The President	The President, or The Honorable Full Name President of the United States	Mr. / Madam President Dear Mr. / Madam President
Former President	The Honorable Full Name	Sir / Madam Dear Mr. / Ms. / Mrs. Last Name
President Elect	The Honorable Full Name	Sir / Madam Dear Mr. / Ms. / Mrs. Last Name
The President's Spouse	Mr. / Ms. / Mrs. Last Name	Dear Mr. / Ms. / Mrs. Last Name
The Vice President	The Vice President, or Vice President Full Name	Sir / Madam Dear Mr. / Madam Vice President
Cabinet Members	The Honorable Full Name (The) Secretary of (Department)	Sir / Madam Dear Mr. / Madam Secretary

	INSIDE & ENVELOPE	SALUTATION
U.S. Attorney General	The Honorable Full Name Attorney General of the United States	Sir / Madam Dear Mr. / Madam Attorney General
The Chief Justice (The Supreme Court)	The Chief Justice (of the United States) The Supreme Court	Sir / Madam Dear Mr. / Madam Chief Justice
Associate Justice (The Supreme Court)	(Mr. / Madam) Justice Last Name The Supreme Court of the United States	Sir / Madam Mr. / Madam Justice Dear Mr. / Madam Justice Last Name
Federal Judge	The Honorable Full Name Judge of the United States District Court for the ___ District of _____	Sir / Madam Dear Judge Last Name
Senator	The Honorable Full Name United States Senate (*Use same form for state senators with the indication:* *The Senate of _____)*	Sir / Madam Dear Senator Last Name
Representative	The Honorable Full Name United States House of Representatives (*Use same form for state representatives and indicate* *name of representative body.*)	Sir / Madam Dear Representative Last Name Dear Mr. / Ms. / Mrs. Last Name
State Governor	The Honorable Full Name Governor of _____	Sir / Madam Dear Governor Last Name
Chief Justice (State Supreme Court)	The Honorable Full Name Chief Justice of the Supreme Court of (State)	Sir / Madam Dear Mr. / Madam Chief Justice
Associate Justice (State Supreme Court)	The Honorable Full Name Associate Justice of the Supreme Court of (State)	Sir / Madam Dear Justice Last Name
Mayor	The Honorable Full Name Mayor of _____	Dear Mr. / Madam Mayor Dear Mayor Last Name
Alderman/Alderwoman Councilman/Councilwoman	The Honorable Full Name Alderman/Alderwoman Full Name Councilman/Councilwoman Full Name	Dear Mr. / Ms. / Mrs. Last Name Dear Alderman/Alderwoman Last Name Dear Councilman/Councilwoman Last Name

Foreign and Diplomatic

	INSIDE & ENVELOPE	SALUTATION
Foreign Head of State	His / Her Excellency Full Name Premier/President of _____	Excellency Dear Mr. / Madam Premier/President
Prime Minister	His / Her Excellency Full Name	Excellency Dear Mr. / Madam Prime Minister

	INSIDE & ENVELOPE	SALUTATION
Prime Minister of Canada	The Right Honourable Full Name, P.C., M.P. (, *add other postnominal letters here*) Prime Minister of Canada	Dear Prime Minister *(Mr. / Madam Prime Minister is incorrect)*
Royalty	*Make inquiry to the embassy of the country for the correct forms of address.*	
U. S. Ambassador	The Honorable Full Name Ambassador of the United States	Sir / Madam Dear Mr. / Madam Ambassador
Foreign Ambassador	His / Her Excellency Full Name The Ambassador of _____	Excellency Dear Mr. / Madam Ambassador

U.S. Military

	INSIDE & ENVELOPE	SALUTATION
In general:	Military titles are numerous. The basic address form is: Rank, Full Name, Service Initials. In the address, rank may be written in full or abbreviated: Major, Maj., or MAJ.	Salutation style is: Dear Rank Dear Mr. /Ms. / Miss Last Name
Services	United States Army (USA) United States Navy (USN) United States Air Force (USAF) United States Marine Corps (USMC) United States Coast Guard (USCG)	
Samples	General (GEN) Full Name, USA Commander (CDR) Full Name, USN Colonel (COL) Full Name, USAF First Sergeant (1SG) Full Name, USA Lieutenant (j.g.) (LTJG) Full Name, USCG	Dear General Last Name Dear Commander Last Name Dear Colonel Last Name Dear Sergeant Last Name Dear Mr. / Ms. / Miss Last Name *(Use Mr., Ms., or Miss for Navy and Coast Guard officers below the rank of Lieutenant Commander.)*
Military Academy	Private (PVT) Full Name, USMC Cadet Full Name United States Military Academy (or) United States Air Force Academy	Dear Private Last Name Dear Cadet Last Name
	Midshipman Full Name United States Naval Academy (or) United States Coast Guard Academy	Dear Midshipman Last Name
Retired Officers	Major (MAJ) Full Name, USA, Retired	Dear Major Last Name

INSIDE & ENVELOPE		SALUTATION

Professional Titles

Attorney	Mr. / Ms. Full Name Attorney-at-Law Or, Full Name, Esq. / Esquire (*Note: If using Esq. / Esquire do not use Mr. / Ms.*)	Dear Mr. / Ms. Last Name Dear Attorney Last Name
Professional Designations: CPA, CLU, etc.	Full Name, CPA, (CLU, etc.) (*Add designations in the order in which they were earned.*)	Dear Mr. / Ms. Last Name
Physician, Dentist, Veterinarian	Full Name, M.D. (D.D.S., D.V.M.)	Dear Dr. Last Name
College / University Officers (with Ph.D.)	Dr. Full Name President (Chancellor, Dean) Full Name	Dear Dr. Last Name
Professor	Dr. Full Name or, Full Name, Ph. D. Professor of _____ (or) Professor Full Name	Dear D. Last Name Dear Professor Last Name

Religious Dignitaries

Pope	His Holiness, Pope Papal Name	Your Holiness Most Holy Father
Patriarch	His Beatitude the Patriarch of _____	Most Reverend Lord
Cardinal	His Eminence, First Name Cardinal Last Name Archbishop of _____	Your Eminence Dear Cardinal Last Name
Roman Catholic Archbishop / Bishop	The Most Reverend Full Name Archbishop / Bishop of _____	Your Excellency Most Reverend Sir Dear Archbishop / Bishop Last Name
Roman Catholic Monsignor	The Right Reverend Monsignor Full Name	Reverend Monsignor Dear Monsignor Last Name
Roman Catholic Priest	The Reverend Full Name	Reverend Father Dear Father Last Name
Episcopal Bishop	The Right Reverend Full Name (, *add academic degrees*) Bishop of _____	Right Reverend Sir / Madam Dear Bishop Last Name
Methodist Bishop	The Reverend Full Name Bishop of _____	Dear Bishop Last Name
Mormon Bishop	Bishop Full Name Church of Jesus Christ of Latter Day Saints	Sir Dear Bishop Last Name
Protestant Clergy	The Reverend Full Name Or, with doctorate: The Reverend Dr. Full Name The Reverend Full Name, D.D.	Dear Mr. / Ms. Last Name Dear Dr. Last Name

	INSIDE & ENVELOPE	SALUTATION
Rabbi	Rabbi Full Name *Or, with doctorate:* Rabbi Full Name, D.D.	Dear Rabbi Dear Rabbi Last Name Dear Dr. Last Name
Imam	The Imam Full Name	Dear Imam Last Name

Multiple Names

	INSIDE & ENVELOPE	SALUTATION
Men with Different Surnames	Mr. Ian M. Green Mr. James L. Black Or, Messrs. I. M. Green and J. L. Black Or, Messrs. Green and Black	Gentlemen Dear Mr. Green and Mr. Black Dear Messrs. Green and Black
Women with Different Surnames	Ms. / Mrs. Jane F. Jones Ms. / Mrs. Ann B. Smith Or, Mesdames J. F. Jones and A. B. Smith Or, Mesdames Jones and Smith	Mesdames Dear Ms. / Mrs. Jones and Ms. / Mrs. Smith Dear Mesdames Jones and Smith (*Mesdames refers to multiple adult women married or not, similar to "ladies".*)
A Group of Men and Women	Ms. Ann Smith and Messrs. Ian Green and James Black Messrs. Green, Black, White Mesdames Smith and Jones	Dear Ladies and Gentlemen Dear Ms. Smith and Mr. Green
Physicians in Joint Practice	Dr. Ian M. Green, Dr. Jane F. Jones, and Dr. Ann B. Smith	Dear Drs. (Doctors) Green, Jones, and Smith

Married Couples

	INSIDE & ENVELOPE	SALUTATION
When the woman uses her husband's name, prefers the title "Ms.", or uses her maiden name	Mr. and Mrs. John F. Kelly Mr. John Kelly and Ms. Jane Kelly (*Note: Do not link Ms. to the husband's name: Mr. and Ms. John Kelly is incorrect*) Mr. John Kelly and Ms. Jane Johnson	Dear Mr. and Mrs. Kelly Dear Mr. Kelly and Ms. Kelly Dear Mr. Kelly and Ms. Johnson
Rank: Elected Office, Military Rank	*The person of higher rank is always listed first, regardless of gender:* The Honorable Jane Kelly and Mr. John Kelly The President and Mrs. Kelly Major (MAJ) Jane A. Kelly and Captain (CPT) John F. Green, USA	Dear Senator Kelly and Mr. Kelly Dear President and Mrs. Kelly Dear Major and Captain Kelly
Rank: Professional or Educational Degree	Dr. Jane Kelly and Mr. John Kelly The Reverend Jane A. Kelly and Mr. Kelly	Dear Dr. and Mr. Kelly Dear Reverend (Rev.) and Mr. Green
Both have doctoral degrees	Dr. Jane Kelly and Dr. John Kelly Dr. John Kelly and Dr. Jane Johnson	Dear Drs. (Doctors) Kelly Dear Dr. Kelly and Dr. Johnson Dear Drs. (Doctors) Kelly and Johnson

CHAPTER 26
DIGITAL COMMUNICATIONS

Email, texting, instant messages, and shared calendars can be effective and efficient ways to communicate. Consider the advantages:

- They are incredibly fast.

- They are relatively cheap.

- A large number of people can be reached.

- A record of information is created.

But because they are so easy to access and relatively new, these forms of electronic communication are also ripe for misuse and abuse—as anyone faced with a flood of pointless and irrelevant messages in their in-box can testify. Businesses are wise to implement clear communication guidelines, and employees are advised to seek them out and adhere to them.

THE BASICS: EMAIL AND TEXTS

Whether it is an email to a boss or a text confirming lunch with a new contact—mistakes made with digital communication can have serious consequences for business. Read on for tips on avoiding the most common difficulties many people face and leverage these powerful tools to your best advantage.

Profread, Proofred, Proofread

"I was typing with my thumbs!" is not an excuse for misspellings, grammatical errors, or punctuation mistakes. Your familiarity with such rules should shine through at all times, no matter which communication medium you use. Mistakes take the focus away from the content of the message. If you make mistakes with something as simple as writing, this sends a signal that you may make mistakes in other areas. With all of the digital information at our fingertips, there is no excuse for using incorrect spelling or bad grammar. A quick proofread to correct obvious misspellings, bad sentence structure, or words with unclear meaning is appreciated in every medium.

Don't use a signature line from a mobile device to excuse lazy misspellings. "Please excuse any typos as this was sent from my phone" isn't courteous; it says you are unconcerned with rereading a message you know may have mistakes. Even when a message is composed on a mobile device, spelling, grammar, and word choice matter.

Autofill and Autocorrect functions have become a part of our new digital world. They can both help and hurt. A quick tour of www.damnyou autocorrect.com will give an idea of how smartphones can badly misinterpret what you meant to type in ways that create confusion at best and extreme embarrassment at worst. What may be seen as amusing in your online social life may be perceived as less so in the business world and can be a knock on your professionalism. Always take the time to reread your messages before you hit Send or Post.

Tone

Tone matters, too. People hear your tone of voice in your writing and it will affect how they interpret the meaning of your message.

In the absence of other information, interpretation often defaults to the negative. So it's especially important to carefully monitor your tone when expressing criticism in writing, no matter how mild—otherwise, even a simple observation can come across as an attack. Use positive modifiers like "please" and "thank-you" to soften requests and show appreciation explicitly. Avoid using imperative language like "need" and "must" unless you really need to or must.

Attempts at humor can also be difficult without the smile and twinkling eye that lets someone in on the joke.

Reading what you write back to yourself out loud, in your conversational voice, is one of the best ways to check the tone of any message before you send, tweet, or post.

Emoticons, Abbreviations, and All Caps

EMOTICONS. Emoticons help by investing electronic messages with emotional tone. A smiley face with a wink can say, "Just joking, in case you missed it." While such a qualifier can work in a personal message, they are best left out of business messages. If your email or text needs an emoticon to convey your tone, it may be a signal that you should opt for a phone conversation or an in-person meeting or you should rewrite what you have written.

TEXT ABBREVIATIONS. In business, texting is probably the only medium in which the use of text abbreviations is acceptable, but even here they should be used with caution. Remember that clarity of communication is one of the objectives in business. Some substitutions, especially phrases that include expletives, have no place in business. Avoid OMG entirely as it can give offense. Safest route? If it's business, spell it out. The same goes for IMHO for "in my humble opinion," LOL for "laugh out loud," and BTW for "by the way." They are fine for text messages, but beware using them or other abbreviations in an email or other more formal means of written communication. They can appear unprofessional, and there is a chance that your recipient may not be up on text abbreviations. Three that are used frequently in email and texts and are acceptable to abbreviate: FYI for "for your information," EOD for "end of day," and COB for "close of business."

ALL CAPS. Another firmly established online convention is to avoid typing in all capital letters as it sig-

> **TIP:** Before you knock, call, send, post, or tweet, choose the communication medium that best serves the message you want to deliver. Never, for example, send an email letter of resignation. Similarly, don't issue serious complaints or criticisms by text or instant message; instead, try to arrange a personal meeting or a phone call to discuss difficult problems or emotional topics.

nifies that you are shouting your message. You would almost never shout at someone in person, and you should almost never use all caps in a written message. Readability studies also show that all-caps messages are much harder to read.

The Medium Is the Message

With so many communication media to choose from, the medium you choose becomes an important part of the message you send.

- A handwritten note lends extra weight to thanks for a job interview, gift, or meal.

- A well-formatted email résumé sent to a tech firm shows respect for a paperless office culture.

- If you have been working late on a project and have a breakthrough, an email to your boss might be appreciated.

- A less formal text that could reach your boss immediately wherever she is might feel like an intrusion outside of work.

Recovering from a Mistake

So what do you do when you post something you shouldn't have or mistakenly send a private message to your coworker that was intended only for your spouse? Sometimes, even if you can't put the genie back in the bottle, you can still minimize the mistake. Remove offensive content that you are responsible for as soon as you can. Take down photos immediately if someone asks you to. Then apologize to those who were affected by your mistake.

Follow messages that go to the wrong people with an explanation—a misdirected text or tweet followed by a quick "oops," for example, is enough in simple or low-stakes situations. If the mistake is bigger and people are likely to take serious offense or maybe even be fired, you should be sure to try to resolve the situation in person or over the phone.

A quick apology sent via text or email is not enough to fix a truly difficult situation, like a boss mistakenly receiving a disparaging email from an employee. For something like this, you want to make every effort to be seen as part of the solution and not just as the source of a problem. Try to get ahead of a situation like this by talking to the people affected before they learn about the mistake in other ways. Lend weight to your apology by offering it in person. Come prepared with solutions and express your willingness to work to resolve the issue. Don't wait to be found out and confronted with the issue. Everyone makes mistakes. How they are handled says as much, or more, about us than our successes. Take responsibility, fix what you can, apologize for what you did wrong, and move on.

EMAIL

Your ability to handle email well is a big part of your professional reputation. Keep an eye on these areas so your email communications are effective and successful.

Timeliness

People, especially businesspeople, usually expect a reply to email the same day or within twenty-four hours. Make sure people you want to stay in touch with get replies within a day or two at the most.

Subject Line

The subject line of your email is like the headline on a newspaper—it is what gets it read. A descriptive subject line increases the chances of your email being opened by identifying the purpose of the email. Proofread your subject line as it is part of your first impression. Building good subject lines makes your emails easy to identify, sort, and prioritize.

Cc vs. Bcc

The carbon copy vs. the blind carbon copy. You want to remain open and honest in your communication. Use the Cc to let the recipient know who else has received a message. Only use the Bcc to protect email address privacy or for big email lists where every recipient does not need access to the entire list. While there are a few business situations where Bcc works—a lawyer who Bcc's his administrative assistant with an email that should be printed and put in a client's file—in most cases Bcc is seen as a subterfuge and should be avoided.

> **TIP:** Click on the sender's name to verify the email address—if it's not the legitimate address of the person you know, then delete the email.

Reply vs. Reply All

Few business etiquette topics push people's buttons like the overuse of Reply All. Don't use Reply All when doing the following:

- Responding to a meeting invitation
- Expressing thanks to the sender
- Continuing an email chain with the sender only

Don't Accept Packages from Strangers

Don't open attachments from people you don't know or even from people you do know if you are not sure about the contents. It is worth it to check if a colleague really sent you some new software rather than infect your computer and possibly your business's network with a virus.

Keep an Eye on Your Junk

Understand all the levels of junk-mail filtering that your email system uses. Specifically, pay attention to the different criteria levels for spam and for how long messages stay in your spam filter before being cleared.

The only thing more remarkable than the amount of spam sent every day is the skill with which most junk filters keep it from ever reaching any of us. Occasionally, a legitimate email will get tagged as spam, so it is worthwhile to check your spam folder on a regular basis to recover emails you wish to keep.

Personal Use

While most companies will overlook the occasional use of work email accounts for personal communications, regular and ongoing use can land you in hot water. Other companies restrict the use of their business email accounts to company business only. Using company accounts and company time to regularly take care of personal business is a common complaint from management. If you do a lot of personal emailing—sending pictures, links, jokes, and messages to friends and family or to support a private business venture—then keep an email account separate from your work account and use it only when not on work time.

Salutations, Sign-Offs, and Mass Mailings

Formal	Informal
Dear	Hello/Hi
To whom it may concern	Greetings
	Good morning/ afternoon

There's no denying that an email is inherently more informal than a typed letter sent via snail mail—but that doesn't mean you can forget all about appropriate salutations. In fact, treat the first email in an exchange with someone as you would a short letter to set an appropriate tone for business. Even with close colleagues with whom you email back and forth frequently, it is thoughtful to employ some sort of salutation, at least on your first email of the day. In subsequent emails, use your common sense: If you're firing ideas back and forth every few minutes—the equivalent of instant messaging or a verbal conversation—then it's acceptable to drop all salutations.

The same goes for signing off on an email. For supervisors, clients, and upper management, a formal sign-off is required—"Thank you/Caitlyn"—whereas for closer colleagues, you may opt for a more abbreviated or informal sign-off—"Thanks, C."

Formal	Informal
Sincerely yours	Cheers
Sincerely	Thanks
Kindest regards	Best
Best wishes	Thank you
Regards	
Cordially	

What about when you're sending out a mass email to a hundred associates? The greeting can be generic—"Dear All" or "Greetings, everyone" or "Hello, team"—while the sign-off should be the same as for an individual email.

TEXTING

The immediacy of texting has made it a go-to choice for a new generation of professionals. While texting enhances business communications, it can also cause communication headaches when not used appropriately.

CONTROL YOUR SMARTPHONE

One of the best ways to ensure that a text message won't bother you late at night or at the movies or on a date is to turn off your smartphone. Don't let your phone control you. Instead, be in control of it.

Setting Boundaries

Start by talking to your colleagues about how they use texting, especially when you are new to a job. You want to be sure that you are texting someone who uses the medium before you start texting to communicate something work-related.

PERSONAL SPACE

Many people see texting as something for personal use and might interpret work-related texts as an intrusion on private time. For some, a work-related text after 9 PM had better be an emergency! Yet, for others, it might be the preferred way to get a message. There is no set rule, so consider (and discuss, if necessary) these boundaries before texting after hours.

STAYING CONNECTED

Whether you prefer to keep all your work communications confined to email or would rather receive work-related messages outside the office via text is up to you. Either is okay but establish your preferences and boundaries with your coworkers. If you prefer not to be texted about work, offer other ways to reach you in an emergency or to contact you if a work-related issue arises—traditional phone calls and email directed to a mobile device are both options. If you like to do work via text, let people know what hours are reasonable to send you messages.

ON THE GO

Don't be that person who is always nose deep in the phone furiously tapping away and ignoring the people around her. Be careful in your quest to stay connected that you don't close off the rest of the world. Work texting can allow your job to take over your life if you are not careful. Ask any spouse who has to share a bedroom with someone constantly texting or emailing for work from a mobile device if it's an intrusion into private life. Set limits before it becomes a problem for you—and be sure affected family members agree with your personal policy.

PERSONAL USE AT WORK

It is worth mentioning the amount of work time that is lost to texts and messaging services. Because they are silent and can be sent relatively quickly, the seduction of sending personal texts from work is great. Just like too many personal calls can negatively impact your work reputation, so can too many texts. Show restraint during work hours; keep the personal texting to an absolute minimum.

Accountability and Confidentiality

Texting and instant messaging have become important business communication tools. Just like you need to keep confidential work emails that are sent to your mobile device secure and, as a best practice,

password-protected, the same care needs to be taken with texts that contain valuable work information. Be sure that your mobile device is password-protected and that you can turn it off, lock it, or wipe it clean remotely if you should happen to lose or misplace it.

SHARED CALENDARS

Shared calendars make coordinating meetings and checking colleague availability easy. But there are a few things to keep in mind about maintaining your calendar and sending meeting requests.

Keep your calendar up-to-date. This means syncing your smartphone to it regularly as well.

Be sure to note all appointments, including personal ones, so that others know if you are available. While some personal appointments, such as lunch with a friend, pose no problems on a shared calendar, others, such as dates, doctor's visits, or personal appointments for something like a bikini wax may be perceived as too much information by others. Use the privacy feature to mark personal appointments. This allows you to see the appointment's details, but others see only "Private" marking your calendar.

Meeting requests may be sent to find out if a time is available or to confirm one previously agreed upon. Either way, reply promptly when you receive one. If you are sending out a notice, first check any colleagues' calendars, and check time zone differences for conference calls. Watch out for Arizona and Hawaii, which do not use daylight savings time.

CHAPTER 27
SOCIAL NETWORKING

While digital communications have blurred the lines of work–life balance in terms of your availability, social networking has added personal branding and image questions to this balance. First, who are you representing: yourself or your company? It becomes critical to know which hat you are wearing. Ethical questions about how you spend your time while you're on the clock come into play: Facebook posts for your company are one thing; for yourself, another. And even if you don't use social networking for work or during work hours, it's entirely possible that whether you are aware of it or not, you may bump into colleagues, bosses, clients, customers, and vendors on social networks outside of work.

You define yourself by images, videos, and words when using social networks. This takes the meaning of work–life balance to a whole new level and requires that you think carefully about how you present yourself or represent your company. This doesn't mean you have to scrub your personal life online free of opinions and interests, but it does mean you need to be able to stand by your words and images if someone in your professional life were to see them.

SOCIAL NETWORKING AFFECTS BUSINESS DIRECTLY

The Internet allows us to get information quickly that once took hours to find, and to conduct business in ways that were impossible to imagine just a decade ago. Sports scores, market updates, streaming video, the latest news and celebrity gossip, music, movies, chat rooms—it's all just a click or a keystroke away. The problem is, much of this isn't work-related—and as a result employers are increasingly frustrated by the loss of productive work to web and social media surfing, and they are monitoring workplace Internet use.

Social "Notworking" by the Numbers

Here's how social networking directly affects business: The National Business Ethics Survey of Social Networkers, which was conducted in 2012 by the Ethics Resource Center, reports that nearly three-quarters of the workers over age thirty report taking part in social networking at home or at work. Additionally, 72 percent of social networkers report spending at least some time social networking at work *every day*, while 30 percent admit to spending an hour or more a day social networking at work.

> **TIP:** Don't expose yourself or your company by viewing questionable material on company issued equipment either through your personal Internet access or through online access provided by the company.

What is more problematic and questionable is that the time spent social networking is not time spent social networking for the business. The National Business Ethics Survey of Social Networkers report says:

> Very little of the online time is work-related. One-third of those (33 percent) who spend an hour or more of the workday on social networking say that none of the activity is related to work. Another 28 percent say just a small fraction (10 percent of their online time) has something to do with their job. **In other words, a growing number of workers are getting paid for time spent on personal interests.**

Another revelation in the report is what active social networkers (those who spend more than an hour a day social networking) share about their workplace:

> Six of ten ASNs (Active Social Networkers) would comment on their personal sites about their company if it was in the news, 53 percent say they share information about work projects once a week or more, and more than a third say they often comment, on their personal sites, about managers, coworkers, and even clients. As a result, **workplace "secrets" are no longer secret, and management must assume that anything that happens at work, any new policy, product, or problem, could become publicly known at almost any time.**

Bottom line: You aren't being paid to spend time on your own social networking profiles. If you're allowed to visit social networking sites during work hours or use social networking for work purposes, save personal use for breaks only.

No Privacy

As with email, there is no privacy protection for on-the-job Internet surfers. Employers can monitor and audit their employees' computers for Internet use, checking on sites visited, time spent at each site, and materials downloaded.

An employee who accesses salacious material or engages in sexist, racist, or other prejudiced online conversation is engaging in clearly inappropriate behavior and puts not only himself but also his company in jeopardy of sexual harassment and discrimination charges or defamation actions.

SOCIAL NETWORKING— FOUR KEY TIPS

Whether you're posting photos or comments to Facebook, building a profile on LinkedIn, posting a video to Instagram, creating an image for yourself on Pinterest, how you interact online will reflect on you. You are out there for the world, not just a few close friends, to see. Four key pieces of advice pertain to the entire social networking world and will help you to build a positive image of yourself with everyone who interacts with you or looks at you online.

Online Privacy Is an Illusion

Just about everything that happens in the digital world has the potential to leave a permanent fingerprint and can be seen by virtually anyone. While privacy protections on social networking sites can help to manage access to what you share online, don't assume they are ironclad.

The public and permanent nature of digital communication offers users a challenge and an opportunity. With all of the connections that happen online you never know just where your message is going to end up, which can be fantastic if you're trying to go viral or get the word out, or it could lift the veil of anonymity and all of a sudden something you assumed was private can be seen by everyone.

Offering Criticism Online—Think Twice

If you are thinking of using social networking to offer criticism of another person, think twice. Here's why:

- Criticism is difficult to deliver and the first step in doing it well is to do it in private. Doing it online is the antithesis of doing it privately.

THE BULLETIN BOARD RULE

Use the "bulletin board rule" as a check to remind yourself of this reality. Before you hit Post or Send, ask yourself if you would be comfortable putting what you wrote up on the bulletin board at the office for anyone to read. If you wouldn't be comfortable, then don't hit Post or Send.

CONSISTENCY = TRUST

You want the image that appears on your online pages to be consistent with the image others have of you. When your personal and professional brands are consistent, your colleagues, clients, and prospects can have confidence that the person being presented is really you. But when the image varies significantly, you will lose the trust of people who are counting on the professional image you have presented to them: a boss who is considering you for a promotion or a company that is considering your application for a job or a prospect who is considering engaging you for work.

- Criticism online can very easily be misinterpreted, especially in the absence of facial expressions, body language, or tone of voice.

Online Posts Are Judged

"Judged" doesn't mean scored to see who is best; it means everyone—not just your friends—will see what you post and form opinions. And their opinion of your opinion may be very different from your opinion of your opinion.

You Are Responsible for Your Online Image

Not only are the comments and images you post your responsibility, you should make sure you regularly monitor the images other people share of you and the comments in which you are referenced. When you see a photo tagged with your image that you object to, first remove the tag (you can do this) and then contact the person who posted the image and ask her to remove it, too (only she can do that). Similarly, if someone writes something that portrays you in an unfavorable light, ask him to remove the post or delete the reference to you in it.

SOCIAL NETWORKING GUIDELINES

When faced with the reality that employees will be using social media online and that their use may or may not be related to business, companies would be well advised to establish a social media policy and communicate it clearly to every employee. Everyone in your company needs to have a clear understanding of what the standards are for using social networking tools in a professional context and what the company's policy is about personal social networking on company time. Specifically, businesses need the protection of an explicit social media policy that defines

- Who has control of and access to the accounts that represent the company

- What is allowable and desirable to be posted on behalf of a company

- What is unacceptable

- How to handle or respond to either criticism or crisis

- What an employee of a company is responsible for on their private social media network(s)

- The consequences for infractions or noncompliance

- A process for handling the departure of or transition to a new social media manager

Whether it's company policy or not, there are certain guidelines that you as an individual employee might consider adopting.

The Very Best Policy: Honesty

The heart of most good social media policies is the expectation of honest and forthright use. Whether you are representing yourself or your company, telling the truth is always a good start. Be transparent about who you are and for whom you work. Don't offer critiques or glowing reviews or even engage in a professional discussion without disclosing your connection, monetary or otherwise, to readers. This goes for citizen reviewers and raters on services like Yelp and Angie's List as well as reporters, PR professionals, and others.

Don't Air Dirty Laundry

Don't gripe about bosses, coworkers, clients, or conditions at work. Even if they are not likely to see it, it reflects poorly on you. And chances are the one time you post something that in retrospect you wish your boss hadn't seen is guaranteed to be the time it will come to his attention.

POPULAR SOCIAL NETWORKS

Social networking sites pop up almost daily. Yet there are several that have withstood the test of time. Each has its particular uses and may or may not be the best for business social networking.

Facebook

Though called a social network, Facebook is now also used by many companies, public figures, and causes. To avoid confusion, keep your interactions on your personal Facebook profile social and personal. If you are promoting a business or cause, make a page for the business or event. Keep promotional posts to a minimum to keep the goodwill of those you are connected with.

If you "friend" business associates on your Facebook page, consider making a group that is just for them, allowing you to restrict the content you want them to be able to see.

Twitter

Twitter is a micro-blogging service that facilitates online conversation. Since Twitter is a public site, observe the general rules for making conversation. (See Chapter 22.) Twitter's entire identity is the 140 character limit on posts; it is impossible to overstate how easy this short form makes it to post something before you think. Wait a few minutes, read your post out loud, or get a second opinion before posting anything controversial, angry, or negative. Don't overuse

Q. One of my "Facebook friends" is a man whom I've met two or three times in a professional group. I don't know him very well, but he seems like a rather smart and nice person. Unfortunately, he comments on at least 80 percent of my updates and posts. Most of his comments are pretty relevant, and sometimes funny, but I feel that the amount of feedback I'm getting is disproportionate to our actual relationship.

This Facebook friend seems like a pretty decent person, and I value his online presence, so I don't want to just "unfriend" him or change my privacy settings.

What do I do?

A. It's always difficult when you have to put limits on a relationship. It can leave hurt feelings and resentment if not done carefully.

If you have the patience, first try some benign options. Give it time. Perhaps he's new to Facebook and will reduce his commenting as the novelty wears off. Or you could take a break for a week or two yourself. When you start up again, you may discover that he's found other places to spend his time and therefore comments less often.

TIP: People look for recommendations and the quality of your connection network to assess your profile so it is advisable to develop these elements. Connections aren't about quantity but quality. So link with people you can vouch for.

the @name convention to try to get someone's attention. For each self-promotional tweet, try to engage with others or promote others at least three times.

LinkedIn

LinkedIn is the primary *professional* social network. People think of LinkedIn as an online résumé, but it's worth keeping your profile current even when not actively networking or looking for a job. Your profile should have a professional looking head shot and at minimum information about where you went to school and have worked. (For more on LinkedIn, see "LinkedIn," page 36.)

Instagram

Instagram functions as a shared photo and video album. Learn to manage your privacy settings and sharing preferences. Don't publicly share images or videos that show you in a negative light. (See also "Consistency = Trust," page 283.) This means risqué subject matter or anything involving intoxicants. It also means content that is too private for such a public forum.

PINTEREST

While Pinterest is often used for personal fun, many companies and individuals are using it for marketing purposes. There are a few points of etiquette to keep in mind when pinning:

- Be respectful. Pinterest is about sharing inspiration and creativity, so keep comments positive. If you don't like something, simply refrain from repinning or liking it, or stop following the board or pinner who shared it. Instead, stick with what you do like about a pin: "Love the use of color!"

- Give credit where credit is due, be it an author, company, designer, photographer, or anyone else involved in an image's creation.

- If a site has a "pin it" button, it's a clear sign they welcome you to use the images posted there. If a site has blocked visitors from pinning its images, respect that decision and refrain, even if you see a way to obtain the image another way.

- When pinning, take the time to click through to verify the original link. Regrettably, some pinners will misdirect users for their own purposes. If a pin links to an unrelated site, skip the pin and scroll on.

- Never copy and paste entire posts or articles from someone's blog or site to share as your pin description.

- Don't pin from search engine results. Pins from general image searches don't allow other pinners to find out the link or page from which the image came. If you find an image through a Google Image search, click through to the link and pin from there, including any source information you find. Pins from other image sharing sites like Tumblr can be tricky to source because so many people reblog from each other. Keep clicking back through the posts to find the original post.

- For the sake of the entire Pinterest community, report inappropriate pins.

- While there is no exact cap on the number of repins you can make from someone else, stop well short of culling his or her entire collection. Follow the "golden rule" and only repin as much as you would be comfortable having repinned from you.

- You don't have to follow everyone who follows you, but it's worth at least checking out his or her boards to see if you might want to return the favor. It's not rude to pick and choose among boards from a pinner you want to follow. It's also okay to "unfollow" or decline an invitation to pin to someone else's board.

PART SIX

ON THE ROAD

CHAPTER 28
THE THOUGHTFUL TRAVELER

While it's nice when a host handles your business travel planning for you, the ability to be self-reliant both in planning and execution is important to getting to your destination successfully. Another is the importance of carefully choosing what to take along—a habit that helps make trips glitch-free. For men and women caught in the headache of making travel plans, packing, and preparing for whatever business awaits them, etiquette is probably the last thing on their minds. After all, isn't behaving well a given? The answer should be yes, but business travelers will have more success when they take a few extra considerations into account.

Just as important as your laptop and carry-on is remembering to respect the rights of fellow travelers, including coping cheerfully with the growing frustrations of airplane travel and keeping your phone calls in check. The smoother things run on a business trip (and the less annoyance you cause), the easier it is to focus on the trip's objectives.

BE SELF-RELIANT

Unless a corporate travel office is handling your travel arrangements, build self-reliance into all your plans.

- Once the date and time of the visit are set, tell the people you are visiting that you'll make your own hotel reservations. Or if your company has a travel department or an affiliation with a travel agency, leave the planning to those reservationists. If your host insists on making them herself, let her do so; the hotel chosen will no doubt be in a place convenient to you both, which is what you want.

- The on-site business center is a valuable hotel amenity, equipped with copiers, fax machines, computers, and Internet access—all for the benefit of businesspeople. Ask the reservationist about special services of this kind and any other perks for the business traveler, and also check to see if they are included in the room charge or come with an additional fee.

- Concierge floors add value to a hotel stay with special areas set aside that have snacks, beverages, hors d'oeuvres, and even a quick breakfast available for guests.

- If your children are traveling with you, ask about babysitting services and creative programs to keep children occupied.

- If you're going to meet a client at your hotel, arrange in advance for the use of a meeting room. A note of caution: Having a business meeting in your hotel room is usually considered too personal these days, especially when it is with a member of the opposite sex.

- If the journey is a long one, plan to arrive in town the day before the meeting so that you'll be refreshed and at your best. If you have an appointment scheduled for the day you arrive, book a flight that leaves plenty of room for unexpected delays. Let the host know you are arriving on the day of the meeting and that you will keep her apprised of your travel progress. The same holds true if you're driving: Get an early start.

- If you are making your own arrangements for traveling from the airport to the hotel and if you must go straight from the airport to your meeting, think twice about taking a taxi; the line at the taxi rank may be long on a busy day. A safer alternative, if cost permits, is to arrange for a car service; the driver knows your destination in advance and will be waiting when you arrive.

- If you're scheduled to give a presentation, plan on arriving the day before. Take any visual aids with you, including equipment for presenting them, or send your materials ahead or arrange for the equipment to be available to you. Don't assume that the office you're visiting has an overhead projector for your slides, for example. (See Chapter 12 for more information on being prepared for a presentation.)

- When all of your arrangements are finalized, prepare an itinerary for the person you are visiting, your office, and your family. Include the following:

  - Your flight schedule, with flight numbers and times of departure and arrival

  - The name, address, and telephone number of your hotel

  - The times and locations of your meetings, with telephone numbers where you can be reached

- The name and telephone number of the contact person in the office you're visiting
- Your cell phone number

TROUBLE-FREE CLOTHING

Pick out the clothes in your wardrobe that are best suited to business travel. They should be lightweight (unless the climate dictates otherwise), wrinkle-resistant, and stylish but not flashy.

- Wear comfortable shoes, but take along a better pair for business meetings and evenings. Leave the sneakers at home.

- Men can choose to wear or pack their jackets. A business jacket without the matching suit pants while traveling is okay.

- Pack enough underwear and socks or panty hose for each day; don't rely on having the time to rinse out small items at night. Hotels do have laundry services for guests who will be there for an extended stay.

- Make sure you have everything you need in your cosmetic or shaving kit in containers of three ounces or less; unlike leisure travelers, business travelers often can't afford the time to buy items they forgot. If you do forget something, before trying to find a nearby drugstore, ask at the front desk if they have any complimentary toiletry items.

- If exercise is part of your daily routine, pack your workout gear or swimsuit.

- Pack a collapsible umbrella.

What to wear on a plane? Both men and women may be tempted to wear their not-so-best jeans and sneakers for the flight, especially since they know they'll be squeezed into a tight seat and could run into delays. But by dressing in business casual for travel (yes, even *dress* jeans with a jacket works), if a checked bag is lost, you won't have to arrive at a meeting looking as if you've just come from mowing the lawn or shopping for groceries. Remember, too, that airlines cater to business travelers. Look the part by dressing appropriately, and you may find you get an added measure of service.

DIFFERENT CLIMATES, DIFFERENT STYLES, DIFFERENT TIMES OF DAY?

Choosing a travel wardrobe becomes trickier when you travel to a part of the country where the climate is different from your home region. You might assume, for instance, that if you're going to the Deep South, you'll find businessmen in short sleeves in summer. But you probably won't, since business dress codes are fairly standard throughout the country, with long-sleeved shirts the rule. Guard against clothing missteps by asking the advice of workmates or friends who are familiar with the region's customs, or ask the receptionist at the office you will be visiting.

If you are making a presentation or attending a meeting at another company, wear your usual business clothes; then wait until you are invited to before removing your jacket.

Dressing for evening calls for more attention. Men might learn, for example, that a blazer is expected with the usual khakis-and-sport-shirt uniform worn for casual events. Likewise, in some places, women dress more formally in the evening than during the day with, say, a beaded top instead of a twin set; accordingly, a woman should pack a dressier garment than she might be wearing for her business dealings. As a practicality, those who travel frequently can invest in one of the stylish daytime-to-evening outfits that are designed with the traveling businesswoman in mind.

EN ROUTE

Trains, planes, and automobiles: Each of these modes of transportation presents its own set of concerns for the business traveler.

Up, Up, and Away

Airline travel is complicated by (1) the penchant airlines have for changing their rules; (2) the fact that in the post-9/11 world, airports have stricter rules regarding security; and (3) airlines are charging fees for every convenience and comfort, from carry-on bags to extra leg room. Take note: If there's one place on earth where an ordinary citizen must always follow directions, it's an airport.

LUGGAGE AND ID. So there won't be any surprises, before you pack your bags check with the airline regarding size limits for carry-on luggage and the number of pieces allowed. You will be asked for a photo ID when you check in and will be barred from boarding if you can't produce a driver's license or some other form of photo ID. (International travelers must present a valid passport.) If a glitch does occur, you can exhibit your first courteous act of the trip by not arguing with airline employees or TSA personnel or making a scene. To avoid problems, get in the habit of jotting down a checklist of essential articles and then running through it before you leave for the airport—wardrobe items, toiletries, business papers, and personal documents, with your appropriate ID at the top of the list.

IN THE AIR. As amazing as it seems, the bad behavior of some passengers qualifies as a threat to safety, with alcohol often to blame. Notorious cases abound: the man who wrestled with an attendant for a liquor bottle, shouting obscenities; the enraged woman who knocked an airline attendant to the floor because there were no more snacks; and incidents even more appalling. As for minor incivilities, you might as well just grin and bear them. If you don't respond to bad behavior with similar reactions, your journey will at least *feel* a lot smoother. Any truly unacceptable behavior, however, should always be reported to the flight attendant.

Some Airplane Dos and Don'ts

- **DO** tell the flight attendant if you need to deplane quickly because of a tight connection. It may be a futile request, but maybe he or she will be able to move you to a seat closer to the front just before landing.

- **DO** carry on at least a brief conversation with the stranger next to you but only if you are sure he invites it. Conversely, politely cut off unwelcome chitchat by excusing yourself to read a magazine or to do your work.

- **DO** be sympathetic to the plight of the middle seat occupant, especially with the use of the armrest.

- **DO** use earbuds or headphones to listen to music—but keep the volume down.

- **DO** be careful about what movies you watch on your computer that the content won't be, at least visually, problematic for the person sitting next to you.

- **DO** treat airline attendants politely. Be patient when you make a request, say "Please" and "Thank you," and thank them when you deplane. Remember: People will always appreciate a smile.

- **DON'T** try to board before your row number or group is called.

- **DON'T** try to push ahead of fellow passengers while walking down the boarding ramp, and be careful not to block the aisle for more than a few seconds when putting luggage in an overhead compartment.

- **DON'T** crush other people's belongings in an overhead compartment to make room for your own. If there's no room for your luggage, ask the flight attendant for help. If he has no solution,

---

WOULD YOU MIND MOVING . . . ?

Increasingly, families that aren't seated together request if a single person wouldn't mind moving so the family can be next to each other. The frustrating part of being asked stems from the fact that the single person may well have paid a premium for that aisle seat and the family that wasn't willing to pay to get seats next to each other is now making their thrift the single passenger's problem.

The other side of the coin is that the single person may be sitting next to a young child who doesn't have a parent next to him to control him.

Frankly, the situation is bad for both the person making the request and the person who is being asked to move, but the real culprit is the airline for its constant effort to squeeze every last dollar it can out of the traveling public.

There is no sure bet answer. The single traveler will have to assess the pros and cons of the particular situation. But he should remember that it is his decision to make and he should not feel compelled to change just because he has been asked.

---

accept that you must gate-check the bag; personnel are usually standing by to make sure it gets into the cargo hold.

- **DON'T** embarrass the helpless parents of a crying child. If a noisy infant or restless youngster disturbs you, leave your seat and scout the plane to see if a vacant seat is available. If, as a rule, you find crying babies intolerable, add earplugs or noise canceling headphones to the items in your carry-on bag.

- **DON'T** overdo the alcohol. Watch your drinking or avoid it altogether, especially if you're going to attend a meeting after arriving. No matter how liberal your corporate culture, you don't want to be met by a colleague—or even more important, a client—with liquor on your breath.

On a Train

Businesspeople who travel between major cities in the same general part of the country have the luxury of choosing rail over air. Naturally, the tenets of courteous airplane travel apply equally to travel on a train, whether for a business trip or the daily commute. One becomes even more key: the use of electronic devices. Unlike airline passengers, railroad travelers are able to use their personal cell phones to conduct business, ring up friends, or check the football scores if they want. A simple rule for cell phone use: If using the phone will disturb the people around you in any way, don't do it. And if you do use it, don't talk about anything confidential or personal. (*Note:* Many trains now have designated "quiet cars," on which use of cell phones or other electronic equipment is prohibited.)

On the Road

It's stating the obvious to say that someone driving to another town for a meeting should allow plenty of time to reach their destination. If you realize you're going to be late, pull to the side of the road and use your cell phone to give your estimated time of arrival. Notification enables your clients or colleagues to continue with their own routine until you arrive. Not only will they appreciate your thoughtfulness, but your own anxiety will also be relieved.

The important thing to remember here is that distracted driving leads to accidents. Most assuredly, texting tops the list of distracted driving, but using a cell phone to make or receive a call takes your mind off the task of driving, even when using hands-free devices. Distracted driving can also occur when you try to tune the radio or check your GPS device for the next turn. If you have a passenger, have him perform these tasks. If you are by yourself, consider stopping to do them rather than endangering yourself and others on the road.

In a Taxi or Limousine

Time was, out-of-town arrivals at an airport or train station had to be wary of literally being taken for a ride by unscrupulous taxi drivers. Now, however, the fares between most airports and major train stations and nearby destinations are strictly regulated, with the standard charges posted both at taxi stands and in the cabs themselves. Always reconfirm this fare before stepping into the taxi. For extra certainty, call ahead to your host or hotel to check on taxi availability and rates as well as the best route to your destination.

PAYING. Make sure you have small bills in your wallet in case the driver isn't able to make change; although it is the driver's responsibility to be able to change at least a $20 bill, this doesn't guarantee he or she can. Tip the driver 15 percent of the fare.

POINTERS FOR CAR PASSENGERS

A car passenger traveling with fellow business-persons should watch his or her p's and q's. Jabbering on about something can distract the driver, who may be reluctant to tell you so. You'll have to use your experience or intuition to gauge the appropriate level of conversation. Other hints:

- Don't lose yourself in your laptop unless there's urgency to make a deadline that the driver shares. Withdrawing completely is as discourteous as talking someone's ear off.

- Before turning on the radio, ask your companions' permission and what kind of station they prefer.

- Use your cell phone only when really necessary or when a business call is being made on behalf of you and any others in the car. If you are the driver, remember that safety comes first. Texting is a less intrusive option for a passenger.

- Do not smoke, especially in someone else's car. If you must have a cigarette, wait for a rest stop.

CAR SERVICE. Being held up getting a taxi can be avoided altogether by arranging to have a car or limousine service pick you up at the airport or train station. These services allow you to pay by credit card, with the cost determined up front—which means no surprises. Better still, the car will be ready and waiting when you arrive, relieving you of having to scramble to find a taxi. At the time of booking ask about the gratuity policy and if it has already been added to the bill.

ALL-DAY SERVICE. Travelers with hectic schedules should consider a third alternative: hiring a car and driver for a full day or even the whole trip. The driver will be at your service for as long as necessary, patiently waiting at the curb whenever you have to be picked up. This kind of arrangement doesn't come cheaply, but the peace of mind you gain may be worth the extra cost.

TRAVELING WITH YOUR BOSS

If you find yourself setting off on a business trip with the boss, keep two words in mind: *respect* and *deference*. Holding doors, seeing to it that she has the more comfortable seat, and letting her initiate a conversation shows an unspoken understanding of your respective ranks. Unless your executive traveling companion insists on doing them herself, you should take charge of various tasks—hailing cabs, checking in at the hotel, making restaurant reservations, and tipping service people. Stay on your toes in all regards: Traveling with the boss gives you the opportunity not only to let her get to know you better but also for you to demonstrate your abilities.

AT YOUR DESTINATION

No matter how weary you feel, be gracious as you check in at your hotel. If you have to make any special requests, a polite demeanor will get you further

than a brusque one. If, say, you failed to reserve a meeting room in advance and one isn't available, co-operation and a smile may secure you a table in the dining room or cocktail lounge during off-hours.

Remember these tips as you check in and get settled:

- For safety's sake, don't confirm your room number aloud when you are given your key, electronic or otherwise.

- If you find something unsatisfactory about your room, call the front desk and ask for a change, giving the reason: The room is too noisy, too close to the elevator, or has a poor view. Most hotels will try to accommodate your requests, depending on availability of a comparable room.

- Call your host to let him or her know you've arrived. Confirm the time of your meeting: "I'll be there at eight o'clock sharp tomorrow morning. Look forward to seeing you then!"

INTERACTING WITH HOTEL STAFF

Large hotels have full-service staffs to assist their customers. Although the staff may be extremely deferential and willing to handle most requests, don't treat them as servants. Instead, make a point of being courteous and don't skimp on tipping. Not only is this the right thing to do, but word also spreads about rude or difficult guests, who can expect no more than the minimum of attention. (See also "How Much to Tip," page 300.)

In some hotels you'll find a fridge full of snacks and beverages there for the taking. The guest selects an item and checks it off an attached bill; the mini-bar and food costs are then added to your room charge at checkout. (Some mini-bars automatically charge when the item is removed.) There should also be an attached price list. Look it over carefully: The markup for this convenience is considerable, and if you aren't careful, it will add a surprising amount to your bill. The same holds for in-room phone calls, which can carry substantial premiums; check all phone tariffs before making a call. Using a prepaid phone card or your cell phone may be a wise choice if you plan on making extensive use of the phone.

DINING OUT

On a business trip, dining out is an inevitable part of the package, whether the occasion is a business meal or a social one. If you find yourself dining solo in your hotel, don't feel awkward. A book, magazine, or screen device will keep you occupied while you're waiting for your food. If you use a smartphone to read a book, set it to silent ring so a call doesn't disrupt other patrons. (For a full discussion of dining out, see Chapter 18.)

When You're the Host

When you're the visitor but are playing the host for a meal, call the hotel in advance of your arrival and ask for recommendations. You'll want a place that's reputable enough to do your company credit but reasonable enough so that you won't have to watch what your guests order. You can check out these suggestions online. Even if your expense account has no limits, avoid very expensive restaurants, which could make guests feel uncomfortable or out of their league. When calling for a reservation, it's fine to ask the average cost of a meal or what the price ranges are for main courses, appetizers, and wine. Having made reservations, you'll also find it easier to resist suggestion by the person you are visiting of a restaurant that is too pricey.

If your dining partners are customers or clients, it's understood that you will pay the tab. Use a credit card, having made sure beforehand that the restaurant accepts the one you plan to hand over. (Although it's the rare restaurant that doesn't take credit cards, never take a chance; the embarrassment of being caught without enough cash is one of the business traveler's worst nightmares.) Also, consider arranging for payment beforehand. It's a great feeling to be able to leave the table without spending time reviewing the check or figuring the tip. Instead, your focus is on your guests.

If you and your guests have overcoats, check them and pay the tip ($2 for the first coat and $1 per additional coat) when you leave.

When You're the Guest

It is likely that you'll be invited to dinner by the business associate you're visiting, which means that he or she expects to pay. Accept graciously, even if your expense account is the bigger one.

Even if you're taken to a five-star restaurant, be modest in what you order. Never go straight to the highest end of the menu, which might put your host in an uncomfortable position down the road. (See Chapter 18 tips for ordering and suggestions from the host. For tips on attending private clubs, the theater, and sporting events, see Chapter 19.)

HOW MUCH TO TIP

Whether to tip—and how much, of course—is always a matter of concern when you're traveling on business. For starters, remember three key things:

1. Always tip discreetly.

2. The longer the task takes or more involved the service, the larger the tip should be.

3. Don't tip too much; anyone who flashes tip money or lavishes inappropriate tips on waiters, doormen, or anyone else will come across as crass.

Some Specific Guidelines for Tipping

SKYCAP AT AIRPORT. The standard tip for the skycap who checks your bags at curbside is $2 for the first bag and $1 per additional bag.

TAXI AND LIMOUSINE DRIVERS. The standards for tipping cab and limousine drivers vary from place to place. Unless you're in a cab with someone who can tell you what's customary, assume a 15–20 percent tip will be appropriate. Be sure you have enough change and small bills on hand at all times so that you and your companions can get out of the cab without delay.

DOORMAN. It's not necessary to tip a hotel or restaurant doorman on arrival unless he takes your bags out of the car and readies them for the bellman. Follow the rule of $2 for the first bag and $1 per additional bag. If he hails a cab for you, tip him $1 to $2. If the doorman has been particularly helpful during your stay, you may decide an extra $5 is in order.

BELLMAN. When the bellman arrives at your room with your luggage, give him $2 for the first bag and $1 for each additional bag he has carried.

HOUSEKEEPER. If you happen to see the person who cleans your room, you may hand her an envelope with your tip and a thank-you. If you are staying for one night, you can leave a tip on the desk in the room with a note: "Thank you, Housekeeping." If you are staying for a longer time, leave a tip each day, as the personnel may change. The standard is $2–$5 for each night.

CONCIERGE. In large hotels, this is the staff member to ask for help with theater tickets or dinner reservations; a $5–$10 tip will do for these services or any other special help. Whenever the concierge gives you directions around the hotel or the city, no tip is expected.

RESTAURANT STAFF. See "Tipping," page 201.

CHAPTER 29

CONVENTIONS, TRADE SHOWS, AND OTHER OFF-SITE EVENTS

While most of your time is spent at your office or with a client, from time to time you may find yourself traveling off-site to a convention, a trade show, a seminar, or possibly a course for management training. Whatever the reason, just because you are away from your usual place of business doesn't mean you can ignore the basic tenets of business etiquette. In fact, because you are off-site and because you are representing your company, you should focus that much more on making sure your actions reflect positively on you and your company.

GETTING DOWN TO BUSINESS AT TRAININGS OR SEMINARS

In a word, go prepared. (See also "Premeeting Preparation," page 139; and "If You're Attending," page 142.)

- Review the agenda or schedule beforehand. You might discover that a subject you feel passionate about or something from which your department could benefit is the focus of one of the seminars and decide to get involved. List the points you want to make (if only in the Q&A period), and arm yourself with any facts and figures needed to back up any information you plan to put forward.

- If you have questions you want answered or issues you think worth bringing up, write them down. Then rehearse asking them, editing as necessary for conciseness. Rambling on at the mike won't win you points with anyone present and may make you sound less professional.

- Learn as much as you can about the principal speakers, not just by reading their biographies in the program but also by asking colleagues what they know about the speaker or doing some online research. This will allow for a more meaningful conversation if you happen to be introduced to one of them.

Once the event is in progress, observe three important rules:

1. The first and most obvious is to show up for the meetings, sessions, or classes you're scheduled to attend. Even if the topic isn't all that pertinent to

your daily work back home, you have the obligation to participate after money has been spent to get you there.

2. The second rule is to be on time. Coming in late is disruptive and casts a poor light on you and your company—the name of which, remember, is clearly written across your name tag.

3. Make a point of taking your own notes, since relying on the minutes to be distributed later can be a big mistake. Also, many of the points and insights you find important may be overlooked by the minutes taker.

Networking

Off-site events, especially conventions and trade shows, offer the perfect opportunity to network. During breaks, make it a point to meet people from other companies or from out-of-town branches of your own firm. It may be tempting to spend all your time with your friends from the home office, but if you do, you're missing key opportunities. Remember: The very fact that you and the strangers around you work for the same company—or in the same field—means that you have something in common. You never know what business can come from just one conversation. (See also Chapter 11.)

TRADE SHOWS

Crowds, banners, music, noise, and all those handouts: An atmosphere this overwhelming can grow wearying after a while, making it all the more important for exhibitors who tend booths to keep their cool and treat even casual browsers as their best customers. As an exhibitor, remember that you are seen not as an individual but as the embodiment of your company.

Nuts and Bolts

Large companies that have major exhibition booths have a team that will do the setup, but small companies require the people who man the booth to set up the display as well. Before you leave for the trade show, try setting up the booth so you know what to do when you arrive at the trade show.

At the trade show, the trade show staff will deliver everything you have sent to your designated space. But setup is your responsibility, so arrive with lots of time in hand and don't leave setup until the last minute. Inevitably, it will take longer than you think.

Work out a schedule with coworkers: Stagger breaks so everyone has a chance to eat lunch and rest their feet. Make sure your schedule ensures your booth always has someone available. Preferably, enjoy your snacks and lunch away from your booth so visitors aren't greeted by the sight of people in your booth eating.

For the sake of your fellow colleagues, be punctual when it is your turn to take over the post. Getting sidetracked at a huge show is easy, and keeping people waiting can cause a ripple effect for some time afterward.

What to wear? Many reps wear the company uniform, from the logo-emblazened polo shirt and khakis all the way to the suit. Be neat and professional in your clothing and grooming.

Appreciate the different working styles and strengths of your coworkers. You can learn a lot from the way an experienced coworker engages prospects.

WHAT'S A DAY'S WORK ON A BUSINESS TRIP?

Q. I was sent on a two-week business trip by my company. During the trip, we had no days off. In fact, every day we were there we probably worked anywhere between ten and twelve hours, including the Fourth of July and weekends. Should I expect my company to provide extra vacation time to me for working weekends and a holiday for a span of two weeks?

A. Your expectation is reasonable. You should talk to your manager about compensation for the extra hours you put in. Before having the conversation, check your company's employee manual for any policies regarding comp time or extra pay for extra hours worked on a business trip. If there is a policy, use it as a basis for your request. If there isn't, use your situation to demonstrate the need for a policy to avoid confusion in the future.

In general, it's better to ask about compensation before going on a business trip. It's much easier to ask about it as part of the planning than to go to your manager after the fact.

With Prospective Customers

At a trade show, it's the norm for people to make snap judgments when they pause at a booth. This means that it's doubly important for you to use good business etiquette as you demonstrate your product or talk about your services. Do the following when meeting potential buyers or clients at your booth:

- Dress as if you were meeting an important client back at the office.
- Always stand when talking with visitors.
- Shake hands with each new visitor.
- Express interest in the person.
- Give visitors your undivided attention.

The trickiest part of your job is when you're faced with the task of balancing several customers at once without offending any one of them. Have business cards at the ready, and use them to momentarily satisfy any visitors waiting their turn. Similar to putting someone on hold on the telephone, utter a quick

---

"WHICH WAY TO THE SNACK BAR?"

Considering the number of people streaming by your booth, it is inevitable that you'll be asked for directions to restrooms, snack bars, the lost-and-found, and yes, the often-elusive information booth.

The wise booth tender will make sure he or she can politely provide the needed answer, even if the directions are to a competitor's booth. On the first day, make yourself familiar with the layout of the floor by taking a walking tour, with the show directory as your guide. Then keep the directory close at hand for the rest of the show. When people who find themselves without a directory ask the way to a specific company's booth, look up its number and respond cheerfully. Your kindness to a stranger might open up a conversation that could lead to interest in your product.

"Please excuse me" to the person you're talking with, turn to the bystander, and hand him or her a card and say, "Would you mind waiting for a moment? I'll be right with you." If you see that a colleague is free, direct the prospect to her. Or, if possible, quickly set up an appointment to meet later in the day.

Even if you're making small talk with a potential customer, it's not a good idea to invite another prospect to join in unless your intuition tells you otherwise: The best approach is to give undivided attention to one person at a time. The same rule applies to product demonstrations. If someone is standing by observing, that's fine—but you should direct your demonstration to the person you're dealing with at the moment. At the same time, make it clear to the other person that you'll be with him or her as soon as you have finished.

Don't forget to collect your prospect's information. Most likely you'll have a device to scan his badge, but it never hurts to ask for a business card as well. It's also a good idea to find out when and how your prospect would like to be contacted. As soon as you can, jot any notes on the back of the card or in the scanner about your prospect. You can use this information to personalize your follow-up.

With Other Exhibitors

If you attend trade shows regularly, more than likely you'll be acquainted with many of the booth tenders from other companies. While you'll no doubt want to catch up with them, and perhaps make plans for the evening, remember that your focus is on the trade show attendees and bringing in business. The less time you spend with old friends, the more time you'll have to meet with potential customers.

Following Up

While you might pursue your hot leads with a phone call, most likely you will be following up by email. Write a personalized note to each prospective customer you talked with as soon as possible or within a week of the show at the latest. Tell the recipient how nice it was to meet him, and that you hope the interest he expressed in your product will someday result in an order. A reference to a nonbusiness topic you discussed—a new grandchild, for example—further personalizes the note and lets it stand out from the norm. Make sure your subject line references your company and the trade show because your prospect may not recognize just your name: Acme Dynamite: 2016 Minerals and Mining Convention.

HOW MUCH FUN?

Because attending an off-site event usually means traveling to another city or a resort, a social element is always present. After hours the atmosphere is definitely social—if not downright party time. Hospitality suites—rooms rented by participating companies to provide their delegates with a space where they can relax and entertain—feature anything from free food and drink to DJs. Golfing and group excursions to restaurants, tourist sites, and shows are other standard activities.

While the chance to have fun is an integral part of any off-site event, don't let your hair down too far. The last thing you want to be is a stick-in-the-mud, but bear in mind that your conduct reflects on your company—after hours as well as during the formal proceedings. Remember, too, that what happens in Vegas doesn't always stay in Vegas.

TRAVELING WITH YOUR SPOUSE

It's great when your spouse or partner can accompany you an out-of-town event, either on your nickel or the company dime. So there are no misunderstandings between the two of you, review the event schedule so your partner knows when you are on duty and what events he or she may attend, and what any dress requirements are. Supportive spouses make an effort to learn something about whatever topics are the focus of the convention, allowing them to join in conversations in a reasonably knowledgeable way. Making this effort demonstrates an appreciation of the event's actual purpose.

Although wives, husbands, and significant others are free to entertain themselves during the day, the company may be hosting evening receptions or other events that everyone is expected to attend. After-hours activities not sponsored by the company—a trip into the entertainment district, for example, or a group visit to a club—are another matter, and neither the delegate nor spouse should feel an obligation to take part. Dancing away to the wee hours at the hottest new nightclub in town may be an experience to remember, but it may also have consequences the next morning, when there are meetings and conferences to attend.

EVENING EVENTS

Sometimes you'll be invited to participate in evening events, which may be a chamber of commerce mixer or a full-blown formal charity event. In either case, you want to make sure that you're prepared and that you represent yourself and your company positively.

While there is a lot of social to these events, ultimately it is a business that is sponsoring or hosting you.

RSVP. Remember to respond to the invitation or get your tickets for the event. Nothing is more embarrassing than showing up and realizing you can't attend because you forgot to purchase or pick up your tickets or your name isn't on the guest list.

DRESS APPROPRIATELY. Make sure you know the attire recommendations for the event. If you need to call the organizer and ask, that's fine, but make sure you leave yourself enough time to acquire the right outfit. If it's a formal, black-tie charity ball you don't want to show up in casual attire.

DON'T FORGET. You'll want to remember your business cards and possibly your checkbook (if you'll be donating to a charity that night).

"HELP! I'M TRAPPED!"

With all the good intentions, you start to work the crowd at a chamber of commerce mixer. Soon you find yourself trapped in a conversation by John Windbag. He is simply talking a blue streak and you can't escape. What do you do?

Excusing yourself to get a refill may end up with his following you to the bar. Your best bet is benevolent honesty. Gently interrupt and explain, "John, I'm enjoying our conversation, but my manager expects me to mix and mingle. Perhaps we could catch up again later. It's been nice talking with you." And then smile and step away.

PREPARE YOUR DATE. If you are bringing a date to the event, prepare him for what to expect—handshaking, introductions, small talk, business talk—as well as what the event is for, what to wear, and what might take place during the event.

LESS IS MORE. Remember that while the event might be amazing, you want to keep your party self reeled in a bit; go easy on cheering on a performer, dancing out on the floor, grazing at the buffet, or ordering at the bar.

THANK YOU. Write a thank-you note to the hosts or organizers the next day to let them know how much you enjoyed the event.

AT COMPANY RETREATS

Company retreats are often for networking within your company's larger structure, team building, or as a thank-you for all the hard work you and your colleagues put in. While they have a much more relaxed atmosphere than trade shows and other events, it's still important that you (and your spouse) maintain a professional image while on the retreat.

Participation

The company has paid for you to attend this event. Usually a retreat is meant to help strengthen the bonds between coworkers, so it's important to participate in whatever events the company has arranged. If that means attending a ropes course to help establish trust and team-building skills, then participate and gain as much as you can from the exercises. The coworker who sulks or comments about how lame the exercises might be does herself no favors by demonstrating that negativity is her go-to emotion.

Evening events might be formal and you may be allowed to bring a spouse. Since this event is a little more social than your average after-work affair, it's okay to enjoy the food and entertainment, but as always remember not to overindulge. It's one thing to cheer on a performer or exclaim how amazing the buffet is, it's another to jump up on stage or take multiple large platefuls of food.

Your spouse or partner should be ready to engage in conversation, and remember, you don't have to keep it all to business: Talking about hobbies and interests is a great way to build bonds with your fellow coworkers.

When it comes to swag—the gifts or freebies some companies give out at retreats—remember to take according to the rules. If it's two pairs of sunglasses per employee, don't load up on three or four just because they are there or no one's looking.

Thank You

Remember to write a thank-you note to the retreat organizer soon after you arrive back home. These events are no small undertaking and you'll stand out as an employee who understands what the company has just done for her and is willing to acknowledge it.

CHAPTER 30

DOING BUSINESS
IN ANOTHER COUNTRY

Americans tend to take their way of doing things with them when they travel abroad, including business practices. While globalization and the Internet are rapidly breaking down barriers between countries, often the way business is done abroad is still strictly local. Take this statement very seriously: Understanding the local business etiquette is the essential starting point for everything else you hope to accomplish. The major differences you encounter will often have less to do with negotiating tactics and decision making than with how effectively you are able to communicate with your foreign counterparts, how well you understand the social aspects of doing business with them on their turf, and how much you appreciate and respect the customs of the culture you are entering.

When traveling to a new culture, the importance of personal consideration takes on a whole new dimension. As a guest, it's incumbent on you to respect and follow the customs of your host—many of which may be quite different from what you're used to.

RULE 1

Since customs can vary even within a country, the most important thing you can do in this regard is follow the lead of those around you and ask others for guidance when necessary. As a thoughtful traveler you can make things easier for your host by doing some preliminary research on the basic customs of the place you're planning to visit.

Here are some basics for doing business around the world:

- Do your homework. Consult a reputable, up-to-date travel guide, the embassy of the country you will visit, or the US Department of State for information on business and cultural customs. If your visit entails high-level meetings or formal cultural events, consider hiring a guide and/or interpreter.

- At the very least, know something about the nation's history; whether there is a national religion and what it is; the form of government; the significance of any national holiday that falls during your visit; a few words and phrases in the native language; the currency and exchange rate.

- Find out if the country you are visiting requires a visa, where and when you acquire a visa, and how much it will cost.

- Personal assistants typically act as gatekeepers for executives, and treating these employees with the utmost politeness is essential when scheduling appointments, which should be done well in advance and confirmed a few days before.

- Be patient. It may take a number of meetings, and even several visits to the country, to conclude your negotiations. It's vitally important that you never express any impatience or anger at the tempo of the proceedings.

ATTITUDE

It's important to keep an open mind when traveling abroad. You may have heard comments about the place you are going to visit and they may cloud your opinion about the people there. There's a big difference between stereotyping and generalizing about a culture. When you stereotype you apply characteristics to every member of that culture. Doing so is a mistake because obviously not everyone is alike or holds the same views. Instead, think more in terms of generalizing. When you generalize, you recognize that a majority of the people in a culture may act or think a certain way, but you respect that each person is an individual and may have a different approach

than that of the majority. For instance, you may have heard that people in a certain country are routinely late for an appointment, but that doesn't mean the person you are meeting with will automatically be late and that therefore you don't have to arrive on time, either. That individual may not adhere to the norm of his or her culture or that person may be showing respect for you and your culture by being on time.

Travel Warnings

One of the first steps you should take before venturing abroad is to find out whether there are any State Department warnings relating to your destination. The State Department gives you not only warnings of political unrest but also updates on currency, entry regulations, driving conditions, and more. (For more information, visit the State Department website at www.travel.state.gov/travel.)

That done, you should prepare an itinerary for your hosts, your office, and your family. (For details on what to include in the itinerary, see page 292.)

CUSTOMS AND CULTURE

At a minimum you should know some basic facts about the country you're visiting, including its geography, history, and political system. When you exhibit more than a passing knowledge, you impress your hosts and all others you meet with your appreciation of the nation, the culture, and the individuals themselves. Because you have taken the time to delve deeper, it demonstrates that you are serious about forming a relationship. Understanding the differences between your culture and theirs and respecting those differences will impact your ability to conduct business successfully. Best advice: Do your research and be prepared.

Information on Cultures

Start your search on the Internet, which offers a wide array of sites where you can find key facts and explore specific areas of a country's culture. Once you arrive at your destination, keep abreast of local events by tapping into regional English-language news media.

Most every country has its own website with factual information, legal information, entry information, and tips about customs. Alternatively, the Central Intelligence Agency has reams of information on its site about countries around the world (www.cia.gov/library/publications/the-world-factbook). The State Department also has descriptive information about most of the countries around the globe (www.travel.state.gov/travel).

Talk to a Colleague

A fellow American who has had experience doing business at the same company or in the same set-ting or country can be an excellent resource to tell you what to expect. If your company has an office in country, contact it before your trip to be sure about customs and attire.

ACQUAINT YOURSELF WITH THE SOCIETY

What precisely should you learn ahead of time when visiting another country or culture?

Basic Facts

Start with the basics first:

- The form of government
- Names of key political people
- National religion, alternatives, and any that are forbidden
- National holidays and days of rest. Take note of religious and secular holidays. You don't want to ask for a business appointment on July 14 in France—that's Bastille Day (equivalent to Independence Day in the United States)—and neither do you want to attempt to conduct business in Jerusalem on a Friday afternoon, when everything closes in preparation for the Jewish Sabbath.
- Dietary customs and laws

Know Laws and Customs

Above all else, be vigilant in your understanding about laws concerning drugs and alcohol. A prescription or over-the-counter drug that is legal in the United States may be illegal for you to bring into another country.

Similarly, alcohol is strictly forbidden in some countries, such as Saudi Arabia. You do not want to be caught with it there; penalties can be harsh.

Other customs and laws you should be aware of before leaving include:

- **Personal behavior.** Specifically, know the limits of public displays of affection. Even holding hands could be viewed as questionable conduct.

- **Gender issues.** For example, should you, as a man, offer to shake hands with a Muslim woman? Answer: Don't initiate a handshake; rather, wait for the woman to offer her hand first. If she does, then it is appropriate to shake hands.

- **Inappropriate material.** Pornography is obvious. But be careful of materials that could imply you are promoting a religion, political party, ideology, or lifestyle.

- **Touching and personal space.** Different cultures have different levels of comfort about touching and how close it is appropriate to stand. Americans, for instance, are generally uncomfortable if people stand closer than eighteen inches to them, whereas in other cultures people stand much closer or even farther apart.

Customs Around Time

Workweeks, business hours, and expectations of punctuality vary widely around the globe. Northern European countries follow a weekly and daily schedule not dissimilar to the Monday–Friday, nine-to-five model, but in southern European and some Latin American countries, it's commonplace for business to come to a halt for several hours at midday, resume late in the afternoon, and continue into the evening. In Muslim countries, Friday is the Sabbath day and the five-day workweek runs from Sunday to Thursday. In Israel, Saturday is the Sabbath day, with the five-day workweek beginning on Sunday and ending on Thursday.

Punctuality is never a fault in any country. On the other hand, don't take offense if you are kept waiting, even for several hours. Punctuality is highly valued in northern European countries, where arriving even a few minutes late is considered an insult. In southern Europe and Latin America, people have a more relaxed attitude toward time and are less likely to be punctual for meetings or expect you to be so.

Appearance

Worldwide, business culture places a high priority and value on being well dressed and neatly groomed. For the most part, the business casual look is frowned upon, although formality does vary by profession, especially in Europe. For example, an investment banker would typically wear a suit whereas a newspaper editor might don a jacket and tie. In general, jackets stay on in offices and restaurants, and women wear skirts, not slacks.

These guidelines will suit you well wherever you do business:

- For men, dark suits of gray or blue, with a well-pressed white shirt, a conservative tie, and polished dress shoes are standard. A tuxedo may be required for more formal affairs.

- Women should opt for stylish but conservative clothing—generally a suit (jacket and skirt), neither flashy nor revealing, worn with heels and makeup. Pantsuits and dresses are acceptable but less formal options. Jewelry should be kept to a minimum. For dinner, an elegant conservative dress or skirt and blouse ensemble is appropriate; a cocktail dress or evening gown is the choice for more formal occasions.

A Note of Caution. Acceptability of slacks for women varies from country to country.

In the Arab nations, modesty is most important. In Saudi Arabia, women are required to be completely covered and veiled in public. In less strict societies like the Gulf states, dresses or skirts may be worn, but dresses should be long-sleeved and hemlines should be below the knee and a scarf or other head covering worn when appropriate. While your Arab host may wear traditional desert robes, visiting men should dress in suit and tie unless invited by their host to wear traditional garb.

Where climate, especially heat, is an issue, the emphasis shifts to comfort, but follow your host's lead. Be prepared with a suit in a light or tropical-weight fabric. In Southeast Asia, suit jackets are often taken off as the day heats up, while businessmen in Singapore may forgo jackets completely, wearing only a long-sleeved (or sometimes short-sleeved) shirt and a tie with trousers. For women visiting these countries, a blouse and a skirt is appropriate (with long sleeves and a below-the-knee hemline, in the case of predominately Muslim Indonesia). In India, the casual look of slacks and a short-sleeved shirt is standard for men, but a jacket is advised for initial meetings. Women can wear slacks and a jacket over a long-sleeved blouse, or a dress, provided the hem is below the knees.

Sex, Politics, Money, and Religion

The old saying that you should never discuss sex, politics, money, or religion in polite company applies twice over in foreign countries. Sex as a topic (in the sense of gender as well as in the sense of sexuality) is definitely off-limits.

Politics is a hot topic in much of the world—usually too hot to touch. Never criticize the leaders or government of your host country, and never criticize your own. If, as is likely, you're quizzed about American politics or policy (either national or international), aim to inform with facts, not opinions. Remember, too, that a businessperson is more of an ambassador for his or her country than is a garden-variety tourist.

Religious customs are an important concern as well. For example, in Thailand, it's sacrilegious to photograph any statue or other image of Buddha; in Saudi Arabia, be aware that your Muslim host must stop to pray several times during the day. By respecting the orthodoxies and conventions of the culture you are visiting, you show respect for your host, and that can translate into more successful business dealings.

PRACTICAL CONCERNS

What do passports, visas, credit cards, currency, and other paraphernalia of overseas travel have to do with polite behavior? Nothing in themselves—but your lack of attention to such items can disrupt your visit (and wreak havoc in some cases), creating embarrassment for you and inconvenience for your hosts. The following information may save you considerable hassles once you embark on a business trip:

- If you lose your passport in the United States, notify the nearest passport agency or Passport Services in Washington, DC. If the loss occurs in a foreign country, report it to the nearest US embassy or consulate or the local police department.

- It's easier to replace a lost passport if you photocopy the data page ahead of time and keep the copy along with a spare passport-size photo in a separate place when you travel.

- Certain countries will not allow you to enter without a visa. To find out whether a visa is required and how to obtain one, call the consulate or embassy of the country you plan to visit, not an agency of the United States; the responsibility to grant and issue visas is the country's alone. If the country you are visiting issues visas at the airport when you arrive, be sure to bring several passport-size photos of yourself in case it is needed for the visa.

- Check to see if your destination has ATM service readily available. Many airports have conveniently located ATMs where you can get funds in the local currency even before you get your baggage. If ATMs won't be available, try to change some of your US currency at a bank before you leave and bring some additional US currency along with a couple of credit cards.

- If they request it, let your credit card companies know when you're traveling, and where. Given the eagerness of credit card companies to prevent fraud, the computer may reject your

card in a new, faraway place, reading it as possibly stolen.

- If you use a corporate credit card, make sure your company authorizes your use of it abroad; otherwise, it could be rejected, too.

- Photocopy your credit cards before you leave, and carry these copies separately from your cards. If a card is lost or stolen, you'll have the number on hand to report it.

- Take along copies of the toll-free numbers of your credit card companies.

BUSINESS CARDS

What should you put on your business card for the convenience of your international colleagues?

- Because honorifics are important in foreign countries and people use them, your name should be preceded by "Mr.," "Mrs.," "Ms.," "Dr.," "Rev.," and so forth.

- List your title—as well as your function—after your name. If you function as the associate director of training for the human resources department, it's appropriate to give an additional title if you have one, such as assistant vice president. In case your title or position is one that a foreigner might not understand, consider putting a "plain English" version in parentheses—for example, "CFP (Certified Financial Planner)."

- Don't omit your title, even if it's a junior one. In many countries, particularly in Latin America, hosts who don't know your title won't know how to treat you or whom they should designate to do business with you. But avoid any temptation to exaggerate your position—being found out could have serious consequences, even to the point of wrecking the planned negotiations.

- Have your business card printed in English and, on the opposite side, in the language of the country you are visiting. It is an instant sign of respect for those whom you will meet. Be sure to have your card checked for form and spelling by a native speaker.

Exchanging Business Cards

In many countries, the exchange of cards follows a certain protocol.

There may be a designated time for presenting cards—for example, at the beginning of a meeting or after you've been introduced. In some countries,

> **TIP:** Note that in many countries the standard business card is larger than an American card. Either bring a larger case or have a separate case to store these cards.

good manners dictate that you present the card with both hands, or with the foreign-language side up.

When you receive a card, don't just stick it in your pocket. Read it right away and then place it in your own card case or briefcase. Don't stuff it into the back pocket of your pants like a wallet.

Whenever you present your card, do so respectfully, handing it directly to the person, not just leaving it on a table for the person to pick up. In Latin America, business cards can be presented during the greeting if done so discreetly. Throughout Asia, after greeting someone, present your card foreign-language side up. In China, South Korea, and Japan, hold it with both hands and take your host's the same way. In Africa, present your business card with your right hand to each person upon meeting him or her.

FORGING PERSONAL RELATIONSHIPS

In many countries, forming personal relationships will be an all-important part of your business dealings. While socializing, your hosts get to know you. Through patience, you'll establish trust—an important element in your foreign counterparts' decisions to do business with you. Conversely, if you appear too eager to talk business, they may think you begrudge the time you spend with them and that you don't value the relationship.

Learn to be the gracious guest, starting with your self-taught mini-course on the culture of the country. Answer questions about American life in a way that can't be perceived as boasting. Don't be surprised if the conversation turns to music, gardening, good places to vacation in winter, or preferences in wine or beer. Such sociability does not, however, give you permission to ask personal questions; Americans' readiness to "open up" is not typical of the rest of the world. Even longtime friends or associates do not usually share personal information about themselves or their families.

The Importance of Names and Titles

While in the United States we may be relatively casual in our approach to forms of address, in other countries the ways of addressing people are more formal. In your written communications, always include salutations and closings. When speaking to someone, defer to the formal. It's always easier to address a person either in writing or in person by their title and last name and then switch to the more informal than it is to mistakenly refer to a person informally only to discover that doing so was a form of disrespect.

Deferring to Age

In many cultures, age signifies seniority. Show respect to businesspeople who are older than you are—even those in a lower position. Notice how those you are with treat their elders and follow suit.

Address elders by title and last name as a measure of respect. Be deferential, holding the door for them

---

USE PROPER TITLES

Always address people by their proper titles. "Señor" and "Madame" are straightforward, but others can be confusing—for example, when in England, don't automatically call a dentist "Doctor"; surprisingly, "Mr." or "Ms." is the proper title. An engineer in the United States is known simply as "Mr." or "Ms.," but in South America, Europe, and Asia, address him or her as "Engineer." In many European countries, "yes" and "no" never stand alone as answers but are always followed by a title: "Oui, madame," "Non, signore."

In most countries outside the United States, it will be a long time before you're on a first-name basis with your host and others you meet formally—perhaps never. Let your overseas business colleague suggest using first names, but do not do it yourself.

---

and allowing them to be seated first. If you happen to be younger than anyone around, dress and act in the most mature manner you can.

Respecting Work Ethics

In many places, family and private life, not work, are the most important parts of the businessperson's world. Even if you feel you could close the deal if you and your host were to work for an extra couple of hours, resist the temptation to suggest it; it's likely to be either rejected or resented. Never interpret this difference in attitude to mean that your foreign counterparts are lazy or indifferent. They may be every bit as serious and meticulous about their work but may simply have a different attitude toward timing than many Americans have; in general, closing shop for the day is not seen as a reason for feeling guilty.

Speaking English Abroad

American English is loaded with idioms and eccentric phrases, and people who speak English as a second language may be familiar with all or none of them. While you may think they understand what you're saying, they may be hearing something else. Conversational bloopers may make for funny stories over the dinner table, but when you're in a business situation they can have serious consequences. Do everything you can to help other people understand you and to make your conversation in English clear for them.

- Speak clearly and not too quickly, enunciating carefully.

- Don't talk in a loud voice—it won't make you better understood.

- Don't use slang, regionalisms, colloquialisms, or euphemisms. For example, saying that something is "a slam dunk" or "a no-brainer" may elicit a puzzled look.

- Make sure that your overseas counterpart has the same understanding of all business and legal terms as you. It may be that in your field the same terminology is used worldwide—but you shouldn't assume so.

- When using numbers in a business discussion, it may be necessary to write them down and show them, since numbers can be expressed verbally in different ways.

- If your host seems at all puzzled or hesitant as you're speaking, pause immediately and rephrase what you just said, and if your host is still puzzled, then ask what it is that he doesn't understand.

Understanding Body Language

Two thoughts about body language: (1) Know what your body language is saying to others, and (2) learn how to read other people's body language. Although your facial expressions, stance, and gestures are basic to communication, they are also easily misunderstood. For example, in the United States, looking directly at the speaker's face in a meeting shows that he or she has your full attention, but in Asian countries, making extended eye contact is considered impolite. Staring could be deemed disrespectful if a person is your superior in Asia, Africa, or Latin America. Even in the United States, extended eye contact or staring is rude.

Gestures are similarly perilous. For instance, in the Middle East showing the bottoms of your feet is an insult. You'll also be well advised to check on local customs before pointing with your finger or snapping your fingers in public. Beckoning with a curled index finger is widely considered offensive as well. All three gestures are considered offensive in India.

In addition, the following gestures should be avoided unless you're absolutely sure that they have the same meaning in your host country as in the United States:

- Thumbs up—generally considered obscene in the Middle East, except in Iraq where it means "perfect"

- The "okay" sign (making a circle with your thumb and forefinger)—considered obscene in Japan and elsewhere
- V sign with palm toward you—considered rude
- V sign with palm away from you—can mean victory or peace

A good guidebook on your host country will include information on what gestures to avoid.

GREETINGS

Greetings vary around the world, but as a visitor you should greet others according to local custom and in a respectful manner. After all, this is how you will begin your relationship. The following are the typical greetings you will encounter.

Handshakes

The standard greeting throughout Europe is the handshake, for both men and women. It is usually polite for a woman to extend her hand first. Most people from the Continent shake hands before and after each meeting, whereas in Great Britain a single introductory shake is sufficient. A Western-style handshake is the standard greeting in Turkey and Israel, but in other Middle Eastern countries you can expect a warmer, more effusive greeting, with the hand often grasped and held rather than shaken. Arabs may also hug or kiss each other. A gentle, warm handshake is the accepted form of greeting across Africa—different ethnic groups may have their own subtle variations—and you should shake the hand of everyone in the room when you arrive and when you leave.

Generally, these guidelines may be followed when shaking hands:

- Use a firm handshake—about the amount of pressure you would use to hold a doorknob. But be careful: In Asia and the Middle East even this level of firmness is considered aggressive.
- Two or three pumps. Then disengage and step back slightly.
- Let a woman offer her hand to you first, especially in Muslim countries.

(For a full description of how to shake hands, see "The All-Important Handshake," page 129.)

Kisses

Kisses are offered both between men and between women in a variety of cultures. The kiss is more of an air kiss, cheek to cheek. In some cultures it is once on the left cheek and once on the right. In others, such as in the Middle East, men who are friends greet each other with three or more kisses.

Hugs

From bear clutches to slight shoulder touches, hugging varies throughout the world. Even in the United States where hugging, especially among men, was not a practice, it is becoming more commonplace in social situations and between businessmen who know each other well and haven't seen each other recently.

Greetings in Other Countries

As you travel the world you will find that greetings vary from country to country.

The Japanese understand that their custom for greeting is different from Western-style handshaking. Even though they bow to each other, Japanese may offer to shake hands with a Westerner. This is a courtesy; since their greetings are ritualistic, complicated, and based on rank, it would be very easy for a Westerner to commit an unintentional faux pas.

In China, a gentle bow of the head and a handshake are appropriate. In Indonesia, the handshake precedes a slight nod or bow.

The traditional Thai salutation is the *wei*—palms together at chest level with head inclined in a slight bow. The same holds for South Korea and the Philippines. However, Westerners are likely to be greeted with a handshake.

In India, a handshake is standard for everyone. In general, avoid touching your host after the initial greeting.

Greetings in Africa are generally long, effusive, and endlessly upbeat—implying that everything in life is fine. Be prepared to do a good deal of casual chatting, designed to build rapport, before getting to your agenda; pushy business dealings are considered rude in Africa.

PERSONAL SPACE AND OTHER BASICS

Be careful not to stand too close to people you are visiting or reach out and touch them until you know their cultural norms.

SPACING YOURSELF. The distance maintained between yourself and others is important; getting too close or moving too far away can be misconstrued as unwanted familiarity or standoffishness. In the United States, people are most comfortable standing at least eighteen inches apart, while northern Europeans and Asians expect more space between. Latin Americans like to stand closer to the person with whom they are talking than you may be used to. Southern Europeans also have a more intimate personal comfort zone, preferring to stand about two feet apart when they converse.

TOUCHING. While North Americans don't engage in casual touching, Latin Americans and southern Europeans may casually touch your arm during conversation or even tap you with a finger to make a point. Don't pull away—it's considered rude. In Middle Eastern, Southeast Asian, and Pacific Island nations, a man may even find his male host taking his hand. Do not misconstrue these gestures, but don't try to initiate them, either.

Speaking in a Foreign Language

It is a courtesy to your foreign hosts to have some small familiarity with their language—knowing at least the words for "please," "thank you," "you're welcome," "good morning," "good afternoon," "good night," "hello," and "good-bye." Learn basic phrases such as "Where is the restroom?" or "How much does that cost?" Carry a pocket foreign-language dictionary so that you can look up words and communicate with people who may not understand English.

USING TRANSLATORS AND INTERPRETERS

While English is often used for international business dealings, there may be times when negotiations will be conducted in the language of the country you're visiting. Unless you are fluent in this language (and oftentimes even if you are), you'll want an interpreter present.

The word *interpreter* usually brings to mind those phenomenal men and women who translate as the speaker speaks, their words following at a fast clip. Known as simultaneous translators, they are not the kind of interpreter the average businessperson uses. More widely used are consecutive interpreters, who speak after the speaker has completed a few sentences. To make sure you get what you bargained for, use only professional translators. To avoid a conflict of interest, make sure that they are in your employ, not hired by your counterpart. Ask for recommendations from friends who have done business in your destination, or see whether your company can handle the hiring.

Before the Meeting

To let your interpreter get acquainted with your way of speaking, spend some time with her beforehand. This will also help you to gauge whether your interpreter's English is idiomatic. Go over the agenda for the meeting, and make sure she can handle technical as well as business terms. Be sure the translator is aware of who the participants will be at the meeting and their rank and titles.

Prepare visual aids, if possible, to clarify and reinforce your and your translator's spoken words. Use both languages on charts and graphs, which can also serve later as confirmation of what you said. Acquaint your interpreter with the visual aids before the meeting.

Also, make sure to let your interpreter know the appropriate dress for the occasion. If you think she should wear business clothes, say so. In general, your interpreter's clothing should be subdued and unobtrusive; it is you, not she, who's the center of attention. If the occasion is formal, ask her to wear a formal dress; for a male interpreter, ask him to wear black-tie attire or at least a dark suit.

At the Meeting

The translator is usually seated at the table between the two major players who need her—for example, you and your host. On more formal occasions, such as a dinner, she will sit slightly behind them. Although she does not expect to join you in eating dinner, see to it that she has a meal either before or after the occasion.

When you speak through an interpreter, many of the same rules apply as when you speak English with a nonnative speaker:

- Speak slowly and distinctly, avoid slang and regionalisms, and watch the host for signs that he's tuning out. Always address the listener, not the interpreter.

- Keep your sentences short, and speak only a few before stopping for translation.

- Intermittently ask your host whether he is clear about what you're saying or has any questions. Be expressive as you speak, and show concentration as you listen. Smile, but don't tell jokes; despite your interpreter's best efforts, humor rarely translates well.

- Don't interrupt your interpreter, but also don't hesitate to stop the meeting to ask her about anything that isn't clear to you.

After the Meeting

When the meeting is over, have the interpreter go over what was said and her impressions of your counterpart's reactions. Ask her to tell you about any non-verbal cues she noticed during the discussion. Also ask her about anything you did not understand. Finally, draft and circulate to all participants a report in English of the conclusions or agreements reached during the meeting.

DINING AND DRINKING

Whether you are the guest or the host, be prompt. As the host, make arrangements in advance. If you need help finding a suitable restaurant, ask for the

---

> **TIP:** If you find yourself being served a strange dish anywhere, eat it whether or not you like it—or even know what it is. One travel expert suggests that you never ask what animal the dish came from—it's easier to down a sheep's eyeball when it remains unidentified.

---

hotel concierge's assistance. When ordering dinner or wine, you may ask your guests if they can suggest local specialties.

In many cultures, an invitation to a dinner must be accepted—not to do so would be considered rude. If you are unfamiliar with dining customs, watch your host or dinner partner and copy what they do. Otherwise, use your best table manners. Respect the dietary customs of the country, and if you are being hosted, don't request food or drink that may be contrary to your host's practices.

A few other standard table customs will stand you in good stead:

- Generally, keep your hands above the table.

- If you're traveling to China or Japan, you should learn to handle chopsticks—and know the etiquette varies in different Asian countries.

- Handle food with your right hand, especially in the Middle East, Asia, and Africa where the left hand is symbolically unclean.

- As a guest, wait until a host talks business.

- Thank your hosts graciously following your meal and again with a handwritten note delivered the next day.

Chopsticks

If you are traveling to the Far East, it is a good idea to learn to use chopsticks and to learn the chopstick etiquette of the particular country you are visiting, as customs vary. In general, use one hand to manipulate your chopsticks, and just as you don't play with

FOREIGN-LANGUAGE TOASTS

If you have to give a toast to an overseas host, or you want to make a toast to someone visiting the United States who speaks a different language, make a point to learn his or her country's traditional toast—which is usually the equivalent of "To your health!" or "Cheers!" Following is a sampling of international toasts, with their pronunciations shown in informal phonetics; capital letters indicate the syllable(s) to stress.

Language	Toast	Pronunciation
Cantonese	Yungsing	YOUNG-SING
Czech	Nazdravi	nahz-DRAHV-ee
Dutch	Proost	PROWST
Finnish	Kippis	KIP-pis
French	A votre santé	ah-votruh-san-TAY
German	Prosit	PROHST, with guttural R
Greek	Stin egia sas	steen -ee-YAR -sahs
Hebrew	L'Chayim	luh-CHI-um, with guttural CH
Hungarian	Egeszsegedre	eh-geh-sheh-GEHD-run
Italian	Salute	sah-LOO-tay
Japanese	Kampai	KAHM-PYE
Korean	Gan bei	kahn-BAY
Malaysian	Slimat minim	seh-lah-maht MEE-noom
Polish	Nazdrowie	nahz-DROH-vee-ah
Portuguese	Brindare	brin-DAR-ray, first *r* slightly trilled
Russian	Na zdorovie	nahz-doh-ROH-vee-ah
Scandinavian*	Skål	SKOAL
Spanish	Salud	sah-LOOD
Thai	Choc-tee	chock-DEE
Turkish	Serefe	sheh-REH-feh

*Danish, Swedish, Norwegian

---

your fork, don't play with your chopsticks. It is also considered impolite to wave them or point them at someone. Never stick your chopsticks vertically into a bowl of rice because in many Asian cultures this is only done during funeral rites. Some other tips for using chopsticks correctly:

- It is impolite to spear items with your chopsticks.
- Don't use your chopsticks to serve yourself food from a common bowl.
- It's okay to bite in half dumplings or other small items too large to eat in one bite.

- Once you've used your chopsticks, rest them on chopstick rests or the edge of your plate, not directly on the table.

Toasting

Except in Muslim countries, drinking usually accompanies dining—and drinking calls for toasting. (Remember that if you're a nondrinker, this is one time that your host should show his understanding; it's perfectly fine to toast with a drink that is nonalcoholic.) For occasions that are somewhat formal, you should have a toast prepared in advance unless you're an accomplished extemporaneous speaker. Make it short and gracious, acknowledging the hospitality of your host. Wherever you are, etiquette calls for the host to make the first toast, so you can take your cue from him. Don't attempt a humorous toast—it could be misunderstood or considered in bad taste.

When drinking informally, you may be expected to utter a short one-word or one-phrase toast—"A votre santé" (to your health) in France, or just "Santé" (health); in Germany, "Prosit" means the same.

Americans unaccustomed to toasting may find themselves drinking more than they intended, so beware.

GIFTS

Become familiar with gift-giving customs and protocol, which vary greatly from country to country. Consider who is receiving the gift, their status, what types of gifts are acceptable, and how and when it should be presented. Gifts fall into two categories, those given in a social setting, say when visiting someone's home, or those given in a business setting, as a token of goodwill. Do some research before you choose either—customs and prohibitions can vary widely and be surprising. For example, giving your Russian hostess a dozen roses would be a mistake because in Russia an even number of flowers is given only at a funeral. For the same reason, a mantel clock is a poor choice for your Chinese business partner because in Chinese the words for "clock" and "death" are virtually identical. Even color carries meaning in some countries. Whereas in the United States white is a color of joy, elsewhere in the world it symbolizes death. Put as much care into the wrapping and presentation of your gift as with your choice of gift.

In countries outside the United States, many rules pertain to the giving of gifts, and failing to follow them is a serious breach of etiquette. One rule common to virtually all countries is to have the gift beautifully wrapped. Quality wrapping paper with a beautiful ribbon and bow are perfect for the gift itself. If you need to transport the gift, use a high-quality bag for carrying it.

Pay particular attention to customs regarding when to give a gift and when to open a gift as these customs vary across the globe. Similarly, find out ahead of time if you should open a gift in front of the giver or if etiquette dictates opening it later.

Here's a sampling of gift giving expectations and caveats:

- The Japanese give and expect gifts on numerous occasions, and the wrapping is perhaps as important as the present itself.

- In some Asian countries, clocks and handkerchiefs symbolize mourning and are not given as gifts.

- The French appreciate music or a book; American best sellers are a good choice.

- In any country, it would be hard to go wrong giving a fine pen or pen-and-pencil set or a coffee-table picture book with an American theme.

- Whether here or abroad, never give liquor to someone in the Muslim community.

- No leather gifts for Hindus.

- Don't give food items to an Orthodox Jew as they may not be kosher.

- Gifts of clothing, perfume, or cosmetics are in poor taste almost everywhere.

DOING BUSINESS— A QUICK TOUR

You've gotten your visa, chosen your wardrobe and gifts, read up on your host country, prepped your materials, and now you can get down to business. The way business is conducted also varies by region and culture, and as the guest, you will want to understand and respect your host's style of doing business.

Europe

As you move from the north of Europe to the southern regions, the most obvious differences in manners concern time and space. Scandinavians, Germans, Britons, and other northern Europeans place a very high value on punctuality, whereas standards are looser in the southern regions. Generally, business appointments should be scheduled at least two weeks in advance. In northern countries, the meeting will start on time and stick to the scripted agenda. Business entertaining tends to take place at restaurants, and while business may be discussed before and after, different countries have different attitudes about discussing business during the meal. It's frowned on in Germany and in England, but not in Scandinavia or the Netherlands. In France, the food will share center stage with any business discussion.

In southern Europe, while you should arrive on time, don't expect that your host will. Meetings may start late and there may be little attempt to come to a quick conclusion. Patience and courtesy are key. The evening meal, usually at a restaurant, plays a larger role in business dealings and many go on late into the night. Hospitality is a tradition, so you may expect to be treated by your host.

In eastern Europe, more advanced planning may be needed to set up visas and appointments. As businesspeople are generally cautious, it may take multiple meetings or visits to come to a conclusion. Hospitality is also valued, and long, lavish dinners are the norm.

Latin America

In Latin America, all business meetings should be arranged at least two to three weeks in advance and even a month or two in advance in some cases. Confirm the time before you make your travel reservations and again before you leave.

Personal connections are very important, and you may need an introduction from a third party—a mutual friend or a bank or law firm. Showing up at a business or government office without an appointment is unacceptable.

Latin Americans like to conduct business at a leisurely pace, preferring to establish a friendly relationship before moving on to work matters. When business discussions do start, they tend to proceed relatively slowly; two- or three-hour meetings that may segue into a business lunch are not unusual. It may take a number of meetings, and even several visits to the country, to conclude your negotiations. It's vitally important that you never express any impatience or anger at the tempo of the proceedings. Hospitality is prized, and you may be hosted to meals at private homes or in restaurants. Do not discuss business on these occasions unless your host brings it up.

The Middle East

In the Middle East, all appointments are generally scheduled for the three intervals between the first four prayer sessions of the day. Since the traditional emphasis on hospitality can cause delays, meetings may be scheduled for a time of day rather than a specific hour. In either case, arrive on time—but don't expect your counterpart to follow suit. Throughout the Middle East, it is customary to make visitors wait. The exception to this is Turkey, which tends to follow Western time schedules. In the Middle East, meetings generally start with extensive small talk, designed to establish friendship and trust, and you can expect lengthy conversations, multiple participants, frequent interruptions, and numerous cups of coffee or tea.

The role of host is taken seriously, and there's a good chance your host will entertain you at his home at a lavish feast. Be sure to sample everything.

Asia

Asia is the most culturally diverse region on earth. Each time you get off an airplane in Asia, you can expect to encounter a whole new set of customs—including language, manners, religion, and social outlook. Decisions tend to be reached by consensus, which takes time. In general, no agreement is final until each issue is resolved to everyone's satisfaction. Not surprisingly, one of the supreme Asian virtues is patience.

Try to make all appointments in Asia as far ahead of time as possible—two months is the advised lead time in some countries. Punctuality is critical and highly valued; arriving even just a few minutes late to a business engagement is considered an insult. It's customary in China to send a list of your delegation before every meeting, along with a detailed agenda. The Japanese, too, like to set the agenda beforehand and then stick to it.

Meals form the core of business entertainment and eating together is considered essential for building good relationships, so all invitations should be accepted.

Africa

Throughout Africa, great importance is placed on establishing warm, friendly relations between business associates. It makes sense to enjoy the process, since business dealings on the African continent tend to proceed at a significantly slower pace than in Europe and the United States. Make all appointments a month or two in advance and call a day or two before to confirm. A letter of introduction from a mutual acquaintance will help pave the way. Try to schedule meetings first thing in the morning, before the midday heat. Arrive on time to every meeting, but don't expect the same from your host. Keeping visitors waiting is standard practice in many countries. Interruptions may be common, and since before-business socializing can delay the start of business discussions, meetings generally extend beyond their scheduled length, so leave plenty of time between appointments. You can generally expect to be entertained, either at a restaurant or a private home. (See "Greetings in Other Countries," page 317.)

INDEX